Militarized Currents

Militarized Currents

Toward a Decolonized Future in Asia and the Pacific

Setsu Shigematsu and Keith L. Camacho, Editors

Foreword by Cynthia Enloe

 University of Minnesota Press
Minneapolis
London

Chapter 3 was previously published in *The Contemporary Pacific* 6, no. 1 (1994): 87–109; reprinted with permission from the University of Hawai'i Press. Chapter 6 was originally published in *Asian Survey* 39, no. 2 (1999): 310–27; reprinted with permission from the University of California Press. Portions of chapter 9 were translated by Teresa A. Algoso from an essay in Japanese by Naoki Sakai, "Sōzō to Jendā" (Image and gender), in *Keizoku suru shokuminchishugi* (The continuation of colonialism), ed. Iwasaki Minoru, Okawa Masahiko, Nakano Toshio, and Lee Takanori (Tokyo: Seikyusha, 2005), 276–90. Chapter 10 was originally published in Korean in Insook Kwon, *Daehan minguk eun gundae da* (South Korea is the military: Peace, militarism, and masculinity with gender perspective) (Seoul: Cheongnyun Press, 2005).

In chapter 1, lyrics from "Pupu 'O Ewa" are printed courtesy of Criterion Music Corporation; copyright 1962.

Copyright 2010 by the Regents of the University of Minnesota

All rights reserved. No part of this publication may be reproduced, stored in a retrieval system, or transmitted, in any form or by any means, electronic, mechanical, photocopying, recording, or otherwise, without the prior written permission of the publisher.

Published by the University of Minnesota Press
111 Third Avenue South, Suite 290
Minneapolis, MN 55401-2520
http://www.upress.umn.edu

Library of Congress Cataloging-in-Publication Data

Militarized currents : toward a decolonized future in Asia and the Pacific / Setsu Shigematsu and Keith L. Camacho, editors ; foreword by Cynthia Enloe.
    p. cm.
Includes bibliographical references and index.
ISBN 978-0-8166-6505-1 (hc : alk. paper) — ISBN 978-0-8166-6506-8 (pb : alk. paper)
 1. Militarism—Pacific Area—History—20th century. 2. Militarism—Social aspects—Pacific Area. 3. Imperialism—History—20th century. 4. United States—Foreign relations—Pacific Area. 5. Pacific Area—Foreign relations—United States. 6. Japan—Foreign relations—Pacific Area. 7. Pacific Area—Foreign relations—Japan. 8. Pacific Area—Politics and government—21st century. 9. Pacific Area—Social conditions—21st century. I. Shigematsu, Setsu. II. Camacho, Keith L.
 DS518.1.M545 2010
 355'.03305—dc22   2009016367

Printed in the United States of America on acid-free paper

The University of Minnesota is an equal-opportunity educator and employer.

16 15 14 13 12 11 10   10 9 8 7 6 5 4 3 2 1

Contents

Foreword — vii
Cynthia Enloe

Acknowledgments — xi

Introduction: Militarized Currents, Decolonizing Futures — xv
Setsu Shigematsu and Keith L. Camacho

I. Militarized Bodies of Memory

1. Memorializing Puʻuloa and Remembering Pearl Harbor — 3
   Jon Kamakawiwoʻole Osorio

2. Bikinis and Other S/pacific N/oceans — 15
   Teresia K. Teaiwa

3. The Exceptional Life and Death of a Chamorro Soldier: Tracing the Militarization of Desire in Guam, ~~USA~~ — 33
   Michael Lujan Bevacqua

4. Touring Military Masculinities: U.S.–Philippines Circuits of Sacrifice and Gratitude in Corregidor and Bataan — 63
   Vernadette Vicuña Gonzalez

II. Militarized Movements

5. Rising Up from a Sea of Discontent: The 1970 Koza Uprising in U.S.-Occupied Okinawa — 91
   Wesley Iwao Ueunten

6. South Korean Movements against Militarized Sexual Labor — 125
   Katharine H. S. Moon

7. Uncomfortable Fatigues: Chamorro Soldiers, Gendered
   Identities, and the Question of Decolonization in Guam   147
   Keith L. Camacho and Laurel A. Monnig

8. Militarized Filipino Masculinity and the Language of
   Citizenship in San Diego   181
   Theresa Cenidoza Suarez

III. Hetero/Homo-sexualized Militaries

9. On Romantic Love and Military Violence:
   Transpacific Imperialism and U.S.–Japan Complicity   205
   Naoki Sakai

10. Masculinity and Male-on-Male Sexual Violence in the
    Military: Focusing on the Absence of the Issue   223
    Insook Kwon

11. Why Have the Japanese Self-Defense Forces Included
    Women? The State's "Nonfeminist Reasons"   251
    Fumika Sato

12. Genealogies of Unbelonging: Amerasians and Transnational
    Adoptees as Legacies of U.S. Militarism in South Korea   277
    Patti Duncan

Conclusion: From American Lake to a People's Pacific
in the Twenty-First Century   309
Walden Bello

Contributors   323

Index   327

Foreword

Cynthia Enloe

Readers will be reading this collection of insightful articles when Iraq has slipped off the front pages of the world's daily papers and faded from television news screens. Fewer people will be paying attention to Afghanistan's ethnic and provincial groups as they continue to cope with the myriad effects of the multinational invasion. There will be a new U.S. president, and the governments of Japan, South Korea, and the Philippines more than likely will have changed hands. Perhaps even the talk of "empire" will have lost its popular cachet. This will be precisely the right time to read this book, cover to cover—slowly.

Our short attention spans might be tempting us to look away from the scenes of militarized imperial action; nonetheless, as we open this provocative book, Guam will still be under U.S. colonial rule, the Philippines and South Korea will remain subjected to intense American pressures, and Japan will continue to be internally divided over whether to stay under the U.S. protective umbrella or to expand its military even further.

The wheels of militarization, in fact, are greased by such popular inattention. The militarizing processes going on in Asia and the Pacific have been made easier to sustain by our distractedness and our inclination to look elsewhere. We might have imagined that the U.S. government's war on terror was militarizing only those countries chosen for the headlines: Iraq, Afghanistan, Iran, and Pakistan, along with Britain and the United States. Yet, as these attentive contributors show us, individual Okinawans, mainland Japanese, Chamorros, South Koreans, Filipinos, Fijians, and Hawaiians each have been weighing and responding to intense militarizing influences—subtle and blatant—during these same early twenty-first–century years. The seeds of those influences were planted long before September 11 and the military invasions of Iraq and Afghanistan, though they have been fertilized by states' responses to those featured events.

Setsu Shigematsu and Keith L. Camacho consciously bring together here both the big picture and the microscopic view of militarism. They allow us to move between these views. We can enhance our explanatory skills by thinking big in order to think small *and* by thinking small in order to think big. Neither view alone is sufficient if we are to make full and nuanced sense of how militarism works, why it continues to push forward into our personal and societal lives, and how it might be rolled back. Recognizing this dual intellectual imperative—to think big and to think small—has been one of the gifts of feminist analysis. That is why tracking militarism in contemporary Asia and the Pacific calls on us to explore privatized sexualities and governments' military-basing policies simultaneously. That is why, at the same time we are tracking the stubborn entrenchment of militarizing processes in such an expansive region, we have to cultivate a curiosity about both individual memories and organized resistances.

We learn here that each is gendered. Soldiers' sexualities, the iconography of atomic testing, organized support of those surviving elderly women once forced to become wartime sex slaves, local military recruitment, popular mobilizing against external militarizers—if we leave out the politics of femininities and the politics of masculinities in our investigation of any one of these, we are destined to underestimate the complex cultural politics of each and the interactions among them all.

It is all too rare to have Hawai'i and South Korea considered in the same book. It is even more unusual to have them joined together between the same bindings by Guam and Japan. In most analyses, "Asia" is treated as politically and culturally separate from "the Pacific," with the latter getting the short shrift. By contrast, Shigematsu and Camacho deliberately have put the two artificially constructed regions into a common analytical frame: the frame of militarism. Today, at a time when U.S. security strategists (civilian and uniformed) are anointing Guam as a hub of American global military operations, absorbing the contents of this book—connecting Guam's Chamorro women and men to the women and men of Okinawa, the Philippines, Hawai'i, Korea, and Fiji—becomes an urgent enterprise.

In an innovative move, Shigematsu, Camacho, and their contributors are asking us to explore the legacies and linkages between the early twentieth-century Japanese Empire and the present U.S. empire. If you are a Chamorro in Guam, an Okinawan in Japan's southernmost island, a Korean living in the south, a Filipino who has resisted emigration, then your family has experienced both Japanese and U.S. forms of colonial and neocolonial rule. While different in many ways, both forms have been militarizing in their intents: to make use of the local women and men, their economies, and their dynamic cultures to serve the external national security strategists' own objectives. Mainland Japanese have had to think hard about these two legacies as well. Japanese feminists have been among the harshest critics not only of the militarizing effects of the current U.S.–Japan interstate alliance but also of the complicity of ordinary women and men in the emergence of Japanese imperialism seven decades ago.

The contributors add an important caveat at this point: we should be wary of imagining that any imperial process is fueled by externally promoted objectives alone. Nor should we presume that imperially militarized processes operate without reliance on particular masculinized and feminized ideas and practices. Thus, as we set out on this journey—as reading any rich volume is, after all, a journey—we should simultaneously watch the big picture of empires' pursuits of militarization while turning our curiosities to the seeming minutiae of local individuals' own gendered silences, desires, memories, and aspirations.

July 2008

Acknowledgments

Our anthology began with a conversation at the Association for Asian American Studies conference in Los Angeles in April 2005. At that time, Setsu was soliciting papers for an anthology conceived under the rubric of feminism and militarism, which she began in January 2005. Our conversation continued over the next year, and we realized that our research interests intersected in more ways than one. We exchanged significant publications in our fields and deliberated over the ways in which our fields produced and represented knowledge. Increasingly, we became interested in trying to articulate the possibilities for cross-regional research agendas that would further the work of demilitarization across our respective fields of study in American, Asian, Asian American, and Pacific Islander studies. In spring 2006, Keith came on board as coeditor, merging his academic training on U.S. colonialism and militarism in the Pacific Islands with Setsu's research background on transnational liberation movements and feminist critical theory in Asia. The partnership turned out to be a productive one, where we learned from each other and became students of new fields of study. As a result, we have gained a deeper appreciation for the depth of knowledge there is to learn from the work of indigenous, feminist, and people-of-color scholars who are located in places that have been renamed throughout colonial modernity as the Americas, Asia, and the Pacific Islands.

Our present volume on gender, race, and colonialism in Asia and the Pacific Islands is a product of these intellectual and political convergences. We thank several organizations for allowing us to see this anthology through to its completion. The Asian American Studies Center at the University of California at Los Angeles, the Freeman Spogli Institute for International Studies at Stanford University, the University of California President's Postdoctoral Fellowship Program, and the Macmillan Brown Centre for Pacific Studies at the University of Canterbury all graciously provided funds for the planning stages of our volume. We also appreciate the kind assistance of our graduate student researchers, Jolie Chea and Alfred Flores, who helped us to address various administrative and editorial tasks in a timely fashion. Teresa Algoso translated an early version of Naoki Sakai's Japanese article that formed the basis of his essay. We appreciate Daisy Kim's translation work and research assistance with the chapter by Insook Kwon. Our contributors likewise supported us throughout the entire process; their commitment, imagination, and scholarship have been an inspiration. As readers will observe, their contributions reflect the specific and shared intellectual goals of various projects in Asia and the Pacific. We hope they represent the kind of alliances and solidarities that foster critical insights and unanticipated political collaborations.

Along these lines, two seminal articles are reprinted in this volume. We thank the University of California Press for allowing us to feature Katharine H. S. Moon's article, "South Korean Movements against Militarized Sexual Labor," which first appeared in *Asian Survey*. The University of Hawai'i Press also granted permission to reproduce Teresia K. Teaiwa's article, "Bikinis and Other S/pacific N/oceans," which first appeared in *The Contemporary Pacific*. More importantly, we thank Katharine and Teresia for agreeing to participate in our collective dialogue. That their articles are reproduced here—long after their initial circulation—testifies to the enduring relevance and value of radical feminist and indigenous thought and intervention in Asia and the Pacific Islands.

Our efforts, moreover, have benefited greatly from the support of the University of Minnesota Press. We are grateful to all the members of its staff and review boards. Our external reviewers offered productive questions and suggestions for revision that substantially strengthened our introduction and the wider contents of the manuscript. We thank them, too. We especially acknowledge Richard Morrison, our senior editor at the University of Minnesota Press, for his support of the emergent, bridge-building intellectual work we aspire to generate. Adam Brunner also assisted in seeing the project through its various stages; working with him has been a pleasure. We appreciate the expertise of Sarah Breeding, our copyeditor, and Roberta Engleman, our indexer. We also gratefully acknowledge Daniel Ochsner's cover design work. The photograph was taken by Keith Camacho, which is a picture taken from Banzai Cliff on Tinian in the Marianas.

We also thank Vicente M. Diaz, Cynthia Enloe, Takashi Fujitani, David Hanlon, Jean J. Kim, Jodi Kim, Michelle Mason, Naoki Sakai, Laurel

Monnig, Gary Okihiro, Dylan Rodriguez, Geoffrey M. White, and Lisa Yoneyama for their untiring support as colleagues, friends, and mentors. They often pushed us to clarify the aims of our volume, to think through the implications of each chapter, and, more broadly, to challenge the limits of existing paradigms. It should be apparent that our volume is indebted to the pioneering work on colonialism and militarism begun by them.

Introduction

Militarized Currents, Decolonizing Futures

Setsu Shigematsu and Keith L. Camacho

Militarized Currents forges a collaboration that examines how militarization has constituted a structuring force that connects the histories of the Japanese and U.S. empires across the regions of Asia and the Pacific Islands. Foregrounding indigenous and feminist perspectives and the scholarship of people of color, this anthology analyzes militarization as an *extension of colonialism* and its gendered and racialized processes from the late-twentieth to the twenty-first century. By examining how former and current colonial territories of Japan and the United States, such as Guam, Okinawa, the Marshall Islands, the Philippines, and Korea, have been variously impacted by militarization, the articles collected here illuminate how their colonial histories constitute the conditions of possibility for ongoing forms of militarization. This collection thus expands our understanding of how these political geographies across Asia and the Pacific have been militarized, demonstrating how contemporary processes of militarization are linked with residual and ongoing effects of colonial subordination.

In this introduction, we outline why we seek to foster cross-regional dialogues and cross-disciplinary methods of analysis by demonstrating how currents of militarization and demilitarization connect and divide people with potentially common interests. We purposely choose the metaphor of currents to signal how militarization operates across temporal and spatial boundaries, as contemporary military technologies are informed by past and projected imperialist imperatives. Bringing together contributions from sixteen international and U.S.-based scholars, we explore the discursive, embodied, historical, and institutional processes of militarization. Specifically, we focus on how people across Asia and the Pacific Islands have variously been impacted and mobilized by the forces of militarization and how demilitarization constitutes a crucial part of larger decolonization movements.

In the first section of this introduction, we highlight the importance of the relationship between U.S. and Japanese imperialisms in understanding the current state of militarization. We then offer a discussion of how dominant periodizations and paradigms obscure the uneven effects of violence and the embedded heteronormative structures of militarized logics. In this critical assessment, we examine how institutionalized divisions of time (periodizations), configurations of space (regions), and disciplinary knowledge formations (area studies) marginalize counterhegemonic subjects of knowledge. Moreover, we discuss how such knowledge formations obscure the need for resisting the ways that peoples, lands, and waters have been categorized and claimed by imperialist–militarist endeavors. Given the racialized–gendered patterns of mass destruction produced through the advancement of militarized logics, our anthology advances the *current* value of indigenous, people of color, and feminist-oriented demilitarizing coalitions as critiques of and alternatives to militarized worlds of the twenty-first century.[1]

Engendering Empires

The regions now called Asia and the Pacific Islands share a history of colonial rule by Japan and the United States. Imperialist wars initiated by these respective nation-states created wartime and postwar conditions of military invasion, occupation, and violence through which the peoples of these regions have struggled and survived. The parallels and interconnections between U.S. and Japanese imperialisms together constitute an important site of analysis to comprehend the current state of geopolitics, militarized movements, and migrations since the twentieth century. The clashing of the Japanese and U.S. empires variously devastated and made claims to liberate colonized subjects from the other competing imperialist power(s). Despite the formal attempts to demilitarize Japan in the postwar era, the remilitarization of Japan has been on the horizon since the onset of the cold war. Memories of the Asia-Pacific wars continue to haunt current constellations of militarization.[2]

Naoki Sakai, a leading critic of Asian area studies and a contributor to this anthology, argues that American and Japanese colonialisms sustained each other's existence through a "trans-Pacific arrangement." Under the postwar–cold war U.S. security system, he asserts that this arrangement was "marked by the complicity of the United States and Japan that effectively disavowed and continues to disavow the past of colonial atrocities; without this the two countries would not have the relationship as they do today."³ These atrocities and their lingering effects include Japan's militarized sex-slavery system in World War II and the U.S. nuclear-testing campaign in the Marshall Islands in the postwar era. Japan's sex-slavery system exemplifies how militarization operates simultaneously with colonialism, with the creation of "comfort stations" as a *militarized organizing logic* that combined regulated heterosexual rape with the concerns of hygiene and the health of soldiers.⁴ The establishment of comfort stations across the Japanese Empire demonstrates how the militarization of sexuality was a direct outcome of empire building and colonial technologies of rule. As several of our contributors demonstrate, the "comfort women" system was directly linked with subsequent forms of organized U.S. militarized prostitution, pointing to the interpenetration of these imperialist systems.⁵

Memories of such militarized violence traverse the Pacific, as toxic currents and legal cases make their way to the shores of the U.S. coasts and courthouses.⁶ As Lisa Yoneyama's work has demonstrated, redress for Japanese war crimes has recently been raised within U.S. courts by naturalized Asian American subjects, pointing to the transnational attempts for reparations by former subjects of the Japanese Empire.⁷ While not necessarily addressed within the logics of war crimes and redress, Marshall Islanders similarly continue to negotiate with the United States to demand various forms of compensation for the sixty-seven atomic tests conducted in the Marshall Islands.⁸ As Marshall Islanders Lijon Eknilang and James Matayoshi declare, "we continue to fight for justice, as survivors."⁹ While some Asian Americans and Pacific Islanders separately raise the specter of empire in U.S. national and transnational contexts, little work has been done to address and analyze the ways in which such calls for justice, however construed, are also connected through militarized currents and circuits. An attention to the interrelated dynamics between the United States and Japan, including their mutual disavowal of colonial violence, thus helps us to explore the ways in which "rulers, agents, and colonized people shaped empires; and the economic and cultural processes in which imperial formations played a part."¹⁰ In our attention to the specific relationship between U.S. and Japanese empires across Asia and the Pacific, we emphasize the need to tease out the tensions between the specificities of local configurations of colonialism as well as the "homogenizing force and collaborative alliance among various colonizers at different historical moments under shifting geopolitical configurations."[11]

The overseas expansion of the Japanese and the U.S. empires converged temporally as part of a reactive process of inter-imperialist competition. Japan's formal empire building began in the wake of the Sino–Japanese War in 1894 and 1895 with its colonial expansion into Kwantung, Taiwan, and Korea. Japan's earlier annexation of Hokkaido (1869) and Okinawa (1879), as many scholars have argued, "laid the groundwork for later imperialist expansion."[12] Formal colonization of territories proceeded with the acquisition of former German colonies in Micronesia in 1914, which included the Caroline, Marshall, and northern Mariana Islands, followed by World War II conquests in Melanesia and Southeast Asia.

Japan attempted to justify its expansionist policies in terms of an anti-Western imperialism, expressing a conscious attempt to resist and overcome Euro-American colonialisms even as Japan imitated and learned from them. In writing about the specificity of Japanese colonialism, Leo T. S. Ching writes that we must understand the "inter-imperialist relationship that situated and determined the particular form of Japanese imperialism in the world system."[13] The rise of Japanese imperialism was an inter-imperialist configuration of power that was cohered by an attempt to negate its "Western" external forces of constitution.

Japanese discourses of racial and cultural superiority contended with Euro-American discourses of white supremacy, at times seeking to include and assimilate other Asians and at other times redefining an inter-Asian hierarchy.[14] As Gerald Horne argues, the racial regimes of the British and the U.S. empires *enabled* Japanese claims to be imperial liberators and posed a significant ideological threat to Euro-American global supremacy.[15] As is well known, Japan used the slogan of the "Greater East Asia Co-Prosperity Sphere" and called for pan-Asian solidarity. Whatever euphemisms and contorted dialogics were used in promoting Japanese imperialism, perceptions of racial and gendered hierarchies were intertwined with other motives for colonization. As Japanese colonialism spread into the Asian continent and the Pacific Islands, the government simultaneously built the military force required to protect its homeland and its newly conquered resources.[16] Japanese colonialism was fundamentally militarist in character, as evidenced in its violent invasion of territories, from Nanjing to the Philippines.[17] As Lewis H. Gann writes, economic and military expansionism necessitated Japan's "creation of vast defensive networks thrust ever farther outward."[18] In the narrativizing of Japan's militarized colonial history, the semantics of "defense" are deployed to naturalize aggression. By the onset of World War II in 1941, Japan had created a network of militarized sites in the *nan'yō*, or the south seas, to maintain Japan's eastern flank and support Japanese attacks against U.S. colonial possessions in the Pacific, such as Guam, Hawai'i, and Wake Island.[19]

In many respects, Japan viewed the Pacific Islands under its wartime rule as the last bastions of defense against the "east," that is, U.S. colonialism in particular and Western tyranny in general. The logics of strategic deterrence and military necessity were extended to Japan's colonies in East and Southeast Asia, where colonial populations were recruited as militarized labor to protect the Japanese homeland.[20] As subjects of Japan's biopower and governmentality, for example, Takashi Fujitani argues that the conscription of Korean "volunteer" soldiers in 1938 occurred in part because of the intensification of conflicts, the disavowal of racism, and the promotion of shared ancestry between Japanese and Koreans. But it would be Japan's transformation of its racist discrimination toward Koreans from an "unabashed and exclusionary 'vulgar racism' to a new type of inclusionary and 'polite racism' that denied itself as racist" that would lead to the incorporation of Koreans into the multiethnic Japanese Empire.[21] As compared to the U.S. wartime conscription and confinement of Japanese Americans, Fujitani asserts that Japan was similarly "forced to begin a process of including these previously despised populations into their nations in unprecedented ways, while at the same time denouncing racial discrimination and even considering these peoples as part of the national populations and, as such, deserving life, welfare, and happiness."[22] Fujitani's astute observations about the ways in which nation-states govern their subjects through inclusionary forms of racism are instructive for how we might critique the militarization of soldiers' lives and deaths across the Japanese and U.S. empires.

While Japan lost much of its imperial domain and militarized power in the war's aftermath, it later regained its economic hegemony since the 1960s under the protection and dominion of the U.S. military forces based in Okinawa and the Japanese mainland. Supplying the U.S. military through the Korean and Vietnam wars enabled Japan's economic recovery, alongside investments in a variety of fishery, industrial, and trade programs in Asia and the Pacific. Japanese tourist investments and tuna canneries, for example, predominate in some areas of the Pacific.²³ As one recent study demonstrates, Japan is "the largest source of Asian tourists and tourism investment in the Islands."²⁴ Japanese tourism in particular would not have occurred without the nostalgia associated with former Asian settler communities and wartime battlegrounds; the paradisiacal allure of island lifestyles and settings; the American military's presence to assure the "safe" travel of Japanese and non-Japanese tourists; and, increasingly, the advertisement of the Pacific as utopic sites of heterosexist and homoerotic desire.²⁵ Discourses of militarism and tourism are thus inextricably linked in Asia and the Pacific not only by a shared history of American and Japanese imperial violence but also by "a wider network of articulations that create the fundamentally modern tensions between work and leisure."²⁶ Presenting itself as a nation of commerce, travel, and peace rather than as a nation of war, Japan continues to disavow its imperial past and present. With the seventh largest military budget in the world (based on 2008 expenditures), Japan's militarized logics of expansion continue with the drive to change Article Nine of the Constitution and to reform its postwar security treaty with the United States.²⁷ The contorted logics of "defense" have been manifested through the deployment of the Japanese Self-Defense Forces to Afghanistan and Iraq over the past decade.

Japan's perception of these regions as militarily strategic, then, historically and contemporaneously parallels U.S. justifications for the colonization of lands beyond its continental borders. Following from its wars of colonial expansion in Native America, U.S. overseas colonial expansion similarly advanced its own rhetoric of civilization, nationhood, and race.²⁸ Since the Spanish–American War in 1898, the United States colonized islands in the Caribbean and in the Pacific, viewing each possession as a strategic site for advancing American economic and military interests.²⁹ These islands included Cuba and Puerto Rico in the Caribbean, and Guam, eastern Sāmoa, Hawai'i, and the Philippines in the Pacific.³⁰ The United States established coal stations, communication lines, and naval harbors throughout these islands. Colonial forms of education, health, and public policy were imposed in America's overseas empire, racializing nonwhite settler populations as inferior, creating native elite and police collaborator classes, and excluding most native populations from white circles of influence, residency, and power.³¹ Clearly, multiple discourses of othering determined the direction of and responses to American "civilization" projects in the Caribbean and the Pacific.³² The means and effects of anticolonial movements likewise differed across the Pacific, from Filipino armed resistance toward the U.S. military invasion of the Philippines to Hawaiian-organized petitions against the U.S. annexation of Hawaiʻi.[33]

After World War II, Japan's new geopolitical position and image was managed by U.S. imperial designs. In *Perilous Memories: The Asia-Pacific War(s)*, T. Fujitani, Geoffrey M. White, and Lisa Yoneyama argue that the United States presented itself as a "liberator" of Japanese wartime colonialism, attempted to erase narratives of prior Japanese rule in Asia and the Pacific, and strove to make invisible the multiplicity of experiences and remembrances of the war.[34] The imperial myths of liberation create what Yoneyama calls an "already accrued debt" to the United States, which continues to fashion the United States as a "liberator" of Japanese colonialism rather than as a nation of war crimes associated with colonial takeovers and occupations.[35] As evidenced in post–World War II Micronesia, for example, David Hanlon asserts that "Americans expected that their role as liberators would secure a welcome reception and an extended period of goodwill from grateful, needy, debilitated local populations."[36] This interplay of colonial legacies continues to animate a sense of indebtedness to the United States as the "rescuer" for many postcolonial subjects, such as the Filipinos and Chamorros who currently serve in the U.S. military.

Moreover, the United States furthers its national image in its colonies like Guam and Hawaiʻi as familiar, necessary, and normal, attempting to marginalize long-standing calls for indigenous, national, and women's self-determination movements on the one hand and violent histories of American and Japanese imperial conquests on the other.[37] As Elaine H. Kim and Chungmoo Choi argue, because of the installation of U.S. military bases throughout Asia and the Pacific at the end of World War II, South Korea and other former Japanese colonies have "never had an opportunity to decolonize in the true sense of the word."[38] While these self-determination movements have been articulated differently across generations and genders, they must face the difficult task of addressing and critiquing the intersections of American and Japanese colonialism and militarism.[39] Understanding the interconstitution of Japanese and U.S. colonialism is imperative for building transnational decolonization and demilitarization movements. In Okinawa, for example, Okinawan perceptions of American military bases were "formed through constant friction with and bleeding of their own memories of [Japanese] empire, making this base-produced modernity difficult to critique."[40] By promoting "dual decolonization," a position that critiques these imperial histories, Hideaki Tobe states that one can begin "to vanquish the multiple layers of colonialism" associated with American, Japanese, and even Okinawan colonial processes and attitudes.[41]

Taking Tobe's dual-colonization paradigm a step further, we believe that it is imperative to understand local demilitarizing efforts *in relation to* other movements to decolonize Asia and the Pacific Islands. As we write this introduction, Japan and the United States have been negotiating to transfer American military personnel and their dependents from Okinawa to Guam.[42] According to one U.S. military report, the Pentagon chose Guam because the island's location "provides strategic flexibility, freedom of action, and prompt global action for the Global War on terrorism, peace and wartime engagement, and crisis response."[43] While Hawai'i, the Marshall Islands, and Okinawa remain some of the most militarized sites in the Pacific, the U.S. military has begun to amplify Guam's "strategic" significance, underscoring "the increasing geopolitical importance of Asia to Washington as well as the Pentagon's priority to project power from American territory rather than foreign bases."[44] It is now estimated that the Pentagon plans to spend $15 billion in construction and transfer costs, whereas the Japanese government intends to commit $6 billion. In support of these funds, President Barack Obama signed into law H.R. 2647: Defense Authorization Act for Fiscal Year 2010 on October 28, 2009. H.R. 2647 now grants the U.S. military $734 million to fund the construction of military facilities in Guam.[45] Additionally, the U.S. military projects that anywhere from eight thousand to fifty-five thousand American military personnel, along with militarized technologies of surveillance and warfare, will be relocated from one island colony to another by 2012.[46]

Despite the American military's often-secretive disclosures about its relocation plans, news about this move has raised several alarming issues for Chamorros and Okinawans alike. First, Japan and the United States have not allowed Chamorros and Okinawans to participate in this process, let alone entertain the wider question of political status and sovereignty debates in Guam and Okinawa. Second, active American military propaganda campaigns are under way in the islands and elsewhere, depicting militarized departure and militarized settlement in terms of "economic progress" for the indigenous and settler populations of Guam and Okinawa. In particular, the U.S. Air Force and Navy and the U.S. Department of Interior are sponsoring conferences to attract businesses from

Australia, Japan, New York, and San Francisco to consider how they might profit from this massive move of military personnel and technology.[47] Third, while Okinawan women welcome the demilitarization of their bodies and lands, that understanding comes with the knowledge that Chamorros and others will be further militarized in more ways than one. As Ronni Alexander exclaims, "The relocation of US soldiers from Okinawa to Guam might mean relief for Okinawan women but would at the same time threaten the very existence" of Chamorros.[48] With the U.S. military already holding nearly one third of Guam's lands, increased militarization would constrain, if not impede, Chamorro efforts to attain greater cultural, economic, and political sovereignty. Furthermore, Guam and Okinawa have yet to receive governmental apologies, monetary redress, or reconciliatory arrangements for the various deaths, environmental damages, and land displacements committed by American and Japanese military forces since World War II.

At the same time, however, the entire military relocation process has offered opportunities for greater communication, interaction, and solidarity among Chamorro and Okinawan organizations. These collective partnerships and political trajectories are a historical first for both societies, as Guam and Okinawa form new transoceanic alliances in the face of encroaching militarization. Women's groups have especially taken the lead in educating each other about militarized violence in their respective homelands. For example, Guam's Fuetsan Famalao'an has organized numerous conferences, film screenings, and village meetings on the topic of gendered and racialized military violence.[49] At one of the recent village sessions, a supporter for a demilitarized Okinawa recently compared the militarized landscapes of Guam and Okinawa. Representing Okinawa Women Act Against Military Violence, she expressed, "I don't know how much the people of Guam realize the impact of having a big military concentration in a small island. Guam is half the size of Okinawa, where we have 28,000 troops and 22,000 families. The military presence is creating serious problems."[50] One ongoing problem concerns Guam's militarized value as an American "buffer zone" from perceived hostilities in the "East," much like how Japan employed the *nan'yō* as a strategic line of defense against Western colonialism. Nevertheless, the realities of Guam, or any other American militarized territory, becoming another site of military battles or nuclear warfare are real. As Julian Aguon argues, regional and national reports suggest that "Guam is fast becoming the first-strike target in any altercation between the US and China and/or North Korea."⁵¹ As the United States continues to remilitarize areas in Asia and the Pacific Islands, the cases of Guam and Okinawa illustrate the need to analyze their militarized conditions in relation to each other and their intersecting colonial currents. As the efforts of these women's groups demonstrate, cross-regional dialogue can foster opportunities for the sharing of critical information, the creating of transnational solidarities, and the demilitarizing of societies.

Lest our political project for a demilitarized Asia and Pacific be misunderstood as either unique or utopic endeavors, it would behoove us to remember that calls for self-determination are always ongoing, if not highly contested, processes across these regions. While Chamorros and Okinawans form new alliances in ways that can be read as both progressive and productive, this is not to say that their case should serve as a model for demilitarization per se. Although they raise critical questions about the intertwined nature of American and Japanese empires, we should recall that processes of demilitarization are often informed by competing political interests, opposing class, gender, and racial hierarchies, and shifting power relations. In forging any connections among Asians, Asian Americans, and Pacific Islanders, then, we should see these efforts on an issue-by-issue basis so as not to reproduce colonial and militarist structures against others.⁵²

In Hawai'i, for example, Asians and Asian Americans have often assumed hegemonic status by virtue of their significant economic and political occupations, as well as by their majority status as settlers.⁵³ Their identification as "locals" particularly masks the presence of Hawaiians and the Hawaiian sovereignty movement, reifying the myth of "multicultural harmony" so deeply associated with the people of the archipelago. Couched within and against a longer history of white missionary settlements and plantation economies, Asians and Asian Americans frequently contend with what Haunani-Kay Trask calls "intra-settler competition"; that is to say, non-Hawaiian intrasettler claims for equality, mobility, and parity attempt to erode native Hawaiian articulations for political sovereignty, if not for the very restoration of the Hawaiian Kingdom.⁵⁴ Commenting on the roots of intrasettler colonialism, Trask asserts that the "history of our colonization becomes a twice-told tale, first of discovery and settlement by European and American businessmen and missionaries, then of the plantation Japanese, Chinese, and eventually Filipino rise to dominance in the islands."⁵⁵ While an awareness of these uneven power dynamics has risen over the years, as evidenced in Trask's critique of Asian settler colonialism, it remains to be seen as to what kinds of cross-cultural and cross-regional alliances may prove resilient in a post–September 11 Hawai'i.[56] Familiar questions need to be asked: Who has the power to speak for whom and why? What theories and methods of resistance does one advance and why? What kind of knowledge is produced in these efforts, and how might oral, written, and digital forms of communication affect the production, distribution, and representation of such knowledge? Above all, what are the probable advances and potential pitfalls involved in undertaking coordinated cross-regional struggles to secure demilitarized futures?[57]

As the United States directs and leads multinational military alliances in the so-called war on terror, these questions increase in relevance as we critique and confound allegiances to militarized power. With the current U.S.-led invasions and occupations of Iraq and the Middle East, our anthology seeks to analyze how imperialist militarization is sustained through the normalization of militarized subjectivities and desires.[58] As the contributors demonstrate, the United States has historically designated moments of national crisis to naturalize the patriotism and war-waging subjectivities and desires of its populations. With the onset of the so-called war on terror, U.S. Naval Admiral William J. Fallon states that U.S. militarization efforts have consequently increased across Australia, India, Japan, Okinawa, the Philippines, and the United States, as areas that constitute "continuing security challenges" for the United States.[59] The admiral's proclamations are disturbing not only because of America's ongoing militarist expansions but also because of the global nature in which the normalization of mass-militarized violence—American or otherwise—has spread. While our contributors do not offer a uniform conceptualization of the ways in which we can analyze the normalization of militarization, their studies show how militarization may be productively transformed, if not altogether contested and overcome.

We must understand, however, that long before the advent of these recent militarized conflicts, the United States defined its national interests not along the borders of the continental United States but in Asia and the Pacific. Hence to circumscribe our understanding of "America" to the continental United States—as previous paradigms have tended to emphasize—is myopic in terms of the reach of American empire. This circumscription also runs the risk of miscalculating the formative role that

U.S. militarization plays in shaping the historical displacements and migrations of the populations we now refer to as Asian American and Pacific Islander. Asian and Pacific Islander displacements, dispossessions, and migrations to America have been punctuated by U.S. wars in Asia and the Pacific, and thus U.S. war waging has become an integral, if not naturalized, part of the grammar of these (im)migration narratives.

Although transnational studies have marked significant developments in understanding these narratives since the 1990s, these paradigm shifts have not systematically engaged with U.S. and Japanese colonialism and militarization as a *structuring force* of (im)migrations, displacements, and diasporas, much less examined how the latter operates as a specific modality of neocolonialism. Despite the interconnections between these two empires, few studies engage in cross-regional and cross-disciplinary dialogues about them. *Militarized Currents* calls attention to this lacuna by examining how these competing empires engendered and racialized the ongoing conditions of militarization across and through these regions. We trace and interrogate these modes and processes of militarization in increasingly globalized contexts of colonial and neocolonial economies that link militarism to tourism and humanitarianism. In so doing, we embrace the opportunity to interrogate these processes and militarized circuits by forging transregional and transdisciplinary collaborations, which, we believe, can generate potentially transformative methodologies of knowledge production.

Tracing the Colonial Legacies of Contemporary Militarization

There is an abundant array of studies about the histories of militarism and colonialism, respectively. Across fields and disciplines such as diplomatic and military history, political science and international politics, peace and conflict studies, military sociology, and feminist and gender studies, militarism as a political ideology and hierarchical organization of political economy and society has been studied across various national and historical contexts. Classic studies of modern militarism, such as Alfred Vagat's *A History of Militarism: Civilian and Military* (1937), exemplify the liberal view of the importance of the distinction between civilian and military powers and interests.[60] Contemporary scholars of militarism have increasingly emphasized how militarism has evolved far beyond efficiently "winning wars" or preserving national security to become a system of self-perpetuation and self-aggrandizement, such that the distinction between "civilian" and "military" may no longer be as relevant in understanding how militarism operates.[61] In *The Sorrows of Empire*, Chalmers Johnson describes militarism as a "phenomenon by which a nation's armed services comes to put their institutional preservation ahead of achieving national security or even a commitment to the integrity of the governmental structure of which they are a part."[62] As Jean J. Kim astutely points out, "The idea that militarism and civilian life are divorced may mystify the fact that the U.S. is a country constantly at war and constantly in denial of this fact."[63]

While empire building takes on many forms, we recognize militarism as a constitutive institution and ideology of empire. Since militarism still persists in nation-states that are not historically expansive, empire-building nations, we seek to distinguish how current forms of militarization are linked to empire and the racialized gendered legacies of colonialism.[64] Our anthology analyzes these dynamic processes of militarization, their transformations, and emergent technologies with attention to their transpacific conditions.

Over the past few decades, scholarly literature on women in the military and the militarization of women's lives has offered tremendous insight on how militarization requires the cooperation and support of women, such that the notion that militarism remains exclusively a matter for men, or a masculine domain, is no longer tenable. Cynthia Enloe's pioneering work on gender and militarization provides a rich foundation for comparative analyses of the gendered dynamics of militarization and theorizes how militarization operates as a complex process, transforming institutions, economies, and relationships. While we maintain a thematic focus on the gendering practices of militarization, our anthology emphasizes the conjunction of race, gender, colonialism, and empire, extending the analytic trajectory of studies of militarization that have not engaged with its imbrications with colonialism and the gendered, racial structures of neocolonial practices.[65]

Studies of militarism and militarization in the post–cold war era have posited a paradigm shift from modern to postmodern forms of military organization.[66] Whereas the modern military was characteristically composed of both conscripted and professional ranks directed toward winning wars, the postmodern military is said to be less tied to the nation-state, increasingly "androgynous," and more fluid and permeable with civilian society.⁶⁷ The promotion of racial and gender diversity in the military and the increasing use of corporatized militias and contract security companies have been cited as evidence of increasingly expansive strategies of militarization. These shifts correspond and converge with the emergence of neoliberalism and globalization, representing the select incorporation of diversity, hybridity, and flexibility as markers of postmodernity. Such changes within militaries have not remained uncontested. Controversies abound regarding issues such as the commercial privatization of militaries, the recruitment and retention of gays and lesbians in the military, the roles of women in combat, and various forms of sexual harassment in the military.

While recognizing these shifts and rearticulations, our volume interrogates this categorization of postmodern militarization and questions whether gender and racial diversity have significantly or substantively altered heteronormative and racialized relations of power. Although the term "postmodern" (as well as "postcolonial") often denotes a posterior temporal and critical relationship, our volume seeks to demonstrate how *racialized and gendered colonial economies* continue to structure and overdetermine putatively postmodern and neoliberal forms of gender and racial diversity. We therefore pursue the claim that, for many people, colonialism has not ended but has been rearticulated, muted, and unmoored through discourses of neoliberalism, postmodernism, postcolonialism, and "antiterrorism." For example, our contributors investigate how the volunteer entry of indigenous people, (post)colonial subjects, and women into the military is conditioned by heterosexist logics and racialized class structures. By demonstrating how militarization continues to operate as a colonial technology that produces desiring subjects and regulates intimate familial, interpersonal, and sexual relations, our anthology illuminates the (neo)colonial conditions of the global present.

In this era of globalized militarization, we ask to what extent have discourses of gender and race been altered, transformed, and rearticulated? Are extant binary, heterosexist, and heteronormative notions of masculinity and femininity obsolete in the context of emergent militarized gendered economies and bodily practices? In what ways might we need to reformulate a spectrum of concepts that can deal adequately, for example, with *militarized female masculinities*, and in what ways are these racialized?⁶⁸ If contemporary modes of militarization are characterized by an increasing permeability with civilian life, are current practices of resistance to militarization no longer the most effective means of demilitarization?

In an era scholars have referred to as global or globalized militarization, we seek to decipher and contest the ways in which militarization has been normalized as inevitable.[69] Given emergent conditions of local and global militarization, we call for innovative and transformative methods of analysis that might foster coordinated, collective, and even unexpected forms of insurgency to forward the unfinished project of decolonization.

Theorists and writers engaged with anticolonial movements and postcolonial studies have produced a corpus of concepts and analytical tools that recognize the interworkings of race and gender as integral to the historical formation of colonialism and the identities of colonial and postcolonial subjects.[70] Often, due to institutional disciplinary limitations, studies of colonialism have attended to colonial literatures and the problems of anticolonial nationalism without sustained attention to the imbrications between militarism, colonialism, and identity formation. While recent scholarship on Japanese colonialism has demonstrated a "stronger emphasis on the variety of responses and experiences of the colonized," we wish to highlight how these complex conditions and memories inform *current* protests against remilitarization and the resurgence of Japanese militaristic nationalism.[71]

By building on and expanding existing lines of inquiry, this collective project aims to extend our understanding of militarization by demonstrating a cross-fertilization of ethnic and critical race studies, feminist and indigenous analyses, and cultural and transdisciplinary studies of militarization. Teresia Teaiwa's pioneering article, reprinted here, provides insights into the *engendering of nuclear colonialism*. She demonstrates how the Marshallese term "bikini" and images of bikini-clad female bodies function to obscure the unseen effects of U.S. nuclear devastation in Bikini Atoll, the Marshall Islands, as well as project an objectified heterosexual female body. As Teaiwa writes, "Nuclear testing is just one—albeit a most pernicious one—of the many colonial phenomena and processes that affect the Pacific region." These forms of nuclear colonialism not only displace the Marshallese from their homelands but also violently constrict indigenous cultures and ways of life, polluting the surrounding waters and lands and making sustainable fishing and farming challenging for generations to come.[72] As Jibā B. Kabua observes, "We Marshall Islanders must develop political will at every level, in every organization, for every situation, to *manage* the changing times in which we live."[73]

Kabua's call for agency, autonomy, and action are well heeded given that the militarization and nuclearization of the Marshall Islands has increasingly "served to 'nuclearize' and nucleate the Marshallese family structure, re-centering land and power around patriarchal and capitalist structures."[74] These transformations stem in part from a complex past of chiefly rule, imperial hegemony, matrilineal heritage, and indigenous resistance in the Marshall Islands. Teaiwa's article is reproduced here because one crucial aspect of this past—that is, the dual violence of American and Japanese colonialism and militarism—continues to haunt generations of Americans, Asians, and Pacific Islanders in the Marshall Islands in gendered and racialized ways that demand our attention and intervention. Referring to the transnational processes of remembrance and forgetting in the Marshall Islands, Greg Dvorak argues that "we are not asked to remember the mass [World War II] graves where Japanese, Korean, and Okinawan bodies were buried by the thousands, not implored to know where the houses of Marshallese chiefs once stood, and not reminded that this is Marshallese land."[75]

In a global era of heightened nuclear testing and threats, it is prudent that we remember the violence of nuclearism throughout the world, challenge all corporations and nation-states involved in the proliferation of nuclear technologies of death, and examine the gendered and racialized implications of these events on the lives of everyday people. That the United States continues to endanger lives with its presence of nuclear technology and warfare in the Pacific testifies to the American policy view of the region as a place whose populations are of little significance. Japan itself once considered dumping its industrial nuclear waste in the Mariana Trench in the 1970s, choosing to place nuclear toxins far from Japan's population but closer to Pacific Islander populations. Because of international protest, however, Japan was denied access to the Mariana Trench.[76] Indeed, it is precisely this current desirability of the Pacific—a region simultaneously commodified and exploited for its visible militarist and tourist value yet ultimately made invisible in its human diversity and complexity—that warrants our interrogation of normalizing structures of authority and governance and our foregrounding of indigenous forms of contestation and survival. As Teaiwa states, the Pacific "still churns with its colonial and nuclear legacies."

Decolonizing Bodies of Knowledge: A Cross-Regional Dialogue

Our anthology is concerned with Asia and the Pacific Islands, themselves problematic terms, whose boundaries and locales have been shaped by competing histories of colonialism and militarism. They are regions that, when juxtaposed for purposes of policy and research, frequently fall under the rubric of "Asia-Pacific."[77] The Asia-Pacific label is known more for its designation of countries on the Pacific Rim than for countries in the Pacific itself. In this geographical configuration, attention is paid to Pacific Rim countries like Chile, Hong Kong, and Singapore, whereas an examination of countries in the Pacific like Nauru, Fiji, and Sāmoa are often lacking. The Asia-Pacific term, while useful for economic analyses of industries in East and Southeast Asia, Latin America, and North America, often makes invisible the multiplicity of Pacific Islander contributions to these regional economies and polities. As Arif Dirlik observes, "Pacific Islanders, with whom the Pacific was initially identified, have been largely marginalized" by the ideology of Asia-Pacific.[78]

This marginalization has much to do with economic perceptions of Pacific lands and peoples as "small" and "isolated" relative to the Rim countries, hence producing a discourse that trivializes Pacific Islander forms of agency, capital, and labor across the region.[79] Pacific Islanders, though, are not the only societies made invisible by the Asia-Pacific rubric. With its focus on American and Asian "Rim" countries, one might presume that societies from these areas are included in dialogue about the Asia-Pacific. This is rarely the case, as the term actually favors discussions about "commodity flows and military-political relationships that would restructure the Asia-Pacific into a coherent region of economic exchange" and reflects the security interests of the more powerful Rim nations.[80] Peripheral to these debates are the roles of everyday peoples in the appropriation, contestation, or deliberation of regional and global hegemonies. With few exceptions, discourses concerning the Asia-Pacific have been structured around the idea of a region of economic, military, and political interest, as perceived by the Rim countries.[81] This anthology thus forwards counternarratives to the dominant ideology and power relations that are typically obscured through the reification of "Asia-Pacific" by analyzing what Ella Shohat calls the "multichronotopic links" between peoples who inhabit and are variously invested in the transformation of these regions.[82] With its attention to spatial–temporal relations, investigating "multichronotopic links" allows us to recognize implicit nationalisms in the production of knowledge and to challenge the ways in which universities erect disciplinary borders and quarantine interconnected fields of inquiry.[83]

Although the title of the volume might suggest that equal attention is devoted to Asia and the Pacific, we are aware that the volume is weighted heavily toward the Pacific versus East Asia and Southeast Asia. However, our purpose in doing so is not to intervene simply within the existing configuration of American and Asian studies, but rather to dialogue and analyze *across* these academic fields, geopolitical areas, and spatial–temporal relations to demonstrate precisely the artificial nature of such divisions when we consider the transregional movements, maneuvers, and logics of militarization. Our purpose in centering the Pacific in our volume is to provide a rearticulation of how the Pacific has been historically seen by Asian and American studies paradigms as an open frontier to be crossed, domesticated, occupied, and settled. Indeed, such regional divides are linked to the militarized logics of security and thus should be scrutinized cautiously, not mimetically replicated.

Our project therefore questions the effects of dominant paradigms and periodizations that privilege neocolonial forms of knowledge production through the consolidation of area studies during the cold war. For, as Jodi Kim argues in *Ends of Empire*, the cold war is not simply a matter of periodization but has served as a regulatory form of knowledge production.[84] The disavowal of colonial atrocities and ongoing militarized occupations were necessarily linked through a race for global dominance that crushed movements for decolonization during the overlapping postwar–cold war periods. The postwar, cold war, and post–cold war dominant periodizations obsfucate an alternative genealogy of arrested decolonization and demilitarization. In order to further demilitarizing and decolonizing alliances, we call for collaborative strategies of knowledge production that understand the political effects of such regional and national divisions.[85]

In framing the temporal and geographical scope of this anthology, then, we advocate the cautious use of the labels "Asia," the "Pacific" and "Asia-Pacific." After all, centuries of Asian and Western colonial rule have renamed as "feminine," transformed as "other," or altogether suppressed indigenous place names of these regions.[86] For this reason and others, our collection foregrounds hitherto subordinated and postcolonial bodies of knowledge that have remained marginalized and repressed under the imperial regimes of Japan and the United States and their attendant institutionalized divisions of "area studies" knowledge production. Instead, we seek to traverse purposely these constructed areas with a heightened call to engage with the knowledge produced by the peoples that reside and move across these areas. Following the directive of the Tongan scholar Epeli Hau'ofa, we focus on "how people, ordinary people, the forgotten people of history, have coped and are coping with their harsh realities, their resistance and struggles to be themselves and hold together."[87] With our concentration on Pacific Islanders, Asians, and Asian Americans, we draw critical attention to the agents of these societies and to the ways in which they articulate histories of resistance and struggle, foregrounding the perspectives of intellectuals from these regions and locales. Given these broad parameters, we specifically explore the experiences of Chamorros, Filipinos, Hawaiians, Japanese, Koreans, Marshallese, and Okinawans under the nexus of colonialism and militarism. While these peoples and societies do not comprise a comprehensive representation of these regions, we hope that this collection provides both a critique of area studies and a departure point for further transpacific dialogue.[88]

By addressing the interlinked Asian, Asian American, and Pacific Islander relations under the dual histories of U.S. and Japanese empires, we believe that area studies, ethnic studies, and interdisciplinary studies can be enriched methodologically, theoretically, and politically. As the Filipino Pohnpeian critic Vicente M. Diaz asserts, Asian American inquiry "must strive to comprehend the kinds of historical and political struggles that Native Pacific Scholars are trying to articulate, just as Native Pacific Scholars need to understand the specificities of Asian histories as they are bound up with the American imperial project among and amidst Native Pacific Islanders in the [U.S.] continent and in the Islands."[89] These points of convergence, as Yen Lê Espiritu argues, also "demand that we refashion the fields of American studies and Asian American studies, not around the narratives of American exceptionalism, and immigration, and transnationalism, but around the crucial issues of war, race, and violence—and of the history and memories that are forged from the thereafter."[90]

This kind of trajectory can foster discussions not only about U.S. militarization across Asia and the Pacific but also about a move beyond the "afterlife" of area studies paradigms that have been shaped by histories of American and Japanese empires. Paraphrasing Walter Benjamin's notion of "afterlife," H. D. Harootunian and Masao Miyoshi observe that we now face the afterlife of area studies, a perspective that surpasses "the older global divisions inaugurated after World War II that informed the organization of knowledge and teaching of regions of the world outside Euro-America."[91] Neither the nation-state category nor communist studies and modernization studies—paradigms central to the development of area studies—can any longer sustain *as natural* the global divisions of the world.[92] Indeed, as the historian Gary Y. Okihiro notes, the "boundaries separating ethnic studies, American studies, and area studies will be even less distinct than they appear in the present, judging from the movements within those fields," an act embraced and elaborated by the contributors of this volume.[93]

In bringing together a range of scholars and theorists who represent and articulate alternative locations and modes of knowledge production in Asia and the Pacific, *Militarized Currents* thus forwards analyses of militarization emanating from scholars and subjects situated in these colonial and postcolonial locations, introducing a generation of emergent voices who build on the pioneering work of our contributing scholars such as Katharine Moon and Naoki Sakai in Asian studies, and Teresia K. Teaiwa and Jon Kamakawiwoʻole Osorio in Pacific studies, and Walden Bello in globalization studies, among others. In doing so, we aim to create a space for dialogue across and between Asian studies, Pacific studies, feminist and gender studies, and American studies scholars, who might otherwise not be familiar or engaged in scholarship from other fields. We intend to build bridges between different scholars, writers, and activists concerned with militarization and emphasize the potentiality for transregional demilitarized movements.[94]

Part I of our anthology, "Militarized Bodies of Memory," opens with Jon Kamakawiwoʻole Osorio's "Memorializing Puʻuloa and Remembering Pearl Harbor." Given the symbolic significance of Pearl Harbor as the official beginning of World War II, we chose to open with Osorio's article, which provides a countermemory and counterdiscourse to the master historiographical narratives of Japan's "surprise attack" on the United States. By foregrounding the Hawaiian naming of Puʻuloa, the imposed colonial renaming of Pearl Harbor is unsettled. As noted already, the American naming can be understood as a process of militarized colonization inscribing and claiming possession of the altered and now-prohibitive militarized terrain. Osorio begins with Hawaiian song and poetry that recalls another system of values and epistemologies of the place known as Puʻuloa. Through a recounting of his own familial genealogies that intimately connect American militarism with Hawaiian dispossession and anticolonial movements, Osorio eloquently explores the complex dynamics of memory and the different forces of identity formation and divergent desires across four generations of his family.

Osorio's article is followed by Teresia K. Teaiwa's "Bikinis and Other S/pacific N/oceans." We offer a reprint of this 1994 article to emphasize the path-breaking postcolonial critique forwarded by indigenous Pacific Islander scholars like Teaiwa and others whose recognition is often obscured due to the ongoing marginalization of Pacific Islander and indigenous studies within the fields of Asian, Asian American, and American studies.[95] Teaiwa writes that the "bikini bathing suit manifests both a celebration and a forgetting of the nuclear power that strategically and materially marginalizes and erases the living history of Pacific Islanders." Teaiwa's paradigm-shaping analysis of militarist, nuclear, and touristic discourses on Bikini Atoll, Marshall Islands, demonstrates the feminization and sexualization of nuclear colonialism, elaborating how empires have been engendered through the deformation and violation of Pacific Islander bodies, whose bodies of memory are too rarely seen or heard.[96]

Following from Teaiwa's thematics of visibility and invisibility, Michael Lujan Bevacqua marks the invisibility of Guam historically and contemporaneously as representative of what he describes as the "banal coloniality" of its official "organized unincorporated" status as a U.S. territory. In his chapter, "The Exceptional Life and Death of a Chamorro Soldier: Tracing the Militarization of Desire in Guam, USA," Bevacqua analyzes the high levels of Chamorro military participation and patriotism by elaborating a genealogy that connects the production of Chamorro desire to join the military to the century-long legacy of colonization. A diasporic Chamorro writer, poet, and scholar, Bevacqua's chapter challenges the normalization of the U.S. military presence that occupies more than one third of the landmass of Guam. Bevacqua incisively theorizes the uncanny and haunting residues of the intermingling of deaths of Chamorro soldiers and the desire for subjecthood for those who live and die in the immediacy of the U.S. colonial militarized presence.

Vernadette Vicuña Gonzalez's chapter, "Touring Military Masculinities: U.S.–Philippines Circuits of Sacrifice and Gratitude in Corregidor and Bataan," theorizes the intertwined economies of tourism, militarism, and colonialism as a thread that links the economies of Hawaiʻi, Guam, and the Philippines. Gonzalez meticulously analyzes the raced and gendered visual narratives of the American military in two touristic sites in postcolonial Philippines: Corregidor Island and Bataan. In her reading of these two tourist destinations, Gonzalez demonstrates how racialized masculinity and heroism are deployed in appeals to "remember properly." In these two sites, the act of touring historical battlefields and military routes is simultaneously an emotional and ideological remembering of a benevolent

American protector and an erasure of Japanese imperial violence and occupation. This act, as Gonzalez asserts, provides a selective reiteration of the Philippines' continuing "special relationship" with the United States as its former colonizer. In these intensely patriotic places, monuments that portray the homosocial bonds of men at war, mutual suffering, and interracial camaraderie of American and Filipino soldiers demonstrate how masculinized heroism and imperial nostalgia function in narrativizing how occupiers and empires are engendered and remembered.

The four chapters in part II, titled "Militarized Movements," thematize how social movements and migrations of bodies have been simultaneously militarized, racialized, and sexualized. The chapters here demonstrate how militarization operates as a transnational structuring force that has remained undertheorized as a process that has defined, shaped, and regulated Asian and Pacific Islander displacements and diasporas and the formation of transnational resistance, demilitarization, and decolonization movements that cross these regions. Thus, while we emphasize that militarization moves beyond the institution of the military, as a transregional and global force, we wish to highlight how it is also a force that structures subjectivity and human relations in the most intimate forms. That is to say, we underscore how militarization operates as a regulating logic and institutionalized practice in terms of familial and sexual relations and infuses and structures various political, resistance, and decolonization movements. All the chapters here demonstrate as well how the dual colonial histories of Guam, Korea, Okinawa, and the Philippines from the late nineteenth century to the twentieth century articulate through contemporary political movements for demilitarization as part of the longer process of decolonization.

This part opens with Wesley Ueunten's chapter, "Rising Up from a Sea of Discontent: The 1970 Koza Uprising in U.S.-Occupied Okinawa." Ueunten provides a transnational perspective on Okinawa's past and ongoing militarized colonial condition. As a territory that has been colonized by Japan and the United States and continues to remain under de facto shared rule by the U.S. military and the Japanese government, Okinawa represents the coarticulation of this complementary and dual neocolonial system. Despite the fact that Okinawa comprises only 0.6 percent of Japanese national territory, 75 percent of U.S. military bases in Japan are concentrated in Okinawa. Although Okinawa was officially reverted from U.S. military governance back to the Japanese government in 1972, its economy, territory, and peoples remain subordinate to the U.S. military's commanding presence that occupies approximately 11 percent of its lands and 19 percent of Okinawa's main island. Ueunten's chapter explores the shared links between Okinawan, African American, and Third World movements in response to U.S. imperialism and militarism. Central to this chapter is an analysis of the Koza Uprising by Okinawans on the night of December 20, 1970. In the midst of the rebellion, Okinawans purposefully refrained from harming African American soldiers, saying that they were "the same as us." Ueunten's chapter explores a shared Third World consciousness against U.S. imperialism that bridges U.S. racial politics and Okinawan discontent under U.S. military rule as an aftereffect of Japanese colonialism. As an Okinawan diasporic scholar and activist, Ueunten's work demonstrates how Okinawan colonial identity can be productively examined in relation to people of color in the United States who have been incorporated into and have lived under the conditions of U.S. militarism.

Ueunten's chapter is followed by a reprint of Katharine Moon's instructive article, "South Korean Movements against Militarized Sexual Labor." Moon's chapter rigorously demonstrates the overlapping conditions and complicities among the Korean government, the Japanese "comfort women" system, and the U.S. military in regulating the sexual exploitation of specific classes and groups of South Korean women. In this chapter, Moon comparatively analyzes the historical context and politics of two movements against militarized sexual labor, namely, the *chŏngsindae* movement (also known as the comfort women movement) and the *kijich'on* movement, the movement that is concerned with the conditions of sex workers in U.S. military camptowns. Through her analysis of these two movements, Moon examines the many connections that link the formation of these movements, which include the colonial occupation of Korea by Japan and the military occupation of South Korea by the United States. As Moon's work indicates, some of the same women who were *chŏngsindae* (comfort women) for the Japanese imperial system later became sex workers for the U.S. military. Moon's pioneering research on the militarization of sexual relations in South Korea brings to bear how the violent and coerced militarization of women's sexuality can lead to the formation of new political movements.

Keith L. Camacho and Laurel A. Monnig's coauthored chapter, "Uncomfortable Fatigues: Chamorro Soldiers, Gendered Identities, and the Question of Decolonization in Guam," analyzes the formation of militarized masculinities in Guam. Specifically, Camacho and Monnig explore the interrelated processes of militarization and masculinization among Guam's Chamorro men in the U.S. Armed Forces. This chapter foregrounds the voices of decolonization activists, military recruiters, and soldiers who speak to the complex conditions of their gendered incorporation into the U.S. military and how they struggle against and with their subordinated status. This chapter illustrates unexpected forms of resistance that militarization produces at the nexus of militarized masculinities and demilitarization movements. Camacho and Monnig argue that the processes of militarization and decolonization are constitutive states of contradiction and pose questions for possibilities of resistance against U.S. militarism in Guam and elsewhere.

Continuing on the thematic of racialized masculinities, Theresa Cenidoza Suarez's chapter, "Militarized Filipino Masculinity and the Language of Citizenship in San Diego," examines the multiple and competing meanings of heteronormative manhood among Filipino navy veterans and their families. Suarez examines how Filipino masculinity is constructed within a transnational context overshadowed by U.S. military culture and U.S. imperialism. Specifically, she explores how Filipino militarized masculinity emerges as a necessary and tenuous construction and not exclusively as a male-gendered or male-gendering project. Rather, Suarez argues that Filipino masculinity is constituted through the co-constructions of heteronormative womanhood and childhood, roles imagined and lived within a transnational domestic sphere inescapably militarized and domesticated. Suarez's chapter does much to demonstrate how Filipino American migration to the United States has been regulated through processes of militarization, which she theorizes as constituting "militarized diaporas."

The final part of the anthology, "Hetero/Homo-sexualized Militaries," brings together four chapters that examine the sexualized economies produced and regulated by military practices. This part begins with Naoki Sakai's chapter, "On Romantic Love and Military Violence: Transpacific Imperialism and U.S.–Japan Complicity," which cogently describes the historical, political, and philosophical intimacies between Japanese and U.S. imperial projects. Sakai's chapter theorizes how the relationship between the colonizer and the colonized—which is mediated through the threat and use of military violence—is narrativized and practiced in heterosexualized terms. Sakai discusses how the underlying and constant threat of violence along with the imminent threat of rape is repressed, converted, and represented in the cinematic form through an economy of heterosexual romance that produces the spectrality of love and seduction. Sakai's chapter does much work to elaborate the relationship between American and Japanese imperialism and how the "universality" of Japanese colonial discourse must be subordinated to the status of a particular in contrast to the reiterated claims of American imperialist universalism. Sakai's chapter provides a historical and theoretical contextualization of the connections between contemporary forms of militarization in South Korea and Japan in relation to Japanese colonialism in Korea and the U.S.-supported militarization of Japan and South Korea.

Insook Kwon's chapter, "Masculinity and Male-on-Male Sexual Violence in the Military: Focusing on the Absence of the Issue," offers the first English-language translation of her groundbreaking study of male-on-male sexual violence in the contemporary South Korean military.[97] Kwon examines the conditions of such male-on-male sexual conduct and homoerotic practices based on surveys and firsthand interviews with military personnel. She also analyzes the mass media and the official military responses to this phenomenon, commenting on the reasons for the public silence surrounding this issue. Given South Korea's mandatory conscription system, Kwon's feminist-informed analysis concludes that the sanctioned masculinity in the military—and how it is practiced and engendered—should be a major issue for those concerned with gendered inequality and sexual violence.

Kwon's chapter is followed by Fumika Sato's pioneering work on women in the Japanese Self-Defense Forces.[98] Sato's chapter, "Why Have the Japanese Self-Defense Forces Included Women?: The State's 'Nonfeminist Reasons,'" analyzes how and why women have been incorporated into the Japanese Self-Defense Forces (SDF) from the 1950s to the present. In her chapter, Sato argues that the feminization of the SDF through its incorporation of women is not motivated by feminist reasons, but that the institutional logic remains heterosexist. Sato's study of the gendering of the SDF provides a salient example of how the feminization of the marketing of the SDF works to create the image of the Japanese military as "peace-makers." As a Japanese feminist scholar, Sato's study also provides a useful counterpoint for considering the significant difference in Japanese feminist responses to women's incorporation in the military compared to U.S. liberal feminist arguments for women's equal treatment and opportunity in the military.

Sato's chapter, along with Kwon, Suarez, Gonzalez, and Camacho and Monnig's work, is one of five chapters in the volume that focuses on gendered, militarized, and racialized identities. While the chapters by Suarez, Camacho and Monnig, and Gonzalez demonstrate the intersectional approach to racialized gender and colonialism representative of an emergent generation of scholars, their juxtaposition with the work of Kwon and Sato also reveals the methodological discrepancies and gaps between methodologies (in both area studies and social sciences) that do not emphasize the racialization of gender or the insights of queer studies. Nevertheless, we see the inclusion of such work as valuable precisely in order to generate cross-disciplinary and transregional dialogues across the Pacific with scholars working outside the U.S. academy.

Patti Duncan's chapter, "Genealogies of Unbelonging: Amerasians and Transnational Adoptees as Legacies of U.S. Militarism in South Korea," draws from a body of feminist scholarship on U.S. militarism in Asia. Duncan's chapter analyzes representations of the experiences of Amerasian children of military camptown women and the transnational adoption of their children as part of the legacy of U.S. militarism in South Korea. As the nation that has the highest rate of transnational adoptions, Duncan argues for an analysis of the relationship between "unidirectional" adoption and Amerasian children, given the latter's presumed association with the militarized sex industry and the U.S. occupation of their homeland. The militarized sexual relations between U.S. military personnel, sex workers, and civilians produces children that are the living reminders of continuing occupation. Militarization is thus a force that has produced generations of abandoned and adopted multiracial children through militarized sexual relations. Within this context, the militarization of bodies and subjectivities continues to incite new alliances in the current struggles to demilitarize the future for generations to come.

Bello's closing chapter, "From American Lake to a People's Pacific in the Twenty-First Century," maps out the current expanse of what he calls America's "transnational garrison state" as it impacts Asia and the Pacific. But more importantly, Bello's chapter offers a vision of alternatives to U.S. militarism that is increasingly showing signs of strain throughout these regions and forwards a case for demilitarizing and denuclearizing the "Asia-Pacific." By concluding this collection with this call for demilitarization, we want to affirm the power of people's struggles for decolonized futures that expand beyond the places currently named "Asia" and the

"Pacific." It is our hope that the future direction of research and scholarship will also converge and combine with the efforts to demilitarize the currents of empire.

Notes

1. Andrea Smith, "American Studies with America: Native Feminisms and the Nation-State," *American Quarterly* 60, no. 2 (2008): 312.

2. As Sabine Frühstück's work illuminates, negotiating the history and representations of the Imperial Japanese Army is very much integral to contemporary processes of rearticulating the identity of the Japanese Self-Defense Forces. Sabine Frühstück, *Uneasy Warriors: Gender, Memory, and Popular Culture in the Japanese Army* (Berkeley: University of California Press, 2007).

3. See Naoki Sakai's chapter in this volume, "On Romantic Love and Military Violence: Transpacific Imperialism and U.S.–Japan Complicity." See also Naoki Sakai, "'You Asians': On the Historical Role of the West and Asia Binary," *The South Atlantic Quarterly*, "Millennial Japan," 99, no. 4 (2000): 789–817.

4. Yuki Tanaka, *Japan's Comfort Women: The Military and Involuntary Prostitution During War and Occupation* (London: Routledge, 2002); "The Comfort Women: Colonialism, War, and Sex," Special Issue of *positions: east asia cultures critique* 5, no. 1 (1997); *Journal of Asian American Studies* 6, no. 1 (2003); George Hicks, *The Comfort Women: Japan's Brutal Regime of Enforced Prostitution in the Second World War* (New York: W. W. Norton & Co., 1985).

5. See the chapters by Katharine H. S. Moon (chapter 6), Naoki Sakai (chapter 9), and Patti Duncan (chapter 12).

6. Lisa Yoneyama, "Traveling Memories, Contagious Justice: Americanization of Japanese War Crimes at the End of the Post-Cold War," *Journal of Asian American Studies* 6, no. 1 (2003): 57–93.

7. Ibid.

8. Lijon Eknilang and James Matayoshi, "Rongelap Survivors," in *Life in the Republic of the Marshall Islands: Mour ilo republic eo an majōl*, ed. Anono Lieom Loeak, Veronica C. Kiluwe, and Linda Crowl (Majuro, Marshall Islands: University of the South Pacific Centre and Institute of Pacific Studies, University of the South Pacific, 2004), 130.

9. Ibid., 131.

10. Craig Calhoun, Frederick Cooper, and Kevin W. Moore, "Introduction," in *Lessons of Empire: Imperial Histories and American Power*, ed. Craig Calhoun, Frederick Cooper, and Kevin W. Moore (New York: The New Press, 2006), 1.

11. Leo T. S. Ching, *Becoming Japanese: Colonial Taiwan and the Politics of Identity Formation* (Berkeley: University of California Press, 2001), 19. An example of

such a collaborative alliance is cited by Mark Selden and Laura Hein. "The United States also used Okinawa as a nuclear arsenal throughout the postwar era, both before and after reversion, with secret Japanese government approval" (22). Laura Hein and Mark Selden, "Culture, Power and Identity in Contemporary Okinawa," in *Islands of Discontent: Okinawan Responses to Japanese and American Power*, ed. Laura Hein and Mark Selden (Oxford: Rowman & Littlefield, 2002), 1–35.

12. Alexis Dudden, "Introduction," in *Japan's Colonization of Korea* (Honolulu: University of Hawai'i Press, 2005), 2.

13. Ching, *Becoming Japanese*, 24.

14. Li Narangoa and Robert Cribb, "Introduction: Japan and the Transformation of National Identities in Asia," in *Imperial Japan and National Identities in Asia, 1895–1945*, ed. Li Narangoa and Robert Cribb (New York: Routledge, 2003), 1–22.

15. Gerald Horne, *White Supremacy and the Japanese Attack on the British Empire* (New York: New York University Press, 2004), vii.

16. Andrew Gordon, *Labor and Imperial Democracy in Prewar Japan* (Berkeley: University of California Press, 1992), 23.

17. Nicholas Tarling, *A Sudden Rampage: The Japanese Occupation of Southeast Asia, 1941–1945* (Honolulu: University of Hawai'i Press, 2001).

18. Lewis H. Gann, "Western and Japanese Colonialism: Some Preliminary Comparisons," in *The Japanese Colonial Empire, 1895–1945*, ed. Ramon H. Myers and Mark R. Peattie (Princeton, N.J.: Princeton University Press, 1984), 502.

19. Mark R. Peattie, "The Nan'yō: Japan in the South Pacific, 1885–1945," in *The Japanese Colonial Empire, 1895–1945*, 203; Tomiyama Ichiro, "The 'Japanese' of Micronesia: Okinawans in the Nan'yô Islands," in *Okinawan Diaspora*, ed. Ronald Y. Nakasone (Honolulu: University of Hawai'i Press, 2002), 57–70.

20. Aiko Utsumi, "Korean 'Imperial Soldiers': Remembering Colonialism and Crimes against Allied POWs," in *Perilous Memories: The Asia-Pacific War(s)*, ed. T. Fujitani, Geoffrey M. White, and Lisa Yoneyama (Durham, N.C.: Duke University Press, 2001), 199–217; Michael Weiner, *Race and Migration in Imperial Japan* (New York: Routledge, 1994).

21. Takashi Fujitani, "Right to Kill, Right to Make Live: Koreans as Japanese and Japanese as Americans During WWII," *Representations* 99, no. 1 (2007): 17.

22. Ibid., 33.

23. Jane C. Desmond, *Staging Tourism: Bodies on Display from Waikiki to Sea World* (Chicago: The University of Chicago Press, 1999), 13.

24. Ron Crocombe, *Asia in the Pacific Islands: Replacing the West* (Suva, Fiji: IPS Publications, University of the South Pacific, 2007), 171.

25. American Friends Service Committee, "AFSC Hawai'i Gay Liberation Program: Activist Materials Addressing Tourism," *GLQ: A Journal of Lesbian and Gay Studies* 8, no. 1–2 (2002): 211.

26. Teresia K. Teaiwa, "Native Thoughts: A Pacific Studies Take on Cultural Studies and Diaspora," in *Indigenous Diasporas and Dislocations*, ed. Harvey and Charles D. Thompson (London: Ashgate, 2005), 16.

27. Japan ranked seventh in military spending in 2008, after the United States, China, Britain, Russia, and France, and tied with Germany to account for 3.2 percent of the world's military expenditures, according to the Stockholm International Peace Research Institute. China's military expenditure surpassed Japan's for the first time in 2006, making China the largest military spender in Asia. Petter Stålenheim, Noel Kelly, Catalina Perdomo, Sam Perlo-Freeman, and Elisabeth Sköns, "Military Expenditure," in *SIPRI (Stockholm International Peace Research Institute) 2009 Yearbook: Armaments, Disarmaments and International Security* (Oxford: Oxford University Press, 2009). Available at http://www.sipri.org/yearbook/2009/05/05A (accessed December 5, 2009).

28. Joanne Barker, "For Whom Sovereignty Matters," in *Sovereignty Matters: Locations of Contestation and Possibility in Indigenous Struggles for Self-Determination*, ed. Joanne Barker (Lincoln: University of Nebraska Press, 2005), 4.

29. Ediberto Román, *The Other American Colonies: An International and Constitutional Law Examination of the United States' Nineteenth and Twentieth Century Island Conquests* (Durham, N.C.: Carolina Academic Press, 2006), 33.

30. For a selection of key essays on Pacific issues, see David Hanlon and Geoffrey M. White, *Voyaging Through the Contemporary Pacific* (Lanham, Md.: Rowman & Littlefield, 2000).

31. See Eileen H. Tamura, *Americanization, Acculturation, and Ethnic Identity: The Nisei Generation in Hawaii* (Urbana: University of Illinois Press, 1994); and Catherine Ceniza Choy, *Empire of Care: Nursing and Migration in Filipino American History* (Durham, N.C.: Duke University Press, 2003).

32. Julian Go, "'Racism' and Colonialism: Meanings of Difference and Ruling Practices in America's Pacific Empire," *Qualitative Sociology* 27, no. 1 (2004): 44.

33. On these subjects, see respectively, Paul A. Kramer, *The Blood of Government: Race, Empire, the United States and the Philippines* (Chapel Hill: The University of North Carolina Press, 2006); and Noenoe K. Silva, *Aloha Betrayed: Native Hawaiian Resistance to American Colonialism* (Durham, N.C.: Duke University Press, 2004).

34. T. Fujitani, Geoffrey M. White, and Lisa Yoneyama, "Introduction," in *Perilous Memories: The Asia-Pacific War(s)*, 3.

35. Lisa Yoneyama, "Traveling Memories, Contagious Justice," 81.

36. David Hanlon, *Remaking Micronesia: Discourses over Development in a Pacific Territory, 1944–1982* (Honolulu: University of Hawai'i Press, 1998), 24.

37. Kathy E. Ferguson and Phyllis Turnbull, *Oh, Say, Can You See?: The Semiotics of the Military in Hawai'i* (Minneapolis: University of Minnesota Press, 1999), xiv.

38. Elaine H. Kim and Chungmoo Choi, "Introduction," in *Dangerous Women: Gender and Korean Nationalism*, ed. Elaine H. Kim and Chungmoo Choi (New York: Routledge, 1998), 3.

39. Nomura Koya, "Colonialism and Nationalism: The View from Okinawa," in *Okinawan Diaspora*, 112–19.

40. Hideaki Tobe, "Military Bases and Modernity: An Aspect of Americanization in Okinawa," *Transforming Anthropology* 14, no. 1 (2006): 93.

41. Ibid. See also Nomura Koya, *Muishiki no shokuminchishugi* (Colonialism's unconscious) (Tokyo: Ochanomizu Shoten, 2005).

42. See Scott Saft and Yumiko Ohara, "The Media and the Pursuit of Militarism in Japan: Newspaper Editorials in the Aftermath of 9/11," *Critical Discourse Studies* 3, no. 1 (2006): 81–101.

43. Society of American Military Engineers, *Guam Military Build-up Program* (Washington, D.C.: U.S. Government Printing Office, 2007), 2.

44. Eric Schmitt, "Secretary Gates Visits Guam Military Base," *The New York Times*, May 30, 2008, http://www.nytimes.com/2008/05/30/world/asia/31guam.html?partner=rssnyt&emc=rss (accessed November 23, 2009).

45. See "Obama OKs 734M for Buildup," *Pacific Daily News*, October 30, 2009, http://www.guampdn.com/apps/pbcs.dll/article?AID=/200910300300/NEWS01/910300327 (accessed November 23, 2009).

46. Julian Aguon, *The Fire This Time: Essays on Life under U.S. Occupation* (Tokyo: Blue Ocean Press, 2006), 10.

47. "Guam Hosts Talks on Military Buildup," *Air Force Times*, August 24, 2007, http://www.airforcetimes.com/news/2007/08/ap_guambuildup_070824 (accessed July 1, 2008).

48. Ronni Alexander, "Confronting Militarization: Intersections of Gender(ed) Violence, Militarization and Resistance in the Pacific" (paper presented at the 49th annual meeting of the International Studies Association, San Francisco, Calif., March 26, 2008).

49. *Fuetsan famalao'an* literally means "the strong women" in English.

50. Mar-Vic Cagurangan, "Activists Bare Report on GI Atrocities Against Japanese," *Marianas Variety*, January 28, 2008, 1.

51. Aguon, *The Fire This Time*, 9.

52. J. Kehaulani Kauanui, "Asian American Studies and the 'Pacific Question,'" in *Asian American Studies After Critical Mass*, ed. Kent A. Ono (Malden, Mass.: Blackwell Publishing, 2005), 134.

53. Jonathan Y. Okamura, *Ethnicity and Inequality in Hawai'i* (Philadelphia: Temple University Press, 2008), 62; Candace Fujikane and Jonathan Y. Okamura, ed., *Asian Settler Colonialism: From Local Governance to the Habits of Everyday Life in Hawai'i* (Honolulu: University of Hawai'i Press, 2008).

54. Haunani-Kay Trask, "Settlers of Color and 'Immigrant' Hegemony," *Amerasia Journal* 26, no. 2 (2000): 4.

55. Ibid., 2–3.

56. Dean Itsuji Saranillio, "Colonial Amnesia: Rethinking Filipino 'American' Settler Empowerment in the U.S. Colony of Hawai'i," in *Positively No Filipinos Allowed: Building Communities and Discourse*, ed. Antonio T. Tiongson, Jr., Edgardo V. Gutierrez, and Ricardo V. Gutierrez (Philadelphia: Temple University Press, 2006), 140.

57. Vilsoni Hereniko, "Indigenous Knowledge and Academic Imperialism," in *Remembrance of Pacific Pasts: An Invitation to Remake History*, ed. Robert Borofsky (Honolulu: University of Hawai'i Press, 2000), 86.

58. See Mary L. Dudziak, ed., *September 11 in History: A Watershed Moment?* (Durham, N.C.: Duke University Press, 2003).

59. William J. Fallon, "Statement before the House Armed Services Committee on U.S. Pacific Command Posture," House Armed Services Committee, March 9, 2006, 3. H.R. 2647: Defense Authorization Act for Fiscal Year 2006, 109th Congress.

60. Alfred Vagats, *A History of Militarism: Civilian and Military* (New York: Meridian Books, 1959). Revised edition of 1937 edition.

61. Ismael Hossein-Zadeh writes, "The power and influence of militarism is exercised indirectly, that is, through formally civilian organs of the state structure" (27). Ismael Hossein-Zadeh, *The Political Economy of U.S. Militarism* (New York: Palgrave, 2006).

62. Chalmers Johnson, *The Sorrows of Empire* (New York: Metropolitan Books, 2004), 23–24.

63. Kim emphasizes for the importance of maintaining "a critical perspective on the function of this division; to judge the content, practices, and quality of phenomena assigned to both [civilian–military] categories; and to analyze the ethical dilemma of maintaining or challenging (or both) the practical outcomes that the existence of the category 'military' facilitates." We thank Jean Kim for this comment.

64. Many scholars have deployed the term "militarization" to emphasize the *process* by which formerly nonmilitary aspects of society, culture, and economy become increasingly influenced by militaristic values (Vagats, *A History of Militarism*). Cynthia Enloe writes, "Militarization is a step-by-step process by which a person or thing gradually comes to be controlled by the military *or* comes to depend for its well-being on militaristic ideas. The more militarization transforms an individual or society, the more that individual or society comes to imagine military needs and militaristic presumptions to be not only valuable but also normal. Militarization, that is, involves cultural as well as institutional, ideological and economic transformations." Cynthia Enloe, *Maneuvers: The International Politics of Militarizing Women's Lives* (Berkeley: University of California Press, 2000), 3. Glen Hook's definition emphasizes the relevance of understanding how

militarization is a transnational process: "The concept of militarization can be used to bring into critical focus the increase in size, strength or influence of the military as a dynamic process with international or even transnational implications" (18). Glenn D. Hook, *Militarization and Demilitarization in Contemporary Japan* (New York: Routledge 1996); Catherine Lutz, *Homefront: A Military City and the American 20th Century* (Boston: Beacon Press, 2001); Catherine Lutz, "Making War at Home in the United States: Militarization and the Current Crisis," *American Anthropologist* 104, no. 3 (2002): 723–35.

65. Despite the growing body of literature on gender and the military, Gwendolyn Hall has pointed out that there persists a dearth of analyses that examine the intersectionality of how gender and race are continually at work in structuring the composition, evaluation, and representation of the military. Although Hall is specifically concerned with the lack of attention to women of color in the U.S. military, we can extend her critique to how studies of gender-related issues in the military have often neglected the ways in which gender is racialized and the ways in which race is gendered. Gwendolyn Hall, "Intersectionality: A Necessary Consideration for Women of Color in the Military?" in *Beyond Zero Tolerance: Discrimination in Military Culture*, ed. Mary Katzenstein and Judith Reppy (Boston: Rowman & Littlefield, 1999), 143–62. See Setsu Shigematsu, Anuradha Bhagwati, and Eli Painted Crow, "Women-of-Color Veterans on War, Militarism and Feminism," in *Feminism and War: Confronting Feminism and Imperialism*, ed. Robin Riley, Chandra Mohanty, and Minnie Bruce Pratt (London: Zed Press, 2008), 93–102.

66. Charles Moskos, John Allen Williams, and David Segal, ed., *The Postmodern Military: Armed Forces After the Cold War* (Oxford: Oxford University Press, 2000).

67. Ibid., 1.

68. For a pioneering study of "female masculinity" see Judith Halberstam, *Female Masculinity* (Durham, N.C.: Duke University Press, 1998); Judith Halberstam, "The Good, the Bad, and the Ugly: Men, Women, and Masculinity," in *Masculinity Studies and Feminist Theory: New Directions*, ed. Judith Kegan Gardiner (New York: Columbia University Press, 2002), 344–67.

69. Asbjorn Eide and Marek Thee, ed., *Problems of Contemporary Militarism* (London: Croom Helm, 1980). See also Peter Wallensteen, Johan Galtung, and Carlos Portales, ed., *Global Militarization* (London: Westview Press, 1985); Cynthia Enloe, *Globalization and Militarism* (New York: Rowman & Littlefield, 2007).

70. Some classic studies we refer to are Frantz Fanon, *Black Skin White Masks* (New York: Grove Press, 1967); Edward Said, *Orientalism* (New York: Pantheon Books, 1978); Ann McClintock, *Imperial Leather: Race, Gender and Sexuality in the Colonial Contest* (New York: Routledge, 1995); Ann Laura Stoler, *Race and the Education of Desire* (Durham, N.C.: Duke University Press, 1995); and Ann Laura

Stoler, *Carnal Knowledge and Imperial Power: Race and the Intimate in Colonial Rule* (Berkeley: University of California Press, 2002).

71. Sandra Wilson, "Bridging the Gaps: New Views of Japanese Colonialism, 1931–1945," *Japanese Studies* 25, no. 3 (2005): 295. Shin and Robinson's volume seeks to demonstrate the "complexity and diversity of colonial modernity, hegemony and identity formation" in colonial Korea (18). *Colonial Modernity in Korea*, ed. Gi-Wook Shin and Michael Robinson (Cambridge, Mass.: Harvard University Press, 2001). Ichiro Tomiyama, "Japan's Militarization and Okinawa's Bases," trans. Wesley Ueunten, *Inter-Asia Cultural Studies* 1, no. 2 (2000): 349–56.

72. Jibā B. Kabua, "We Are the Land, the Land Is Us: The Moral Responsibility of Our Education and Sustainability," in *Life in the Republic of the Marshall Islands: Mour ilo republic eo an majōl*, ed. Anono Lieom Loeak, Veronica C. Kiluwe, and Linda Crowl (Majuro, Marshall Islands: University of the South Pacific Centre and Institute of Pacific Studies, University of the South Pacific, 2004), 187.

73. Ibid., 189.

74. Greg Dvorak, "'The Martial Islands': Making Marshallese Masculinities between American and Japanese Militarism," *The Contemporary Pacific* 20, no. 1 (2008): 69.

75. Ibid., 79.

76. See Crocombe, *Asia in the Pacific Islands*, 168, 341–42.

77. Arif Dirlik, "The Asia-Pacific Idea: Reality and Representation in the Invention of a Regional Structure," *Journal of World History* 3, no. 1 (1992): 56.

78. Ibid., 56.

79. See Epeli Hau'ofa, "Our Sea of Islands," *The Contemporary Pacific* 6 (1994): 147–61.

80. Rob Wilson and Arif Dirlik, "Introduction: Asia/Pacific as Space of Cultural Production," in *Asia/Pacific as Space of Cultural Production*, ed. Rob Wilson and Arif Dirlik (London: Duke University Press, 1995), 6.

81. Dirlik, "The Asia-Pacific Idea," 56.

82. Ella Shohat, "Area Studies, Gender Studies, and the Cartographies of Knowledge," *Social Text* 20, no. 3 (2002): 69.

83. Ibid.

84. Jodi Kim, *Ends of Empire: Asian American Critique and the Cold War* (Minneapolis: University of Minnesota Press, 2010).

85. The East Asia–U.S.–Puerto Rico Women's Network Against Militarism is an example of such a transregional demilitarizing effort. We affirm the need to create transregional alliances to further what Kuan-Hsing Chen points to as the "incomplete project of decolonization" (47). Kuan-Hsing Chen, "Introduction: The Decolonization Question," in *Trajectories: Inter-Asia Cultural Studies*, ed. Kuan-Hsing Chen (New York: Routledge, 1998), 1–53.

86. Nerissa S. Balce, "The Filipina's Breast: Savagery, Docility, and the Erotics of the American Empire," *Social Text* 24, no. 2 (2006): 90.

87. Epeli Hau'ofa, "Epilogue: Pasts to Remember," in *Remembrance of Pacific Pasts: An Invitation to Remake History*, ed. Robert Borofsky (Honolulu: University of Hawai'i Press, 2000), 458.

88. Shirley Hune, "Through 'Our' Eyes: Asian/Pacific Islander American Women's History," in *Asian/Pacific Islander American Women: A Historical Anthology*, ed. Shirley Hune and Gail M. Nomura (New York: New York University Press, 2003), 11.

89. Vicente M. Diaz, "To 'P' or not to 'P': Marking the Territory Between Pacific Islander and Asian American Studies," *Journal of Asian American Studies* 7, no. 3 (2004): 184.

90. Yen Lê Espiritu, "Thirty Years AfterWARd: The Endings That Are Not Over," *Amerasia Journal* 31, no. 2 (2005): xviii.

91. H. D. Harootunian and Masao Miyoshi, "Introduction: The 'Afterlife' of Area Studies," in *Learning Places: The Afterlives of Area Studies*, ed. Masao Miyoshi and H. D. Harootunian (Durham, N.C.: Duke University Press, 2002), 14.

92. Bruce Cummings, "Boundary Displacement: The State, the Foundations, and Area Studies during and after the Cold War," in *Learning Places: The Afterlives of Area Studies*, ed. Masao Miyoshi and H. D. Harootunian (Durham, N.C.: Duke University Press, 2002), 265.

93. Gary Y. Okihiro, *The Columbia Guide to Asian American History* (New York: Columbia University Press, 2001), xiv.

94. The editorial collaboration between Setsu Shigematsu and Keith L. Camacho, who are respectively trained as an Asian–Japan studies–Asian American studies feminist scholar and as a historian of Pacific Islander Studies is an example of the kind of cross-disciplinary and cross-regional dialogues we hope to generate.

95. See Vicente M. Diaz and J. Kēhaulani Kauanui, "Native Pacific Cultural Studies on the Edge," *The Contemporary Pacific* 13, no. 2 (2001): 315–42.

96. Teresia K. Teaiwa, "On Analogies: Rethinking the Pacific in a Global Context," *The Contemporary Pacific* 18, no. 1 (2006): 73.

97. Translation from the Korean language publication, chapter 5 of *The Republic of Korea Is the Military* (Paju City, Korea: Chungnyunsa, 2005), 247–82.

98. Sato Fumika, *Gunji soshiki to jendā: jieitai no joseitachi* (Military organization and gender: the women of the self-defense forces) (Tokyo: Keio University Press, 2004).

I

Militarized Bodies of Memory

1

Memorializing Puʻuloa and Remembering Pearl Harbor

Jon Kamakawiwoʻole Osorio

"Hui"

    Pūpū (a`o `Ewa) i ka nu`a (nā kānaka)
    E naue mai (a e `ike)
    I ka mea hou (o ka `āina)
    Ahe `āina (ua kaulana)
    Mai nā kūpuna mai
    Alahula Pu`uloa he ala hele no
    Ka`ahupahau (Ka`ahupāhau)
    Alahula Pu`uloa he ala hele no
    Ka`ahupāhau, Ka`ahupāhau
    Nani Ka`ala hemolele i ka mālie
    Kuahiwi kaulana a`o `Ewa
    E ki`i ana i ka makani o ka `āina
    Hea ka Moa`e eia au e ke aloha
    Kilakila `o Polea noho i ka `olu
    Ia home ho`ohihi a ka malihini
    E walea ana i ka `olu o ke kiawe
    I ka pa kolonahe a ke Kiu

    (Shells of `Ewa throngs of people
    Coming to learn
    The news of the land
    A land famous
    From the ancient times
    All of Pu`uloa, the path trod upon by

> Ka'ahupahau
> All of Pu'uloa, the path trod upon by
> Ka'ahupahau
> Beautiful Ka'ala, sublime in the calm
> Famous mountain of 'Ewa
> That fetches the wind of the land
> The tradewind calls, "Here I am, beloved"
> Majestic Polea in the coolness
> Home delightful to visitors
> Relaxing in the coolness of the kiawe
> And the soft blowing of the Kiu wind)[1]

Third-year Hawaiian-language students spend a good deal of both semesters reading and translating—or I should say, puzzling over—the stories, or mo'olelo, from *Lei Momi o Ewa*, written by Sarah Keli'ilolena Nākoa.[2] Of all the texts that confront and confound the Hawaiian-language student, this one indeed is the most difficult. Her writing is elegant and precise and filled with allusions and idioms that are not familiar to our generation of native Hawaiian people, whom we refer to as Kanaka Maoli.

Auntie Sarah was born in 1911 in Waimalu, whose streams fed into Pu'uloa, known to most people today as Pearl Harbor. Many of the particular names of places in the ahupua'a[3], in which the naval base at Pearl Harbor is located, have disappeared or have been turned into street names and names of barracks and entrances to the shipyard. We cannot see these places as Nākoa saw them in her youth, as delightful ocean fronts and fishing places, patrolled by the powerful female 'aumakua Ka'ahupahau, or refreshing springs like Honokawailani where water lilies flourished and where another kūpua, or demigod, in the form of a long-haired girl, watched as she and other keiki[4] from the areas played in the springs.

Pu'uloa has become unfamiliar terrain to us, much like the language of our elders and for some of the same reasons. The terrain itself is altered: streams have been interdicted and redirected by culverts and ditches, springs have disappeared, whole ecosystems that fed the once rich Ewa coastline have been strangled or neutered, and, in any case, many Hawaiians, unless they join the armed services or the large corps of civilian workers at Pearl Harbor, generally find the place forbidding. There are military police and, now, heavily armed patrols that guard the entrances to

Pearl Harbor, and most of us go there only on some kind of business. The U.S. Navy certainly prefers it that way.

Several years ago, I was recruited to a teaching position at West Oʻahu College, and, largely out of a sense that no opportunity should go uninvestigated, my wife and I toured the campus with the humanities chair. The thing that struck us first was that I would forever be looking down at the fleet of U.S. warships, the symbol of American power and the symbol of our dispossession, as long as I worked there. I decided they could not pay me enough. But in a sense, Pearl Harbor is that visual and kinetic reminder not only of our loss—and by "our" I mean Kanaka Maoli—but of our helplessness as well. It is not that the ships and armed soldiers themselves are menacing so much as it is the sense that they belong to that place now and we do not.

If I were a geographer, I would mark the dynamics of changing landscapes, especially such forceful changes as are represented by military bases and how the military uses land. Traditional place names, or wahi pana, have vanished, and in their places are names of former army and navy officers, American presidents, and even American battlegrounds far from these islands. If I were an environmentalist, I would rather describe the hundreds of polluted sites in the Pearl Harbor area, acknowledged by the navy but unaddressed for decades, and discuss the threat of toxic leaks into the aquifer that threaten the whole population of the island.[5] Any Kanaka Maoli political economist could focus on the tremendous impact that Pearl Harbor makes on public policy and the dependency of the local economy on military spending.

As a historian, I am interested in all of these things, but mostly as they pertain to how we should understand not just the navy's but America's presence in these islands today. It is not a simple thing to understand. I was born in the postwar world. My sister, the oldest, was born a few days after the Japanese unconditional surrender aboard the USS *Missouri*, and my older brother and I were born several years later. What we knew of the war was typical family lore of the time: how my grandfather, an American ex-doughboy of German descent, had married my half-Hawaiian, half-Chinese grandmother and had four children, including my mother, the eldest; how he, a civilian fireman, had been called to duty at Pearl Harbor on the morning of December 7, 1941; and how, before he left the house, he handed a loaded twenty-five caliber pistol to my grandmother and instructed her to use it on the girls and herself if the Japanese invaded.

Shall I tell you that, in my early childhood years, the notion of the Japanese Americans in Hawai'i as the enemy was a subtle theme of my upbringing? This was not so much so from my grandfather born in Dayton, Ohio, on my mother's side, but from my strongly Republican family on my father's side, whose connection to the sugar plantation hegemony has actually been described by historians before me. My father's father emigrated from Portugal at the age of nine and came to a Hawai'i dominated by race and class divisions that were enscribed within the plantation society itself. Portuguese were not free of the stigma of contract labor, yet, as Caucasians, they could not be easily lumped with the Chinese, Japanese, and Filipino workers who outnumbered the Haole Caucasians and Kanaka Maoli in Hawai'i by 1900.[6]

When Lawrence Fuchs wrote *Hawai'i Pono: A Social History of Hawai'i* in the 1960s, he focused on the ways in which plantation owners and other businessmen used racial theories and xenophobia to maintain their political power on election days and to weaken the labor union movements in the 1930s. Laboring-class Hawaiians and Portuguese were invited to join with wealthy Republicans at the polls to prevent Hawai'i from being taken over by the "Yellow Peril," and collective bargaining was consistently understood as a tactic for Japanese political gains. For my family, on both sides, by 1941 the navy and the army had come to represent the stalwart and powerful struts of an American society that would never allow the islands to become a part of Japan.

Both my father and his brother served during World War II, and my uncle retired as a civilian worker in the U.S. Air Force. My mother's brother joined the U.S. Army as did thousands of AJAs—Americans of Japanese ancestry—though his loyalty was not questioned as theirs was.

I wonder if his loyalty—I am speaking here of Leroy Kay, Jr.—should have been questioned. He was born in 1928, a mere generation after close to forty thousand signatures of Kanaka Maoli were affixed to petitions begging the United States not to annex Hawai'i[7] and the beginning of the American occupation. Of course his father was born an American, but his mother was not, and all the family members of his grandparents' generation signed those petitions, and all considered themselves loyal to the queen and subjects of the Hawaiian Kingdom.

I wonder how it is that so many young Kanaka men were so quickly dispatched into military service while suspicions of Japanese lingered almost as long as martial law in Hawai'i. My mother and her siblings were half German, but the Army made no special battalion for Americans of German ancestry in the territory. We Kanaka were counted on and trusted to be loyal Americans, while Japanese here were subject to search and seizure and every display of their Japanese heritage would be discouraged by the general social disapproval as well as, more astonishing to the Issei, by the rejection of that heritage by their own young men and women, the Nissei and Sansei who came of age in 1941.

Ask my father about the war and he will tell you about his service in the merchant marine and the attack on the convoy in which he served by a German submarine in 1945. But my mother also had interesting and compelling stories that revealed so much about life here in Hawai'i. She told me once of how she came across a high school friend of hers, a young Japanese woman, the day after Pearl Harbor was bombed. Her friend wept all day and could not speak to anyone. My mother wanted to console her but had no idea what to say. She would also speak of the different children in her family born to cousins who had slept with American servicemen gone and forgotten. The children were hānai (adopted) by some of the older couples in the family and life went on. My mother also spoke of the blackouts in Honolulu, the air raid sirens, the air raid marshals who patrolled streets and made sure that houses had been prepared for blackouts, and, of course, she spoke about the rationing, which, coming on the heels of the Great Depression, seemed not so large a thing.

I will tell you something I remember myself. When, as children, we stayed at my grandfather's house in Kaimuki, I used to scratch the paint off of the windows with my fingernails. It was a kind of dull green water-based paint that covered every pane in the house, although by the time I was around, monograms and messages had been scratched into its surface, providing an interesting record of my cousins, my mother, and her siblings. But in so many ways I was scratching at the opaque film that separates the reality of my parents' generation from my own. Their experience of war, unlike mine but also unlike the majority of other American civilians' in 1941, was direct and personal. *We* were attacked, not just the Pacific fleet. If the Japanese were to invade, we would be the victims of their bombs and occupation. Our beaches were strung with barbed wire, and our high school seniors—especially from my own alma mater, Kamehameha schools—were taken from their classes and immediately employed as coastal watchers.

For all of the sacrifices that the public in Hawai'i were called to perform, it is also clear that a kind of political unity was forged. There was a common enemy, and our parents quite clearly saw the American flag as their flag, the destroyed battleships as theirs, too, and the young men killed as their young men. Indeed, perhaps the vulnerability of the fleet and the vulnerability of all those young men may have been the solder that linked Kanaka Maoli to their American occupiers. Did we make the epistemological leap to the belief that they had died for us, defending us from the Japanese menace? Or perhaps, was it by gazing into their fearful, shell-shocked eyes that we found a common humanity and forgave them for their arrogant taking of our land and dignity?

There is no question that my parents and countless other native Hawaiian men and women were willing to sacrifice their lives, putting off their marriages for the sake of the war, enduring martial law, enlisting and leaving and dying for the country that had taken their birthright. How else was there to explain the expectations of that generation of Kanaka Maoli that seem so close to those of any American family in the 1940s: that someday they would win the war and earn not only peace but also a profound prosperity. One of my early memories is standing in the kitchen with my mother and hearing her sing this song, the tune and words still seared into my brain nearly half a century later:

> When the lights go on again all over the world
> And the boys are home again all over the world
> And rain or snow is all that may fall from the skies above
> A kiss won't mean "goodbye" but "Hello to love"
> When the lights go on again all over the world
> And the ships will sail again all over the world
> Then we'll have time for things like wedding rings and free hearts
>   will sing
> When the lights go on again all over the world
> When the lights go on again all over the world[8]

That period in my family's life seemed exciting to me, and I grew up with a fascination for the Pacific war, reading every history book, every novel, every comic book I could lay my hand on that dealt with the Pearl Harbor air raid and its aftermath. My love of history was forged on those events. By the time I was ten years old I knew the dates and places of practically every naval engagement in the Pacific between 1941 and 1944.

I knew the names of the Japanese carriers sunk at Midway and even the American cruisers and destroyers sunk in The Slot during the battles for Guadalcanal. I read constantly at home, on weekends, and even during school, hiding a book on great carrier battles behind my math text while my classmates learned to divide fractions without me.

All things considered, I should have become a militarist. But my generation's defining war was Vietnam. Vietnam was almost a sideshow to the civil rights movement, the hippies and rock music, and the drugs and cults of youth that seemed much more real to us—at least to those of us lucky enough not to get drafted—than the war was. Far away and mediated through television, Vietnam did not unify our generation nor bind us to the generation before. Perhaps not coincidentally, neither did that war demand our full attention. As for sacrifice, it seemed that all we were asked to give up was our young men and our skepticism about our political leadership.

I think of how different the wartime civilian mentality was then compared with our mentality today in the war on terror. I consider the vast difference between the notion of rationing—sacrificing creature comforts for the war effort—versus George Bush's early exhortation to continue to consume and that it was virtually through our actions as consumers that we would continue to proclaim our liberty and win the war. Can we even listen to a song like "When the Lights Go on Again" without some secret mirth about the incredible naïveté of the lyrics? Did not some of you readers, when you heard the song, begin to analyze the symbolism of lights going on and of electrical power and major oil companies being at the root of World War II? Yet wasn't my mother just thinking back about the blackouts, the fearfulness of the skies, and the anxiety for her future husband when she sang the song to me?

I was about the same age as my mother in that memory in the 1970s when hundreds of my contemporaries, young men and women, most of them Hawaiian, participated in protests of the U.S. Navy's occupation of Kahoʻolawe and the navy's near destruction of that island. Eventually they were joined in this protest not so much by members of their parents' generation but by their grandparents, or kūpuna. The elders in the Protect Kahoʻolawe ʻOhana (PKO) provided spiritual comfort and practical knowledge to the young people who willingly risked their liberty and their lives by placing themselves on Kahoʻolawe as a buffer between the bombs and the island.

"Kaho`olawe"

Ha`aheo wale ho`i `oe
E Kaho`olawe `āina kaulana
Ho`oheno ana 'oe
Me ka hinahina
E aloha i ke ko a ka wai
I ka`i mai ua anu kâua
A luna au
O Kaho`olawe
Ahuwale nâ pua hinahina
Lua`ole nahano a ka makani
O ke Kiu Ke`e ia
A`o nâ pali
Ha`ina `ia mai
Ana ka puana
Nohona a mana`o mai
`O au e ke ho

(You are proud, indeed
Kaho`olawe, famous land
You are so cherished
With your hinahina
Enjoy the water
We seek shelter from the chilly rain
High
On Kaho`olawe
Abundant, the hinahina blossoms
Incomparable, the breeze that blows
The wind named Kiu Ke`e
Of the cliffs
Tell
The refrain
My thoughts return to my home
And my friends)[9]

After four accesses between 1976 and 1977, scores of young people had been arrested, several incarcerated, and two young men had died on that island. Their sacrifices, coupled with the miserable dénouement of

America's war in Southeast Asia, created a strong public aversion to what had once been a hegemonic military presence in Hawaiʻi. In 1980, the U.S. Navy signed a consent decree with the ʻOhana essentially agreeing to share the island with the protest movement, to limit sharply the training and the use of live ordnance on the island, and to revegetate the island.

In the following years, the PKO escorted thousands of people to Kanaloa for religious exercises, work, and educational accesses. Kahoʻolawe had also been greatly transformed by the military presence from a once productive land with streams, springs, and native plants to a parched land with few trees and bushes and a perennial waistline of red mud around its shore. Those of us who have seen firsthand the result of military "stewardship" have formed a fairly indelible opinion of the militarization of Hawaiʻi and tend to regard the U.S. military's objectives and practices as counter to everything that we think of as Hawaiian. To this day, heroes among native Hawaiians tend not only to be great conquerors like Kamehameha but also people like Liliʻuokalani, who peacefully opposed the American military occupation of Hawaiʻi in 1893, and George Helm and Kimo Mitchell, young Hawaiian men who died on Kahoʻolawe in 1977.

"Hawaiian Soul"

> I can recall the way
> Your voice would fill the room
> And we would all be stilled
> By your melody
> And now your voice is gone
> And to the sea belongs
> All of the gentle songs
> That you had harbored
> Hawaiian Soul
> How could you leave us
> You've not been lost at sea
> You're only wandering
> Hawaiian Soul
> We sing your melodies
> And send them out to sea
> You know the harmony
> They say before you left

To seek your destiny
That older voices called
And drowned your laughter
But I believe you knew
What you would have to be
A beacon in the storm
To guide us after[10]

There is no simple analysis of the native Hawaiian's perspective on warfare in general or the American war machinery in particular. Opposition to the U.S. military presence can be profound and freely verbalized even within families in which one or more of the wage earners are employed by the armed services. Hundreds of young men my age enlisted or were drafted into the army, and many families have long histories of military service spanning generations. We come from a warrior society, and I do think that certain values tend to resonate between Hawaiians and soldiers—discipline, self-sacrifice, and a willingness to commit to a deserving leader.

Ultimately, battle and warfare dignifies in the most peculiar fashion. Between the fraudulence of personal and national ambition that create arenas of slaughter and the obscenity of slaughter itself, there is, nevertheless, the possibility of a kind of grace between soldiers, a recognition of likeness that most of us, engaged in professions that do not require their kind of sacrifice, will never know.

I would like to perform one last mele, taken from a chant composed to commemorate the warriors of Oʻahu who fell from the Pali in the face of Kamehameha's advance almost 150 years before the samurai in their fragile aircraft descended into Puʻuloa. In one part of this mele the falling warriors are seen as a flower drooping over the face of the cliff, and the perspective of the invading warriors expresses a great love, respect, and aloha for those who are fighting, losing, and dying.

"Waikā"

Kū akula ʻoe i ka malanai a ke Kīpuʻupuʻu
Nolu ka maka o ka ʻōhāwai o ʻUli
Niniau ʻeha ka pua o Koaie
ʻEha i ke anu ka nahele o Waikā
A he aloha e.[11]

As a historian I have a perspective on my parents' war and on the country for which they fought and sacrificed. It is just a generation, and I see this all so differently than they did, which answers for me the question of whether in the space of a single generation our people could go from Hawaiian patriots to American soldiers. Rather than seeing the fleet as our protector, I wonder why so much of our land on this island of Oʻahu, nearly 25 percent, is part of a military base. I think that the United States has created a target on these islands to make certain that the first place attacked will not be part of their homeland. And I see the basing of their Stryker Brigade as one more threat to the peace and security of my own Kanaka Maoli people.

But I can easily understand not only how my parents can have such different perceptions but also how they see mine as ridiculously stupid. It is not that the major oil companies did not have a huge stake in Japanese adventurism or that Roosevelt may have known the attack was imminent, but that these understandings are decidedly beside the point. What matters to my parents about Pearl Harbor is that it moved their whole generation to act decisively and heroically, and it is that moment in their lives that defines them as a people and continues to define the way they see the world half a century afterward.

So it is also true for me and the postwar generation with whom I grew up that the events of our youth helped to define our lives, and what we grew up with is a measure of cynicism and self-glorification that our parents often find difficult to comprehend. Realizing that causes me to wonder what sorts of definitions my children will grow up with and how events in the present are shaping them.

My teenaged children gave amused looks to one another as I began to practice the song "When the Lights Go on Again," although my eight-year-old daughter—bless her heart—began to try to sing it with me. None of them will understand that the genre of this music is as foreign to me as Bob Dylan is to them but that I am intimately connected to it because my mother sang it to me and signified how deeply meaningful this music, her memory, and her history was to her.

Thus I can understand how cultural meanings are transferred between generations—imperfectly. Whatever it was that drew my parents to solidarity with American soldiers and sailors simply did not cross the boundaries of our generation whole. Thus, I need to remember that my attitudes about the meaning of their presence here will not cross into my children's lives as thoroughly as I might wish.

But I would like to take them to Pā'au'au, Polea, and Honokawailani and show them how a landscape can be so thoroughly altered as to seem alien. I would remind them that it is still their 'āina, their land, and that it is within their power, if not to physically reclaim it, to nevertheless reclaim it spiritually and emotionally. It is impossible to say for certain what the future holds, but we can certainly hold on to the things that we know and feel, and we can continue to remember them for our own sakes if not for our children's.

Notes

1. *Hawaiian Music and Hula Archives*, http://www.huapala.org.

2. Sarah Keli'ilolena Nākoa, *Lei Momi o 'Ewa* (Honolulu, Hawai'i: Sturgiss Printing Co., 1979).

3. Translated into English, "land division."

4. Translated into English, "children."

5. Pat Tummons, "Use of Islands by Armed Forces Leaves No Stone Unturned," *Environment Hawai'i* 2, no. 2 (1992): 4–7.

6. Robert C. Schmitt, *Demographic Statistics of Hawai'i* (Honolulu: University of Hawai'i Press, 1968), 120.

7. Noenoe Silva, *Aloha Betrayed: Native Hawaiian Resistance to American Colonialism* (Durham, N.C.: Duke University Press, 2004).

8. Eddie Seller, Sol Marcus, and Bennie Benjamin, "When the Lights Go On Again (All Over the World)," performed by Vaughn Monroe and His Orchestra, 1943.

9. Emma Bishop, "Kaho'olawe," *Hawaiian Hula Archives,* http://www.huapala.org. This song was written in the 1870s and describes a beautiful and hospitable island, a very different island than the one seen today after decades of navy misuse.

10. Jon Osorio and Randy Borden, composers, "Hawaiian Soul," from *Hawaiian Eyes*, Hilo, Mālama Media. This song was written on the day in March 1977 when the search for the missing Helm and Mitchell was called off and the two were presumed dead.

11. This interpretation is taught by Aaron Sala, recording artist and graduate student in ethnomusicology at University of Hawai'i–Mānoa who teaches music and Hawaiian identity at the Kamakuokalani Center for Hawaiian Studies. His interpretation of this mele is used here with his permission.

2

Bikinis and Other S/pacific N/oceans

Teresia K. Teaiwa

Specific Notions

What does the word "bikini" evoke for you? A woman in a two-piece bathing suit, or a site for nuclear-weapons testing? A bikini-clad woman invigorated by solar radiation, or Bikini Islanders cancer ridden from nuclear radiation? The sensational bathing suit was named for Bikini Atoll. This was the site in the Marshall Islands for the testing of twenty-five nuclear bombs between 1946 and 1958. Bikini Islanders testify to the continuing history of colonialism and ecological racism in the Pacific basin. The bikini bathing suit is a testament to the recurring tourist trivialization of Pacific Islanders' experience and existence. By drawing attention to a sexualized and supposedly depoliticized female body, the bikini distracts from the colonial and highly political origins of its name. The sexist dynamic the bikini performs—objectification through excessive visibility—inverts the colonial dynamics that have occurred during nuclear testing in the Pacific, that is, objectification by rendering invisible. The bikini bathing suit manifests both a celebration and a forgetting of the nuclear power that strategically and materially marginalizes and erases the living history of Pacific Islanders. The bikini emerges from colonial notions that marginalize "s/pacific" bodies while genericizing and centering female bodies.

For Pacific Islanders the name "Bikini" evokes memories and visions of a s/pacific historical and contemporary political reality. Nuclear testing is just one—albeit a most pernicious one—of the many colonial phenomena and processes that affect the Pacific region. In 1980 the United

Nations reported that more than two hundred nuclear bombs and devices had been detonated in the Pacific, but this figure did not include nuclear *missiles* launched into the Pacific by the United States, the Soviet Union, and China.[1] Britain exploded twelve nuclear bombs on Johnston Atoll between 1958 and 1962 and in the 1950s conducted twelve tests at Monte Bello, Emu, and Maralinga in Australia. Since 1966, France has tested forty-one atmospheric bombs and continued to test underground at Moruroa and Fangataufa until 1996.[2]

The New World Times reported tests at Moruroa in June and November of 1990, bringing to 130 the total of underground tests there since 1975. *The New World Times* also reported Professor M. Hochstein, director of Auckland University's Geothermal Institute, as saying that the shafts at Moruroa may contain about a hundred times the amount of radioactive material dropped on Hiroshima.[3] Nuclear testing in Australia and French Polynesia profoundly affects the health and welfare of indigenous peoples. In April 1992, France announced a twelve-month suspension of its nuclear tests in the Pacific, with the possibility of extension if other countries joined in a moratorium.[4] Although both the United States and France signed the Comprehensive Test Ban Treaty in 1996, their nuclear-powered (and armed) vessels continue to patrol the ocean. Current global political realignments and the development of nuclear capabilities in Brazil, India, Iran, North Korea, Pakistan, and other countries have complicated the configuration of both the nuclear arms race and the antinuclear movement. The Pacific Ocean, however, still churns with its colonial and nuclear legacies. Bikini epitomizes these legacies.

Bikini

On a Euro-American map, Bikini Atoll is located at 165 degrees east of Greenwich or 15 degrees west of the international dateline, between latitudes 10 and 20 degrees north of the equator. The atoll surrounds a lagoon some 40 kilometers long and 20 kilometers wide, and is composed of twenty-six islands—Bikini being the largest—covering a surface area of 7 square kilometers. Bikini Atoll is part of the Republic of the Marshall Islands, former colony of Germany, Japan, and the United States. The republic is currently linked in "free association" with the United States.[5]

The Marshall Islands became a part of the U.S. Trust Territory of the Pacific as a result of Japan's defeat in World War II. The most horrific component of U.S. military strategy during the war was the nuclear bombings of Japan at Hiroshima and Nagasaki on August 6 and 9, 1945. Within the subsequent context of a cold war with the Soviet Union, the United States proceeded to further test and develop its nuclear and naval powers on and around the Pacific islands entrusted to it by the United Nations.[6] The United States decided to test at Bikini for several strategic reasons: The area was under its control; the islands were in a climatic zone free of storms and cold temperatures; the lagoon was large enough for a fleet of target vessels; the population of Bikini in 1946 was between 166 and 170 people—small enough to be relocated with relative ease; and, ultimately, Bikini—and the Marshall Islands in general—were at least five hundred miles from all sea and air routes, distant enough that ensuing radioactive contamination would not endanger "heavily populated areas."[7]

The U.S. military secured the cooperation of the Bikinians in vacating their island by appealing to their sense of Christian duty.[8] On February 10, 1946, the Islanders were told by the military governor that Bikini would be used for "the good of mankind and to end all world wars."[9] By March 7, 1946, after repeatedly reenacting for camera crews their "consultation" with the military governor, the Islanders departed for the temporary home of their choice on another atoll, Rongerik, just over a hundred miles east of Bikini. The nuclear project, code-named Operation Crossroads, could then be implemented. Some forty-two thousand U.S. military personnel—twenty of whom were women—were on hand for the two tests conducted on July 1 and July 25.[10] The U.S. military went on to conduct other nuclear tests on Enewetak Atoll and to establish a support base on Kwajalein. During this period, the people of these atolls, and others like Rongelap and Utirik, were subject to radiation, displacement, or both.[11]

Since 1946, the Bikini Islanders have experienced the many troubles attendant on relocation—or *dis*location. Within a year Rongerik proved inappropriate because its lagoon and plant life could not support the Bikinian population. The move to Rongerik had also placed the Bikinians under the jurisdiction of a paramount chief, a fact that did not please them. Subsequently the Islanders were sheltered at the military base on Kwajalein Island. In 1948 they were moved to Kili Island, and in the 1950s the U.S. government awarded them $25,000 in cash plus a $300,000 trust fund for full use in their homeland. This monetary compensation provided some relief, but eventually the Bikinians faced more population pressures on Kili as their numbers grew to three hundred by 1970.[12] Furthermore, their desire to return to Bikini was still strong, for they had a specific physical and spiritual relationship to their homeland that the colonial government could not fully appreciate.[13]

In 1968, after the Atomic Energy Commission declared the island safe, U.S. President Lyndon B. Johnson guaranteed the Bikinians return, but the island was still dangerously radioactive because of the twenty-three nuclear tests conducted there between 1946 and 1958; it would take a minimum of thirty to sixty years for some areas to be safe again.[14] When the United States finally admitted that the island was still unsafe, the Islanders were forcibly evacuated again in 1978.

At this time, Bikini Islanders are scattered throughout the Marshall Islands, with most living on Kili, Kwajalein, or Majuro.[15] Numerous claims had been filed against the United States as the Islanders became afflicted with radioactivity-related cancers and birth defects. A radically altered version of the Compact of Free Association between the Republic of the Marshall Islands and the United States, approved by the U.S. Congress in 1986, allocated a $150 million trust fund for nuclear victims from four atolls—Bikini, Enewetak, Rongelap, and Utirik—exposed to radiation during the testing period.[16] Bikinians subsequently filed a $450 million lawsuit against the United States, to which the U.S. Congress responded in 1988 by approving a $90 million trust fund for cleaning up and resettling Bikini.[17] Although the Bikinians may attempt to take the U.S. government to court again, it is not likely they will achieve much more than this. The Bikini Islanders' resettlements have been troubled by environmental, social, economic, political, physical, and emotional considerations.

Bikinis

In 1946 French designer Louis Reard launched a sensational two-piece bathing suit.[18] The bikini, as it was christened, celebrated the Allied efforts in World War II. Fashion historians have noted that European vogues in revealing clothing tend to coincide with periods of war: "Fashion is always at its most provocative during or after times of war, for the excellent reason that, from the woman's point of view, there is more than a good chance of a lot of eligible males turning up their toes at any minute (one night at the Duchess of Richmond's Ball, the next day carnage at Waterloo) so speed is of the essence in the sexual come-on message."[19] Clothing and fashion, of course, can be manipulated by both individuals and society. A woman may choose to expose her body for attention, but society also has investments in such display.

In the context of war, society has an ideological stake in the reification of female bodies when male bodies are being sacrificed heroically: "During the First World War women were urged to inspire and distract the boys as they marched off to battle or came home on leave. A new coquettishness began to affect female swimwear as daring exposures overtook everyday dress and corsets were abandoned. Collar-bones and elbows, ankles and calves came into view on the street, and evening dresses, suspended by the thinnest straps bared even the armpit. *On the beach, instead of fending off masculine attention with massive yardage, it now became entirely respectable, even a tinge patriotic, to begin cautiously to gratify the searching male gaze.*"[20] The bikini bathing suit found its position in this fashion ideology.

While being liberated from earlier cumbersome swimsuits, bikini-clad women[21] joined other variously clothed—or unclothed—model female images pinned up for a heterosexual male gaze: "A system of power . . . authorizes certain representations while blocking, prohibiting or invalidating others. Among those prohibited from Western representation, those representations denied legitimacy, are women. Excluded from representation by its very structure, they return within it as a figure for—a representation of—the unrepresentable (Nature, Truth, the Sublime, etc.). Yet in being represented by, women have been rendered an absence within the dominant culture."[22] The mass production and distribution of seminude female images are forms of sacrifice—or symbolic atonement—that substitute and domesticate the unrepresentable chaos of nuclear war: "The original scientists working at Los Alamos took bets among themselves as to whether they would ultimately have a 'boy' or a 'girl,' that is, a success or a dud. A success it was, and the 'fathered' (by J. Robert Oppenheimer) bomb was nicknamed 'Little Boy.' A few years later, the bomb underwent a sex change operation: the device dropped on the Bikini Islands was nicknamed 'Gilda' and painted with an image of sex symbol Rita Hayworth."[23] The sacrifice of the Islanders and military personnel during nuclear testing in the Pacific cannot be represented without threatening the legitimacy of colonial power, so nuclear technology becomes gendered and domesticated. In the end the female body is appropriated by a colonial discourse to successfully disguise the horror of the bomb.

Edward Said describes such a colonial discourse as positioning the West as actor as well as spectator and the Orient (or, for our purposes, the exotic) as passive reactor or malleable site.²⁴ In this sense the bikini offers a female body as affirmation of a colonial gaze. The bikini politically negates the female body by exposing it, but, by its mass exposure in the bikini, the female body also negates the history of s/pacific bodies.²⁵ The bikini-clad woman is exotic and malleable to the same colonial gaze that coded Bikini Atoll and its Islanders as exotic, malleable, and, most of all, dispensable.

The bikini is, in effect, more about European and American sex–gender cultural history than about Pacific Islanders. But the bikini's seminudity also reflects a conjunction between conceptions of the neoclassical and the South Sea noble savage that began in eighteenth-century European imagination. After his 1768 voyage, French explorer Bougainville explicitly compared the Tahitians with ancient Greeks: "I never saw men better made, and whose limbs were more proportionate: in order to paint a Hercules or a Mars, one could nowhere find such beautiful models." A naked young Tahitian girl on the deck of his ship appeared, "as Venus . . . herself to the Phrygian shepherd having the celestial form of that goddess."²⁶ Eighteenth-century artistic representations of Venus were lent validity by documentations of European encounters with scantily clad South Sea Islanders. When early bikini-clad women were hailed as "Venuses," the bikini's genealogy seemed *noble*: "The most simple way for society to get away with practically anything, or practically nothing, was to pretend that their fashions were inspired by some great bygone age. Thus when confronted with accusations of indecency they could pretend an innocent hauteur towards anyone who complained . . . the most extraordinary displays of flesh have been permitted under the justification that they were 'classically inspired.'"²⁷ The bikini exoticized generic female bodies by constructing them as references to a Grecian golden age and a South Sea paradise; in this genealogy the more immediate colonial and nuclear ancestry was conveniently marginalized. (By "generic female body," I mean a body that emphasizes femaleness and implies heterosexuality over and above any other specificity of social identity.) As a result of emphasizing continuity between the Euro-American past and the Pacific Island present, this genealogical construction masked the ruptures caused by their convergence.

If, at its birth, the bikini offered white bodies the opportunity to become tanned, colored, or otherwise marked as exotic, bikini-clad bodies have subsequently become "natural" props in a scene of leisure. American media representations of the bikini, like *Entertainment Tonight*'s bikini specials, emphasize the desirability of an idealized female body.²⁸ While some women in the United States have recognized that the representation of women in bikini bathing suits undermines their efforts at redressing sexism,[29] the sinister implications of the bikini go beyond sexism. The bikini's deep structural symbolism is significantly repressed in its popular manifestations.[30]

The appropriation of the name "Bikini," a s/pacific site of trauma and dispossession, for a sexy generic bathing suit functions as fetishism. By using the fetish as a theoretical framework I do not intend disrespect to those objects Westerners have labeled fetishes or those that have embedded sacred meaning for indigenous peoples. I intend rather to critique the type of fetishization that objectifies and vulgarizes otherwise meaningful subjects. Several critics have warned of the remystifying abilities and the dangers of making a fetish out of the concept of fetishism.[31] Nevertheless, this chapter mobilizes a concept such as the fetish to describe a(nti)historical and sexist elements of European and American cultural constructions and political processes in the Pacific.

In *Civilization and Its Discontents*, Sigmund Freud discussed a process by which the fetish stopped the memory in traumatic amnesia: the fetish is a conceptual substitute for a penis (for Freud, the mother's) that "should normally have been given up, but . . . is precisely designed to preserve it from extinction . . . [The fetish] remains a token of triumph over the threat of castration and a protection against it."[32] I take nuclear weapons as the ultimate phallic *and* castrative symbols for specific national cultures within a global political context.[33] The bikini bathing suit functions as a token of triumph (a fetish for Western Europe and the United States) over the threat of castration by enemy nations and as psychic protection against the horror of their own destructive powers.

The simultaneously reified and repressed multiple symbolisms of the bikini-as-fetish resonate with aspects of Julia Kristeva's psychoanalytic framework. Kristeva discussed woman's position as "both 'inside' and 'outside' male society, both a romantically idealized member of it and a victimized outcast. She is sometimes what stands between man and chaos, and sometimes the embodiment of chaos itself."[34] Through assumptions of its significance on a generic female body, the bikini represents sex–gender ideologies produced in Western Europe and the United States. A bikini-clad woman visually embodies and denies both sexual and nuclear chaos.

As Freud maintained, there is "an aversion, which is never absent in any fetishist, to the real female genitals."[35] The bikini exposes everything but the breasts and the pubic area. While the breasts are tantalizingly emphasized, pubic hair is considered fashionably deadly if not concealed: women are encouraged to shave or wax their bikini lines. The fetishistic aversion to real female genitals extends to female body hair—solidifying the relationship between the bikini-clad woman and the classical female nude, which is never portrayed with pubic hair. The classical fetishization of the female body converges with contemporary fetishization of the bikini-clad body.

As a commodity, the bikini exceeds its material utility and begins to mediate social—that is, gender and colonial—relationships.[36] Although a traditional Marxist analysis would focus on the commodity's evolution from product of human labor to "idol of the marketplace," I am more interested in the process that alienates the colonized referent of the commodity. To this end, I find a discussion by Emily Apter particularly illuminating. She comments on literary representations of the commodification of exotic others in a French fin-de-siècle novel, *La Goutte d'or*. Idriss, a Maghrebian man, sells a polyethylene cast of himself to a Parisian department store and is subsequently recruited as a model to stand in the store window performing a few angular and spasmodic gestures to promote the sale of the casts: "In the mirror reflection of a thousand, identical department-store mannequins, one can extract a political critique of the alienated, colonized, North African self. In this sense, fetishism 'buys back' its political redemption. Though Idriss may be prostituted, frozen, and reified, his dead stare (Medusa's head) gives back to consumer society the very alienation that consumer society has inflicted on him."[37] The relationship between the commodity (the mannequin) and its colonized referent (Idriss) in this case is direct; the bikini on the other hand has two colonized referents, and privileges (however minimally) one (generic South Sea noble savage) over the other (dispossessed Bikinians). The mass-produced and mass-marketed bikini simultaneously transcribes and erases the dispossession of the Bikini Islanders onto millions of female bodies. Although Apter sees some redemption in such a paradox, the emptiness of commodity consumption is only benign if we ignore the malign effects of the bikini's companion commodity, the bomb.

Toward Nuclear-Free and Independent S/pacific Bodies

The bomb and the bikini are colonial military and neocolonial tourist technologies respectively, and as such they have a profound impact on s/pacific bodies. I would like to take some time here to explain my notion of the s/pacific body. Barbara Christian criticized French feminist theorists' position of the body as the generating source of knowledge because they "return to the old myth that biology determines everything and ignore the fact that gender is a social rather than biological construct."[38] I agree with Christian insofar as constructions of biological inferiority have legitimized the historical oppression of many people. I hold, however, that the body is the site of physical and social experience and, as such, cannot be denied the potential for generating liberative knowledge. For, as Elizabeth Spellman has noted, somatophobia, or fear and disdain of the body in Western thought, has been associated historically with intellectual superiority.[39] The s/pacific body emerges for me as a site for comprehending specific social and physical environments and for apprehending generic colonial technologies of marginalization and erasure.

The decolonization of s/pacific bodies is intimately woven into island women's activism.[40] Women have been in the vanguard of many Pacific Island sovereignty movements. Perhaps most exemplary of women-initiated decolonization in the Pacific is the group of Belauan women, *Otil a Beluad*, who have consistently organized resistance to U.S. and domestic pressures to amend the antinuclear constitution of Belau.[41] The nuclear presence in the Pacific, however, is only one symptom of the everyday multiplicity of (neo)colonial onslaughts on s/pacific bodies. Pacific Island women also organize around issues of health, environment, substance abuse, and domestic violence for the sovereignty of s/pacific bodies. Activist efforts counter colonial notions that attempt to marginalize and erase them: the romantic notion of a nude South Sea Islander and the militaristic notion of islands as expendable spaces for nuclear testing.

Because nudity and nuclear testing both take on moral and ethical dimensions, Christianity—the most overtly popular religion in the Pacific—figures prominently in any discussion of both the colonization and the decolonization of s/pacific bodies. If we remember that the Bikinians surrendered their island out of Christian charity, we must also acknowledge that Christian organizations of predominantly indigenous women are instrumental in the Nuclear Free and Independent Pacific movement (NFIP).[42] Christianity's role in the Pacific has certainly been ambiguous.[43]

Early encounters between men (and women) of the cloth and naked natives were marked by violence.[44] By the late eighteenth century, European Christians had determined that the islands were purgatorial rather than paradisical, and that the noble savage was really ignoble: Islanders needed both salvation and civilization, and mostly they needed to be clothed.[45] The missionaries swathed s/pacific bodies in cotton laplaps, mother hubbards, and short trousers. Clothing functioned as a device of colonial social control, not only by eliminating nudity, but also, in colonial Papua for instance, by distinguishing appropriate dress for Islanders from appropriate dress for Europeans.[46]

As tourism has become a primary industry for many of the postcolonial Pacific Island nations, Islanders are increasingly exposed to sun-seeking and seminude "First-Worlders." In general, Islanders are wryly amused by contemporary Euro-Americans' various states of undress: "It's an irony that the white man who came to us puritanically stiff and overdressed, now wears hardly anything on the beach on a summer day or on a Sunday afternoon. He has even gone further that that: he now streaks through the streets or the parks in America or Europe, and some countries plan to set aside certain areas and beaches for nudists only . . . So who is playing naked now? I hope we have taught the white man a lesson in innocence and healthy living!"[47] Most Islanders, influenced by Christian modesty, wear bathing suits that are considerably more voluminous than the bikini. The *lavalava*, *pareo*, shorts and a T-shirt, and even dresses (for women), rather than the bikini, are the most common attire for Islanders at the beach.

In a tourist economy, the beach becomes the principal site of leisure—and a clichéd backdrop for bikini-clad tourists. Of course, tourism also affects Islanders' perceptions of themselves and their environment, and increasing numbers of upwardly mobile Islanders—especially in Fiji, Hawai'i, and Tahiti—may be seen lounging leisurely on the beach in their bikinis. There is a bitter irony in the transformation of the beach and the production of the bikini, for in Marshallese "bikini" means "beach," and for the Bikini Islanders the beach was the space they crossed to surrender their island for the nuclear tests of the United States.[48]

Organized protest against nuclear testing in the Pacific began in 1970 when the Committee Against Tests on Moruroa (ATOM) was formed in Suva, Fiji. Its membership came from the Pacific Theological College, the University of the South Pacific, and the Fiji Young Women's Christian Association. When ATOM organized the first Nuclear Free Pacific conference in Suva in 1975, the Pacific Conference of Churches was its principal cosponsor.

NFIP gained momentum with subsequent conferences in various island states: Pohnpei in 1978, Hawai'i in 1980, and Vanuatu in 1983, the most recent being held in Suva in 1991.⁴⁹ A loosely organized information and lobbying network, NFIP encompasses trade unions, private aid organizations, environmentalists, disarmament lobbies, women's collectives, and Christian groups.⁵⁰ Australian scholar Stewart Firth described its successes in his book *Nuclear Playground*:

> Its lobbying has helped dissuade the Japanese, so far, from dumping radioactive waste in the deep ocean trenches off the Northern Mariana Islands in the northern Pacific; and because of the movement's complaints, the military forces of Australia and Japan no longer bombard the island of Kahoʻolawe during annual exercises with the Americans, in deference to the cultural significance of the island to native Hawaiians. Who would have predicted in 1980 that within six years the independent countries of the South Pacific would be seeking to establish a nuclear free zone? Or that the ANZUS Treaty would be in abeyance because the New Zealanders refused to be defended by nuclear weapons? Or that the forces in favour of the nuclear free constitution in Belau would have resisted the U.S.A. for so long?⁵¹

NFIP has adopted a radical platform that advocates independence and sovereignty movements in the Pacific. These include supporting the Kanak independence struggle in the French colony of New Caledonia and opposing the Indonesian government's policy of transmigration and genocide in its colony, West Papua.⁵²

NFIP operates on the premise that whatever happens in one part of the Pacific Ocean affects the whole ocean, the continentals living on the edge of it, and the Islanders living in the midst of it.⁵³ Since the nuclear specter first appeared in the Pacific—Hiroshima and Nagasaki in 1945 and Bikini in 1946—it has spread its poison at an alarming rate.

The biggest stumbling block for Pacific Islanders in lobbying internationally is that they constitute a very small portion of the world's population. By 1986 statistics, the total population of the Pacific Islands was 4,952,470.⁵⁴ The size of Bikini Atoll's population was a significant factor in making it a site for nuclear testing. When addressing the future of the U.S. Trust Territory of the Pacific Islands in 1969, Henry Kissinger made a comment for which he has become notorious in the Pacific: "There are only 90,000 people out there. Who gives a damn?"⁵⁵

This is all about bodies—but vastly different ways of finding meaning in bodies. There are more bikinis being sold globally every summer than there are Bikinians receiving compensation for dislocation and exposure to radioactivity. While practically every slick nightclub in Waikīkī holds a weekly bikini contest, the NFIP movement organizes annual commemorative and educational events on March 1, which is designated Bikini Day.

S/pacific N/oceans

What are we to make of these bizarre juxtapositions? The bomb and the bikini remind us of the militarist and tourist notions that shaped a particular historical moment in the West and continue to shape the contemporary Pacific Islands. At their inception, the bomb and the bikini reflected a supreme ambivalence in Western thought: the valorization of woman as nature, the abom(b)ination of nature manifested by military and scientific technology, the naturalization of racial difference, and the feminization or domestication of military technology. How else can we explain the influx of images of women as sex symbols, the persistent development of nuclear weapons technology, the racist paternalism toward colonies and territories, and the psychological domestication of nuclear technology except as a peculiarity of Western culture and history? More to the point, how are we to deal with this peculiarity? I am tempted to conclude this chapter with a simple demand for a moratorium on the production and display of bikini bathing suits to coincide with a moratorium on the production and testing of nuclear weapons. But while I do believe that such a demand is warranted, the more immediate purpose of this particular academic exposition is to develop a critical understanding of cultural artifacts and representations of the Pacific Islands.

Military, economic, racialized, and gendered histories converge in the bikini bathing suit with far-reaching ideological and material implications. In this chapter I have attempted to explore and elucidate some of these implications by selectively applying Marxist, psychoanalytic, and feminist theories. Marxism and Freudian psychoanalysis are particularly illuminating lenses through which to view commodities or fetishes like the bomb and the bikini. Feminist approaches provide a crucial critique of the gendered social relations, representations, and audience reception that surround the bikini's particular history. But although they may effectively describe processes of violence and commodification, largely Eurocentric theories must remain ornamental to narratives that interrupt dominant historical and cultural constructions of islands as military bases and tourist sites.

Faced with a thesis as disturbing as the bomb and the bikini's erasure of specific (Bikini) Islander history, I have had to acknowledge both destructive and life-sustaining histories. The Bikinians and other Marshallese Islanders are at a distinct disadvantage in negotiating terms with the U.S. government. Remembering and rearticulating the history of Bikinians' forced migration and exile is a beginning form of resistance to the ideology that created both the bomb and the bikini. I believe that the hope for most specific Islanders is in collective resistance to military and tourist encroachments; this is why I have retold a history of the NFIP movement. With its commitment to indigenous rights and support from and for women's organizations, the movement embodies a history that radically challenges military and, especially, tourist notions of the island Pacific's significance. NFIP's history is informed by what I call "s/pacific n/oceans"—an explicitly politicized version of what some call the "Pacific Way." S/pacific n/oceans honor the specificities of Islander experience, recognize the generic effects of (neo)colonialism on all Islanders, and are committed to political and cultural cooperation at the regional level. Together the histories of specific islands and s/pacific n/oceans surround cultural artifacts and representations of the Pacific and erode the generic constructions on which both military and tourist industries depend.

Notes

I am grateful to Setsu Shigematsu and Keith Camacho for inviting this chapter as a contribution to this important volume. An early version of this chapter was presented at the ninth Pacific History Association Conference in Christchurch, New Zealand, in December 1992. It was subsequently published as "bikinis and other s/pacific n/oceans," in *The Contemporary Pacific* 6, no 1 (1994): 87–109 and was reprinted in David Hanlon and Geoffrey M. White, ed., *Voyaging the Contemporary Pacific* by Rowman & Littlefield in 2000. Although the chapter has been edited for this volume, it is important to note that information, sources, and analysis in this chapter are specific to the temporal context of its production and publication. I accept responsibility for any and all remaining problems.

1. Stewart Firth, *Nuclear Playground* (Honolulu: University of Hawai'i Press, 1987), ix.

2. Suliana Siwatibau and B. David Williams, *A Call to a New Exodus: An Anti-Nuclear Primer for Pacific People* (Suva, Fiji: Lotu Pasifika Productions, 1982).

3. "Testing Continues on the Polynesian Islands," *New World Times*, Winter 1990, 29.

4. "France Suspends Nuclear Testing until 1993," *San Jose Mercury News*, April 9, 1992, 17a.

5. Giff Johnson, "Marshall Islands: Politics in the Marshall Islands," in *Micronesian Politics*, ed. Ron Crocombe (Suva, Fiji: University of the South Pacific, 1988), 67–85.

6. Firth, *Nuclear Playground*.

7. Robert C. Kiste, *The Bikinians: A Study in Forced Migration* (Menlo Park, Calif.: Cummings, 1974), 27.

8. Ibid., 18. Bikinians first encountered Christian missionaries in 1908.

9. Ibid., 28.

10. John Stone, *Radio Bikini: A Film* (Carmel, Calif.: Pacific Arts Corps, 1988), 88. The U.S. forces observed the tests from the edges of a twenty-mile perimeter around ground zero. The effects of radioactive exposure on the observers have not been acknowledged by the U.S. government. In Stone's film, a former naval corps member talks about the life-threatening physical ailments afflicting him since he observed the tests.

11. Ibid.

12. Firth, *Nuclear Playground*.

13. Laura Hyun-Yi Kang has pointed out that the ease with which the colonial United States dislocated the Bikinians arose out of its generalization of islands—"one island is just like another"—and its denial of the subjectivity of colonized others (personal communication, 1992).

14. Micronesian Support Committee, *Marshall Islands: A Chronology, 1944–1978* (Honolulu, Hawai'i: Micronesia Support Committee, 1978).

15. Firth, *Nuclear Playground*.

16. Johnson, "Marshall Islands."

17. Ibid.

18. Graeme Donald, *Things You Didn't Know You Didn't Know* (St. Leonard's, Australia: Unwin, 1985).

19. Prudence Glynn, *Skin to Skin: Eroticism in Dress* (New York: Oxford University Press, 1982), 96. Most of Glynn's feminist analysis may seem moralistic and somewhat simplistic, but it has a certain political effectiveness. Other aspects of her discussion are more nuanced, including her attention to male fashion and fashion's relationship to church and state.

20. Anne Hollander, "Swimsuits Illustrated," *American Heritage*, July–August 1990, 58, emphasis added.

21. When the French first introduced the bikini bathing suit to the United States, models were reportedly uneasy about their tops slipping off, their bottoms hitching up, and their pallid skin being exposed. See "The Trouble with the Bikini," *Life*, no. 27, 1949, 65–66.

22. Craig Owens, "The Discourse of Others: Feminists and Postmodernism," in *The Anti-Aesthetic: Essays on Postmodern Culture*, ed. Hal Foster (Seattle, Wash.: Bay Press, 1983), 59.

23. Jane Caputi, "The Metaphors of Radiation: Or, Why a Beautiful Woman Is Like a Nuclear Power Plant," *Women's Studies International Forum* 14, no. 5 (1991): 426.

24. Edward Said, *Orientalism* (New York: Vintage Books, 1978). Incidentally, the South Seas was sometimes conflated with the Orient or "East" by seventeenth-century Europeans. As Bernard Smith observes, a contemporary reviewer of the pantomime *Omai* wrote, "This pantomime is founded on an Eastern tale"; he also described a Tahitian *marae* in the pantomime as a "repository for the bodies of the Eastern kings in Otaheite" (93). Bernard Smith, *European Vision and the South Pacific, 1768–1850* (Oxford: Oxford University Press, 1960). Such conflations illustrate just how randomly and generically Europeans imagined their exotic "others."

25. John Berger has discussed how a ruling class mystifies history by making art inaccessible to the general populace (11). John Berger, *Ways of Seeing* (London: Penguin Books, 1972). This chapter works on a variation of his thesis: when the general populace sees so much of the bikini, history is still mystified.

26. Smith, *European Vision and the South Pacific, 1768–1850*, 25.

27. Glynn, *Skin to Skin*, 96.

28. CBS's *Entertainment Tonight* featured a series on the bikini that included stories on people who had made fortunes either by designing and marketing the bikini or by promoting beach bikini contests (November 8, 1991). The "ideal" female bodies displayed in bikinis in this series become generic commodities for the titillation of a male gaze and the enticement of a female consumer.

29. ABC's *A Current Affair* (November 27, 1991) reported on a conflict between female employees and the Stroh's Corporation over the company's use of a "Swedish" bikini team in its beer advertisements.

30. On ABC's family sitcom series *Growing Pains*, the adolescent character, Ben Seaver, has a poster of bikini-clad women in his bedroom. The poster is entitled "Island Girls," but all of the women are white.

31. Emily Apter, *Feminizing the Fetish: Psychoanalysis and Narrative Obsession in Turn-of-the-Century France* (New York: Cornell University Press, 1991).

32. Sigmund Freud, *The Standard Edition of the Complete Psychological Works* (London: Hogarth Press, 1961), 153–55.

33. For a psychoanalytic discussion of the bomb, see Brian Easlea, *Fathering the Unthinkable: Masculinity, Scientists and the Nuclear Arms Race* (Concord, Mass.: Pluto Press, 1983); for a feminist critique of military strategic discourse, see Carol Cohn, "Clean Bombs and Clean Language," in *Women, Militarism, and War: Essays in History, Politics, and Social Theory*, ed. Jean Bethke Elshtain and Sheila Tobias (Savage, Md.: Rowman & Littlefield, 1990), 33–55.

34. Terry Eagleton, *Literary Theory: An Introduction* (Minneapolis: University of Minnesota Press, 1983), 190.

35. Freud, *The Standard Edition of the Complete Psychological Works*, 154.

36. My use of Marxist analysis here is superficial; Marx's earlier work on alienation and the transformative power of money might inform my analysis differently, but I have focused only on the first volume of *Capital*. Karl Marx, *Capital*, vol. 1, trans. Edan and Cedar Paul (New York: E. P. Dutton, 1962).

37. Apter, *Feminizing the Fetish*, 12.

38. Barbara Christian, "The Race for Theory," in *Gender and Theory: Dialogues on Feminist Criticism*, ed. Linda Kauffman (New York: Basil Blackwell, 1987), 233.

39. Elizabeth Spellman, *The Inessential Woman: The Problems of Exclusion in Feminist Thought* (Boston: Beacon Press, 1988).

40. Spellman demonstrated the shortcomings of feminist theories that construct sexism and racism as separate and unequal processes of oppression (ibid., 117). Pacific Island female activists and academics seem to approach colonialist racism and sexism as coterminal forces. See Laura Marie Torres Souder, *Daughters of the Island: Contemporary Chamorro Women Organizers on Guam* (Lanham, Md.: University Press of America, 1992); and Haunani-Kay Trask, "Fighting the Battle of Double Colonization: The View of an Hawaiian Feminist," *Ethnies, Human Rights and Tribal Peoples: Renaissance in the Pacific* 4, no. 8–10 (1989): 61–67.

41. Teresia K. Teaiwa, "Microwomen: US Colonialism and Micronesian Women Activists," in *Pacific History: Papers from the 8th Pacific History Association Conference*, ed. Donald H. Rubinstein (Mangilao, Guam: University of Guam, 1992), 125–42; and Meikam Weera, "Palau Trusteeship Council Petition," *International Work Group for Indigenous Affairs Newsletter*, September–October 1991, 28–29.

42. NFIP in its turn supports indigenous women's organizing; for example, it cosponsored the conference "Wahine Maoli: Sisters in Solidarity" for native Hawaiian and American Indian women at the University of Hawai'i at Mānoa, March 8, 1992.

43. Historically, missionaries and colonial agents worked closely, as in the case of Hawai'i; contemporarily, the lines between church and state have been blurred, for example, in the legislative and legal battles over abortion in predominantly Catholic Guam and in Colonel Sitiveni Rabuka's claiming of divine inspiration for a two-year period of martial law in Fiji.

44. According to Hempenstall and Rutherford, the earliest missionaries to the Pacific Islands were Spanish Jesuits who landed on Guam in 1668 (98). Peter Hempenstall and Noel Rutherford, *Protest and Dissent in the Colonial Pacific* (Apia, Sāmoa: University of the South Pacific, 1984).

45. In *European Vision and the South Pacific*, Smith explains that the *Duff*, a vessel enlisted for a British Methodist project, embarked for Tahiti in 1796, marking the beginning of the second and most extensive wave of missionary efforts in the Pacific (104).

46. As Woolford explains, missionaries and colonial officials imposed a hierarchy of clothing on native people: shoes were denied to many Islanders as they had been to African American slaves; Papuan men were expected to wear short trousers or laplaps but would be penalized, usually by flogging, for donning a shirt (9–10). Don Woolford, "Blacks, Whites, . . . and the Awful Press," *New Guinea and Australia, Southwest Asia and the Pacific Islands*, January 1974, 4–25.

47. Tunumafono Apelu Aiavao, "Who's Playing Naked Now? Religion and Samoan Culture," *Pacific Perspective* 12, no. 2 (1983): 9.

48. An idea to create a marine park out of Bikini lagoon and the twenty-one vessels sunk during the 1946 atomic tests received publicity in the 1990s. Needless to say, the transformation of "a nuclear graveyard" into a tourist site that might generate revenues for Bikinians seems both symbolically and materially bankrupt. See John L. Eliot, "In Bikini Lagoon Life Thrives a Nuclear Graveyard," *National Geographic*, June 1992, 70–82.

49. Firth, *Nuclear Playground*, 133.

50. Ibid.

51. Ibid., 134.

52. Ibid. For a history of Indonesian policy in West Papua, see Carmel Budiardjo and Liem Soei Liong, *West Papua: The Obliteration of a People* (Surrey, United Kingdom: TAPOL, the Indonesian Human Rights Campaign, 1988).

53. For this reason NFIP has formed alliances with Pacific-Rim groups in Japan and Canada. See Firth, *Nuclear Playground*.

54. See South Pacific Commission, *South Pacific Economies Statistical Summary* (Noumea, New Caledonia: South Pacific Commission, 1993).

55. Kiste, *The Bikinians*, 198.

3
———

The Exceptional Life and Death of a Chamorro Soldier

Tracing the Militarization of Desire in Guam, ~~USA~~

Michael Lujan Bevacqua

Hacha: Living (Un)Exceptional Lives

The banal ambiguity of Guam's political existence, along with other sites such as Guantánamo Bay, either signals the coming of empire or already marks quietly its passage.[1] But, as opposed to Guantánamo Bay where the de- and reterritorialization of empire can be seen in much clearer and camera-ready terms, Guam is important precisely because its political existence represents forms of banal coloniality that continue to evade even the sharpest critical eyes.[2] It is spectrally indistinct, meaning that whatever specters of colonization or injustice it conjures up, they remain the type that do not haunt. If a brave new world of cosmopolitanism and global democracy arrived tomorrow, it is more than likely that Guam's status as a distantly imagined appendage to the American empire will remain untouched and unquestioned.

Since September 11, Guam has been a magnet for military activity and buildup. Posturing by President George W. Bush and his administration that troops in Europe will be redistributed through Asia and the Pacific in anticipation of "hot spots" in the region has only increased Guam's value as a forward military outpost. Despite Guam's status as one of the world's last official colonies, this increased militarization of the island has registered little to no protest on an international or national level. In American media, what little coverage does exist assumes either that the stationing of more bombers or fighters on Guam is routine or that the mere mentioning of Guam, as a "dot on the map," should make the inhabitants feel fortunate for the "extra" attention.³ In Guam, the local media uncritically celebrates these increases by reprinting military press releases and writing glowing editorials.

On the edge of American empire and the margins of international sovereignty, the banal yet exceptional existence of Guam can be instructive in the more subtle ways that militarism works. On an island where the U.S. military controls one third of the territory and has a century of militarization and colonialism in support of its occupation, we see the effects of militarizing impulses and inconsistencies on the bodies, the gazes, and the desiring of Chamorros, its indigenous people.⁴

Given this position, it would be an understatement to say that Chamorros on Guam live an ambiguous and indistinct existence. Although they are American citizens, by virtue of their residence in Guam they do not receive all the subsequent rights, such as a vote for president or representation in the U.S. Congress. Although they are geographically and politically distant from Washington, D.C., the federal government has plenary powers over Guam, meaning absolute and total control over the island.

This control over Guam has at least been theoretically contested by the United Nations (UN), which continues to list Guam as one of the sixteen remaining non–self-governing territories of the world. These non–self-governing territories are sites where the UN's mission to "eradicate colonialism" from the world and to provide colonized peoples paths to self-determination remain unfinished.⁵ For the past two decades, Chamorros have made regular pilgrimages to the UN in New York City to testify on the state of their island before the UN Fourth Committee and UN Special Committee of 24. These Chamorro delegations also call upon the United States to recognize and see through its obligation to decolonize the island.⁶ The position of the United States on this UN mandate is unsurprisingly ambivalent. During the testimonies provided for the Fourth Committee in October 2006, a member of the Guam delegation, Victoria Leon Guerrero, noted that the representative of the United States who was present in the room while they testified would not look at them or even acknowledge that they were there: "From where we were sitting, the U.S. representative had to turn his head in order to look at us . . . He never turned, never looked at us. That's how the United States government relates to the people of Guam."⁷ The same could be said for how the United

States refuses to respect, or even accept openly or publicly, that the island and its people have any right to decolonization.

Although at present the majority of the island's residents, both Chamorro and non-Chamorro, are uncertain over what they would want next for their island in terms of political status, or if a change is even possible or advisable, there has nonetheless developed a small but determined decolonization movement on Guam.[8] The trips to testify at the UN are only a single component of this movement, which has also focused on local educational campaigns, protests at both the government of Guam level and the federal level, and the building of solidarity with other indigenous peoples around the world and those struggling under the weight of American militarism or colonialism. This movement is composed of numerous organizations, some of which have been fighting for decades, such as *I Nasion Chamoru* or Organization of People for Indigenous Rights (OPI-R), and some created just recently, such as *Famoksaiyan*.[9]

Despite this growing movement to confront the United States over its colonial hold on the island and the frequently confusing place that Chamorros occupy in relation to their colonial master, they continue to be represented, both internally and externally, as one of the most patriotic semi-American ethnic groups.[10] The high levels of Chamorro participation in the U.S. military are often cited to make this point.

Since 1944, Chamorros have joined the military in record numbers. At one point in 1980, the U.S. Department of Defense estimated that 5 percent of Guam was in the military, which according to one editorial writer was twelve times the national average.[11] Chamorros have also made regular appearances in major U.S. conflicts over the past century, their starring role coming during the Vietnam War where they and Guam held the distinction of possibly having the highest killed-in-action rate per capita.[12] With the current war in Iraq still being waged, most of America's military recruitment offices are having problems meeting their quotas; Guam's recruiting centers, on the other hand, are doing just fine and are regularly recognized for their superb work.[13] In fact, at present, four of the U.S. Army's twelve highest recruitment "producers" can be found in Guam.[14]

The received opinion as to the source of this patriotic attachment is World War II.[15] In 1941, Guam was invaded and occupied by Japan. After thirty-two months of brutal occupation, during which hundreds of Chamorros were starved, beaten, and killed, America returned in 1944 to "liberate" its colony.[16] Since then, July 21 of each year celebrates the reinvasion of Guam as "Liberation Day." Considered the island's largest holiday, and even celebrated by Chamorros throughout the world, it is most visibly commemorated by a huge parade full of beauty queens, ranks upon ranks of U.S. National Guard members, and more military hardware than the film *Saving Private Ryan*.[17]

It is from this U.S. "liberation," this gesture of benevolent concern for its colonial citizens, that most in Guam explain the high levels of public and phatic patriotism, military and civilian loyalty and devotion. As one Chamorro, a major who teaches in the Reserve Officers Training Corps program at the University of Guam, put it, "My service is payment for a debt. I was taught since I was young about how we were liberated, and this is the least I can do."[18]

The first section of this chapter will deal with this simple genealogy of Chamorro patriotism by forming a possible counter genealogy, which will connect the colonization of Guam and U.S. strategic interests in the island to Chamorro militaristic impulses. The second section will build off of this point by looking at Chamorro military participation as the embodiment of a secret lack that Chamorros are forced to shoulder on behalf of the United States, as well as at the limits and possibilities for resistance when this service performs an important function in maintaining the United States as a nation.

Hugua: The Life(s) and Death(s) of a Soldier

Since the current U.S. war in Iraq began in 2003, three Chamorros have died there. The first was Christopher Rivera Wesley, killed on December 8, 2003.[19] The second, Michael Aguon Vega, died a few months later on March 20, 2004.[20] Jonathan Pangelinan Santos would be the most recent Chamorro to die on October 15, 2004.[21]

In this particular war, the bodies of the dead are not allowed to be photographed as they return home. This is no doubt an attempt on behalf of certain powerful figures to contain and limit the potential political meaning that these bodies might create and thereby exorcise any unfriendly specters, which are hardly patriotic and do not stay on message but always necessarily accompany the dead.[22] Thus the bodies disappear; the bones, the blood, the skin, even the very death knell itself crushed and bent out of meaning in order to run American patriotic machinery. But this sort of use, this disappearance, does not mean death. For death as we all know means ghosts—ghosts that cannot be controlled, cannot be subdued. Ghosts that can only be silenced through an escape to life.[23]

In the film *Weekend at Bernie's*, we see the two main characters go through an elaborate charade to convince those around them that their boss who passed away at the beginning of the weekend is not dead.[24] The protagonists carry him with them, pretending he can walk; move his head up and down to communicate with others; and even set up contraptions so he can wave at people jogging by.[25] All of this takes place precisely because of the denial of death and the fear of what this particular death might mean.

Freud and *The Interpretation of Dreams* might make an important reflective point here. In one of his collected dreams, a father, who fell asleep while at vigil over his son's coffin, dreams of his dead son. In the dream the father is approached by his dead son, who, covered in flames and smoke, reproached the father saying, "Father, can't you see that I am burning?" The father then wakes up to see that a candle has fallen and his son's clothes have actually caught on fire.[26]

The most obvious interpretation is that the external stimuli of the heat and the fire manifested in the father's dream and forced him to wake up. The Marxist Lacanian Slavoj Žižek, however, maintains something a bit more complicated. When confronted with the horrifying reproach of his son, the father wakes up, *precisely so that he can continue to dream*. In other words, in order to dodge the potential guilt over his son's death, the overwhelming guilt that had been haunting him in his dream, he escapes into waking life but only to continue to dream a denial of that death.[27]

Today, we are all haunted in similar ways, but with a slight twist. We confront this haunting most profoundly in the images of fallen soldiers. In Guam's media, for example, I saw the desperately creative ways that the deaths of these soldiers could be dodged. That is to say, I saw how their bodies could be reanimated, whether through discourses on sacrifice, discourses on American-ness, or discourses on terrorism and mortal danger. Their deaths are denied most often as a form of sacrifice, sometimes beautiful, sometimes justified, but always important and necessary. They are representations that persist after their bodies are hidden, their death denied, and they arrive at our doorsteps buried in newspapers or attached to e-mails in our inboxes. They are images of soldiers in full regalia, standing tall, serving proudly, but they nonetheless seem to scream out to us, *"Can't you see that I am living?"*[28]

A phatic cry and a hint at a co-opting are taking place. In Guam, this exhuming and rehumanizing of the dead Chamorro soldiers create powerful forces for maintaining patriotic devotion among Chamorros toward the United States. "Resurrection" is the ideal word for this process because this will ultimately rely on the "divine structure" of American hegemony. This process thus will not produce *kantan minatai*, or dirges, but instead create patriotic proverbs and devotional beatitudes to the United States. The dead and the death do not speak here; they are instead spoken for, spoken through, as a sort of ventriloquism through which patriotism takes place.[29]

One might call this chapter some sort of habeas corpus intervention. One might also call this chapter a questioning of the claims upon the body that deny the death and seek to obliterate the ghosts of injustice. But my intent here is not to claim the bodies of three Chamorros in the same way. Such a claim would produce similar crass results. The ethics of death imply that it is not the dead that can or must speak but the death itself; all that one says on behalf of the dead or through them is merely a cushion for the traumatic gaps in the symbolic network that this death threatens to reveal.[30]

On Guam I would call this a *surahånu* intervention. *Suruhånus* and *suruhånas* are traditional healers, some of whom have regular conversations with *taotaomo'na* in Guam, or the spirits of Chamorro ancestors.[31] I am not a *surahånu*, mind you, but instead this text is acting as my medium, that is, my means of trying to start a conversation with the deaths of these Chamorros.[32]

Tulu: Incongruent Infantilization

It's best to begin with images of the three Chamorros who have died fighting in Iraq. Due to the huge numbers of Chamorros in the U.S. military, images such as these are common throughout Guam's households and media. Chamorro homes are often filled with images of family members proudly serving their country with their *boyo'* haircuts or bald heads. Guam newspapers and television overrepresent such images, creating special pages, inserts, or segments that actively construct their productive power. The intersections within the images sometimes contest but more often reinforce overarching hegemonic notions in Guam.[33] Most often, soldiers stand proud and strong before American flags, making concrete connections between masculine sexuality, authority, and the U.S. nation.[34]

In some photos local icons such as ancient Chamorro warriors are used for unit logos, allowing too perfect a union between apparently "indigenous" masculinities (i.e., proud warrior-like behavior) and American military service. Sometimes they are images of soldiers receiving decorations from white commanding officers or family members, all conferring certain forms of visibility and recognition. Soldiers in the field, often operating high-tech weaponry or standing sure and certain of presence and dignity, exude agency and purpose.[35]

These representations play huge roles in making American military interests locally readable and desirable. Despite the dozens of miles of intimidating fences around Guam, which mark military and civilian territory, and the thousands of miles that lie between these Chamorros, their homes, and Washington, D.C., and the Pentagon, these images blur those demarcations, linking sometimes subtly and sometimes concretely the fate of Chamorros in Guam with the U.S. military. These representations meld an array of generic but nonetheless emotionally potent citations of things such as home, family, and values and provide the U.S. military, and service in it, as the means to defending and protecting such imagery. The effect is that, through military service, not only is the colonial gap between a Chamorro and the United States overcome but also an intimacy is forged. As a result, the "home" that soldiers serving abroad are staunchly defending becomes far more than just *Nåna* and her *Fina'tinas Chamorro*, but Uncle Sam and his military status quo as well.[36]

The image of Christopher Rivera Wesley is taken from a tribute Web site for the fallen American soldiers in Iraq. He is dressed in full battle gear in the deserts of Iraq. He is, as one Chamorro stated it to me, "doing a man's work . . . and willing to die a man's death."[37] The few photos I found of Wesley either were of this nature or had him in civilian clothes with his sister and mother. On one site his mother had posted her gratitude for whoever had started a memorial page for her son.[38] Many sites, however, did not feature photos of him at all.

The critical impetus for this chapter came when a similar patriotic Web site had a startlingly different image of Wesley. In this photo, Wesley is the only child among hundreds of other soldiers fully adult and fully uniformed.[39] The contrast was too sharp to ignore: Wesley appears as the immature, civilian-clothed, smiling child, while all others present stern faces and are pumped full of all the agency that uniformed military personnel are meant to imply.

There are many responses one can have to something like this. Racist! Infantilization! Stupid white people![40] As charming as these statements can be, after staring at this photo of Wesley, I set them aside as unproductive. The use of this childish image might be, but need not be, malicious, and to fixate on that might miss a more important, fundamental incongruency. A mistake had been made in the use of this photo, but probably not the one that most would recognize.

I recalled a quote from a *Doonesbury* comic during the initial days of the Enron (non)scandal. Ari Fleischer, the Bush mouthpiece, is asked, "What did Ken Lay get for his $550,000 in contributions to Bush?" The answer: nothing. The response: "Nothing? Isn't that a breakdown in the system?"[41]

It was then that I realized what mistake had been made and what I was stumbling upon. As this image of a "Chamorro child" stared at me, I realized that each time a Chamorro joins the military, a secret contract is being signed. In exchange for their service, their sacrifice, they are to receive a set of very important and unique clothes, the military uniform. Hardly just any uniform, this one seems to pulse with powerful meanings. It is a uniform woven from the fabric of adulthood, stitched up tightly with strength, masculinity, agency, visibility, and voice.[42] Wesley at the minimum was supposed to have evaded this representation. Because of his service he was supposed to escape this infantilization, this childish representation, that continues to haunt Chamorros both in Guam and in the halls of government offices in Washington, D.C.[43]

Fatfat: Instructional Presence and Absence

It was cognitive dissonance over Wesley and his infantilized representation that forced me to rethink and reappropriate what has become a commonly used image in Chamorro scholarship. This image, titled "More Like His Father Everyday," first appeared in *The Guam Recorder*, a Guam naval newspaper, in 1912 to illustrate the successes of the U.S. Navy in "civilizing" the Chamorro (see Figure 3.1). In seminal Guam texts such as *Colonial Dis-Ease: US Navy Health Policies and the Chamorros of Guam, 1898–1941* by Anne Perez Hattori, it is used to illustrate the paternalistic and racist nature of the U.S. colonization of Guam. While this interpretation is vital, I now see this image as a possible sinthome through which the patriotic economy of Guam, which pushes Chamorros to join the military, is run.[44]

Figure 3.1. "More Like His Father Everyday," originally published in The Guam Recorder, a Guam naval newspaper, 1912

Uncle Sam, ever benevolent, stands atop advancement. His dark, ambiguously dressed and sexed Chamorro child stands atop the gifts of his presence. In time the image seems to suggest that the Chamorro might reach up to the level of his father.

From 1898 to 1941, Guam was ruled by an autocratic military regime run by a succession of naval governors whose power was basically absolute. To facilitate their control over Guam's civilian Chamorro population, different programs of civilizing and spheres of naval influence were created, in particular around health care, politics, and education.[45] I tend to concentrate on education the most in my work, for it is in this process that the formal and obscene desires of the colonizer can be best explained.[46] The techniques of instructional presence and absence can also be best visualized here.

The formal aspects of the colonizer are easily identified and openly admitted to. They fall under the logic of assimilation or incomprehensible othering. From the beginning of the American colonization of Guam, "benevolent assimilation" was an openly acknowledged endeavor that was articulated differently by each successive naval governor.[47] Incomprehensible othering can be found most prevalently in the early years of naval rule in Guam, whether in medical texts that pronounced Chamorros as disease ridden and provided warnings for sailors on contact with natives of the island's jungles or in naval governor's reports that described Chamorros as free from the "ambition or the desire for change or progress."[48] The commonality is that they both admit to a movement of the colonized, whether further away from or closer to the colonizer.

It is here, within this obscene economy and forms of instructional absence, where the deep-tissue colonizing takes place and where the ideological terrain of Guam is drastically changed. This is where a gap, a void, an absence is forced to be interpreted. This is the place where instructional presence, such as the idea that "Education is important," forces an informing of an absence, such as the prohibition, and thus lack, of Chamorro language in schools, the lack of anything Chamorro related in curriculum, and the intense hygienic invasions into and upon the Chamorro body.[49] The absence is given meaning based on the presence, the often-silent teaching, of lessons of Chamorro incompleteness, inadequacy, dirtiness, impossibility, invisibility, and nakedness.[50] Thus we find the specter of the U.S. colonized subject, the "disembodied shadow" from the *Insular Cases* at last coming into being, if such a thing can come into being.[51]

This is where the importance of the obscene desire is revealed, that is, the desire for the nonteleological thing. Colonizing impulses and military demands intersect to desire the thing that cannot and will not disrupt or threaten the colonizer. In Guam we see the desire for the nonteleological thing in the responses to the movement of Chamorros along the spectrum of naval comfort and anxiety.[52] The avowed civilizing of Chamorros led to their incessant demands for more rights.[53] The savage othering of them created even more fear in the navy as Chamorros thus became more associated with the fearful realm of the outside in Guam, such as the jungle, which was perceived to be full of disease and danger.[54]

Lima: Attaining Agency

Returning to the image of Uncle Sam and his Chamorro child, we can pick it apart based on its formal and obscene elements. For those who have eyes only for the formal side of things, an obvious teleology is implied. Upward movement, or improvement, will come if Uncle Sam's mandates are followed and obeyed. But in the details the obscene desire can be teased out. The use of the child is common to these types of representations, but the use of the child and the blocks refers to the stripping of any internal or natural development from the child. The child will not grow or move on its own, meaning that all the agency or movement, up or down, is presupposed by colonial interventions.

At the most basic level, this can be expressed through the rephrasing of a quote from *Monty Python's Life of Brian*: "All right, but apart from sanitation, medicine, education, wine, public order, irrigation, roads, the fresh-water system and public health, what have the Americans ever done for us?"[55] The encompassing and the assuming of all (most importantly, positive) possibility can be found in a statement such as this. Anything beyond the United States, anything that could surpass its grasp, its authority, is easily marginalized or obliterated. To even ask the question of what could or should exist otherwise is quickly overwhelmed by the litany of American colonial projects. The implication is obvious: for the Chamorro there can be nothing save for that which America has or will provide.

But what must be pointed out here is that the nonteleological thing can never really be created. Constant negotiation takes place, which forces and allows movements and both expected and unexpected forms of agency and resistance. But just in the metaphoric power of the image, in this desire unrealized but nonetheless present, we find powerful impacts.

The impossibility, the collection of absences imposed upon the Chamorro through this colonization, was not peaceful or placid. The opposite of existence is not, after all, nonexistence but insistence.[56] The Chamorro pushed into this position bears these insistent, traumatic marks of incompleteness, of *chattaotao*, which is Chamorro for the state of being not quite human.[57] This (im)positioning is closely linked to the maintenance of Guam as a strategic military zone. Since its capture in 1898, the colonization of Guam by the United States has been run on twin, interwoven desires: first, that the island's strategic space needs to be controlled and, second, that the Chamorro needs to be remade into something that does not and will not tamper with this control.

The Secret Guam Study by Dirk Ballendorf chronicles a number of reports and studies conducted by the U.S. State Department, Department of Defense, and Department of Interior during the 1970s regarding the future of Guam and Chamorros in relation to the United States. One report emphasized the importance of Guam's strategic space and the need to continue to control it, as well as the necessity to shape the identity of the island and Chamorros to meet this goal.[58]

Chamorros trapped by these desires often find themselves in a horrifying position. Patricia Taimanglo's dissertation on Chamorro intergenerational trauma, "An Exploratory Study of Community Trauma and Culturally Responsive Counseling with Chamorro Clients," contains many statements by Chamorros to this effect, which express the daily distress of confronting one's existence as being determined by and derived from a distant and disinterested colonizer. As one Chamorro states, "We're not actually human beings but tools . . . We're no different than the piece of land up at NAS or Anderson Air Force Base."[59] As another Chamorro articulated to me angrily, "We are only human when the Feds want us to be."[60]

These colonizing marks insist much on behalf of interests hardly local to Guam. They insist that the invisible become visible, that incompleteness become completeness. They insist upon seeking out a trajectory, and in order to maintain U.S. control over Guam and the identity of Chamorros, the processes of colonization in Guam establish their own easy, simplistic means by which Chamorros can hitch themselves once again to a teleological train.

Returning to the image of Uncle Sam with his nearly naked Chamorro, the means that comes first to mind is the clothes offered to Chamorros by service in the military. The wearing of the uniform is the easiest escape from the chaos of this apparently eternal childhood outside of society and deprived of a conventional identity. But more important than infantilization and nakedness, these clothes have a way of not erasing but covering up the colonial markings upon the Chamorro body, making them somehow different in source and providing the Chamorro with a feeling of ownership over them as opposed to just being cruelly defined by them. It is in the uniform that so much that is otherwise difficult or unattainable can be easily grasped or attained.

Here I will discuss briefly three ways in which the uniform can provide an aura of completeness for Chamorros: voting, visibility, and voice. As a colony, no one who resides in Guam, Chamorro or otherwise, can vote for president. This is just one simple discontinuity that can be dodged by joining the military, as active members can vote anywhere, whether in Guam, Guantánamo, or Iraq.[61] Thus even the most simple, token form of political agency can be easily attained.

As for invisibility, the media in Guam has long practiced its own forms of instructional absence.[62] One need only to look through the run of Guam's longest running newspaper, the *Pacific Daily News*, to see it.[63] As one of many colonizing institutions in Guam, its main function is to make readable American frames and strategic desires in and for Guam. However, in addition to this, it has traditionally provided daily lessons in Chamorro visibility and invisibility. For decades the primary way in which a Chamorro, outside of a politician, could grace its pages was through military service. This was particularly so during the 1960s and 1970s where images of Chamorros in uniform heading off to or returning from basic training or heading off to and returning from Vietnam often filled entire pages. Nearly all of the seventy-eight Chamorros who returned dead from Vietnam were given an image and half of the space on the cover page of the *Pacific Daily News*.[64] What these types of images affirmed, which similar newspaper sections strengthen today, is the authenticity and naturalness of a very particular form of Chamorro identity. This is an identity that is defined primarily through patriotism and military service and is seen as the key to achieving local and national recognition and visibility through its regular appearance in media such as newspapers.

Lastly is the issue of voice. The Chamorro who joins the military is able at last to occupy that voice of universality in American discourse that only select groups and individuals within the United States can hold. That voice is the one that can speak for all and, more importantly, prevent others from speaking.

In my conversations with Chamorros in the military, this dynamic is often too easily apparent when difficult topics, such as war or the decolonization of Guam, are broached. Midway through these discussions I find the rug under my right to speak has been quickly pulled out with statements such as "I am fighting to protect your right to say those things!" Whenever the position of the United States in Guam is questioned, the soldier, with his ability to lay a personal claim on nearly all speech, can ensure that that critique is either retracted or made suspiciously ungrateful. Thus, through military service, American-ness can be assured for those who desire it, and they can literally become the voice of America in Guam.

Gunum: Resistance and Commissary Privileges

It must be noted, before this chapter sounds too much like a twisted existential advertisement for literal human recruitment, that these are perceived receivables—that is, they are the tendencies in the ideological terrain in Guam that push and pull Chamorros in different directions. While military service might appear to be the best possible means for attaining agency and mobility and finding a comforting human fullness to salve their otherwise impossible existences, the reality is that Chamorros who join the military often find themselves discriminated against, whether for promotions or by unruly white soldiers who refuse to salute a "brown soldier."[65] Often, their American-ness can continue to be questioned, despite their history of service.[66] Even using Vietnam as a historical narrative, where Chamorro patriotism and love often goes unquestioned, many soldiers, in addition to their physical war wounds, brought back with them angry memories of racism and being hazed by white soldiers forcing them to prove they were not "gooks."[67]

The uniform comes with a lot of costs, one of which in particular I'd like to discuss. This service can in some ways solve the problems of Chamorro impossibility by giving individuals minute and token forms of presupposed agency. But the cost comes in the form of the sacrifice that must be shouldered by Chamorros in their covering up the lack of the colonizer.

While presenting a paper at the *Sovereignty Matters* conference in New York City in April 2005, I discussed the need for the radical act in Guam in order to break out of the colonial and liberal deadlock that exists there.[68] The radical or authentic political act is a certain type of move that, in its acceptance of the void of a particular choice, is able to change the very coordinates from which it is acted.[69] I mentioned specifically an act by the late Angel Santos from the activist group *Nasion Chamoru*.[70] Before Guam's media and military police, Santos and several others jumped a military fence. The act was radical precisely because the men who jumped accepted the void that their act created around them. They accepted the fact that neither their culture, nor their people, who felt they were "troublemakers," nor the law (the military from whom they could only expect violence or death) would protect them.[71] Thus, when they arrived at the other side of the fence and were arrested by military police, the ground beneath them had changed drastically, making all manner of once unthinkable and maladjusted acts against the federal government or military routine and normal.

In response to my talk, one person in the audience remarked that maybe another good way of resistance, instead of jumping the fence, was to get in a truck, drive through the military gate, get to the other side, buy a whole bunch of food and anything else, and then drive out. The implication of this act is to subvert the system or abuse it from within through military service.

This is an important form of resistance and one that even I have used to get cheaper chicken and drinks. But it is extremely problematic, and not because it is consorting with the enemy or because it taints some notion of "pure" indigenous resistance, but more so because this is one of the many acts of resistance that are presupposed by the colonizer. This method of resistance is one that the colonizing process itself sets up, and the acceptance of this position by the Chamorro soldier might serve a larger national function.

Fiti: Living the Lack of the Other

Those who live in liminality and encounter and breathe it in all its visceral and banal forms are the ones who know best these lacks. It is us in the colonies, the zones of indistinction, the often-unexceptional states of exception, who know what the colonizer lacks best. It is these lacks that we are forced to live.

The claim that America rides the crest of empire in the ways that it thinks locally but acts globally can be too easily complicated by a place such as Guam.[72] As "America in Asia," as "Where America's Day Begins," as "Where America's Empire Begins," in Guam we find the inconsistencies of the American nation, which are thus transformed into the secret lack that Chamorros are forced to embody.[73] The military means through which the position of the disembodied shade can be escaped are built upon the keeping of this secret. We can see this best exemplified in the

Chamorro soldier and his or her sacrifice, which is, at the most basic level, a gesture made on behalf of the other in an attempt to cover up their lack, their inconsistency.[74]

One can see this clearly in the deaths of the three Chamorro soldiers in Iraq. In newspapers and television reports on the deaths, no mention is made whatsoever about Guam's colonial status. Family members interviewed seem to care little that their child, nephew, or cousin was sent to war without people on Guam having any representation in the political bodies that sent him or her there. Instead, thick, juicy platitudes about defense of freedom, defense of the democracy, and, thus, defense of the Guam home front against terrorists were invoked.[75]

In a way, the donning of the uniform comes with its own hidden teleological purpose or function, which is served in the death of a Chamorro. Those deaths become the generally small, but nonetheless potent and productive, point of strange and enchanting affirmation, that is to say, the loyal liminality, the exceptional acceptance of an exceptional state. It is the devotion of those who are not supposed to be devoted, the care of those who are not supposed to care. Articles about Chamorro loyalty to the United States during World War II build off this point. One article titled "THESE ARE AMERICANS" states that "there are no more patriotic citizens than the liberated natives of Guam. After 32 months of Jap bestiality, they know for sure what it is worth to be Americans."[76] The Chamorro, who at that time was not even a citizen, who was treated like a child at every level, whose potential political rights were discussed in terms of threatening national security, and whose island was destroyed by both the Americans and Japanese, nonetheless is filled with love.[77] Agueda Johnston, a Chamorro educator from prewar Guam, was asked by an American news reporter in 1944 how she felt after her island had been destroyed by the American reinvasion. She answered very patriotically that she did not care—all that mattered was that the Americans had returned.[78]

In the perceived patriotism of those who by admission are not supposed to be patriotic, we find an important idea in the maintenance of the American nation.[79] The Chamorro soldier is thus the one who willingly and loyally shoulders the indigenous sacrifice, which covers up the inconsistency in the American nation.[80]

Gualo: What to Do with the Uniform

It would irresponsible for me to end on such a sour note. Resistance is not futile. It is necessary and it is taking place all the time. But there are numerous tricks to finding it and even more to make it transformative. To conclude, I will discuss two possibly productive sites of resistance for Chamorros in Guam seeking to resist militaristic impulses and also to form means through which radical resistance itself can take place.

One of the least told stories in Guam is that of the Insular Guard, an all-Chamorro semimilitary force created before World War II.[81] These men had uniforms and they received pay and blessed commissary privileges, although significantly less than what their white counterparts received. When the Japanese invaded in 1941, some of these men fought valiantly against them, and some even died. Many of them, however, ran.[82] There exists a monument in Guam's capital today that honors those valiant defenders. If anything, I think there should be a monument to the deserters, to those who ran.[83]

Lastly, during the later years of the Vietnam War, after dozens of Chamorros had died, thousands had served and come back, and many had gone back again, the island's patriotic luster was beginning to fade. Daily, trucks, overloaded with a seeming infinite number of bombs, could be seen on the island's main roads moving between the island's naval and air force bases. One mother, sick of the death and the war, implored her son not to go to Vietnam. Her son, drafted and feeling as though he had no choice, told her he had to go, that he would be fighting for her. When the boy woke up the next morning, he found that his mother had not believed him and that, during the night, she had hid his uniform.

Postscript

Since the initial submission of this chapter, the Chamorro death toll has changed and so has the way it is being reported. As I am updating this chapter in November of 2009, sixteen Chamorros and non-Chamorros from Guam and the Commonwealth of the Northern Mariana Islands (CNMI) have died in the Iraq War. In media accounts in Guam and in Micronesia, this figure is often subsumed into a larger category, namely soldiers from Micronesia (from Guam, the CNMI, the Federated States of Micronesia [FSM], Palau, and the Republic of the Marshall Islands) who have died in the American war on terror.[84] In this larger context, the number of dead soldiers from the region skyrockets to thirty-nine in all.

These statistics are jarring considering that the population of this region of the world is less than six hundred thousand and that close to half of those who have served and died from Micronesia are not U.S. citizens and would not even be considered "semi-Americans."[85] Despite the already startling nature of these statistics, they achieve their true impact if you combine these deaths from the Micronesian region with twenty-seven other deaths, which together come from the "American" political community that has the highest per capita killed-in-action rate of the United States. This community can be found scattered across tens of thousands of miles from the Western Pacific into the Caribbean in hundreds of islands, all administered by the U.S. Department of Interior. It is America's insular empire, a sea of its colonies, encompassing all the previously mentioned islands of Micronesia as well as American Sāmoa and the U.S. Virgin Islands.[86]

Despite their small populations and small sizes, these islands do nonetheless lie at the tip of America's military spear. In the case of Guam, we see this geographically and in strategic military terms. But these islands, despite the distances between them and their distances from Washington, D.C., or the Pentagon, are all bound together by incredible military enlistment rates and these equally incredible killed-in-action statistics. There is much more critical work to be done in bringing together these insular areas and in theorizing what role these hypermilitarized and exceptional positions and bodies play in the production of the United States and its power.

Notes

The subheadings in this chapter *(hach*a, *hugu*a, *tul*u, etc.) are ancient Chamorro numbers. In modern Chamorro they have been replaced with Spanish numbers *(un*o, *d*os, *tre*s, etc.). I use them to number section headings in my written work as a small gesture of decolonization.

1. Michael Hardt and Antonio Negri, *Empire* (Cambridge, Mass.: Harvard University Press, 2001).

2. The key is how and if things can fit. In a talk at University of California, San Diego, about Guantánamo Bay and the "enemy combatants" detained there,

titled "Where Is Guantanamo?" Amy Kaplan concluded her genealogy of American empire by stating that there should be an international movement to shut down Guantánamo and its noxiously spectral juridical and political status. While I agree with this prescriptive point, my response to her title of "Where Is Guantanamo?" is "Where Is Guam?" While an international movement to shut down Guantánamo seems to be possible, could an international movement to decolonize Guam (or any other banal colony) ever exist? Probably not, precisely because of Guam's own spectrally indistinct status and because decolonizing Guam will always be thought of as being too small a task or not providing high enough stakes. At present, it seems that the epistemological hierarchies that inform movements or projects such as these will always leave out a site like Guam. Amy Kaplan, "Where Is Guantanamo?" (lecture, University of California, San Diego, April 28, 2005).

3. Tom Perry, "Dot on the Map Retains Large Strategic Stature," *Los Angeles Times*, January 28, 2002.

4. The indigenous people of Guam are the Chamorros. The island was first colonized by Spain in the seventeenth century with the establishment of a Catholic mission. As a result of warfare and disease, more than 90 percent of Chamorros died within the next four decades. In 1898, Guam was taken by the United States as a spoil of the Spanish–American War. The island would be run for the next forty years by a U.S. military dictatorship. In 1941, the United States abandoned Guam to the Japanese military, which held the island for more than two years, resulting in the death of more than six hundred Chamorros. Guam was retaken in 1944 after a massive bombing campaign by the U.S. military, destroying the island's main villages. After six years of continued military rule, in response to protests both in Washington, D.C., and in Guam about the island's political status, an Organic Act was created for Guam in 1950, which gave Chamorros American citizenship and some protections under the U.S. Constitution. To this day, Guam continues to be an unincorporated territory, a colony of the United States. See Political Status Education and Coordinating Commission, *I Magobetna-na Guahan: Governing Guam, Before and After the Wars* (Agaña, Guam: Political Status Education and Coordination Commission, 1993).

5. As of 2002, the United Nations General Assembly lists sixteen entities that are still colonies or non–self-governing territories: Western Sahara, Anguilla, Bermuda, British Virgin Islands, Cayman Islands, Falkland Islands (Malvinas), Montserrat, St. Helena, Turks and Caicos Islands, U.S. Virgin Islands, Gibraltar, American Sāmoa, New Caledonia, Pitcairn, Tokelau, and Guam. The United Nations, "Non-Self-Governing Territories Listed by the General Assembly in 2002," The United Nations Web site, http://www.un.org/Depts/dpi/decolonization/trust3.htm (accessed December 1, 2009).

6. "Guiñifen i Mañainå-ta (The dreams of our ancestors)," *Minagahet Zine* 6, no. 1 (2008): 22.

7. Aaron Glantz, "Natives of Guam Decry US Expansion Plan," *Antiwar.com*, http://www.antiwar.com/glantz/?articleid=10156 (accessed December 13, 2006).

8. Michael Lujan Bevacqua, "Everything You Wanted to Know about Guam but Were Afraid to Ask Žižek" (master's thesis, University of California, San Diego, 2007).

9. *I Nasion Chamoru* translates into "The Chamorro Nation" and is a grassroots organization, first started in 1991, and has been most notable in forcing the Governor of Guam to implement the Chamorro Land Trust Act, which provides land for lease to landless Chamorros. OPI-R is an activist organization comprised primarily of professionals and scholars who were central in creating the tradition of dialogue and outreach to the United Nations. *Famoksaiyan* translates to either "the place or time of nurturing" or "the time to paddle ahead and move forward." It was started at a conference in San Diego in 2006 and has since conducted different educational campaigns on decolonization and the militarization on Guam in both Guam and in the Chamorro diaspora.

10. Patricia Taimanglo Pier, "An Exploratory Study of Community Trauma and Culturally Responsive Counseling with Chamorro Clients" (Ph.D. dissertation, University of Massachusetts, 1998), 151–55. The use of an American inclusive does not quite sit right with me, as there are too many discontinuities in Guam and in its relationship to the United States for me to call Chamorros "Americans" without supplying a book-length footnote. Michael Lujan Bevacqua, "These May or May Not Be Americans: The Patriotic Myth and the Hijacking of Chamorro History in Guam" (master's thesis, University of Guam, 2005). Despite enthusiastic admissions of patriotism from Chamorros themselves, the discontinuities are not only difficult but often impossible to speak around. While eating dinner at Denny's in Guam with my family, I pointed out to my nephews and niece that all the white people were sitting in at the center tables, which are much bigger than the ones we were at against the wall. My nephew Dylan responded, "Oh, I see Uncle Mike, those tables are for the Americans and these tables are for us."

11. Joe Murphy, "Guam Military Role Highest in Country," *Pacific Daily News*, July 10, 1980, 15.

12. Robert Underwood, "Afterword," in *Campaign for Political Rights on the Island of Guam* (Saipan, CNMI: Commonwealth of the Northern Mariana Islands Division of Historic Preservation, 2001), 210.

13. For example, Mark Pieper, "Award Recognizes Marine Corps Recruiters on Guam," *Pacific Daily News*, November 17, 2003, or "Military Milestones," *Pacific Daily News*, February 17, 2004.

14. James Brooke, "On Farthest U.S. Shores, Iraq Is a Way to a Dream," *New York Times*, July 31, 2005.

15. If collective-thought consensus forms artifacts, then the text that has formed to represent supposedly the collective beliefs of Chamorros regarding their relationship to the United States and its military was written by a white disc jockey on Guam named Jeff Evans. Written for a Liberation Day special of Guam's version of *TV Guide*, it uses almost too perfectly the language that seems to forever bind Chamorros devotionally to the United States. Jeff Evans, "Liberation . . . The New Generation Many Meanings to Many People," Special Advertising Section, *TV GUAM*, July 21, 1996.

16. For the most comprehensive and extensive historical account of the Japanese occupation of Guam see Tony Palomo, *Island in Agony* (Hagatña, Guam: Self-published, 2004).

17. Cecilia Taitano Perez, "Liberation Day: A Re-Telling," in *Kinalamten Pulitikat: Sinenten I Chamorro: Issues in Guam's Political Development: The Chamorro Perspective* (Hagatña, Guam: Political Status Education and Coordination Commission, 1996), 70–77.

18. John Taitano, interview with the author, University of Guam, ROTC Building, Mangilao, Guam, October 13, 2002.

19. Therese Merto, "Chamorro Killed in Iraq," *Pacific Daily News*, December 12, 2003.

20. Therese Merto, "Funeral for Guam Native Set," *Pacific Daily News*, March 7, 2004.

21. Katie Worth, "Santos' Death Mourned," *Pacific Daily News*, October 20, 2004.

22. James Rainey, "Unseen Pictures, Untold Stories," *Los Angeles Times*, May 21, 2005.

23. Avery Gordon, *Ghostly Matters: The Haunting of the Sociological Imagination* (Minneapolis: University of Minnesota Press, 1997).

24. The methodological logic of using *Weekend at Bernie's* or similar "pop culture" texts comes from Slavoj Žižek's work, where he follows the recommendations of Walter Benjamin that a "theoretically productive and subversive procedure" is "the reading of the highest spiritual products of a culture alongside its common, prosaic, worldly products." Slavoj Žižek, *Looking Awry: An Introduction to Jacques Lacan though Popular Culture* (Cambridge, Mass.: MIT Press, 1991), vii.

25. The hope of course being that the thing that is obviously alive cannot have any ghosts. But hauntings persist always, as is evidenced in the film *Ghost in the Shell 2: Innocence*. Far different than the usual humanity versus machine or a cyborg or machine with an identity crisis, the film's ontological exploration is enhanced with the unsettling introduction of dolls. In them and similar figures of indistinction, we encounter the disturbing doubts over whether the thing that is obviously alive really is and, alternatively, the possibility that a lifeless object might

actually live. *Ghost in the Shell 2: Innocence*. DVD, directed by Mamoru Oshii (Bandai Visual Company: Tokyo, Japan, 2004).

26. Slavoj Žižek, *Did Someone Say Totalitarianism?* (London: Verso, 2001), 195.

27. Ibid., 196.

28. This is the traumatic reproach that must be woken up from to be avoided. The plenitude of platitudes that come afterward seeks to destroy this recognition of unethical treatment of the death/dead. This relates to Lacan's statement as to why the dead return to haunt us: *because they were improperly buried*, a point that Žižek illustrates through horror films such as *Night of the Living Dead* or Stephen King novels such as *Pet Sematary*. Žižek, *Looking Awry*, 22–23.

29. In Guam this can best be exemplified through a 1968 editorial from Joe Murphy in Guam's longest running newspaper, the *Pacific Daily News*. In the piece, Murphy creates a fictional dialogue between a young Chamorro, who had died in Vietnam, and his mother. In the dialogue the young soldier professes his love for the United States, proclaiming its greatness and saying he will kill anyone who says otherwise. Joe Murphy, "Pipe Dreams," *Guam Daily News*, March 12, 1968, 19.

30. The text where I derive most of my ideas about the ethics of death is Jacques Derrida, *The Work of Mourning* (Chicago: University of Chicago Press, 2001). What I mean by the term "ethics of death" is, what is the ethical treatment of the dead? How does one speak to or for someone after they can no longer respond, except within yourself? An essential element in these ethics is the understanding that each death possesses only a singular meaning, that ultimately it in and of itself means nothing. Each death holds the potential to reveal the gaps in the symbolic order, or the fact that the Big Other does not exist, and that the world around us doesn't not possess any inherent order. All that we say for the dead, or say about the dead is in essence our efforts to cushion ourselves from this truth.

31. Lawrence J. Cunningham, *Ancient Chamorro Society* (Honolulu, Hawai'i: The Bess Press, 1992), 102, 152.

32. This is where my ethics come in. I cannot emphasize enough that it is their deaths that I am interested in. I am not attempting to rewrite the lives of these Chamorros and transform them into militant Chamorro nationalists. I am instead looking at the larger structural/cultural issues, the ideological tendencies in Guam that push Chamorros into the military and then lay claim upon their lives and their meaning when they die. Department of Chamorro Affairs, *Chamorro Heritage: A Sense of Place* (Hagatña, Guam: Department of Chamorro Affairs, Research Publication and Training Division, 2003).

33. Sometimes these images can contest dominant hegemonic narratives and understandings. For example, the inclusion of the family within the image is extremely productive but can, however, complicate things greatly. Nicole Santos told me of a serviceman that she interviewed for whom the inclusion of the

family in the military image presented a nagging problem. What if, this serviceman thought, it came down to it that one day it was the U.S. military versus the people in Guam, for whatever reason? Which side would he be on? Defending his "country"? Defending his family? Nicole Santos, interview with the author, University of Guam, Mangilao, Guam, July 15, 2004.

34. Thousands of Chamorro females are also in the military; they are photographed in similar postures and backdrops. How does this reinforce or complicate dominant discourses? Furthermore, how are *matan inosensia*, or "faces of innocence," received? What I mean by this are faces such as Jonathan Pangelinan Santos, where he looks directly at the camera, face somewhat level (as opposed to chin up slightly), not with a proud smug countenance but instead an uncertain one. Do photos of Chamorro females in the military challenge characterizations of these images as masculine or strong? From the research that I have done into these types of images, I find that they perform a powerful patriotic function. With Jonathan Pangelinan Santos, for example, we see the active creation of a worthy sacrifice and a worthy role model, as the language of loyalty intersects between family anecdotes (of the young man not wanting to go but going anyway) and his young, uncertain, but nonetheless loyal, face. See Nicole Adapon Santos, "The Paradox of Guam: Brief Essays on Culture, the Military and a U.S. Pacific Territory" (master's thesis, University of California, Santa Cruz, 2007).

35. This is a very important divide in representations of the "others" of the world, in particular in the realm of movies and video games. In franchises such as *Splinter Cell*, *Metal Gear Solid*, and *Medal of Honor*, we can see how race, nation, and technological prowess intersect to make slogans such as "Army of One" powerful and productive by providing literal situations where an army of one American (with the help of all the technological and rational superiority the West can offer) can take on multitudes of terrorists or enemy soldiers.

36. *Nåna* means "mother." *Fina'tinas Chamorro* means "Chamorro cooking." The collapsing of these interests is vital in getting people to go to war, as evidenced by the e-mails I often receive from Chamorros fighting in Iraq. In 2004, just a few days after the third Chamorro had died in Iraq, I received a group e-mail from another Chamorro fighting there. Interestingly enough he made no reference to freedom or liberty but instead situated his impetus for fighting and for "fighting harder" in knowing that he was defending us, his friends and family "back home." Roland Ada, personal communication, October 20, 2004.

37. Anonymous, e-mail to author, December 29, 2003.

38. Tim Rivera, "Fallen Heroes of Operation Iraqi Freedom: Army Spc. Christopher J. Rivera Wesley," *Fallen Heroes Memorial*, http://www.fallenheroesmemorial.com/oif/profiles/wesleychristopherjrivera.html (accessed December 17, 2004).

39. MilitaryCity.com "Honor the Fallen," http://www.militarycity.com/valor/256929 (accessed December 18, 2004; site now discontinued).

40. This litany is not meant to be completely facetious. I included these statements precisely because of the way people initially reacted when I would share my reading of the images. I fear that this has become the standard "U.S. people of color" critique nowadays and something that must be gotten past. While these readings might be initially important, they become easily fetishized and prevent any further critical work from taking place.

41. Gary Trudeau, *Peace Out Dawg! Tales from Ground Zero* (Kansas City, Mo.: Andrews McMeel Publishing, 2002), 102.

42. This section was inspired by, but has nothing to do with, Slavoj Žižek's discussion of Judith Butler's discussion of Hegel's master and slave dynamic. Slavoj Žižek, *The Ticklish Subject: The Absent Centre of Political Ontology* (London: Verso, 1999), 265.

43. Any discussion about political maturity often drips hypocritically with the infantilization of the other. Those seeking a good example of this need only visit any senator or congressional representative office in Washington, D.C., and discuss with them Guam's possibility of becoming a state. If you aren't completely pandered to or dismissed, then a discussion around unreadiness for that sort of political obligation will take place. Government corruption will be discussed, as will the inability of Guam to become "economically self-sustaining." Of course what will be gracefully negated from this conversation is any meaningfully mention of any similar inconsistencies within America itself.

44. A sinthome, as opposed to a symptom, is something that does not just signify a system but offers a point through which the system can be unraveled. It is the imaginary point through which an entire ideological network is knotted and thus offers a means through which the system itself can be undermined. Žižek offers as an example of a sinthome, "single unemployed mother." It is a point where, according to him, "all the lines of predominant ideological argumentation (the return to family values, the rejection of the welfare state and its 'uncontrolled' spending, etc.) meet" (176). Žižek, *Ticklish*.

45. Political Status Education and Coordinating Commission, *I Magobetna-na Guahan*. For politics see Penelope Bordallo Hofschneider, *Campaign for Political Rights on the Island of Guam, 1898–1950* (Saipan, CNMI: Commonwealth of the Northern Mariana Islands Division of Historic Preservation, 2001). For health care, try Anne Perez Hattori, *Colonial Dis-Ease: US Navy Health Policies and the Chamorros of Guam, 1898–1941* (Honolulu: University of Hawai'i Press, 2004) and Christine Taitano DeLisle, "Delivering the Body: Narratives of Family, Birth and Pre-War Pattera" (master's thesis, University of Guam, 2001).

46. Education was compulsory for most of the navy's forty-three-year autocratic rule over Guam. Policies on compulsory education changed depending on the time period. In some eras, children could easily be excused from school if they could prove their family needed them on their farm. The required ages also changed, slowly

increasing as time went on and the educational system became more streamlined. Michael Lujan Bevacqua, "Chonnek Guatu, Halla Magi: Chamorro Identity and American Colonialism and Pre-War Guam" (Unpublished paper, 2003).

47. Robert Underwood's "The Colonial Era: Manning the Helm of the USS *Guam*," *Islander Magazine*, May 22, 1977.

48. Hattori, *Colonial Dis-Ease*, 19–22, 39–60; Governor of Guam George Dyer, *Annual Report*, 1904, 2–3.

49. In my master's thesis at the University of Guam, I encountered numerous examples of Chamorros confronted by these intersections. One such equation is as follows: if education is important, and in school I am not educated about my island, my language, my culture, then none of these things must be important. This of course raises the question, could the opposite take place? Could an absence inform a presence? This is where negotiation takes place. For many young Chamorros, the fact that they and their parents did not exist in the schools forced them to critique actively their lessons in civilizing and Americanizing. For a fictional telling of this see Melissa San Nicolas Taitano, "Stars and Stripes and bonelos aga' Forever," *Latte: The Essence of Guam* 1, no. 1 (May 1995): 68–69. As this story displays, the most contested point for children attending these schools was what the instruction meant about their parents. Did the lessons mean that their parents were dirty? That their parents were backward? That their parents were stupid?

50. I've made attempts at interrogating several of these (non)states. For inadequacy/inferiority, see Michael Lujan Bevacqua, "Nihi ta fan Agululumi: Inferiority and Activism Amongst Chamorros," *Galaide* 2, no. 1 (2003): 1–2, 5. For impossibility, see Michael Lujan Bevacqua, "Impossible Cultures: Missed Representations, Chamorros and the Decolonization of Guam" (paper presented at the 3rd Annual Graduate Student Conference of Ethnic Studies in California, University of California, Berkeley, March 4, 2005). For incompleteness, see Michael Lujan Bevacqua, "'Decolonization Is Like Giving Ourselves a Lobotomy!' Discourse of the Chattaotao Chamorro of Guam" (paper presented at the 33rd Annual National Association of Ethnic Studies Conference, Chicago, Illinois, March 25, 2005).

51. *Downes v. Bidwell* 182 US 244, no. 507 (1901), C. J. Fuller, dissenting.

52. The key to this is the way strategy was written into U.S. Navy documents in Guam. Requests for more civil rights by Chamorros were constantly responded to with not only a formal "you are not ready" but also an informal discussion on how such a move could pose strategic dangers for the United States in Guam. There is a constant tension in how the native should be treated, which leads to a desire for not the close-thing, not the distant-thing, but the thing that will not move: the thing that will not threaten by becoming too close or by moving too far away and out of sight and knowledge.

53. This was evidenced in an anecdote from Governor Dorn (1907–1910). He recalled how one day a Chamorro had appeared in the governor's palace demand-

ing that Chamorros be given a "bill of rights." Dorn asked the Chamorro if he knew what a bill of rights was, but he didn't. Dorn then called a meeting of the native "chiefs" and asked them if they all wanted a bill of rights for Chamorros. They all agreed. He then asked them what a bill of rights was, and none could explain to him what it was. Hofschneider, *Campaign for Political Rights*, 54–55.

54. At one point, this led to the creation of a leper colony in Guam, which, due to the inexperience of the navy in identifying leprosy, actually ended up quarantining dozens of Chamorros who didn't have leprosy at all. In 1911 the navy went so far as to deport eighteen of them to a leper colony in the Philippines to die. Hattori, *Colonial Dis-Ease*, 61–90.

55. I stumbled upon this quote in Slavoj Žižek, *Iraq: The Borrowed Kettle* (London: Verso, 2004), 69–70. I use it here to describe "negation of a negation" in a colonial space, whereas Žižek used it to discuss negation of a negation in politics, most specifically in the diverse and possibly contradictory political stances of Tony Blair.

56. Slavoj Žižek, *Welcome to the Desert of the Real* (London: Verso, 2002), 22.

57. Bevacqua, "Decolonization is Like."

58. Dirk Ballendorf and Howard Willens, *The Secret Guam Study: How President Ford's 1975 Approval of Commonwealth Was Blocked by Federal Officials* (Mangilao, Guam: Micronesian Area Research Center, 2005).

59. Pier, "An Exploratory Study," 149.

60. Ed Benavente, interview with the author, *I gima'-na* (Benavente home), Mangilao, Guam, March 27, 2004.

61. This example may seem trifling, considering how little votes mean in the U.S. empire. But in reality it does carry a lot of symbolic value, and some of it derives from the pathetic ways that Chamorros and people on Guam are tokenistically placated. For example, people in Guam do cast votes for the president of the United States. These votes are counted and published, but they mean nothing. Guam has no Electoral College votes, so these votes are worth the paper that they are published upon; that is, they mean nothing, except as a tokenistic gesture to feign an inclusion. Similarly, the delegate for the U.S. Congress from Guam (like the delegates from the other colonies) cannot vote in session, only in committee. At one time, however, the delegates were allowed to vote and be counted, but only so long as their votes did not affect the outcome of the vote. So in landslide votes delegates count, but when the vote is close, their votes were taken out of the total.

62. Not much research has been done on the media in Guam, but one place to start would be Ronald Stade, *Pacific Passages: World Cultures and Local Politics in Guam* (Stockholm: Stockholm Studies in Social Anthropology, 1998).

63. The *Pacific Daily News* was started in 1945 by the U.S. Navy as the *Navy News*. It came into private hands in 1950, however its intimate relationship with the interests of the U.S. Navy has hardly changed since then. This is most evident

in the editorials and opinion pieces by Joe Murphy, a retired white military man who worked for the *Pacific Daily News* as an editor and is currently a columnist. Since the 1960s, he has been the most aggressive presence in the paper for ensuring that the naturalness of the military presence in Guam be questioned as little as possible. He does so through heavy yet surprisingly digestible ideologies about pragmatic and no-nonsense speech. His pieces are written in straightforward prose, always professing to get straight to the point, which always centers around how Guam needs the United States, most specifically in the form of military bases and as something ideal to emulate, in order to survive. Through Murphy's pieces we can see well the function of the newspaper and more specifically the voice of the editor in a colonial space, namely as a mouthpiece or local translator for divine colonial mandates. It is on the page that the limits of discourse are often set, whether it be for what fairness means, what patriotism is, what culture should be, and so on. All of this is accomplished by positioning itself as the "defender of American values" in Guam.

64. From 1950 to 1970, the *Pacific Daily News* was called the *Guam Daily News*.

65. Ed Benavente, interview with the author, *I gima'-na* (Benavente home), Mangilao, Guam, March 25, 2002.

66. Perez, "Liberation Day," 85.

67. Pier, "An Exploratory Study," 151–55.

68. My use of the term "act" is far from orthodox Lacanian or even Žižekian. In my presentation I used the act to discuss the resources of resistance in Guam, which must be conserved if this type of act is ever to take place. This framing of the conversation is necessary because of the way that the liberal and decolonial deadlock in Guam is built around the preventing of any and all acts. One can think of both the liberal and decolonial deadlocks as the perception of "history's end," where the best of all possible worlds has been reached and thus balance must be kept in any and all ways to ensure that this golden status is kept and maintained. Therefore all radical or potentially transformative positions must be negated or moderated so as not to threaten this "status to end all statuses." The liberal deadlock is the image of the United States as the superlative "liberal democracy." The decolonial deadlock is the refusal to admit to the need for any transformative decolonization. Naturally these statuses are always undergoing some change, but these changes are always already presupposed to have happened, meaning that in essence they never happened but always already were. Thus the perceptional glories of these deadlocks are maintained through regimes of negation of negation. Any radical element is quickly negated and dismissed, but when pieces of that radicality are incorporated in subtle ways, the second negation takes place, negating this very incorporation. Žižek, *Iraq*, 79–81.

69. Ibid.

70. Angel Santos was one of the founding members of the Chamorro activist organization *I Nasion Chamoru* and its first *Maga'lahi*, or "chief." He was instrumental

in getting land for landless Chamorros, as well as inspiring a generation of Chamorros to speak out against the excesses of both the local government and the federal government in dispossessing Chamorros from their lands. He was elected to Guam's legislature several times. He passed away in 2003.

71. Robert Underwood, "Consciousness and the Maladjusted People of Guam," in *Chamorro Self Determination*, ed. Laura Souder and Robert Underwood (Hagatña, Guam: Chamorro Studies Association, 1991), 135–41.

72. Žižek, *Iraq*, 19–20.

73. These are three slogans that are invoked to capture the meaning of Guam. They provide a quick insight into the island's identity. The first two were first created by the tourism industry on Guam in hopes of marketing Guam as a piece of America just on the edge of Asia, or as a unique and exotic part of the United States. The third slogan has recently come into prominence by those critical of American policies in Guam and by those working toward decolonization as a response to the banal tourist slogans that celebrate the American-ness of Guam.

74. Žižek discusses how this operates in films such as *Beau Geste* or *Dangerous Liaisons*. Žižek, *On Belief*, 67–70. Another function of the sacrifice is the sacrifice not to cover up the inconsistencies of the other, but to sacrifice precisely to determine whether there is an "other" or not. Semi-Americans are familiar with this, as its actualization is "spontaneous citizenship." The Chamorro who sacrifices to prove that America does really exist is thus "spontaneously" awarded Americanness. The article that I will discuss further down is evidence of this process. The maintaining function of this process is powerful because even if the other desires attached to the sacrifice are not fulfilled, the colonizer is nonetheless humanized as someone who does respond, someone who is not just a disinterested colonizer but someone who cares.

75. In earlier drafts of this chapter I used quotes from the newspaper articles over the soldiers' deaths to discuss this point. I later decided that to make this point in that way was insensitive and could only come off as me criticizing explicitly and directly the way family and friends on Guam mourned this loss (and also reproduces the whole "colonized as dupes" discourse). In an effort to respect the dead, but nonetheless interrogate the death, I chose to frame it in this way.

76. Crecencis Cespedes, ed., *America to the Rescue* (Hagatña, Guam: Self-published, 1994), 48.

77. U.S. Congress Senate Committee on Territories and Insular Affairs, *Hearings before a Subcommittee of the Committee of Territories & Insular Affairs on S. 1450, a Bill to Confer United States Citizenship upon Certain Inhabitants of Guam & Extend the Naturalization Laws Thereto*, 75th Cong., 1st sess., 1937; Don Farrell, *Liberation–1944* (Tamuning, Guam: Micronesian Productions, 1984), 181.

78. Cespedes, *America to the Rescue*, 48.

79. It is interesting to look at the way the deaths of semi-Americans are represented in the media and then dissected and discussed in general public discourse. Whether it be Chamorros, other islanders from Micronesia such as Yapese or Palauans, or American nationals from Asia or Latin America, each death on the battlefield provides a restrained yet welcome site of national jouissance. In *Looking Awry*, Žižek talks about how nationalism is built upon a collective organizing of enjoyment through shared national myths. In this way, ethnic tension within the nation always boils down to the ethnic other who is threatening our national means of enjoyment yet at the same time possesses some secret enjoyment, which only he/she/it has access to. Žižek, *Looking Awry*, 165. What we see in the war deaths of semi-Americans is a sort of shortcut, or a patriotic perversion. The enjoyment of the ethnic other is necessarily secret, but what these deaths seem to imply is a means of accessing it. Thinking about the quote by Agueda Johnston after the American return, here we see the apparent access. When one of these soldiers dies patriotically, the secret enjoyment of the ethnic other is revealed to be the United States or to be a love of the United States and its means of organizing enjoyment.

80. Indigenous sacrifice refers to the type of erasure that allows a vertical antagonism to become a horizontal one. For example, conflict between groups separated vertically in terms of power, claim, or authority (such as a dominant group to the marginalized or indigenous person to the settler) is usually transformed by erasing the claim of the subordinate groups while conserving the position of their vertically opposed antagonists and creating a new terrain of conflict in which all groups appear to continue to be different and oppositional but are now arranged in a horizontal way (e.g., multiculturalism). The shift is thus from a terrain of competing universals to one where each group is just a different side of a dominant universal.

81. *The Defense of Guam*, 50th Anniversary (Defense of Guam) Planning Committee, 1994. This was a program created by the government of Guam in order to celebrate the fiftieth anniversary of Guam's reoccupation by the United States by retelling the story of the Insular Guard soldiers who fought the Japanese in 1941.

82. Bevacqua, "These May or May Not Be Americans," 102–8.

83. Hardt and Negri, *Empire*, 205.

84. Brett Kelman, "Guam Honors War Dead," *Pacific Daily News*, May 27, 2008.

85. Blaine Harden, "Guam's Young, Steeped in History, Line Up to Enlist," *The Washington Post*, January 27, 2008.

86. The U.S. Department of Interior, "Fallen Heroes in the War on Terror from the OIA's Insular Areas," http://www.doi.gov/oia/Firstpginfo/islanders_in_the_military/heroes.html (accessed December 6, 2009).

4

Touring Military Masculinities

U.S.–Philippines Circuits of Sacrifice and Gratitude in Corregidor and Bataan

Vernadette Vicuña Gonzalez

Corregidor Island and Bataan are the hallowed grounds of American World War II valor in the Philippines. Located in the northern region of the Philippines, these two sites, evocative of American World War II martial heroics, function to capture the tourist imagination and conceal histories of imperialism, military violence, and long-standing occupation. As such, they elude the kinds of critique that are more commonly leveled at active or former military bases, particularly feminist critiques of the sex industries that link both tourism and militarism in the Pacific.[1] Unlike their infamous comrades, the former Subic Bay Naval Base in Olongapo and Clark Air Field in Angeles, Corregidor and Bataan escape the seamy reputations and realities that structure militarized sites. This chapter examines how gendered and racialized discourses of war, heroism, and nationhood are deployed by and through the rearticulation of Corregidor and Bataan as tourist attractions and the kinds of ideological labor these discourses perform. In particular, by actively linking Corregidor and Bataan to the ostensibly "demilitarized" former U.S. military sites of Clark Air Field and Subic Bay Naval Base, this chapter remaps the shifts in the modalities of American militarism in the Philippines.

This specific intervention is situated within a broader project that seeks to interrogate the links between military and touristic ideologies, cultures, and technologies of mobility and surveillance in the nineteenth- and twentieth-century Asia-Pacific, where I argue that the "roots" and "routes" of the U.S. military presence and of tourist itineraries are mutually constitutive.[2] Today, as institutions and industries, the military and tourism are interwoven into the everyday and taken-for-granted routines and logics of both local and global life. They have become matter-of-fact explanations for themselves (and each other).³ Because of this, the interrelationships between tourism and militarism need to be better unpacked in order to lay bare the complex connections between these two very gendered formations of domination. Following Inderpal Grewal and Caren Kaplan's call for a postmodern feminist analysis to "articulate the relationship of gender to scattered hegemonies such as global economic structures, patriarchal nationalisms, 'authentic' forms of tradition, local structures of domination, and legal-juridical oppression on multiple levels,"⁴ this exercise elaborates the gendered intimacies between militarism and tourism and seeks to lay bare the stakes in their mutually beneficial relationship.

In the densely intertwined and constructed economies and cultures of tourism and militarism that constitute Corregidor and Bataan, modern gendered fantasies of liberation, mobility, and security are conjured up that support the postcolonial fictions of neoliberalization in Subic Bay and Clark. That is, while the United States has since officially left its former colony's territories, a reterritorialization of these former military reservations within the new economic structure of tourism has rendered American military history solely within the "good liberation" framework. Connecting Corregidor and Bataan, two of the most sentimental sites of Allied masculine heroics, to Subic Bay and Clark, the two most infamous and ignominious, this chapter establishes a continuity of the logics of militarization in the Philippines and traces the shifts in the modalities of militarization that continue to organize U.S.–Philippine relations.

Corregidor, an island fortress in Manila Bay, was initially established as a military zone by the Spanish conquistadors and later taken over by the United States after the War of 1898, when the United States effectively took over the colonial reins of the archipelago. It achieved international renown during World War II when General Douglas MacArthur used it as the Allied headquarters before the fall of Bataan to the north and the consequent loss of the island to Japanese invaders in 1942. When MacArthur and the Allied forces returned to retake the Philippines and the rest of the Pacific in 1945, Corregidor, along with Bataan, became inextricably tied to narratives of freedom and liberation.

In contrast, Subic Bay and Clark are names that are much more fraught with the complex and complicit political economy of military occupation rather than the straightforward heroic narrative of Corregidor and

Bataan. Subic Bay, like Corregidor, was initially established by the Spanish as an arsenal and repair facility for its navy. Once the United States took over as the colonial administrator, however, Subic Bay Naval Base ("Subic Bay" hereafter) became a major naval facility, one of the largest in Asia. Clark Air Field ("Clark" hereafter) was established soon after the U.S. occupation of the islands and grew to be one of the largest and most developed American overseas bases. Though both bases played important roles during World War II, Subic Bay and Clark are equally infamous for the kind of off-base "entertainment" economies, as well as patterns of gendered violence, that are generated by the military—hardly the stuff of ideal American public relations.

Following World War II and Philippine independence in 1946, the United States and the Philippines negotiated and signed the Military Bases Agreement, which was essentially a hundred-year lease that allowed the U.S. military to continue to occupy the Philippines. This was amended in 1966, with stipulations that the lease would run out in 1991. In 1991, in a resurgence of nationalist fervor, the Philippine Senate rejected an extension of the Military Bases Agreement, and the bases were handed over to the Philippine government. When the United States "returned" the bases to the Philippines in 1991, there was a lively public debate over the symbolic and material significance of the departing American military presence.

Despite, and probably because of, their role in this debate, as the price and prizes of U.S. military occupation, Subic Bay and Clark have never attained the kind of unsullied Allied narrative of liberation and rescue that permeate Corregidor and Bataan. The former have since been developed as special economic zones under public–private partnerships and now function as commercial and tourist hubs for the neoliberalizing economy of the Philippines. In their incarnation as special economic zones, the fates of Subic Bay and Clark rise and fall with the Philippines' troubled political and economic situations. By critically rearticulating the relationship between Corregidor and Bataan's heroic narrative, particularly as retold within a touristic framework, to Clark and Subic Bay's shifting identities as special economic zones, I hope to provide an alternate reading of the narrative of American uplift that continues to structure all four sites.

Tours of Corregidor and Bataan, with their saturated narratives of masculine sacrifice and valor, serve as alibis for the unfreedoms that are produced by continued U.S.–Philippine collusions. Taking the particular examples of Corregidor and Bataan, I explore how violent geographies of U.S. militarism are masked by sentimental narratives of masculinity through the mechanisms of tourism. Touring military masculinities, then, as the title of this chapter suggests, entails the production and consumption of the raced and gendered visual narratives of the American military within a touristic framework. At the same time that it is underpinned by the monuments and histories of American occupation, this particular iteration of military tourism operates as an explanation for continued relations of "brutal domination" made possible by such mechanisms as the Visiting Forces Agreement.[5] I argue that the contemporary economic fates of Subic Bay and Clark are very much tied to the successful marriage of tourism and militarism in Corregidor and Bataan. Indeed, the ways in which the touristic narratives of American rescue and liberation in Corregidor and Bataan are framed and consumed are crucial to the enterprise of legitimizing broader militaristic–touristic relations in the Philippines' unstable neoliberalizing economy. The military, particularly the continued U.S. presence, serves as a guarantor for potential investors.

Indeed, this ostensibly postbase era has seen broader U.S.–Philippine military cooperation than ever before, with U.S. economic investments tied to the security relationship long established by the 1951 U.S.–Philippines Mutual Defense Treaty. In 1998, the Visiting Forces Agreement, or VFA, a bilateral agreement between the United States and the Philippines, allowed the U.S. military to have access to Philippine airports and ports for fueling, repairs, supplies, and rest and recreation. In effect, it allowed for the continuance and increasing importance of military relations between the two nations. Under the VFA, the United States has made ship visits to Philippine ports and conducted combined military exercises with Philippine forces. Current Philippine President Gloria Macapagal-Arroyo, indeed, was the first foreign leader to lend her support to former U.S. President George W. Bush's declared war against terror. In many ways, Clark and Subic Bay have reverted to their former structures as U.S. military outposts. The convergences, then, between the economies of militarization in Subic Bay and Clark and the touristic practices that Corregidor and Bataan hope to produce serve to secure a particular international relationship of inequality and collusion.

"Demilitarization" Reconsidered

In 2003, Richard Gordon, the Philippines' current Secretary of Tourism, former mayor of Olongapo (the location of Subic Bay Naval Base), and former chair of the Subic Bay Metropolitan Authority charged with the base's transition to a freeport economy, announced a plan to produce tourists out of soldiers in order to stimulate the country's beleaguered tourism industry. His strategy: to recruit American soldiers who were already "visiting" the Philippines under the aegis of the VFA as more active and conscious tourists. Hoping to tap into and create nostalgia for former playgrounds and to build up a new touring market for the still-struggling special economic zones that were formerly U.S. military reservations, Gordon's proposal also included an invitation to servicemen formerly based in Subic Bay and Clark to return to their old haunts for a reunion. Producing tourists from soldiers, Gordon's plan tapped into the sentimental journey of remembering and gratitude instilled by a sedimented history of U.S. military occupation in the Philippines and hoped to profitably overlap the circuits of militarism and tourism in the Clark and Subic Bay special economic zones in historically familiar ways.

This militarized tourism strategy not only deploys historically masculine and heterosexist modes of travel but also puts into play what Patricia Goldstone calls discourses of "making the world safe for tourism."[6] In the Philippines, discourses of "security" have historically been tied to the necessary presence of the American military machine (gendered masculine and racialized white) protecting a feminized, brown Pacific. In Gordon's model of a secured (in both senses of the word) market for tourism, colonial ideologies of travel and militarism are neatly folded into neocolonial economies of desire and transnational structures of world policing. Having long championed the continued development of the Subic Bay economy during his stint as mayor of Olongapo and leader of Subic Bay's transition from a military base to a special economic zone, Gordon embodies a heteropatriarchal statesmanship that frames the formal removal of the bases as a kind of victory for the people of the Philippines yet returns it to the former structures of economic dependence that characterized it during U.S. occupation. In tandem with the continuing relations between the United States and the Philippines that contradict official narratives of demilitarization, Gordon's strategy practices a statecraft that produces the post-1998 military formations between the United States and the Philippines as good liberation and one that is necessarily guaranteed by continuing U.S. military presence. This effectively and efficiently taps into the still-dominant Allied rhetoric of Corregidor and Bataan, which, not coincidentally, he also promotes as tourist destinations under the Department of Tourism's new campaign. In effect, in his role as Secretary of Tourism, and in his prior involvement with Subic Bay, Gordon participates in a larger statecraft of transforming a history of death, violence, and American occupation into a narrative of (neo)liberation and military cooperation for the good of both nations. Indeed, his strategy to produce Subic Bay and Clark's new, improved touring soldier–subject was timed in anticipation of U.S. President George W. Bush's 2003 visit to the Philippines to secure further cooperation for the U.S. and the Philippines' armed relations against terror and to guarantee a future where such subjects continue to occupy and tour the Philippines.

Gordon's disingenuous call to recruit tourists from the ranks of soldiers also elided the robust state-sponsored sex tourism trade that flourished before the U.S. military's official withdrawal in 1991 and that still exists today under the VFA.[7] Emphasizing instead the "legitimate" types of tourism that the special economic zones are attempting to get off the ground, Gordon's strategy sanitized the present-day product of what Cynthia Enloe notes as the collusion of "Philippine nationalism, land reform and demilitarization" in the region.[8] As noted earlier, however, characterizing the post-1991 era as one of demilitarization is certainly premature and misleading. What has happened instead is that, under Gordon, the Philippine Department of Tourism has actively produced a state narrative of military tours that was disarticulated from the seamier history of American military occupation even as such histories continue to structure the present, particularly in Subic Bay and Clark.[9]

On the national and global stage, Gordon's dream of a militarized tourism ambitiously attempts to interpellate soldiers as legitimate tourists in legitimate tourist sites located in former U.S. base territories. However, the success of Gordon's project is enmeshed in the effectiveness of more suitable sites of American military memorialization in the Philippines, which he has specifically promoted as tourist destinations since his ascension as Secretary of Tourism. Part of Gordon's quest to elevate the role of tourism in the Philippine economy rests on the appeal of what Renato Rosaldo has named "imperialist nostalgia," or "a pose of 'innocent yearning' both to capture people's imaginations and to conceal its complicity with often brutal domination."[10] This stance of imperialist nostalgia is squarely located in a historically familiar orientalist framework that continues to structure the contemporary relationship between the United States and the Philippines. The hybrid soldier–tourist subjects conjured in Gordon's complicit fantasy are the exemplars of the privileged subject of modernity: the masculine, Euro-American traveler who is at once a symbol and arbiter of state power and violence.[11] These tourist subjects invoked in Gordon's plan to drum up business operate as a fetish to conceal the very conditions that make their presence possible: the tourist sites that they are imagined to inhabit are sites of past and present violence and occupation. For many people whose livelihoods continue to revolve around these militarized economies, such tourist-friendly manipulations of history serve to enhance the contrast between the rhetoric of uplift and cooperation and the realities of complicit and often-violent survival.[12] I argue that the imperialist nostalgia invoked in these militarized–touristic spaces, particularly periodized around World War II and its grand narratives of brotherhood, suffering, and salvation, make this transition possible. The recovery of the heroic, rooted in and running throughout these desiring and nostalgic "new" economies of tourism and commerce and backed up by the continued armed collusion between the United States and the Philippines, make the erasure of past and present violence possible.

In his work on tourism and militarism, Geoffrey M. White points out the cultural, economic, and political links between World War II military tours and modern tours framed by these war memories, as well as the production of loyal and grateful native subjects for the easy assurance of the touring soldier. For White, the return of military veterans to commemorate the Battle of Guadalcanal in the Solomon Islands constituted a "second invasion" that became a contested site of transnational memory making.[13] Following White, I will ask questions about how new kinds of (trans) national, class, and political alliances are forged through the masculine narratives of military sacrifice that saturate these spaces and about what kinds of remembering publics are produced by these military–touristic narratives. How are racialized masculinities in Corregidor Island and Bataan central to the ideological work done by historical and contemporary projects of tourism and militarism in the postcolonial Asia-Pacific? I argue that in Corregidor and Bataan, the freedoms of touring are ineluctably linked to the sentimental logics of martial citizenship and sacrifice.

Overlapping Dominations of Tourism and Militarism

My research is situated in the transnational critical inquiries into militarism and tourism begun by Cynthia Enloe, Teresia K. Teaiwa, Geoffrey M. White, Kathy Ferguson, Phyllis Turnbull, and others.[14] This body of work calls for analytical attention to the ways in which historical and present-day militarizations are intimately tied to patterns and practices of travel. Going beyond a mapping of the overlapping geographies of militarisms and tourisms, my project analyzes the ways in which they are mutually constituted under the aegis of imperialism and globalization. I argue that the ways in which tourisms and militarisms operate today, with their regulation and control of the quotidian, are not only throwbacks to colonial projects of civil discipline but also constitutive facets of modernity. By linking militarism and tourism more overtly, I hope to point out that they have a particular resonance and specificity in outlining a version of globalization that makes militarization more palatable and more profitable.

Linking or likening tourism to colonial modes of domination is certainly not new. Many scholars have used colonial–imperial models to explain the unevenness of tourism as an industry and culture. Dennison Nash laments the loss of sovereignty implied in catering to metropolitan tourist desires.[15] Tourism as a form of imperialism is inseparable from the fact that it is the fastest-growing global industry, particularly for less-developed countries and regions. As a developmental strategy, it represents the imposition of lending policies dictated by supranational organizations like the World Bank and International Monetary Fund. In exchange for loans, many Third World countries gamble on the quick foreign exchange promised by the growing, if volatile, tourism industry to generate investment confidence and cash. Martin Mowforth and Ian Munt emphasize that these supranational organizations are in effect enforcing economic colonialisms, "relegat[ing] the role of the national government to one of providing the necessary infrastructure, leaving it more indebted than before . . . [and] offering free trade zones for tourism companies wishing to build and operate resorts."[16] Indeed, the World Tourism Organization (ironically, also the WTO) describes the potentials of tourism as "liberalization with a human face," with particular benefits for women.[17] For many of the women (and men) in Subic Bay and Clark's militarized economies, tourism's humane liberalization has fallen short of its promises.[18]

These justificatory logics structure the continuing presence of the American military in the Pacific: jobs, stability, and foreign exchange. While militarism as a form of domination often goes unquestioned, here I am interested less in the "guns and troops" aspect than in Cynthia Enloe's claim that "the military is only one part of the story of militarization."[19] Militarization is also a process of exerting ideological, political, and cultural control in order to normalize the presence of the military, prioritize its needs, and centralize its role in defining and defending "national security." The steady and continued militarization of life in the Philippines thus begets the parallel erosion of local sovereignties; exacerbations of class, race, and gender asymmetries; and environmental degradations brought on by tourism.

Yet tourism also enacts power through the social processes, transactions, and ideologies that recall sedimented histories and cultural practices of colonialism. In the American tropics of the Philippines, the diverse practices of colonial travel, with their accompanying discourses of gender and racial differences and technologies of display, discipline and shape the ways in which contemporary cultures of tourism operate.[20] These practices work hand in hand with the overarching logics of tourism that frame it as a panacea for struggling economies.

Steeped in nostalgic discourses of heroic suffering and sacrifice, Corregidor and Bataan take on new life within tourist circuits. In these intensely patriotic places, monuments that portray the homosocial bonds of men at war and the mutual suffering and interracial camaraderie of American, Filipino, and other soldiers temporarily suspend histories of segregation, disenfranchisement, complicity, and racial violence. Grief, shame, awe, and euphoria are employed in soliciting gratitude for heroic, masculine American soldier–citizens, ushering their inclusion into the imagined national family through sacrifice, dismemberment, and death even as the American state holds off on the actual fulfillment of these promises for those on the fringe of the national imaginary. Visitors pay their respects to the dead, take part in an overdetermined ritual of remembering, and are "touched" by sacrifice. The bodily management of visitors works alongside the selective and layered construction of memory and nation, carefully crafting a nostalgic and heroic space that produces a grateful tourist subject.

Barbara Kirshenblatt-Gimblett, theorizing on the heritage industry, describes it as "a mode of cultural production in the present that has recourse to the past."[21] Working within logics similar to imperialist nostalgia, heritage produces the past as a product for consumption. In the case of Corregidor and Bataan, as with other heritage sites, however, "remembering is a prelude to forgetting."[22] This partial amnesia, concealing histories of imperial domination and violence, is, in the end, the tourist commodity. Within the neocolonial economy of the Philippines, where the U.S. military still occupies a dominant role, the politics of producing state-sanctioned memories for public consumption is a crucial element in fashioning the continuing relationship between the United States and its former colony. Writing about the politics of memory around the Asia-Pacific wars, T. Fujitani, Geoffrey M. White, and Lisa Yoneyama argue that "these new opportunities for remembering are imperiled by a variety of factors. The powerful discourses of national, ethnic, and racial unity, the linear and teleological narratives of anticolonial struggles and emancipation, patriarchal and masculinist nostalgia for community and sexual ownership, and the conditions of transnational capitalism are only some of the forces that threaten to obscure and domesticate unsettling memories at the century's end."[23] Thus, while the contested terrains of war memories provide moments where the past "flashes up at a moment of danger," they can also become fodder for complicit and competing discourses.[24] For spaces that are overwhelmingly structured by discourses of patriarchy, nationalism and "liberation," such dangerous moments are managed to a minimum. Moreover, in the post–September 11 reframing of geopolitics, touring memorialized military spaces becomes a necessary aspect for recruiting civilians into the narrative of liberation. Situated within the Allied–Axis framework of World War II histories, the production and consumption of Corregidor and Bataan as tourist sites play handily into the discourses of the war on terror, further reproducing Kirshenblatt-Gimblett's mode of remembering-as-forgetting.

Military Heroics as Tourist Attractions

The next part of this chapter examines the gendered and racialized politics of memory and modernity that link and structure the emerging tourist sites of Corregidor Island and the Bataan Death March memorials in the Philippines. The military tourism scenes in Corregidor and Bataan perform critical ideological labor—contributing to what Neferti Xina M. Tadiar has called the "fantasy production" of dominant transnational imaginings about the Philippines.[25] To this end, the act of touring

Corregidor and Bataan is a re-membering (in the multiple senses of the word) of American colonial and neocolonial geographies.

In emphasizing the centrality of the sentimental, ostensibly historic American militarism in these sites, I also hope to connect the symbolic guardianship of the Philippines' "Big White Brother" to the neoliberal ideologies that underpin the development of tourism in the postcolonial Third World. By providing spaces where public memorialization of heroic military action took place, these highly charged touristic moments gesture toward the necessary centrality of state-sponsored and condoned militarism even as the market has eroded the state's other public functions. In other words, what tourists tour in Corregidor is not *just* a historic site but also a story about continuing American–Philippine relations that casts contemporary American-style neoliberal policy in the familiar role of hero. The imaginative labor that Corregidor and Bataan perform as tourist sites, then, is inseparable from the exploitation of material labor at the nearby export-processing zones in Bataan, Clark, and Subic Bay, also former U.S. military "reservations." These military bases reconfigured as commercial hubs rearticulate colonial discourses of uplift, modernity, progress, and salvation in their militarized, privatized borders much in the same way that these narratives are circulated and consumed on Corregidor and Bataan.

On Corregidor Island, the juxtaposition of various monument parks commemorating the different players involved in its defense, occupation, and retaking has produced a semiotic jungle that is nevertheless overrun with a dominant Allied heroic narrative. Bataan, less overwhelmingly monumentalized, is a minimalist mapping of Allied suffering at the hands of the Japanese army. In these two sites, the act of touring historical battlefields and military routes is simultaneously an emotional and ideological remembering of a benevolent American protector, an erasure of imperial violence and occupation, and a reiteration of the Philippines' continuing "special relationship" with its former colonizer.

Reconstructed as memorials during the Marcos era, these two linked sites have since been reappropriated by subsequent political administrations and reinserted in alternative narratives of valor and nationhood. For instance, on Corregidor, there is also a monument to the People Power Revolution that ousted the U.S.-backed Marcos regime. Yet the heroic Allied narrative continues not only to structure these commemorative sites but also to elide the contradictions between the World War II American-rescue account and American manipulation during the Marcos years. Part of the potency and continuing durability of these rescue narratives lies in their attractiveness to tourism. What critical links are made possible when we consider the ways in which militarisms and tourisms are intimately intertwined in the neocolonial geographies of the Philippines? Further, the ways in which gender is imbricated in the articulation of militarism and tourism, particularly in the production of transnational memories of masculine heroics, help to produce a tourist-worthy product. In the transnational imaginary conjured by war memories and sustained by touring these same war memories, a specifically gendered and racialized mode of "fantasy production" is at work—one that operates effectively at the emotional and sentimental level that tourism does.

Hero Island

Corregidor Island is a military fortification established by Spanish colonial powers in Manila Bay. It is best known for its role as the sentimental staging ground of the Allied powers' retaking of the Pacific against the Japanese. Today, it is a popular stop on the nostalgic-for-America tour and is often profiled in various publications addressed to the tourist, such as in-flight magazines, tourist brochures, and mainstream newspapers. According to these materials, Corregidor is the "hero island," which must be visited "especially [by] the young, so they will be able to appreciate the sacrifices of their parents and grandparents in defense of the freedom they take for granted today."[26] It is the "island fortress," synonymous with "Dunkirk and the Alamo," whose dramatic and horrific stories are relived again and again.[27] It is, as the Philippine Department of Tourism unironically sells it, the "Island of Valor, Peace and International Understanding."

The memorialization of Corregidor Island as a World War II battle site is inseparable from the sentimental circuit of Allied war memories that insist on the existence and inclusion of stories of Filipino and American brotherhood-through-suffering. By emphasizing this fraternity of war as the official public narrative of U.S–Philippine relations, the masculine heroics of World War II operate to replace American colonialism in the Philippines as *the* formative emotional bond between the Philippines and the United States. Corregidor thus plays a crucial role in this tenuous postcolonial recuperation of the Philippine–American "special relationship," one that relies on narratives of rescue and brotherhood and of American honor in fulfilling heroic promises to its colony. The production of

Corregidor as a visitor attraction is based on nostalgic narratives of masculine suffering and heroism—narratives that play up the almost messianic roles of General Douglas MacArthur and the American "liberation forces" during World War II. From the side of Philippine national memory, Corregidor is the exemplar of the "special relationship" between Filipinos and Americans, a kind of brotherhood forged through ties of gratitude, benevolence, mutual suffering, and triumph. Corregidor occupies a sentimental and emotional place similar to that of Bataan, the better-known, but less tourist-friendly, site of the infamous Death March. These are place names that are highly evocative of brave, young Americans holding off the unrelenting assaults of the Japanese Imperial Army. Touring Corregidor is a trip back to World War II and a trip that engenders gratitude to American colonial benevolence (rather than American colonial violence).

The island, now turned over to the Department of Tourism and the Corregidor Foundation, a private, nonprofit civic organization led by retired Philippine military officers and American expatriates, hosts tours led by Sun Tours, a ferry company that has a virtual monopoly over tourist traffic to Corregidor. The full all-day tour includes lunch, transportation, a guide, and light show and runs a hefty 1,190 pesos per person, a little over $20 American, which by Filipino standards is exorbitant. As a result, the tour attracts foreigners, of whom a majority are American tourists or expatriates, along with some Japanese veterans and overseas Filipinos. Filipino families come here when the only other transportation option, a five hundred–peso tour, reaches a minimum of sixty-five people. The tour itself, with its unapologetic paean to American bravery and grit, is tailored to fit the demographic of elite foreigners and domestic tourists, as well as grateful *Balikbayan* Filipinos who have made their fortune in their adopted lands. Very few World War II survivors are left, but active servicemen continue to tour Corregidor, including veterans from other, more-recent military action.

On this tiny island, stories of American valor are laid on with a heavy hand. The imaginative architecture of this journey is unabashedly coercive. The day-long tour is bookended with documentary films that run on both the outgoing and return legs of the ferry trip. As the first film's overwrought narration (*Fortress of Courage*) and soaring score informs visitors, Corregidor and Bataan were the last American stands in the Philippines against "Asia's greatest war machine" during the dog days of World War II. After General MacArthur's abandonment and twenty-six days of bombing, "The Rock" was finally surrendered by General Jonathan Wainwright. MacArthur's oft-repeated and media-savvy mantra "I shall return" theatrically structures the ultimate American comeback, however. "Like a spider to ensnare its prey," we are told, the "tightening of the web" begins the "liberation of Luzon" and the taking back of lost territories. The narrative of eventual dogged survival, ingenuity, and triumph is capped by MacArthur's return to the island to "pay tribute" to Corregidor. At the end of the film, the American flag goes up. This sets the scene for the tourist to himself "retake" the island, where both the tourist and the destination have been secured by the military sacrifice of American soldiers.

A cannon on the dock greets tourists upon reaching Corregidor, and tourists exit the ferry to a military march. The transportation, reproductions of the trolleys that once crisscrossed the island during its American military administration, is made for touring. The whole island is an overt tribute to Filipino and American symbols of triumph, heroism, and brotherhood, arranged in different sets of parks or monuments and presided over by a gigantic statue of MacArthur. The Filipina tour guide, in perfect English, narrates the history of Corregidor, which was designated a U.S. military reservation in 1902 and was fortified between 1904 and 1922 with guns, batteries, and magazines that have become photo-opportunity stops along the tour.

Constructing an Allied Fraternity

Friendship Park is dominated by a statue of Filipino and American soldiers assisting each other on the Bataan Death March and bordered by markers that record the different battalions that fought during the war (see Figure 4.1). A familiar figure of interracial fraternity, the larger-than-life sculpture embodies the emotional and ideological weight of Corregidor as war monument. Here, American troops suffered with their Filipino comrades during the darkest days of the Japanese invasion of the Philippines and triumphed in the eventual "liberation" of the Philippines. The statue, with its realistic capture of suffering and its idealistic portrayal of interracial brotherhood, signals a kind of innocent camaraderie under pressure: a transcendent theme of empathic humanity.

Yet on this overly monumentalized island, there is no mention of the Philippine–American War that marked the beginning of U.S. imperialism in the Philippines, much less of the thousands of Filipino veterans still

TOURING MILITARY MASCULINITIES · 77

Figure 4.1. Brothers-in-arms. A statue at Friendship Park in Corregidor, depicting Filipino and American soldiers assisting each other on the Bataan Death March. Photograph by author, 2008.

waiting to receive benefits from the U.S. government.[28] The batteries that people climb on and pose by are named after American officers who fought in the Philippine–American war, but the ironies of this early imperial war are easily overlooked by the narrative of World War II liberation. The barracks, in their vine-overgrown ruins, evoke ghosts of young, innocent men sleeping in these quarters and walking in their hallways and not the racial segregation that kept Filipino and American troops and their families in separate quarters and schools on the island. The narrative recollected focuses on American soldiers and not the stewards and servants who attended them. Ironically, the guide informs us that *Gone With the Wind*, with its problematic racial representations, was the last film shown in Corregidor's theater before Japanese invasion. Following Kirshenblatt-Gimblett's schema of an imperfect recollection of the past in the production of heritage destinations, Corregidor's World War II ghosts sanitize what was a violent project of American empire building fifty years earlier. Writing about the Philippine–American War as a site of masculine citizen making, and of war memorials in particular, Oscar V. Campomanes argues that the process of "aestheticizing . . . the actual war is . . . shorn and cleansed of its mess, many costs, and savage malevolence."[29] Producing Corregidor as tourist site allows for narratives and histories of valor and brotherhood but little room for remembering the imperial occupation by American troops in an overseas colony.

American valor and the supporting role of Filipino friendship and bravery are the central elements of Corregidor's monumental architecture. Among the memorials is the Pacific War Memorial, funded in 1964 by U.S. Congressional appropriations.[30] It is a stark white dome with a circular hole at the top through which a shaft of sunlight every May 6 directly illuminates the marble slab below, commemorating the fall of Corregidor. Behind it, a wide walkway leads to a steel sculpture of the eternal flame, mounted on a deck that also provides a view of the ocean. On either side of the walkways are marble panels listing the narrative of World War II, from the "Defense of Hawai'i" to "Philippine Liberation." Not incidentally, the "Philippine Resistance Movement" is praised for their "repeated blows against the armies of the invaders in a heroic fight for the cause of freedom. Their valiant effort contributed greatly to the final liberation of the Philippines." Yet make no mistake: liberation was an American act. American funding for this Philippine monument, particularly during a time when American politics was instrumental in the postcolonial Philippines, is merely an extension of an ongoing "special relationship." Tellingly, former dictator Ferdinand Marcos dedicated the memorial thus: "From this day on, this new edifice on Corregidor will also be a monument of peace. The men whose memory we honor with this memorial fought to make peace, if not possible, an enduring condition of human life. We who now behold it, do so as the living beneficiaries of their sacrifices. We look at this monument with eyes used to the spectacles of a peaceful life; the bright and soaring quality of its architecture symbolizes for us the heights of human achievement that we can reach, not in war but peace."[31] As "beneficiaries" of a peace secured by violence and sacrifice, Marcos reminds us (for his sake and the sake of his foreign sponsor) that we must be thankful for the peaceful life secured by suffering and death. Producing a national memory of militarized security, this memorial links masculine sacrifice with the continued sacrifice of a benevolent American protector. Thus, the "spectacles" of the tourist gaze are adjusted to see only the theatrical narrative of liberation and not the "savage malevolence" of colonialism and neocolonialism.

The museum next to the war memorial is a more compact version of the island itself, with smaller guns guarding the entrance, and dog tags, badges, broken crockery, and utensils standing in for their larger counterparts outside. The menu for the last Thanksgiving before the war makes this a distinctly American space—a sentimental American holiday celebrated on foreign soil for the last time. The domestic scenes evoked in the museum displays belie the inherent violence of soldierhood: these are youthful (emphasizing the sacrifice) and reliable boys just doing their patriotic duty. Photographs capturing heroic poses and prewar innocence line the walls: men in bunks, cleaning guns, talking, and parading. The interruption of war, then, functions in the way of breaking up this homosocial family. It almost seems that the U.S. military occupation of the Philippines was a kind of male-only bonding retreat, and not until rudely provoked did the military respond.

In spaces shared by tourism and militarism such as Bataan and Corregidor, the analytics of power, identity, the state, empire, and capital are borne out in particularly gendered and racialized ways. A photograph in the military museum on Corregidor Island captures what Grewal and Kaplan point out as the "scattered hegemonies" of modernity that are organized and established through gender. This oversize color photograph, taken in 1994, hangs on one of the walls in the museum, which is dominated by black-and-white photographs of U.S. soldiers who were based in Corregidor before World War II. In this image, smiling former presidents of the United States and the Philippines (Bill Clinton and Fidel Ramos, respectively) pose with each other during a tour of the island, capturing a moment within a larger official history of gendered militarism and travel. As masculine prototourists and heads of state, Clinton and Ramos represent the promises of unfettered and secure travel as products of continued state cooperation and increased neoliberal policies. More significantly, they frame the contemporary production and consumption of Corregidor (and, implicitly, Bataan) within the heroic mode of World War II's shared suffering and triumph, structuring military history as a heritage destination. In the photograph, the smiling faces of Clinton and Ramos imply that present-day freedoms—including the privileges of travel—are thus neatly folded in with the dramatic heroism of Corregidor's dead men and the continuing vigilance of mutually supportive militaries in the Pacific. The language of brotherhood—of a fraternity of watchful patriarchs—becomes the guarantor for a modernity characterized by militarism and tourism.

The defense of the island is cast in sentimental, and not strategic–militaristic, terms, much like the narratives that structure the tourist consumption of the island. At this museum, tourists have an opportunity to reflect in silence on the militarized itinerary they have experienced throughout the day thus far. It is an exercise in meditating on the powerful story of sacrifice and an opportunity to identify with the suffering of "our boys." Here, the national family is formed through the international brotherhood of American and Filipino soldiers and headed by the American patriarch who insists on returning to the Philippines to save the "Little Brown Brother." In the museum, black-and-white photographs of American paratroopers during the retaking of the island from the Japanese insist on the drama of the almost-cinematic narrative of liberation. Finally, the color photograph of Fidel Ramos and Bill Clinton punctuates the visual exhibit, completing the narrative arc of Corregidor as a modern militarized tourism site. It is a messianic narrative of sacrifice and loyalty, one that has resonance in the neocolonial ties that continue to structure U.S.–Philippine relations.

The last stop on the daylong tour is the Malinta Tunnel, where a light and sound show of World War II narratives of survival, violence, and sacrifice has been installed. Malinta Tunnel, originally an arsenal and underground hospital, is now the stage for the story of American and Filipino resistance. The tunnel tour follows the main tunnel and uses the lateral tunnels for dioramas and photo slide shows. The life-sized figures in the dioramas rehearse, once again, scenes of soldiers beleaguered by Japanese attacks. Tourists are treated to loud explosions and fog machine effects during what is essentially a summary of what they have heard all day.

At the end of the tunnel and the show, a spotlight falls on the Filipino flag standing opposite the entrance, and tourists stand still for the Filipino national anthem, replaying the American return of Corregidor to the Philippines, and, ostensibly, to them. Today, Malinta Tunnel is blown up again and again as part of a touristic itinerary of remembrance and gratitude. It completes the narrative of sacrifice that visitors have been subject to all day on the tour. Implicitly, tourists are told, Corregidor was returned to its rightful owners by the loyal and noble sacrifice of American troops.

On the boat ride on the way home, we watch Douglas MacArthur's *I Shall Return* video biography. We keep returning, over and over, to sacrifices made, tallying up the dead, appreciating the gift of freedom.

Bataan's Suffering Sublime

The Bataan peninsula, a gray profile guarding Corregidor from the north, haunts the tour of the island in more than one way. Visible from the island, it is the point of reference for another tour of American valor. Bataan's history was and is intimately intertwined with Corregidor's just as the fate of one military stronghold would affect the other. Less accessible as a touristic site than Corregidor's compact and regulatable islandness, Bataan's claim to fame is the "Bataan Death March," the grueling 184-kilometer jungle-and-road trek that American and Filipino prisoners of war were forced to undergo after the fall of Bataan.

Compared to the surfeit of memorials on Corregidor, and belying its greater infamy, Bataan is less tourist ready, less tourist friendly, and less containable. There are no organized tours here, and any visitors who decide to come must organize their own itineraries. The kilometer markers that the Marcos administration put up in 1964 have long since been vandalized or stolen, and the recent move to replace the missing markers is going slowly. These markers are small, blue, and unobtrusive. Standing alone, marking long stretches of road, and interrupted by the occasional (yet not prominent) World War II monument, they do not constitute an easy or compelling tourist attraction, and few tourists come here. Those that do are small groups of soldiers, families of survivors, or history buffs. More tourists (but still not many) see the *Dambana ng Kagitingan* (Cross of Valor) memorial, also built under the Marcos regime, which houses a museum similar to Corregidor's, with marble panels depicting scenes of soldierly bravery and sacrifice.

The memorial, a ninety-five-meter-high concrete and steel cross erected atop a hill with extensive views of the Bataan peninsula, is open for visitors to climb. On this structure, one can survey the landscape and imagine the war played out on the backdrop. Tapping into *the* archetype of Christian masculine sacrifice, the memorial allows visitors to visualize what was made possible by the deaths of American and Filipino soldiers. In particular, over the backdrop of Bataan scenery, one can imagine the already-familiar narratives of suffering, survival, and brotherhood over the landscape. The opportunity to take the obligatory tourist picture from the top of the cross also defines a moment of gratitude, bracketed and shaped by the panels that narrate other moments of soldiery sacrifice that border its base. Simultaneously evoking a landscape of war and sacrifice, as well as enabling a tourist gaze structured by the "spectacles of a peaceful life," the panorama from the cross performs double duty. This implicitly masculine soldier–tourist sublime allows a profound identification with suffering that is inevitably tied to the tourist freedom that the viewer experiences.

In their entirety, these encompassing narratives of Bataan and Corregidor—with their icons of the wounded, tortured soldier and the brave and stoic general—elicit gratitude for the sacrifice entailed in "liberation" by what is now known as "the greatest generation."[32] These narratives, told by memorials, museums housing silenced guns, old photographs and uniforms, ruins of barracks and batteries, and markers on a dusty road, seamlessly merge with cultural repositories of Hollywood movies and History Channel documentaries, World War II fiction and nonfiction, and countless other stories of American stoicism, bravery, and sacrifice that form our cultural imagination. Tourists come armed with these narratives even if they are not particularly military buffs. As the dominant discourses that circulate today, these regimes of truth structure the appropriate sentiments and histories that are allowable in these sites.

Other Military Tours

Yet, in between the repetitions of praise to the loyal, steadfast soldier and the loyal, steadfast military occupier, the other narratives of militarism lie in wait. Its present-day legacies, such as the infrastructures left behind in former military reservations, have been recruited into the business of the export-processing zone, part of which is focused on tourism as a panacea for the continuing ills of the Philippine economy. Thus Gordon's fantasy of turning Subic Bay and Clark into tourist hubs patronized by the soldier–tourist dovetails neatly into the narrative of rescue and uplift that dominates military tourism in Corregidor and Bataan.

In tourism, as well as in these export-processing zones, jobs are provided, "service" learns its place, skills are imparted, and the infrastructure left behind by the benevolent giant serves to continually uplift the struggling "Little Brown Brother." It could not be otherwise, according to the touristic narratives of Bataan and Corregidor. At Clark and Subic Bay Freeports, sites of massive former American military reservations that have now transitioned—with some struggle and hard work on the part of Philippine government officials, former antibase activists, and global capital—into legitimate centers of business and pleasure, neoliberal economies embody this gift from a departing liberator. Yet in even in their ostensible return to the Filipino people, these former military lands constitute another node of neocolonial domination. The imaginative work done by connecting military tours of Bataan and Corregidor frames the way that material labor is seen in these sites.

The Philippines, as the first sponsor of Bush's war on terror and home to former military bases that now unofficially host American troops, continues to be key to the transnational circuits and linkages wrought by and between American military and economic regimes. In the context of this war on terror, touring military sites sets the stage for an appreciation of acts of state militarisms as the advent and arbiter of modernity and the modernization of "other" populations and nations. Iterating gendered and racialized discourses of leisure and labor, war and work, these militarisms are once again affirmed as necessary measures not only to guarantee order and security for the transnational production of goods, as in the export-processing zones, but also to instill safety for routes for travel. The Critical Filipina and Filipino Studies Collective (CFFSC), among other progressive groups like Bayan, Anakpawis, and Gabriela, points out that the intertwined logics of capital and militarism have served to rationalize systematic killings of progressive Filipino and Filipina activists as "terrorists" by Philippine paramilitary forces trained by U.S. troops. According to the CFFSC, "This strategy masks a deceptive and wholly undemocratic campaign to coerce the Philippine people and the peoples of the world into justifying and condoning the brutal military suppression of the legal and collective right to organize against injustice and exploitation" where the remilitarization of the U.S.-controlled world is a project that is tied to "creating new sites of investment and profit and new opportunities for the aggrandizement of unlimited power and wealth for the few."[33]

Thus the tourist narrative of the wounded, brave soldier pushing on, dying, or returning becomes a tourism that not only celebrates the aftermath of that sacrifice (ostensibly U.S.-style capitalist democracy) but also functions as a guarantor, an alibi, for the continued intimacies between militarism, the state, and capital today. Tourism, in this instance, ties itself to an act of gratitude—appreciation for what soldiers gave up, what foreign militaries contributed to, and what is secured today in these unique borderlands.

Inviting soldiers to officially become tourists, as Gordon does, further extends the welcome mat to what might otherwise be legitimately seen as an occupying force. By tying militarism to tourism more securely, a modified yet familiar narrative of benevolence and protection recirculates. In this new narrative, different memories of militarism–tourism are highlighted, such as those of Gordon's ostensibly new soldier–tourist, the epitome of the modern mobile subject. Under the VFA, this new soldier–tourist subject is the ultimate protected subject: at the cost of the Philippine government's sovereignty, American soldiers committing crimes in the Philippines are not under the jurisdiction of local laws. As the new "rescuer"—providing not only tourist dollars for a struggling Philippine economy but also a protective force to guarantee "stability"—the soldier-tourist becomes a new privileged subject of both states. Tragically, the potency of such masculinized narratives of military suffering also submerge contemporary moments of gendered and racialized violence committed on Filipinas, who embody the collateral damage of these new military maneuvers. Against this backdrop of military–tourist modernity, the "incidental" stories of base-related sexual violence are relegated to the footnotes.

Other stories—those that interrupt the protector narrative in particularly gendered and racialized ways—become, in effect, the new (yet historically familiar) sacrifice of the Philippine nation. In November of 2005, a young woman was allegedly raped by six American off-duty servicemen who were acting as tourists (in a karaoke bar) in the Subic Bay Freeport. The six men were in the Philippines taking part in U.S.–Filipino "counterterrorist" training.[34] Yet by no means was this an isolated incident: in 1992, fifty-two cases of rape and physical and sexual abuse were suspended when the United States officially returned the base territories to the Philippines.[35] While a row has followed in the Philippine legislature and the media regarding who has custody of the men and jurisdiction over the crime, the Armed Forces of the Philippines were quick to announce that the rape case would not have any impact on the continuing joint military exercises.

As Anne-Marie Hilsdon puts it, "Masculinity, combat and sex are interwoven in the prostitution industry which has developed near Filipino military barracks and U.S. military bases."[36] This established pattern of near state-sanctioned violence produces a hierarchy of national memory and privileged subjects that taps into the potent resonance of Corregidor and Bataan and the way these liberation narratives have neatly transitioned into a new world order. Hilsdon points out the key role that base tourism, as the fifth most important source of revenue for the Philippines, plays in the economic big picture.[37] Thus tourist and military masculinities bolster each other in the joint exercise of controlling bodies and narratives that interrupt the nostalgic World War II memory of rescue and liberation that continues to inform these militarized spaces today. At stake, then, in the project of transnational memory making in which military tourism takes part, is a gendered project of complicit patriarchies. Bridged by the silencing of these other narratives of violent military tourisms, these state patriarchies produce a vision of a modernity founded on past brotherly cooperation that is guaranteed by the continuing vigilance over these deviant bodies.

These narratives of valor, mutual suffering, and ineluctable liberation and triumph foreground instead the instilled appreciation for what are essentially the leavings of the American military machine. To tour the footprints of the American military today necessarily calls on these acts of gratitude again and, in doing so, allows for the forgetting of other narratives of violence. These gestures and performances of postcolonial thanksgiving are particularly resonant in the contemporary moment, as U.S. militarization in the post–September 11 era rearticulates colonial geographies through ideologies of security, stability, and the "freedom to travel." Military tours function in this moment as a vehicle of imperfect memory, making possible the continuation of gendered nationalisms, militarized society, and violent futures.

Notes

Early versions of this chapter were presented at the 2004 Association for Asian American Studies conference, at the 2005 American Studies Conference, and for the American Studies Department at the University of Hawai'i in November 2005. *Maraming salamat* to Setsu Shigematsu and Keith L. Camacho for the invitation to participate in this project. I am grateful to them, Mimi Nguyen, Lucy Mae San Pablo Burns, Jeffrey Santa Ana, and Lisa Yoneyama for valuable feedback on early versions of this chapter.

    1. For feminist critiques of the institutionalization of sex work by the military, see Cynthia Enloe, *The Morning After: Sexual Politics at the End*

of the Cold War (Berkeley: University of California Press, 1993); Brenda Stoltzfus and Saundra Sturdevant, *Let the Good Times Roll: Prostitution and U.S. Military in Asia* (New York: The New Press, 1993); and Katherine H. S. Moon, Sex Between Allies: Military *Prostitution in U.S.–Korea Relations* (New York: Columbia University Press, 1997). For a general critique of the U.S. military empire, see *The Sun Never Sets: Confronting the Network of Foreign U.S. Military Bases*, ed. Joseph Gerson and Bruce Birchard (Boston: South End Press, 1991); and Chalmers Johnson, "America's Empire of Bases," *Common Dreams News Center*, http://www.commondreams.org/views04/0115-08.htm (accessed October 13, 2005).

2. Vernadette Gonzalez, S*ecuring Paradise: Tourisms and Militarisms in Hawai'i and the Philippines*, unpublished book manuscript.

3. Phyllis Turnbull and Kathleen Ferguson, *Oh, Say Can You See?: The Semiotics of the Military in Hawai'i* (Minneapolis: University of Minnesota Press, 1999).

4. Inderpal Grewal and Caren Kaplan, *Scattered Hegemonies: Postmodernity and Transnational Feminist Practices* (Minneapolis: University of Minnesota Press, 1994), 17.

5. See, for instance, Gwyn Kirk and Margo Okazawa-Rey, "Demilitarizing Security: Women Oppose U.S. Militarism in East Asia," in *Frontline Feminisms: Women, War, and Resistance*, ed. Marguerite R. Waller and Jennifer Rycenga (New York: Garland, 2000), 159–72.

6. Patricia Goldstone, *Making the World Safe for Tourism* (New Haven, Conn.: Yale University Press, 2001).

7. See Saundra Sturdevant, "Who Benefits? U.S. Military, Prostitution, and Base Conversion," in *Frontline Feminisms: Women, War, and Resistance*, 141–58, who points out Richard Gordon's key role in disciplining the laboring bodies of Filipina workers during his stint as the head of the Subic Bay Metropolitan Authority.

8. Cynthia Enloe, *Bananas, Beaches and Bases: Making Feminist Sense of International Politics* (Berkeley: University of California Press, 1989), 39.

9. See, for instance, Anne-Marie Hilsdon, *Madonnas and Martyrs: Militarism and Violence in the Philippines* (Manila, the Philippines: Ateneo de Manila University Press, 1995), who presents findings on the prostitution industry that cropped up in Olongapo and Angeles, sites of Subic and Clark, respectively.

10. Renato Rosaldo, *Culture and Truth: The Remaking of Social Analysis* (1989; repr., Boston: Beacon Press, 1993), 70.

11. Caren Kaplan, *Questions of Travel: Postmodern Discourses of Displacement* (Durham, N.C.: Duke University Press, 1996).

12. Vernadette Gonzalez, "Military Bases, 'Royalty Trips' and Imperial Modernities: Gendered and Racialized Labor in the Postcolonial Philippines," *Frontiers: A Journal for Women Studies* 28, no. 3 (2007): 28–59.

13. Geoffrey M. White, "Remembering Guadalcanal: National Identity and Transnational Memory-Making," *Public Culture* 7, no. 3 (1995): 530.

14. Enloe, *Bananas, Beaches and Bases*; Teresia K. Teaiwa, "bikinis and other s/pacific n/oceans" in *Voyaging Through the Contemporary Pacific*, ed. David Hanlon and Geoffrey M. White (Lanham, Md.: Rowman & Littlefield, 2000), 91–112; David Hanlon and Geoffrey M. White, ed., *Voyaging in the Contemporary Pacific* (Lanham, Md.: Rowman & Littlefield, 2000); and Turnbull and Ferguson, *Oh, Say Can You See?*.

15. Dennison Nash, "Tourism as a Form of Imperialism" in *Hosts and Guests: The Anthropology of Tourism*, 2nd ed., ed. Valene L. Smith (Philadelphia: University of Pennsylvania Press, 1989), 37–52. See also Noel Kent, "A Tourism Society," in *Hawaii: Islands Under the Influence* (Honolulu: University of Hawai'i Press, 1993), 164–84; Jamaica Kincaid, *A Small Place* (New York: Penguin Books, 1988); and Haunani-Kay Trask, "These Lovely Hula Hands: Corporate Tourism and the Prostitution of Hawaiian Culture" in *From a Native Daughter: Colonialism and Sovereignty in Hawai'i* (Honolulu: University of Hawai'i Press, 1999), 136–47.

16. Martin Mowforth and Ian Munt, *Tourism and Sustainability: New Tourism in the Third World* (London: Routledge, 1998), 294.

17. World Tourism Organization, "Liberalization with a Human Face," World Tourism Organization, http://www.world-tourism.org/liberalization/menu.htm (accessed May 9, 2004). This Web site points out that this program follows the UN Millennium Development Goals as well as the WTO's Global Code of Ethics on fair trade and poverty alleviation.

18. See Saundra Sturdevant, "Who Benefits?"

19. Cynthia Enloe, *Maneuvers: The International Politics of Militarizing Women's Lives* (Berkeley: University of California Press, 2000), xi.

20. I borrow the term "American tropics" from the title of Allan Punzalan Isaac's book, *American Tropics: American Imperial Desire and Asian Pacific American Postcoloniality* (Minneapolis: University of Minnesota Press, 2006).

21. Barbara Kirshenblatt-Gimblett, *Destination Culture: Tourism, Museums, and Heritage* (Berkeley: University of California Press, 1998), 150.

22. Ibid., 159.

23. T. Fujitani, Geoffrey M. White, and Lisa Yoneyama, "Introduction," in *Perilous Memories: The Asia-Pacific War(s)*, ed. T. Fujitani, Geoffrey M. White, and Lisa Yoneyama (Durham: Duke University Press, 2001), 5–6.

24. Walter Benjamin, "Theses in the Philosophy of History," in *Illuminations*, ed. Hannah Arendt, trans. Harry Zohn (New York: Schocken Books, 1969), 255.

25. Neferti Xina M. Tadiar, *Fantasy-Production: Sexual Economies and Other Philippine Consequences for the New World Order* (Hong Kong: Hong Kong University Press, 2004).

26. Amadis Ma Guerrero, "Hero Island Corregidor," *Freeman Magazine*, April 1993, 28–29.

27. Frank Taylor, "Corregidor Revisited," *Mabuhay Magazine*, June 1991, 38–44.

28. An article in the March 11, 2001, *Philippine Daily Inquirer*'s Sunday "Lifestyle" section gives an account of the nascent tourism on Corregidor, with a few digs at the irony of the Fil-American Friendship Park: "Never mind if the colonizer has yet to fully honor the Filipino veterans' invaluable contributions to the war effort with a compensation package at par with their American comrades" (Alex Y. Vergara, "The Fall and Rise of Corregidor," G-1, G-4).

29. Oscar V. Campomanes, "Casualty Figures of the American Soldier and the Other: Post-1898 Allegories of Imperial Nation-Building as 'Love and War,'" in *Vestiges of War: The Philippine–American War and the Aftermath of an Imperial Dream 1899–1999*, ed. Angel Velasco Shaw and Luis H. Francia (New York: New York University Press, 2002), 142.

30. Alfonso J. Aluit, *Corregidor* (Manila, the Philippines: Galleon Publications, 2003), 125.

31. President Ferdinand Marcos, June 24, 1968, Pacific War Memorial plaque at Corregidor.

32. Tom Brokaw, *The Greatest Generation* (New York: Random House, 1998).

33. "The War Against the People: U.S. Scholars Denounce Killings in the Philippines and Calls for a World-Wide Action," Statement of the Critical Filipina and Filipino Studies Collective, March 28, 2005, http://cffsc.focusnow.org/05-killings .html (accessed June 25, 2006).

34. "US Marines 'Raped Filipina Woman,'" BBC News, November 3, 2005, http://news.bbc.co.uk/go/pr/fr/-/2/hi/asia-pacific/44-3134.stm (accessed November 17, 2005).

35. T. J. Burgonio and Volt Contreras, "6 US Marines Held for Rape," *Inquirer News Service*, November 4, 2005.

36. Hilsdon, *Madonnas and Martyrs*, 96.

37. Ibid., 97.

II

Militarized Movements

5

Rising Up from a Sea of Discontent

The 1970 Koza Uprising in U.S.-Occupied Okinawa

Wesley Iwao Ueunten

> *Burn, burn, let the whole world burn!*
>
> —Overheard by journalists during the Koza Uprising
> (Takamine, *Shirarezaru Okinawa no beihei*)

I came across an account of a riot that occurred in Okinawa on December 20, 1970, that made its way to the front page of many major American newspapers but then suddenly disappeared from news coverage the next day. In the aftermath of the "Koza Riot," or what I choose to call the "Koza Uprising" because it was not merely a chaotic and mindless fracas (a point about which I will address later; see Figure 5.1), over seventy cars owned by Americans and a few buildings on the huge Kadena Air Force Base, for which the town of Koza served as an entertainment district, were burned by Okinawans. No such violent protest by Okinawans toward U.S. military occupation can be remembered before or since then.

This chapter seeks to examine critically the historical and social context of the Koza Uprising; in doing so, it aims to reveal the nature of a tripartite relationship between Okinawa, the United States, and Japan. That is, the Koza Uprising took place against the backdrop of U.S. imperialism in Asia and its colonial rule over Okinawa. Japan had previously been the colonial ruler of Okinawa after forcibly annexing the former Ryûkyûan Kingdom in 1879. Consequently, the U.S. takeover of Okinawa in 1945 was the transfer of control from one colonial ruler to another. However, Japan has benefited from U.S. colonial rule over Okinawa, as its postwar "economic miracle" was made possible by the U.S. military umbrella concentrated in Okinawa. In the postwar period, then, Japan became a "junior partner" to the United States' hegemonic influence in Asia; Japan's defeat meant that it was forced to acquiesce to a subordinate status under the United States, but it did not mean giving up dominant status over other Asian countries.

Okinawa became the "keystone" in this unholy alliance by allowing Japan to contain the most blatant aspects of U.S. domination in a place far enough away to remain out of the consciousness of the general American and Japanese populations but near enough to offer the benefits of U.S. military presence. Even now, about 20 percent of Okinawa, the main island in the Ryûkyû Archipelago, is occupied by U.S. military bases. About 75 percent of all U.S. military facilities in Japan are located in Okinawa, despite the fact that Okinawa comprises less than 1 percent of the land area of Japan. To put things into perspective, the size of Okinawa is approximately 454 square miles, or almost exactly the size of the city of Los Angeles, and smaller than the island of Kaua'i in the Hawaiian archipelago.[1]

Interestingly enough, the tripartite relationship bred the conditions for the development of a "Third World" consciousness among Okinawans. Given that Okinawa was and still is a colonized space, it is not surprising that Okinawans developed an affinity to other colonized peoples in the world. A Third World consciousness, with strong ties to U.S. movements, also became concrete and interpersonal with the presence of a large number of soldiers, many of whom came from inner-city and working-class backgrounds. Among these soldiers were African Americans, who were disproportionately represented in the Vietnam War. There were also white political activists from the United States with whom Okinawans were in direct contact. Thus, in the midst of the uprising, Okinawans consciously refrained from harming African American soldiers and their property.

However, given that the United States' entry into Asia was from the start a masculine incursion (starting from at least Commodore Matthew Perry's landing in Okinawa in 1853) and that the U.S. military has always been led and "manned" predominantly by males, we cannot analyze Okinawa as merely a colonized and racialized space. Okinawa must be seen as part of a larger network of U.S. military installations and U.S.-friendly countries that catered to the sexual needs of American troops. This network resembles and even overlaps the former Japanese military's arrangement of military installations and brothels (euphemistically referred to as "comfort stations") and the present Japanese system of economic incursions and sex tourism throughout Asia and the Pacific. In this way, both

Japanese and American empires in Asia must be seen as gendered and sexualized projects and projections.

According to 1969 statistics, 7,400 Okinawan women, or about one in every 40 to 50 women in Okinawa aged 10 to 60, were involved in prostitution.[2] Koza, where the uprising took place, was the major site for the bar and sex industry that catered to American troops. Shannon McCune, former civil administrator in Okinawa and later president of the University of Vermont, describes Koza in the early 1970s in *The Ryukyu Islands*: "Koza has little design, being completely dependent for its livelihood on the American servicemen who flock to it while one passes from Kadena airbase, the Marine training camps located to the north and the Army barracks to the south. Koza is a city of bars, pawnshops, 'hotels' and various clothing and souvenir shops. The neon signs and garish billboards are ugly though eye-catching. In recent years the illicit drug traffic has been a major problem. There is truly little of the charm of Okinawa to be found on the crowded streets of Koza!"[3] McCune devotes less than a page in his book to describing Koza, choosing to focus on Okinawa's scenery, quaint history, and interesting culture—aspects of Okinawa that had more "charm." Perhaps the charm of Okinawa lies in its seeming conformity to an Orientalist notion that it is stuck in an "ancient time" and not able to move forward without the West's guidance. Koza with its "neon signs and garish billboards" and "illicit drug traffic" is too modern and, perhaps, too similar to many blighted areas in the United States to be charming. Consequently, Koza uncomfortably reveals the racialized, gendered, and sexualized aspects of the U.S. military presence in Okinawa while reminding Americans of the racialized, gendered, and sexualized aspects of American society itself.

It is perhaps with the desire to believe the notion that Okinawans are stuck in time and in need of guidance that McCune writes about them: "The Okinawans are an island people. The sea, and particularly its typhoons, is ever present in their lives. Insular and isolated, they tend to feel that the whole world revolves about them. In fact, however, the major decisions that have changed their history and their destinies have been made in places far distant from their shore."[4] From the view of island people such as Okinawans, "empire" and "colonization" are not abstract concepts, since they manifest themselves in concrete experiences of death, destruction, diasporization, discrimination, exploitation, and oppression. Resisting empire and colonization is not simply a matter of believing that they

Figure 5.1. Photo of a burning car in the aftermath of Koza Uprising. Photo by Koh Yoshioka, reproduced with permission

do not exist. However, a critical examination of the Koza Uprising reveals the postwar U.S. colonial empire for what it really is: an insular and isolated island in itself.[5] Its existence depends greatly on the fragile idea that the world revolves around it and on its ability to keep from view the seas of discontent on which it floats. This chapter follows the nearly concealed routes on this sea of discontent, connecting the Koza Uprising to the past and to the shared destinies of people from distant shores.

The Koza Uprising

According to U.S. military documents based on local Okinawan civilian police records, at about 1:00 a.m. on December 20, 1970, an American under the influence of alcohol hit an Okinawan pedestrian, who was also drunk, as he was crossing a street in Koza. The victim was taken to the hospital at about 1:30 a.m. and the local Okinawan police began conducting an investigation. The investigation was completed without trouble except for the jeering and hissing of the crowd that had gathered. The trouble began when the police tried to have the offender's vehicle removed from the accident scene. By then the crowd had grown to about two hundred people. According to the report, the crowd began crying out, "Don't turn over the car to the MPs [military police]," "If we permit the car to leave here, we will see the Itoman case repeated again," and "Put [the American offender] under the people's trial."⁶

A few weeks earlier, on September 18, 1970, an intoxicated U.S. soldier driving in the town of Itoman struck and instantly killed Kinjo Toyo, an Okinawan woman who had been walking on a sidewalk. As the U.S. military tried to tow the car involved in the accident away, a crowd of Okinawan civilians surrounded the tow truck and demanded a thorough investigation. Civilians kept a vigil at the accident scene for seven days, but the U.S. military later found the soldier innocent of any wrongdoing. Incidents such as this happened with high frequency in the 1960s, and the death of Kinjo brought the anger of Okinawans to a boiling point. Okinawan civilians thus organized a public demonstration in Itoman that took place only four days before the Koza Uprising.⁷

The Okinawa civilian police went ahead and had the car taken to the Koza police station, driven by an MP officer, with the offender and an unidentified Okinawan woman in the backseat.⁸ Five or six MPs remained to control traffic, but the Okinawan assistant inspector at the scene judged that it was wise to have the MPs leave the scene immediately because of the increasingly unruly crowd. However, the retreat by the MPs led the crowd to become even more aggressive as the group stopped one of the MP cars from leaving, causing its passengers to flee on foot. The crowd kept growing to about five hundred people. At about 2:10 a.m., a car driven by an American approached the gathering, upon which four or five Okinawans dashed out and shouted, "An American car is passing!" and "Kill!"⁹ The original words used by the Okinawans might have been *kuruse* or *takkuruse*, or even the Japanese word *korose*. *Korose* literally means "kill," but the Okinawan *kuruse* or *takkuruse* could mean both "hit" and "kill." Seldom do Okinawans use the word "kill," and, in the case of the Koza Uprising, it is likely that the crowd was threatening to beat up the Americans rather than kill them.

It is imperative here to emphasize that the uprising was not about senseless killing and violence. In fact, the uprising resulted in no deaths, damage to private businesses, or looting. Further, of great importance is the fact that the Okinawans were selective of their targets: in the midst of the mass action, the participants called out to each other not to hurt the black soldiers.[10]

The crowd stopped the American car from moving, and at about 2:15 a.m. they began throwing rocks. A piece of a cement block, the size of a human head, was thrown into the windshield, hurting a person inside. Another similar-sized piece of cement block was thrown through the back window, hurting another person. By that time, the crowd grew to one thousand. At 2:30 a.m., four MPs arrived and began firing shots in the air. The crowd retreated, giving the MPs and the Okinawan police a chance to take the injured persons in the car away. As the MPs and police drove away, however, the crowd went completely out of control and proceeded to split into two groups, overturning cars with yellow plates, or plates with F-numbers, which indicated that they were owned by Americans. They pushed the cars into the road and burned them. The crowd even went onto Kadena Air Base and set fire to some buildings.[11]

The U.S. military's report of the incident said that after the group split, an MP formation fired a volley of warning shots. However, it reported that "a well organized and disciplined group of approximately sixty Local National youths came out of an alley on the west side of Moromi Street in a formation of three columns about twenty persons deep in a quick-time step carrying wicker baskets of rocks and bottles."[12]

According to Aniya Masaaki, the crowd also yelled, "Yankee Go Home!" Women working in bars came out to fill cola bottles with gasoline to feed the fires. The military mobilized about five hundred armed soldiers and tried to stop the crowd with tear gas and fire hoses, but they were repelled by flying rocks. After six hours, about seventy cars had been burned and nineteen Okinawans had been arrested.[13]

The Okinawan mayor of Koza at the time recalled that he had never seen anything like the uprising even though he had lived through World War II: "Even though there were over one thousand people moving about, they did not say anything or make a sound. The group of young ones came, turned over the Americans' cars, and threw cola bottles filled with gasoline on the cars and set them on fire. The people watching folded their arms, sat down, and watched the overturned cars burn. It was really strange."[14] The incident was covered internationally in the news and appeared in major American newspapers on December 21, 1970. For example, a *Los Angeles Times* front-page article was titled, "2,000 Okinawans Storm U.S. Air Base." The *Washington Post* had a photo of burned-out cars on a Koza Street along with two articles on its front page with the headings "Okinawans Battle GIs, Burn Cars" and "Islanders Resent U.S. 'Arrogance.'" The *New York Times* covered the uprising with a photo of "some 80 American cars burning" on page three. Americans became painfully aware of the anger of an island people about whom they knew little beyond such representations of being "quaint" and "docile" as in the popular movie *Teahouse of the August Moon* (1956).

The news of the Koza Uprising quickly disappeared from American newspapers. Any follow-up to the uprising was conspicuously absent from the newspapers that had covered it the day before. Interestingly, some papers reported U.S. plans to reduce the number of troops in Okinawa but made no mention of the Koza Uprising.[15]

Contextualizing the Koza Uprising

> Tou nu yu kara, yamatu nu yu, yamatu nu yu kara amerika yu *(From the Chinese world to the Japanese world, from the Japanese world to the American world)*
>
> —Postwar Okinawan folk song, "Jidai nu nagari" (The flow of the times)

To depart from imperialistic worldviews that cannot understand the seas of discontent from which the Koza Uprising rose up, I invoke the Okinawan concept of *yu*.[16] This term corresponds with the Chinese character 世 (*shi*). The Okinawan concept of *yu*, similar to the Japanese *yo*, corresponds with the English words "world" or "society," but *yu* also refers to a particular era and the social relations of that era. More than the Japanese concept of *yo*, however, *yu* expresses Okinawan historical memory of external introductions and imposition of world orders, world systems, and worldviews. The following contextualization includes Japan's use of force to integrate Okinawa into the Japanese world (*yamatu yu*), the world of war (*ikusa yu*) in the form of the horrific Battle of Okinawa in 1945, and the American military occupation (*amerika yu*) from 1945 to 1972. It must be pointed out here, however, that each *yu* is not in a linear temporal relationship to the others. Rather, *yu*'s coexist, overlap, and interact. For example, Okinawa is now an official part of Japan and has thus returned to *yamatu yu*, but the presence of American military bases needed to protect Japanese economic and political interests still places it clearly within *amerika yu*. *Ikusa yu* is alive in the scars and trauma of the Battle of Okinawa's survivors and their descendants, as well as in attempts by the Japanese government to cover up its military atrocities against Okinawan civilians during the battle. The continued use of Okinawa as a staging ground for wars to protect American and Japanese interests serves as a daily reminder to Okinawans that *yamatu yu*, *amerika yu*, and *ikusa yu* are not just abstract memories of the past.

Yamatu yu (The Japanese World): Japanese Colonization

Ironically, the era of Japanese colonization over Okinawa was spurred by nascent American imperialism in Asia. In 1853, American naval officer Commodore Matthew C. Perry and a fleet of gunboats arrived in Okinawa on its way to force open Japan's doors to trade and diplomacy. In Okinawa, Perry coerced the Ryûkyûan Kingdom to sign a treaty with the United States after having marched his way into Shuri Palace with a company of marines in full dress, two fieldpieces, and a band that played "Hail Columbia!"[17]

Perry left a part of his crew in Okinawa when he departed for Japan. During their stay, an incident took place that foretold the coming injustices and crimes against Okinawan women by American military personnel. The event concerned an attempt to rape an Okinawan woman by one of Perry's crewmembers. A group of local Okinawans later pursued the crewmember, leading him to a precipice where he fell into the ocean and drowned. Upon his return, Perry ordered the trial and punishment of Okinawans who were involved in the death of his crewmember.[18]

Perry's arrival in Edo Bay in 1853, and his gunboat diplomacy, drove home the point that Japan needed to catch up with the West to avoid being colonized by it. This realization led to the overthrow of the obsolete Tokugawa government in 1868 during the Meiji Restoration. Playing a major role in the Meiji Restoration was the feudal domain of Satsuma in the southern region of Japan. In 1609, Satsuma staged a military invasion of Okinawa, known then as Ryûkyû,[19] under the pretense of punishing it for not contributing to Japan's earlier attempts to invade China. The Ryûkyûan Kingdom was allowed to remain in existence, but, for over 350 years, Satsuma used the threat of military force to skim off profits from Ryûkyû–China trade and extract taxes from Okinawa.

Oguma Eiichiro writes that the dual relationship of the Ryûkyûs to China and Satsuma was possible in the international order of East Asia before the introduction of the modern nation-state model. However, when Japan adopted the nation-state model in response to the advancement of Western nations into East Asia in the latter half of the nineteenth century, the dual allegiance status of the Ryûkyû Kingdom became unsustainable. This began the process in which, according to Oguma, "Ryukyuans" became "Japanese."[20]

If it had been simply an issue of Japan's relationship to Ryûkyûs then it is likely that Japan would not have annexed the former kingdom because of the rather strong domestic resistance toward accepting "foreign" Ryûkyûans as Japanese. The reason for Japan's annexation of the Ryûkyûs was national defense. Japan had already secured its northern defenses against Russia by moving into Hokkaido by the 1870s, but it had not secured its southern borders. The annexation of Okinawa in 1879 was the initial stage of the solidification of Japan's southern frontier against the rest of the world.[21]

The assignment of "prefecture" rank to Okinawa barely concealed its status as a Japanese colony. The several thousand Japanese who settled in Okinawa soon after 1879 were mainly from Kagoshima (formerly known as Satsuma before the Meiji Restoration) and Osaka. The government of Okinawa Prefecture was predominantly staffed by Kagoshima men, with the exception of lower officials who were token natives. Commerce was controlled by people from Osaka. Okinawa's sudden inclusion into Japan's capitalistic system created conditions for widespread poverty and suffering. Since sugarcane became a cash crop, much land was appropriated for its cultivation, while less land was used to grow food. Consequently, the Okinawans were forced into an increasingly dependent situation where they grew sugarcane for cash to buy foodstuff from Japan. When world sugar prices dropped after World War I, Okinawans experienced what they call *sotetsu jigoku*, literally translated as "cycad hell," where many people were forced to eat the *sotetsu*, or cycad, to survive. Since *sotetsu* is poisonous if not prepared correctly, many people died from eating it. To make matters worse, the central government overtaxed the Okinawans. In 1882, Okinawa paid 655,279 yen in taxes to the central government, while the government spent only 455,136 yen on Okinawa. Other available figures show that in the ten years from 1919 to 1928, Okinawa paid sixty-eight million yen to the Japanese government, which spent only twenty-three million yen on Okinawa.[22]

The economic exploitation of Okinawa went hand in hand with racial discrimination. Every aspect of Okinawan culture was seen as inferior. Even outside of schools, Okinawan music, dance, religion, and customs were discouraged, while everything that came from the Japanese mainland was seen as civilized, modern, and superior. Okinawan scholar Nomura Koya provides a sophisticated analysis of the link between Japan's forced military annexation of Okinawa and its forced assimilation of Okinawans. He writes, "The military annexation of the Ryukyuan kingdom was part of the territorial expansion of Japanese imperialism and the beginning of colonial violence toward the Okinawans. As have others who have been colonized, the Okinawans were labeled as 'backward,' 'uncivilized,' and 'second-class citizens' by the Japanese from the very beginning of annexation. Since simply discriminating against the Okinawans would only heighten their dissatisfaction and thus make it difficult for Japan to govern the colony effectively, the one issue that surfaced for the colonialists was how to have the colonized identify with Japanese nationalism."[23] Nomura's further discussion reveals deeper aspects of the Okinawan experience under Japanese colonization and paves the way for understanding the affinity that Okinawans later had for Third World consciousness. He writes that assimilation for Okinawans was not simply the process of acquiring Japanese culture. Utilizing the concept of *intellectual colonialism*, which Edward Said used to describe how "the colonized internalize the values and substantive perceptions of the colonizers," Nomura talks about the deep psychological effects of being under Japanese colonial rule. In other words, the inclusion of Okinawans into the Japanese nation-state entailed the internalization of the notion that they were "backward," "uncivilized," and "second-class citizens."

Ikusa yu (The World of War): The Battle of Okinawa

Of further importance to understanding the Koza Uprising is the strong Okinawan consciousness of how being Okinawan—culturally, linguistically, racially, and otherwise—could result in unspeakable death, despair, and destruction during the Battle of Okinawa, which took place from April to June 1945. To protect the "homeland"—of which Okinawa was not considered a part—the Japanese military fought a desperate battle on

Okinawa, in which, as historian George Feifer writes in *The Battle of Okinawa*, some 150,000 *noncombatant* Okinawans died.[24] The final Okinawan death toll, however, is probably higher, since among the dead were many Okinawan teenagers who were recruited by the Japanese Army as soldiers and nurses.

Survivors of the Battle of Okinawa pass down stories of how Japanese soldiers requisitioned cave shelters, food, and water, forcing Okinawan inhabitants to fend for themselves. There are also stories of Japanese soldiers terrorizing Okinawan mothers to smother their crying babies. Further, there are abundant stories of Okinawans being killed by Japanese soldiers for speaking the Okinawan language. This linguistic profiling was seen as necessary by the Japanese military to prevent Okinawans from spying for the enemy.[25]

For example, on April 9, 1945, the Japanese military gave the following order: "From now on soldiers and civilians as well are all required to use nothing but standard Japanese. Those who speak Okinawan will be regarded as spies and receive appropriate punishment."[26] Master Sergeant Kayama Tadashi, who carried out executions of civilians on the off-lying island of Kume, explained his acts in terms of the need to control Okinawans rather than to protect them: "My troops consisted of a mere thirty or so soldiers while there were ten thousand residents. So if the residents had turned on us and sided with the Americans, we would have been finished right away. So . . . we needed to take firm measures. So I conducted executions in order to keep the civilian residents under our control."[27] Death that did not come directly at the hands of either Japanese or American soldiers often came in a more tragic form: forced suicides and honorable deaths in the name of the Japanese emperor. Stories of Okinawans being coerced by the Japanese military to kill themselves in order to escape torture and rape by Americans abound in Okinawa and in the diaspora.[28]

Amerika yu (The American World): American Occupation

Prior to these forced suicides and honorable deaths, plans for the U.S. military occupation of Okinawa were drawn up in conjunction with the U.S. military invasion of Okinawa sometime in the summer of 1944. Fifteen navy and four army officers were dispatched from Washington to Schofield Barracks on O'ahu, Hawai'i, to plan the U.S. military government of Okinawa. Consequently, the combat forces involved in the invasion of Okinawa had the central role of preparing the postwar blueprints for Okinawa.[29] While the U.S. military may have shown more concern for the lives of Okinawan civilians than the Japanese military, U.S. military interests ultimately held the highest priority over the livelihood and liberty of Okinawan civilians. U.S. Brigadier General William Crist, who was responsible for the military government project on Okinawa, announced in a radio broadcast to the rest of the United States that "the first aim of the military government is to make it possible for combat units to concentrate on the war without having to worry about non-combat personnel." He added that "the military government will take measures to provide the minimum relief needed for civilian survival under international law" but "minimize the economic burden on the United States by promoting economic self-sufficiency in the occupied territory." Crist then stated brusquely, "We have no intention of playing Santa Claus for the residents of the occupied territory."[30]

It is with this attitude that the United States invaded and occupied Okinawa in 1945. It did not officially relinquish control until 1972, when it "returned" the islands to Japan. Consequently, Okinawa became a U.S. colony in which the democracy of the Okinawans was sacrificed. In 1950, the United States set up the U.S. Civil Administration of the Ryûkyûs (USCAR) and the Government of the Ryûkyû Islands (GRI). The USCAR was controlled by Washington and oversaw the GRI, which consisted of a USCAR-appointed Okinawan executive and a popularly elected legislature. However, the GRI was clearly subordinate to U.S. interests, as Taira Koji, an Okinawan scholar, writes, "It was clear that civil liberties under the USCAR-GRI regime were inferior to those enjoyed by citizens in any prefecture of Japan under the 1947 Constitution. A matter of symbolic importance was that governors of Japanese prefectures were popularly elected, while the chief executive of the GRI was not. Bills passed by the Ryukyuan legislature were also subject to a USCAR veto. Decisions of the Ryukyuan courts were sometimes reviewed, reversed, or removed from their jurisdiction by USCAR."[31] In the years following the Communist takeover of China in 1949 and the outbreak of the Korean War in 1950, the United States stepped up efforts to expand its military facilities on Okinawa. Land was often taken from Okinawans violently, with the use of guns and bulldozers. An account given by the Okinawa Prefectural Cultural

Promotion Foundation illustrates the brute force employed in obtaining land on Okinawa:

> On 5 December [1953] at 8:15 a.m. the American military bulldozers suddenly arrived. 1,200 residents hurried to the scene, surrounded the bulldozer, and demanded that the bulldozers leave. Then, about one hour later, fourteen or fifteen armored vehicles arrived with four or five light machine guns and more than a dozen heavy machine guns with live ammunition. The residents were surrounded by 350 armed soldiers in full battle gear. The somewhat surreal atmosphere at first gave the impression that it was all being done just for show, but as the circle tightened and the bayonet points began to touch flesh, many began to fear the day would end in a bloody massacre.
>
> Irritated at the obstinate resistance tactics of the residents, the U.S. soldiers finally began attacking the people with their rifle butts, kicking them with their combat boots, and throwing them into drainage ditches, among other things.[32]

Along with these strong-arm tactics, the U.S. military employed dubious "democratic" means to acquire land for military facilities in Okinawa. In June 1956, the Price Report was presented by a special subcommittee of the Armed Services Committee in the House of Representatives, chaired by Rep. Melvin Price. The Price Report that resulted from the special subcommittee's inspection tour of Okinawa led by Price in the fall of 1955 recommended a lump-sum payment to Okinawans for land acquired for U.S. military facilities. The terms of the payment were not acceptable to the Okinawans, and widespread protest swept through Okinawa.[33] In the cold war situation, the protests caused great concern for the U.S. government as evidenced by a Department of State intelligence report. Dated October 26, 1956 (since declassified) and entitled "US Administration of the Ryukyus Enters a Critical Period," the report stated, "If discontent in the Ryukyus continues to grow, the problem could arouse in Asia the highly-charged theme of 'anti-colonialism.' The Communist bloc, exploiting its pretension that decreasing tensions obviate the need for sacrifices in the name of military security, have begun to encourage Asian misgivings over protracted US military government of the Ryukyus and to threaten action in the United Nations."[34] As shown previously, the U.S. military tried to put up a facade of democracy in Okinawa by establishing the GRI. Reminiscent of the Japanese military's disregard for the protection of Okinawan lives and lands, the Price Report unapologetically revealed that the U.S. military had no genuine concern for Okinawan democracy:

> We are in Okinawa because it constitutes an essential part of our worldwide defenses. In Japan and the Philippines, as in other parts of the world, our base tenure is dependent upon the continued existence of friendly governments. In the Ryukyu Islands the circumstances of our political control and the absence of a belligerent nationalistic movement allow us to plan for long-term use of a forward military base in the offshore island chain of the Far East-Pacific area, subject, of course to our own national policy. Here there are no restrictions imposed by a foreign government on our rights to store or to employ atomic weapons.[35]

Important in this historical discussion is the early censorship of Okinawan writers by U.S. occupation authorities. In *The American Occupation of Japan and Okinawa: Literature and Memory*, Michael Molasky provides an informative account and analysis of the work of Arakawa Akira. In 1953, Arakawa founded *Ryūdai bungaku* (Ryûkyû University literature), which was the student literary magazine at the University of the Ryûkyûs. The magazine was closely associated with the protest movement against the U.S. military, as several of its editors were key organizers in it. In 1956, the poem Arakawa submitted to *Ryūdai bungaku*, "An Orphan's Song," was censored by occupation authorities because it encouraged resistance against the occupation. To circumvent censorship, the editors of *Ryūdai bungaku* published the next issue without submitting it for clearance by the American censors. In the cold war environment of the time, the American authorities cracked down on the magazine by recalling copies that had been distributed, banning publication for six months, and expelling four editors who had been part of the protest movement.[36] One of the submissions in the magazine, Arakawa's poem "The Colored Race," threatened the American authorities because it talked about racial discrimination by people from the white race as well as the common subordinate statuses of the yellow and black races. For example, in one part of his poem, he writes,

Your skin, like ours, is not white
A rugged dark brown, it is
the color of iron.
Covering ineradicable welts
from the whip
Your brown skin is
Strong, like stone.
You who are Black
and we who are Yellow,
Together, we are the Colored Race.[37]

In other sections of the poem, Arakawa talks about the racial identities imposed by the dominant whites with pointed references to skin color:

As for "Yellow,"
If you want to call us "Yellow"—
Go right ahead!
We don't mind being the Yellow Race
We are the unadulterated Yellow Race.
Go right ahead! Call us your
"*Yellow Fellow*."[38]

Molasky argues that Arakawa's poem illustrates the arbitrary and changeable nature of racial categories imposed by the white occupiers. He writes that "'The Colored Race' suggests that oppressed peoples perpetuate their own subjugation by internalizing the subjugator's discourse, and the poem attempts to usurp authority from the white occupiers by redefining the language of race."[39]

Up to the 1960s, the presence of U.S. military bases, military personnel, and military dependents brought many disruptive elements into Okinawa. These include the screeching of military airplanes that cause stress to the people living near the bases, the storing of nuclear weapons and nerve gas that always pose the threat of a potential catastrophe, and the committing of crimes by U.S. military personnel toward Okinawans that evoke feelings of stress, fear, and pain. In June 1967, for example, the Okinawan newspaper *Ryûkyû shimposha* conducted a public survey of Okinawan attitudes toward the U.S. military. When asked if the U.S. military bases made Okinawans feel secure, 45.5 percent of the respondents expressed strong anxiety for their safety, whereas 30.0 percent felt "somehow insecure." Only 1.7 percent felt that their safety was assured by the presence of U.S. bases.[40]

Other incidents that happened in the late 1960s illustrate why the respondents would be so strongly concerned with U.S. military occupation. In 1965, a trailer carried by a Lockheed C-130 aircraft fell to the ground and killed an Okinawan schoolgirl. In 1966, a KC-135 jet-fuel tanker skidded at Kadena Air Base, crashed into a car, and killed a man on a nearby highway. In 1968, drinking water and crops were contaminated by a fuel-oil leak from a military pipeline. In the same year, a bomb-laden B-52 headed on a mission to Vietnam failed to take off and exploded at Kadena Air Base. Fortunately, the crash occurred on base and not in a densely populated area or near ordnance storage facilities, which were believed to store nuclear weapons.[41]

Crimes committed against Okinawans by Americans connected to the U.S. military also increased from an already-high number of 973 cases in 1964 to 1,003 cases in 1965. By 1966, the numbers rose to 1,407. Of those totals, "atrocious and violent crimes" exponentially rose from 265 cases in 1964 to 446 cases in 1966.[42] The lion's share of these "atrocious and violent crimes" was against women. Just as in Perry's time, American military interests in Okinawa were a greater priority than the protection of Okinawan women against sexual violence perpetrated by American military personnel. In most cases, Americans who committed crimes against Okinawans were often let go or given light punishment. A sampling of the crimes against Okinawan women by American military personnel in the years from 1969 to 1971 gives us a graphic illustration of the asymmetrical power relations between male American servicemen and Okinawan women. This asymmetry is evidenced in the punishment administered toward American servicemen.[43] Figure 5.2 is a small portion of a much longer list that has now been made available to the public. This list, along with other documents, was introduced to people who attended presentations by Okinawan women activists who traveled across the United States in 1996 after three U.S. Marines raped a twelve-year-old Okinawan girl. While the original list starts in 1945 and ends in 1995, the excerpt includes only the incidents that happened around the time of the Koza Uprising. As with most statistics on crimes against women, this list cannot be said to be complete and, moreover, does not include sexual violence in the form

Date	Description of Crime	Punishment
2/22/69	A twenty-one-year-old hostess is found and her nude body disposed of by a private second-class in an artillery regiment in Koza City.	Arrest, no record
3/3/69	The body of a twenty-year-old hostess is found, and the official autopsy leads to the conclusion that the crime was committed by a general infantryman (GI).	Unsolved
11/?/69 [exact date unknown]	A twenty-year-old woman, returning from her part-time job in Naha City, was raped and stabbed with a knife repeatedly on a public street when she resisted her GI assailant.	Two-month salary cut and discharge
5/28/70	A twenty-one-year-old woman was attacked at her job on a military base in Urasoe City by a GI.	Not guilty Insufficient proof
5/30/70	A high school student is attacked by a U.S. military sergeant, and is stabbed in the abdomen and head in a failed rape attempt. School teachers, women's organizations, and high school students issue a strong protest and the suspect is arrested.	Three-year sentence, demotion
[exact date unknown]	A woman proprietor of a bar is raped when a GI forces his way behind the counter.	Accused is transferred during trial
4/23/71	The nude body of a twenty-two-year-old hostess is found at a grave. The testimony of a witness results in the arrest of a Marine corporal.	Acquitted due to lack of evidence
5/1/71	A forty-one-year-old woman is stabbed to death in Kin Town by a Marine private first class and is arrested after his fingerprints and blood are found.	No record
5/21/71	A junior high school student is raped by a GI in Koza City.	Suspect not found
5/23/71	A twenty-four-year-old hostess is abducted, taken to an abandoned house, and raped on her way to work.	Unsolved
7/10/71	A mentally retarded twelve-year-old girl who is playing in front of her house is gang-raped by three GIs in Ginowan City.	Arrest, no record

Figure 5.2. Crimes committed against Okinawan women by U.S. military personnel, 1969–1971

of prostitution and "consensual" relationships based on false promises by American men of marriage and life in the United States.

From *Yu* to Us: Koza as a Nexus of Internal, External, and Sexual Colonialism

Why would unarmed women and men stage a violent attack against the most powerful military in the world? Why was it that the protesters seemed to have been disciplined enough to overpower the MPs? Because the women working in the bars in Koza quickly produced the Molotov cocktails used in the uprising, had they already been anticipating such an event? Finally, what do we make of participants in the uprising who made a conscious effort to refrain from hurting African American soldiers? Such questions require looking at Koza as a meeting place of U.S. internal colonialism, characterized by racism against African Americans and other nonwhites, and external U.S. and Japanese colonialisms, manifested with impunity in Okinawa. Further, internal and external colonialism cannot be analyzed separately from sexual colonization because the oppression of African Americans and other racial minorities in American history has been inextricably linked to the commodification, exploitation, and subjugation of nonwhite female and male bodies.

The city of Koza did not exist before the American occupation. It developed as a base town that catered to Kadena Air Base, the largest U.S. military base in Asia, in the central part of Okinawa. A large proportion of the people of Koza settled there after having been displaced by the destruction of the Battle of Okinawa and by the construction of Kadena and other U.S. military bases. Others were returnees from Japan's former colonies in Asia and the Pacific Islands. Many of the displaced groups depended economically on the bars, strip clubs, and other components of a recreation industry that catered to young male Americans during the Vietnam conflict.

Koza was where local Okinawan rock bands entertained American soldiers nightly. Surviving the often unruly and violent audiences of soldiers on their way back from the war in Vietnam, a handful of these rock bands became wildly popular among American soldiers for their macho personas that matched their ear-piercing singing, aggressive guitar riffing, and driving bass and drum rhythm making. The ultra masculine personas that Okinawan rock bands developed perhaps also reflected an Okinawan male response to the sexualized and feminized positionality that Okinawa, in general, and Koza, in particular, was forced to hold in East Asian geopolitics. The temporary control that they achieved over American soldiers through their performances was a brief relief from the lack of control they had in their own lives under U.S. military occupation.

While they could captivate their American-soldier audiences in nightly performances, like other Okinawans, Okinawan rock musicians were reminded daily of the sexualized nature of the U.S. occupation and of their powerlessness against American extraterritoriality. For example, in an oral-history interview, one musician talks about how his wife and younger sister were half white because of the American occupation army. The musician also explained how a military jeep driven by an American soldier hit and killed his grandmother as she was waiting for a bus. The driver fled into the military base and was never found. Recalling both his grandmother's death and his participation in the Koza Uprising, he says, "I still don't like Americans. There are good and bad people among them, but I must say that the bad feelings that I have held for them since I was a child exploded in the Koza incident."[44]

Higashionna Tsuneo was born in the Philippines in 1938 and moved to Misato Village after the war and later to Koza. Using the pen name of Higashi Mineo, he wrote a novella entitled *Okinawa no shōnen* (Okinawa boy) in 1971 that was awarded the prestigious Akutagawa Prize in 1972.[45] The novella is a coming-of-age story of the protagonist Tsuneyoshi, whose family returns from Saipan to Okinawa after the war and ends up running a bar in Koza that caters to American soldiers. The bar is actually their family home, and Tsuneyoshi often has to give up his bed to prostitutes and their customers when the bedroom next to the bar was filled. The following is an excerpt from *Okinawa no shōnen* where Tsuneyoshi is awakened by his mother to give up his bed:

"Let them all use one bed together," I said, sitting up.
"Don't be silly! Now hurry or we'll lose this chance to make some money."
Mom unfolded a starched sheet as she rushed me out of bed.
"This sure is a lousy business you're in."
"There's no use complaining. It's how we eat, you know."
"It's still lousy."
It made me want to cry, thinking people would probably do anything to eat. I took my school cap and satchel off my desk and pushed them under my bed out of sight.

"Excuse us," said Michiko. She came into my room leading a soldier by the hand. As she put her arm around his waist, she glanced at me with a faint smile.[46]

Higashionna's writings express the seething discontent of the people of Koza over their racial, economic, and sexual subordination to the occupying U.S. military. Such discontent lay just below the surface of the forced civility that Okinawans had to display toward American military personnel in order to survive as their service providers and entertainers. It is because of this context of discontent that surrounded Okinawan life in Koza that I have chosen to use the word "uprising" rather than "riot" to describe the events of December 20, 1970. My choice of words follows Okinawan historian Aniya Masaaki's insistence on describing the events of that day using the term *minshū hōki*,[47] which can be roughly translated as "popular uprising," "popular revolt," or "popular rebellion." He explains,

> Since this *minshū hōki* was not something planned, had no leaders, and was carried out in response to the course of events at the time, one could call it a *sōdō* [disturbance or riot], but it was not a disorderly *sōdō*. Even though it was an anti-American *sōdō*, it was not simply an exclusionist act. It was instead a response to the unjust and tyrannical rule of the U.S. military.
>
> At the time, the U.S. military could not hold the people down using military force. One could say it illustrated both the strength to fight in response to the 20 years of oppression since the war ended and to the weight of history. [48]

His argument is similar to critiques of the word "riot" when used to describe urban revolts in the United States during the 1960s. For example, Herbert Gans wrote in 1968, "Events commonly described as riots or civil disorders are in reality *spontaneous rebellions*, carried out impulsively by Negroes disenchanted with the way they have been treated by white American society. These rebellions are the natural outcome of the years of anger that have been building up in the ghettos of the nation's cities and towns."[49] Similarly, Robert Blauner wrote that the "ghetto riots" in several urban areas across the United States were not merely attempts by blacks to gain fuller integration into the social order and access to the material benefits that were enjoyed by the majority of American citizens. Rather, "the revolts pointed to alienation from this system on the part of many poor and also not-so-poor Blacks." Blauner's description of "internally colonized" blacks rising up to resist rings similarly to Aniya's explanation for his use of the word *minshū hōki*: "One of the most significant consequences of the process of colonization is a weakening of the colonized individual and collective will to resist his oppression. It has been easier to contain and control Black ghettoes because communal bonds and group solidarity have been weakened through divisions among leadership, failures of organization, and a general disappointment that accompanies social oppression. The riots are a signal that the will to resist has broken the mold of accommodation."[50] In explaining the application of the "internal colony" model to blacks in the United States, Blauner points out that "the classical colonialism of the imperialist era and American racism developed out of the same historical situation and reflected a common world economic and power stratification." That is, the African slave trade weakened Africa and made it less able to resist European colonialism. Slavery also contributed to the accumulation of wealth in America and Europe, which allowed for those areas to develop technological and military superiority over non-Western and nonwhite peoples. This process laid "the basis for racist ideologies that were elaborated to justify control and exploitation of non-white people." Consequently, Western colonization over nonwhite people necessarily entails racism.[51]

Okinawan experiences of death, destruction, and discrimination under Japanese rule no doubt increased their comprehension of American racism in Okinawa. However, the intense daily contact between American soldiers and Okinawans in Koza was also reflected in sophisticated understandings of race, as evidenced by the previously mentioned poem, "The Colored Race," by Koza resident Arakawa. Another perceptive observation of race can be found from the account of a Koza rock musician who himself was half white but identified closely with Okinawan issues: "Up to the 1970s, Teruya was the black town and Center Street was the white town. It was the era of racial discrimination and Orientals were looked at very differently. Yeah, there was discrimination toward Orientals ... Vietnamese people, Okinawan people all looked the same to them (Americans). In other words, they thought of themselves as nationals of a superior country and since they saw Okinawans being of the same race as the people from the country they were fighting, they didn't see us as being equal to them."[52] The black segregated district of Teruya described by the rock musician reveals the irony that the American forward presence in the Far East was to protect and promote freedom and democracy. In fact, many white Americans brought attitudes characteristic of the segregated Deep South. At the time of the uprising, Koza and other base towns in Okinawa were similarly segregated into black and white entertainment districts. Takamine Tomokazu, an Okinawan journalist who covered U.S. military base–related issues, writes that the black section of the town was referred to by white soldiers as the "Bush," while the black soldiers called it "Four Corners" or its original name "Teruya."[53] Okinawans also referred to Teruya as "Mokutangai," or "Charcoal Town," and to the black soldiers as *Teruya seinen dan* or the "Teruya Youth Group."[54]

Takamine's description of the black section of Koza provides a view of intimate exchanges between the black soldiers and Okinawans that no doubt had lasting effects on Okinawan consciousness. For example, in the black section of Koza there existed a group of black soldiers called the Bush Masters who, according to Takamine, wore jackets with a panther embroidered on the back suggesting a connection to the Black Power movement, the Black Panther Party, or both.[55] At its peak in 1969, the group had over one hundred members. The Bush Masters met in a bar in the black section of Koza where they discussed Black Power movement movies and literature that came in from the United States. The group was also a moral force in the black section, protecting white soldiers who wandered into the black section from physical violence. They would also collect money to recompense bars and restaurants when black soldiers did not pay for their meals and drinks. Takamine even writes how the Bush Masters coordinated a blood drive for one Okinawan woman who needed an operation.[56]

Takamine points out other things that tied black soldiers and Okinawans together. Because they tended to be lower ranked and lower paid than white soldiers, the black soldiers consumed local products more than white soldiers. For example, the preferred alcoholic beverages of the black soldiers were Akadama port wine (a cheap Japanese brand), Orion Beer (a locally brewed beer), and Zuisen (a brand of traditional Okinawan liquor). On the other hand, white soldiers often consumed more expensive drinks, such as Heineken, Johnny Walker, Napoleon, and Schlitz. However, the matter was probably more than just economics and involved a feeling of closer affinity that the black soldiers had with the local, nonwhite culture. In the summers when young Okinawans would parade down the streets of

Teruya in the Okinawan *eisa* drum dance, it was a familiar sight to see the black soldiers joining in.[57]

This sense of public affinity between blacks and Okinawans sometimes transmitted into political spheres of resistance as well. The manner in which Okinawans took to turning cars over and burning them (with women working in the bars quickly producing gasoline-filled bottles) can perhaps be contextualized within Okinawans' contact with African American soldiers. This style of protest against oppression on a mass scale is glaringly absent in Okinawa before or since. However, the model for this type of action may have come from an incident that happened a little over a year before the December 20 uprising. On August 30, 1969, a group of fifty or more black soldiers got into a confrontation with some MPs over a trivial incident: the group's anger exploded when an intimidated MP fired his gun. The group overturned the MP patrol car and set it on fire.[58] The incident also seems to be reminiscent of the ghetto riots across the United States that took place between 1965 and 1968, which observers such as Gans and Blauner point out were more than physical acts of violence and looting but rather were "spontaneous rebellions" against the white, racist treatment African Americans experienced in the United States.

However, the relationship between the black soldiers and the Okinawans was not always harmonious. Okinawans were not immune to their own racist attitudes toward black soldiers. Although Okinawan discrimination against black soldiers was no doubt an extension of Japan's internalization of white supremacy, Okinawans' own prejudices against darker skin could be linked to other dynamics. For example, darker skin was not simply associated with the preannexation peasant class; after Japanese annexation darker skin became a marker of the impurity and inferiority of Okinawans vis-à-vis Japanese from the main islands of Japan. Darker skin came to signify "natives" from the so-called primitive places of the Pacific Islands and Southeast Asia.

Further, black and Okiwanan relations were aggravated by the sexualized nature of heterosexual interactions between black soldiers and Okinawan women. Both groups suffered the indignities of colonization and racism. And while the black soldiers were heirs to a long history of white sexual domination over black women, in Okinawa they enjoyed some limited sexual privilege over Okinawan women, a fact that Okinawan males resented. The tensions between the two groups manifested in a scuffle on August 17, 1971, between black soldiers and Okinawans. The scuffle stemmed from an incident in which three black soldiers were refused service in a bar. An altercation followed where the soldiers were beaten up by a group of Okinawan bar employees. The three black soldiers managed to escape and gather a group of about twenty to thirty other black soldiers.

These tensions seem to have already arisen around the time of the Koza Uprising as black soldiers were defying the de facto segregation. For instance, a declassified confidential report made to U.S. Civil Administration of the Ryûkyû Islands, approved with the signature of the Chief of the Counterintelligence Division and dated July 10, 1970, gives us a glimpse of what was happening at the time. The report, entitled "Negro Personnel Reportedly Desiring to Take Over Koza City, Okinawa," stated that "an increasing number of Negroes are frequenting the Gate 2–B.C. Street areas of Koza (which was the 'white' section of the town)." The source of the report, identified as having "furnished reliable information in the past," also described a meeting on July 3, 1970, held in the Gate 2–B.C. Street vicinity in which a speaker "said that the Negroes will take the area over as their own."[59]

Given black efforts to desegregate Koza's "entertainment" district, then, the group of black soldiers mentioned previously consequently marched through the streets chanting antiracial discrimination slogans. The demonstration caused fighting to break out between the black soldiers and the Okinawan bar employees. According to Takamine, the Okinawans were already well organized from earlier base workers' strikes and were able to gather over one hundred people. The Okinawans then chased the black soldiers back into the base. Some of the Okinawans began breaking the windshields of American cars parked near the gate and beating up any black soldier that passed by. The Okinawan police were able to calm the situation down, but, by unfortunate chance, there was a car accident involving a black soldier and an Okinawan. This caused a mob of 1,000 to 1,500 Okinawans to surround the accident scene and the MPs who had come to investigate. The MPs and the black soldier involved in the accident escaped to the Koza police headquarters. The crowd, however, threw bottles and rocks at the headquarters, causing several people to be injured.[60]

Relations between the Okinawans and the blacks were later improved on January 15, 1972, when various black organizations, Latino and white soldiers, and Okinawans took part in a twelve-kilometer march in memory of Martin Luther King, Jr. Okinawans watching the march applauded the participants when they learned about its purpose.[61]

Along these lines of discord and solidarity, a dialogue emerged between blacks, Okinawans, and others regarding the antiwar movement in the United States. Several notable white antiwar activists, including Jane Fonda, came to Okinawa to lead protests against the Vietnam War and U.S. militarism. Within the antiwar movement there were people of color who clearly saw the connection between white racism and the war. For example, Cuban-born Green Beret Alfonso Toledo actively participated in the antiwar movement after being disillusioned by the futility of the war. According to Takamine, he engaged in discussions with other Latino and black soldiers about his antiwar position and about questions of ethnic self-determination.[62] A photo of him at a strike rally of Okinawan base workers in 1971 shows him raising his fist in the air. There are also photos from 1971 showing meetings between black soldiers, white activists, and Okinawan activists. In the background of one such meeting, as shown in Figure 5.3, is the famous poster of Black Panther Party leader Huey Newton sitting in a wicker chair holding a rifle and spear.[63]

Mapping the Koza Uprising in the Sea of Discontent

As previously shown, the forced proximity of Okinawans and African American soldiers in Koza led to both interracial conflicts and mutual understanding. A flyer written in English and Japanese, distributed by African American soldiers to Okinawans in the aftermath of the Koza Uprising, reinforced their shared status:

> So you see we both are in the same situation. With this you see that we have a problem. With every problem there is a solution. Black GI's are trying to become a part of the solution, not the problem. The Black GI's are willing to help and talk to the Okinawans in order to form much better relations between the oppressed groups, because we have so much in common. So why not get our heads together and come up with a solution to destroy the problem. The Black GI's are aware of the situation that brought about the riot, and this was truly a RIGHT-ON-MOVE. That's the only way they'll bend.[64]

From across the ocean, African Americans had already been conscious of what was happening in Okinawa. For example, the January 4, 1969, issue of *Black Panther* reported a rally of three hundred Okinawan university

Figure 5.3. Antiwar–antimilitary activists in Koza, Okinawa, 1971. Photo by Koh Yoshioka, reproduced with permission.

students that demanded the withdrawal of B-52s and the dismantling of U.S. bases. With much admiration of the students in Okinawa, *The Black Panther* reported, "The forceful action of the students threw the U.S. and Japanese reactionary pigs into a panic. The latter sent out about five hundred armed policemen to ruthlessly suppress the demonstrators. Braving the pigs' brutal suppression, the students stormed the base several times and fought bravely with the police."[65] In an age long before the word "transnationalism" became widely used and before faxes, the Internet, affordable international flights, and cheap long-distance phone calls made it easier to travel and communicate between the corners of the U.S. global empire, political movements in the United States were strongly conscious of what was happening in Okinawa. This was evident in the early Asian American movement. Two longtime Japanese American women activists and friends, Minn Matsuda and Kazu Iijima, who wanted to create a Japanese American group in New York for their college-age children, established Asian Americans for Action (AAA) in the fall of 1968. One of its early members was Yuri Kochiyama, a close friend of Malcolm X and an icon of radical politics.[66] In one of its undated publications, AAA urged "the American people to join the people of Okinawa and Japan in demanding the complete removal of all U.S. bases, personnel and military equipment from Okinawa and Japan." It added that "we must insist on liberation and self-determination for the people of Okinawa as for all of the Third World."[67]

Similarly, the Koza Uprising was brought to the attention of the Asian American movement on the West Coast through the radical Asian American publication, *Gidra*, based in Los Angeles. Hatano Terumasa from Japan wrote in *Gidra*, "This action of the people of Okinawa clearly embodied the dawn of a new age, with revolutionary significance equal to the occupation of Shinjuku area (central part of Tokyo) in October, 1968 and the rebellion in Watts."[68] In 1970, pioneering Asian American activist and scholar Yuji Ichioka wrote an article in *Gidra* that was highly critical of the way the conservative Japanese American Citizens League supported the U.S.–Japan Security Treaty and the reversion of Okinawa to Japan.[69] Mike Murase, a *Gidra* staff writer, also examined the adverse environmental and social impacts (with much emphasis on the rape of Okinawan women by U.S. servicemen) of the bases on Okinawa in an article titled "The Keystone of the Pacific." In another *Gidra* article in May 1972, Tracy Okida described the Okinawans as being a "vanguard struggle related to the revolutionary movements of other Third World peoples."[70]

Conclusion

The Koza Uprising is a contradiction in itself: the rampage of "angry," "organized," and "politicized" Okinawans against the U.S. military in the dead of night is at odds with the popular image of Okinawans as "friendly," "pleasant," "agreeable," "gentle," "peace loving," and "passive."[71] However, the contradictory nature of the uprising is part and parcel of other contradictions that arise from Okinawa's particular positionality in global geopolitics. Japan's chronic unwillingness to accept genuinely Okinawans as fellow humans is at odds with its strategic need to keep Okinawans in the Japanese nation-state in order to strengthen Japan's defense against invasions from perceived enemies. The United States' self-proclaimed leadership of the democratic free world is equally and grossly inconsistent with its deprivation of the practice of democracy in Okinawa.

An interesting paradox that arises from these contradictions is worth mentioning. Okinawa is but a small island territory with very limited resources at the fringes of the U.S. empire as well as part of a Japanese national sovereignty that depends on that empire.[72] Okinawans are a relatively small minority group scattered in a diaspora that stretches from Okinawa and mainland Japan to the estimated three hundred thousand Okinawans in the Americas, Asia, and the Pacific Islands. In total, Okinawans perhaps number less than two million. The irony is that, despite Okinawa's peripheral geographical existence and its small population, of which a large percentage has spread to other parts of the world, the United States and Japan have constantly been preoccupied with putting a lid on Okinawan dissent. Still, Okinawans live in and navigate the sea of discontent, despite efforts by the United States and Japan to quell their unpredictable tides. The swiftness in which the Koza Uprising appeared and disappeared from the American media seems to be a case in point: dissent is the Achilles' heel of empire.

Perhaps more threatening is the fact Okinawan women take more leadership roles in antimilitary protests, bridging international connections with women in places where global militarization violates the human rights of women and children, such as Guam, Hawai'i, Japan, the Philippines, Puerto Rico, and South Korea. Okinawan women have also helped to unleash major protest movements in Okinawa as a result of the 1995 rape of a twelve-year-old Okinawan girl, among other pressing issues. In short, Okinawan women are formidable in their role as navigators in the sea of discontent, as they rely on matriarchal Okinawan cultural values that emphasize the sanctity of life and nature while they steer Okinawans toward political alliances with the larger world.

This does not mean that the empire has just lain down and died. On the contrary, it has struck back by actually encouraging Okinawan culture and "worldwide" Okinawan networks. The Japanese government pushed Okinawa to accept, under veiled threats of economic sanctions, the construction of a heliport over a pristine reef in Nago. It "rewarded" Okinawa and the city of Nago by hosting the United Nations G-7 summit at a resort in Nago. Before and during the summit, the Japanese government promoted Okinawa's unique culture (which it suddenly claimed to be Japanese culture) as well as promulgated a version of Okinawan history that emphasized its ancient history as a seafaring nation that linked different countries through entrepot trade. A television drama series about an Okinawan family was also broadcast around the time of the summit. The series was benevolent in showcasing Okinawan music and dance and portraying Okinawans as friendly, warm, wise, and happy-go-lucky people. Understandably, since it was shown on NHK, the government-run broadcasting organ, not once did the series delve into "negative" issues such as discrimination against Okinawans by Japanese, the Battle of Okinawa, or the U.S. military bases.

Despite the new "positive" image that Okinawans enjoyed, it served to direct the Japanese public's attention away from Okinawans' discontent over the presence of U.S. military bases in Okinawa. It also helped to transform Okinawan culture into a commodity for consumption by an increasing number of people who claim to "love" everything about Okinawa, except the U.S. bases. The United States continues to push forward with plans to build a heliport in Nago, and the plan for reducing the military burden in Okinawa is to shift it to Guam.

Now, more than ever, we need to hone our navigating skills.

Notes

Japanese names follow the convention of surname followed by given name.

1. Chalmers Johnson, *Blowback: The Costs and Consequences of American Empire* (New York: Metropolitan Books, 2000), 36.

2. Suzuyo Takazato, "The Past and Future of Unai, Sisters in Okinawa," *AMPO Japan-Asia Quarterly Review* 25, no. 4 (1995): 76.

3. Shannon McCune, *The Ryukyu Islands* (Harrisburg, Pa.: David & Charles, 1975), 162.

4. Ibid., 15.

5. Here I find inspiration from French sociologist Michel De Certeau, who urges us to shift our focus away from the obsession of scientific institutions on analyzing systems that repress individuals to one that examines the practices that take place within and against these systems. The former type of analysis is privileged because scientific institutions study the very system of which they are a part and "conform to the well-known genre of the family story." He writes, "Seeing this elucidation of the apparatus by itself has the disadvantage of *not seeing* practices which are heterogeneous to it and which it represses or thinks it represses. Nevertheless, they have every chance of surviving this apparatus *too*, and, in any case, they are *also* part of social life, and all the more resistant because they are more flexible and adjusted to perpetual mutation. When one examines this fleeting and permanent reality carefully, one has the impression of exploring the night-side of societies, a night longer than their day, a dark sea from which successive institutions emerge, a maritime immensity on which socioeconomic and political structures appear as ephemeral islands" (41). Michel De Certeau, *The Practice of Everyday Life* (Berkeley: University of California Press, 1984).

6. Okinawa-shi Heiwa Bunka Shinkoka (Peace Culture Promotion Section of Okinawa City Offices), ed., *Beikoku ga mita koza bodo* (Koza riot as seen by the United States) (Okinawa: Yui Shuppan, 1999), 22.

7. Aniya Masaaki, "Koza minshu (Koza peoples)," in *Shashin ga toraeta 1970-nen zengo koza hito machi koto anata ga rekishi no mokugekisha* (Koza people, streets, and events around 1970 in photos: you are an eyewitness of history), ed. Heiwa Bunka Shinkoka (Okinawa: Naha Shuppansha, 1997), 187.

8. It is assumed that the unidentified Okinawan woman was with the offender at the time of the accident.

9. Okinawa-shi Heiwa Bunka Shinkoka (Peace Culture Promotion Section of Okinawa City Offices), *Beikoku*, 38.

10. Ibid., 11; and Masamichi S. Inoue, *Okinawa and the U.S. Military: Identity Making in the Age of Globalization* (New York: Columbia University Press, 2007), 55.

11. Okinawa-shi Heiwa Bunka Shinkoka (Peace Culture Promotion Section of Okinawa City Offices), *Beikoku*, 40.

12. Ibid., 118.

13. Aniya, "Koza minshu (Koza peoples)," 187.

14. Takamine Tomokazu, *Shirarezaru Okinawa no beihei: beigun kichi 15-nen no shuzai memo kara* (Unknown truth about U.S. troops in Okinawa: from notes of fifteen years reporting on U.S. bases) (Okinawa: Kobunken, 1984), 68. Translation provided by this author.

15. For example, on December 22, the *Los Angeles Times* and the *Washington Post* both had articles on their front pages titled, respectively, "U.S. to Heavily Cut Forces in Okinawa and Japan by June" and "U.S. Announces Pullout of 12,000 Troops From Japan." Neither of those articles mentioned the uprising. The *New York Times* had an article on the U.S. military's need to keep troops in Okinawa and did have a photo of U.S. military policemen firing tear gas during the uprising. However, right below that article was another editorial about U.S. plans to cut combat forces in Japan.

16. The epigraph cited in this section is taken from Kadekaru Rinsho, one of Okinawa's premier postwar *minyo* (folk music) singers, who used the words in the first verse of a song called "Jidai no nagare" (The flow of the times): *Tou nu yu kara yamatu nu yu / Yamatu nu yu kara amerika yu / Mijirasa kawataru kunu Uchinaa* . . . (From the Chinese world to the Yamatu world / From the Yamatu world to the American world / How strangely this Okinawa has changed . . .).

17. George H. Kerr, *Okinawa, the History of an Island People* (Rutland, Vt.: C. E. Tuttle Co., 1958), 315–16.

18. Francis L. Hawks, *Narrative of the Expedition of an American Squadron to the China Seas and Japan Performed in the Years 1852, 1853, and 1854* (New York: D. Appleton & Co., 1857), 566–67.

19. "Ryûkyû" is derived from Liuch'iu, the name that the Chinese used to describe the island kingdom.

20. Oguma Eiji, "*Nihonjin*" *no Kyokai: Okinawa, Ainu, Taiwan, Chosen, shokuminchi shihai kara fukki undo made* (The boundaries of the Japanese: Okinawa, Ainu, Taiwan, Korea, from colonial control to the reversion movement), 1st ed. (Tokyo: Shinyosha, 1998), 19.

21. Ibid., 20–21.

22. See Aniya Masaaki, "*Kengai dekasegi to kennai ijuu* (Interprefectural sojourning and intraprefectural migration)," in *Okinawaken Shi*, vol. 7 (Tokyo: Sentoraru Insatsujo, 1974), 423–55; and Mitsugu Sakihara, "The History of Okinawa," in *Uchinananchu: A History of Okinawans in Hawaii* (Honolulu: University of Hawai'i Press, 1981), 14.

23. Nomura Koya, "Colonialism and Nationalism: The View from Okinawa" in *Okinawan Diaspora*, ed. Ronald Nakasone (Honolulu: University of Hawai'i Press), 111.

24. George Feifer, *The Battle of Okinawa: The Blood and the Bomb* (New York: First Lyons Press, 2001), xi.

25. Masaie Ishihara, "War Experiences of the People of Okinawa and the Development of the Okinawan Philosophy of Peace" (paper presented at the International Conference on The Politics of Remembering the Asia/Pacific War, East–West Center, in Honolulu, Hawai'i, September 7–9, 1995). The paper cited here is an expanded and revised version of "The Memories of War and the Role of Okinawa in the Promotion of World Peace."

26. Masahide Ota, "Re-examining the History of the Battle of Okinawa," in *Okinawa: Cold War Island*, ed. Chalmers Johnson (Cardiff, Calif.: Japanese Policy Research Institute, 1999), 30.

27. Ibid.

28. As a member of the Okinawa Kenjinkai of San Francisco, I have heard stories of forced suicides and other Japanese military atrocities against Okinawan civilians here in the Bay Area. Most of the members of the Okinawan Kenjinkai are Okinawan women who immigrated to the United States after World War II as wives of U.S. military personnel. Of these members, a large portion experienced the Battle of Okinawa. Despite these accounts and the general consensus of researchers that the Japanese Imperial Army "forced and steered" Okinawan civilians to commit mass suicides, the Japanese Ministry of Education in 2007 instructed high-school textbook publishers to remove references to those suicides from textbooks to be used in 2008. The move by the Ministry of Education sparked a large public uprising by Okinawans, which was highlighted by a protest rally that drew 110,000 people in Okinawa. For a reference in English, refer to "Military 'Forced' Okinawan Mass Suicides: Expert Defies Ministry to Go Public

with Criticism of Textbook Revisionists," *The Japan Times Online*, November 28, 2007, http://search.japantimes.co.jp/cgi-bin/nn20071128a5.html.

29. Ota Masahide, "The U.S. Occupation of Okinawa and Postwar Reforms in Japan Proper," in *Democratizing Japan: The Allied Occupation*, ed. Robert E. Ward and Sakamoto Yoshikazu (Honolulu: University of Hawai'i Press, 1987), 285.

30. Ibid., 289.

31. Koji Taira, "Troubled National Identity: Okinawa," in *Japan's Minorities: The Illusion of Homogeneity*, ed. Michael Weiner (London: Routledge, 1997), 160.

32. Quoted in Michael Molasky and Steve Rabson, *Southern Exposure: Modern Japanese Literature from Okinawa* (Honolulu: University of Hawai'i Press, 2000), 94.

33. The Price Report did not offer a specific formula to determine lump-sum amounts. Instead, it criticized the U.S. military's method of land assessment based on a comparable sales approach as unrealistic because agricultural land was usually kept within family ownership and seldom sold in Okinawa. A somewhat vague alternative method was presented: "It is the view of the subcommittee that in arriving at compensation for land best suited for agricultural production, the United States should give predominate consideration to current agricultural productivity and income data relating to similar lands now in agricultural use in Okinawa." The Okinawan proposal was for annual rental of $8,263,178 for forty thousand acres of land used by the U.S. military plus $14,363,103 as payment for "outstanding claims for destruction of land and property and for incidental expenses and losses incurred as a result of land acquisitions." The Price Report concluded that, under the Okinawan proposal, the market value of the fee title to the property, as estimated by the army, would be paid out in a little over two years as rental payments and other claims. Armed Services Committee, "Report of a Special Subcommittee of the Armed Services Committee, House of Representatives, Following an Inspection Tour, October 14 to November 23, 1955" 84th Congress (Washington, D.C.: U.S. Government Printing Office, 1956), 7651–67.

34. Department of State, Office of Intelligence Research, "US Administration of the Ryukyus Enters a Critical Period," Intelligence Report No. 7366, October 26, 1956.

35. Armed Services Committee, "Report of a Special Subcommittee."

36. Michael Molasky, *The American Occupation of Japan and Okinawa: Literature and Memory* (New York: Routledge), 92.

37. Ibid., 97.

38. Ibid., 97.

39. Ibid., 98.

40. Akio Watanabe, *The Okinawa Problem: A Chapter in Japan–U.S. Relations* (Melbourne, Australia: Melbourne University Press, 1970), 66.

41. Ibid.

42. Ibid., 65.

43. From an unpublished list compiled by Suzuyo Takazato and Harumi Miyagi (n.p., February 1, 1996).

44. Okinawa-shi Heiwa Bunka Shinkoka (Peace Culture Promotion Section of Okinawa City Offices), ed., *Rokku to koza* (Rock and Koza) (Okinawa: Kobundo Insatsu Kabushiki Kaisha, 1994), 167.

45. Molasky, *The American Occupation of Japan and Okinawa*, 55–56.

46. Quoted in Molasky, *The American Occupation of Japan and Okinawa*, 59.

47. My choice of "uprising," rather than "revolt" or "rebellion," is mainly based on aesthetics. "Uprising" connotes the downtrodden standing up against oppression and seems to fit the Chinese characters that are contained in *hoki*, which consists of *ho*, the character for bees or wasps, and *ki*, the character for awakening, rising, and beginning.

48. Aniya, "Koza Minshu (Koza peoples)," 187.

49. Herbert J. Gans, "Urban Riots: Violence and Social Change," *Proceedings of the Academy of Political Science* 29, no. 1 (1968): 42.

50. Robert Blauner, "Internal Colonization and Ghetto Revolt," *Social Problems* 16, no. 4 (1969): 399.

51. Ibid., 395–96.

52. Ibid., 54.

53. Takamine, *Shirarezaru* (Unknown truth about Okinawa), 203.

54. Okinawa-shi Heiwa Bunka Shinkoka (Peace Culture Promotion Section of Okinawa City Offices), ed., *Rokku to koza* (Rock and Koza), 54.

55. Besides the Bush Masters, there were other black groups existing throughout Okinawa such as Black Hawk, Son of Malcolm X, Maw Maw, Afro-American Society, People's Foundation, and Zulu.

56. Takamine, *Shirarezaru* (Unknown truth about Okinawa), 206.

57. Ibid., 209.

58. Ibid., 203.

59. Public Safety Department Records of the Operations Division of U.S. Civil Administration of the Ryukyu Islands, "Negro Personnel Reportedly Desiring to Take Over Koza City, Okinawa." Record Group 260: Records of the United States Occupation Headquarters World War II, National Archives and Records Administration. Box No. 20 of HCRI-PS, Folder 6. Copy obtained from the Okinawa Prefectural Archives in Okinawa, Japan, on November 25, 2009.

60. Ibid., 217–18.

61. Ibid., 219–20.

62. Ibid., 162.

63. Okinawa-shi Heiwa Bunka Shinko (Peace Culture Promotion Section of Okinawa City Offices), ed., *Shashinga toraeta* (Koza people, streets, and events), 63.

64. From photo in Ibid., 66.

65. *The Black Panther*, January 4, 1969, http://www.etext.org/Politics/MIM/bpp/bpp040169_8c.htm (accessed December 8, 2006; site now discontinued).

66. Andrew Hsiao, "100 Years of Hell-Raising: The Hidden History of Asian American Activism in New York City," *The Village Voice*, June 23, 1998, http://www.villagevoice.com/news/9825,hsiao,226,1.html (accessed May 30, 2008).

67. "Implications of the U.S.–Japan Security Treaty," prepared by members of Asian Americans for Action, circa 1970.

68. "Okinawa: A People's Struggle," *Gidra*, April 1971.

69. "JACL and the US-Japan Security Pact," *Gidra*, June–July 1970.

70. "Okinawa Kaiho," *Gidra*, May 1972.

71. These descriptions have been cultivated and promulgated in the writings of eighteenth- and nineteenth-century Western explorers who visited Okinawa, by Hollywood movies such as *The Teahouse of the August Moon* (1956) and *The Karate Kid, Part II* (1984), and by books such as *Okinawa Program: How the World's Longest-Lived People Achieve Everlasting Health—And How You Can Too* (2001).

72. Perhaps not directly linked to Okinawa, but nonetheless a part of "the sea of discontent," was a simultaneous transpacific movement by island people who were similarly displaced, discriminated against, and disaffected. In 1971, a group of immigrant Cook Islanders, Samoans, Tongans, and other Pacific Islanders in Aotearoa, New Zealand, founded the Polynesian Panther Movement (PPM). Many of its members were university students when they joined, and most had grown up in inner-city Auckland. Following World War II, emigration from Pacific islands to New Zealand increased, reaching a peak in the 1960s and early 1970s. The New Zealand government encouraged this immigration as the Pacific migrant workers provided the necessary labor for the country's expanding industries.

The PPM channeled the anger and frustrations of the Polynesian youth in Auckland toward promoting solidarity with the indigenous Māori liberation struggle, expressing positive views of Pacific Islander identities, and working for fundamental, radical change. The PPM published its own newspaper, set up programs to serve the community, and organized and participated in political demonstrations. See Melani Anae, ed., *Polynesian Panthers: The Crucible Years 1971–74* (Auckland, New Zealand: Reed Publishing, Ltd., 2006), 21–58.

6

South Korean Movements against Militarized Sexual Labor

Katharine H. S. Moon

As the twentieth century draws to a close, South Korean survivors of Japanese military sexual slavery (the Japanese "comfort system," or *chŏngsindae*) and activists on their behalf have been noted as some of the most persuasive and omnipresent advocates of women's human rights at international meetings and conferences. Within South Korea, graphic accounts of sexual brutality in wartime have become household news. In 1992, a television drama series, *Eye of the Dawn*, which depicted Korean resistance to Japanese colonial rule, not only included portraits of young women and girls being forcibly rounded up for sexual use in battlefronts, but also made the story's heroine a *chŏngsindae* survivor. She became a spy against the Japanese and therefore a nationalist and patriot. Globally, the *chŏngsindae* issue, as a political struggle regarding women's sex work, is probably the first to receive so much widespread publicity since the international (mostly Western) debates and policy measures ensuing from the scare of white slavery in the late-nineteenth and early twentieth centuries. Numerous academic, literary, and other works on the issue have been rolling hot off the presses,[1] and even women's fashion magazines have been reporting periodically on this newly unearthed history.[2]

This is not to say that the *chŏngsindae* movement (CM) is a success story pure and simple; it is not. Its major demands—official reparation and apology to survivors—still have not been met by the Japanese government, and such demands generally were not supported by the South Korean government.[3] Yet, in terms of raising awareness, presenting formal petitions to governments and international institutions, building coalitions, and obtaining media coverage, the CM has achieved enormous visibility within just a few years.

The CM, however, is not the first women's movement in South Korea to protest and redress sexual exploitation and abuse of Korean women by foreign men. In the 1970s, Korean women activists, some of whom are now fighting for the *chŏngsindae* survivors, protested vehemently against the Japanese government and Japanese society's participation in *kisaeng* tourism (sex tourism) in Korea.[4] Also, since the mid-1980s, a group of Korean women and men have sought to recognize and publicize the plight of U.S. military camptown (*kijich'on*) prostitutes as victims of debt bondage and objects of foreign domination. Yet, these movements never generated or received the kind of public recognition and support, both domestic and international, that the CM has garnered.

The CM and the *kijich'on* movement (KM) originally began together as part of a larger Asian women's human rights movement against the sexual exploitation of women. Professor Yun Chong Ok's groundbreaking research on former *chŏngsindae* women was first publicly presented at the International Seminar on Women and Tourism (held in Seoul and on Cheju Island in April 1988). There, a *kijich'on* woman gave her own testimony about her ordeals as a sex worker. The stated intent of the conference organizers and participants was to challenge traditional conceptions of women's chastity and the socioeconomic conditions that foster the sexual abuse of women's bodies and labor. Representatives from the Philippines, the United States, Canada, England, Japan, Taiwan, Thailand, and South Korea were present. The conference participants aimed to share information on related issues and problems from different parts of the world, especially Asia, to forge women's solidarity as activists and criticize the role of governments and businesses in fostering the trade in women's sex work.[5]

Additionally, at the outset of the conference, the leaders had invited Yu Pok Nim and Faye Moon, founders of a counseling center for camptown sex workers, My Sister's Place, to join forces and support the CM as a cause against militarism and the violation of women's human rights. On the surface, the founders of both movements shared values and concerns that might have made them likely alliance partners in a larger women's movement: both were opposed to the sexual exploitation and abuse of women and were motivated by their nationalism and Christian sensibilities. However, the two were unable to forge a real partnership and went their separate ways, as will be discussed later.

This chapter compares the ideology, leadership, and organization of the two movements in the context of changing civil society in South Korea since the late 1980s in order to account for what Chunghee Sarah Soh characterizes as the CM's "remarkable success in making the 'military comfort women' problem a universal moral issue of women's human rights"[6] and the KM's relatively localized and less-recognized status. The two movements are appropriate for comparative analysis because of (1) the violence, social stigma, and alienation inflicted on both groups of women by foreign troops and Korean society (Koreans have even used the same euphemism—*wianbu*, or "comfort women"—to identify them); (2) the common activist environment and leadership from which they took root; (3) the antiforeign nationalism they espouse; and (4) the impact each has had on the other.

The *Chŏngsindae* Movement (CM) and the *Kijich'on* Movement (KM)

The CM has generally refused to acknowledge the plight of U.S. camptown prostitutes as being parallel to that of *chŏngsindae* survivors, based on the view that the *kijich'on* women voluntarily serviced soldiers whereas the latter did not. However, I argue that there are significant similarities. First, the lasting effects of such sexual labor in terms of bodily damage, social alienation, loss of dignity, shame, and loneliness resonate in both groups of women. Chong Chin Song, professor of sociology and leader of the Korean Council for the Women Drafted for Military Sexual Slavery by Japan (hereafter the Korean Council), describes the personal consequences of *chŏngsindae* life that are common for the survivors: After having returned to Korea,

> they bore guilty consciences, simply because of the knowledge that they had been prostitutes. They suffered from the prejudice and discrimination of their relatives and friends. Many still had venereal disease or from time to time suffered its recurrence . . . Many women subsequently found that they were barren, and many still suffer from . . . womb infections, high blood pressure, stomach trouble, heart trouble, nervous breakdowns, mental illness and so on. The psychological aftermath is far more serious that the

breakdowns or mental disorders . . . haunted by delusions of persecution, shame and inferiority. They tend to retain a distrust and hatred of men . . . People around the women tend to despise them.[7]

The previous statement can be applied verbatim to the plight of U.S. camptown women. Most women, especially of the older generations, suffer from a severe sense of pariah status; they rarely venture into what they call "normal" Korean society (outside the camptowns) and often feel paranoid that others are condemning them. Most hide their *kijich'on* lives from their own families, though most send money home. When they do try to return to their families, they are more often than not rejected. Kim Yang Hyang, in the documentary film *The Women Outside*, recounts her rejection by family members. When she went back to her hometown after having worked in camptown bars, one of her cousins yelled at her, "Don't come around our place."[8] Those with Amerasian offspring also suffer the indignities of racism and ethnocentrism directed at their children from the general Korean population. The children are stigmatized and harassed in schools, particularly those of African American–Korean parentage. In 1992, I met "Sŏnha's Mom" (age thirty-five) and her sister (age thirty) in Anjŏngni, the camptown next to Camp Humphreys. Both were offspring of a Korean woman (from the Korean War era) and two different African American men. Their mother had been a camptown prostitute, as they themselves were. They tried to hide their "secrets" from their (Korean) extended family. Though their skin color and facial features revealed their African American parentage, they were fully Korean in speech, mannerisms, and customs. Yet, they rarely ventured outside the shantytown of Anjŏngni into the larger Korean society.[9]

Many have also suffered from bouts of depression, sexually transmitted diseases (STDs), and unwanted pregnancies. Although the Korean government systematically has established health clinics in or near most major U.S. camptowns (run by the Ministry of Health and Social Affairs) since the early 1970s, the clinics only check and treat women for STDs, not for general health.[10] When the women confront health problems, they are often too poor to get proper medical treatment. Mental health problems seem to be the most difficult for women to overcome. In addition to the social stigma and alienation, many women struggle with physical and emotional abuse by their bar owners, managers, or pimps and their American customers. "Bakery Auntie," who was sixty-seven when I met her in 1992 at My Sister's Place, the counseling and advocacy center in Uijŏngbu, remained continuously distrustful of and nervous around other people. She had had a history of severe physical and psychological abuse by her pimps during her several decades as a *kijich'on* prostitute and had difficulty relating to other people without devaluing herself; one of her greatest fears was that she might die alone. The most extreme cases of violence perpetrated on *kijich'on* women by managers and pimps or U.S. soldiers have resulted in the death of the women; the case of Yun Kŭmi, who had been brutally beaten, mutilated, and murdered by Private Kenneth Markle, has been the most widely published one in recent years.[11]

In some cases, the *chŏngsindae* woman and the *kijich'on* woman might be the very same person. Staff at My Sister's Place noted that a few of the elderly prostitutes they had gotten to know revealed information about Japan in wartime that regular civilians would not be familiar with. Bakery Auntie is one such person: she had lived in different parts of Japan during the war and had "told stories" to the staff about the Japanese. Given that they had already become "fallen women" in their own eyes, feared that their past might be uncovered, and were poor and unmarriageable upon return to Korea, it is not an unlikely possibility that some former *chŏngsindae* women fell into sexual labor for the U.S. military.

There are other significant parallels. Both groups of women come from the lower classes and were uneducated or undereducated; among the *kijich'on* women of the 1950s to the 1970s, those with junior–high school degrees were considered highly educated. Chungmoo Choi points out that "many of the *chŏngsindae* were chosen in order to protect their brothers and fathers from being conscripted into the Japanese military or to keep their families from losing tenant rights."[12] Similarly, accounts abound of camptown women working in the bars in order to support impoverished families, ailing parents, and the university fees of their siblings.[13] In both groups of women, poverty and low-class status, lack of education, and their youth (teens to early twenties) added to their vulnerability of being "recruited" and deceived by flesh traffickers.

The key difference in terms of entry into sexual labor between the two groups is that many *chŏngsindae* women routinely were rounded up and systematically kidnapped into military prostitution whereas *kijich'on* women, as a collective, were not. However, some camptown women were kidnapped by common criminals, and other forms of coercive procurement, such as fraudulent promises by traffickers for well-paying jobs and training, applied to both groups of women. In both the *chŏngsindae* and *kijich'on* systems, rape was often used as a way to "initiate" women into sexual labor.

Furthermore, *kijich'on* women have not been as mobile or "free" as people commonly have assumed. They are beholden to their club owner, manager, or pimp through what human rights activists call the "debt bondage system," whereby they accrue debts to their clubs and must work to pay them off before they can leave. The system is premised on exploitation because club owners will often rent a room and purchase furniture, clothing, cosmetics, and music systems—all deemed necessary for the woman to attract soldiers—before the new woman even arrives at the club but charge women with a "referral fee" for putting her into a new bar and will expect her to pay.[14] In most cases, the women do not have the funds and will borrow from the new employer, who will, in turn, raise her debts. If a woman tries to leave the club without having paid the debt, the owner will send out thugs, "slicky boys,"[15] to bring her back. In 1988, *Mal Magazine* reported that, on average, the sex workers' club debts ranged between one and four million won (US$1,462 and $5,847, respectively, based on 1988 rates).[16]

In some of the older *kijich'on* housing compounds for the camptown women, men or women were placed at the exits to monitor the women's movements. In some of these rooms, as those I had seen in Songsan, "pimp holes" had been cut out of walls in the prostitutes' rooms so that a "monitor" could make sure that the club received payment from the soldier for the sex he received and, simultaneously, that the women were not making plans to escape. Soh points out that "police ordinances of imperial Japan permitted licensed prostitutes the freedom to cease their trade even if the proprietor did not countersign their applications."[17] Ironically, such "freedom" has not applied to the *kijich'on* women living in a sovereign country. For decades, the Korean National Police helped sustain and legitimate U.S. soldier-oriented prostitution by usually taking the side of the club owner when women have tried to run away.[18]

People who learn about the *chŏngsindae* system often are appalled by the level of organization and bureaucratic paperwork that helped regulate the sexual behavior of Japanese soldiers and the female sex slaves. But it is imperative to understand that the *kijich'on* system is highly regulated and sustained by official policies and practices of the U.S. military and the Korean government. Although *kijich'on* women work out of private businesses, all such nightclubs, bars, and tea houses catering to U.S. military personnel must be licensed by the Korea Special Tourist Association, which has been an arm of the Korean government. Moreover, in order to work in the bars, a woman must register her name, address, and other vital information with the local police and the local STD clinic. She must go to the clinic, operated by the Ministry of Health and Social Affairs, for regular gynecological and blood examinations in order to keep her STD card valid. The card in turn serves as a work permit. The U.S. military also has kept extensive files on *kijich'on* bar workers as a way to "track" the "source" of STDs that their men may contract.[19] Some U.S. military commands in the 1950s and 1960s even conducted their own gynecological checks on prostitutes as a way to check the spread of venereal disease (VD). In the 1970s, some commands provided medical supplies to Korean VD clinics to assist in the regulation of sex workers.[20]

Not only are there striking parallels in the exploitation and suffering experienced by both groups of women, but also both social movements grew out of the leaders' Christian concern for these women who were physically, emotionally, and socially compromised. The 1988 International Seminar on Women and Tourism was organized by Korea Church Women United, an umbrella organization for Christian women activists, which has supported both movements. Yu Pok Nim and Faye Moon, founders of My Sister's Place, began their outreach work in the U.S. camptowns as part of their missionary work. Yu had studied theology at a Korean seminary and Moon, the wife of dissident activist Rev. Moon Dong Hwan, had a background in social work and counseling. Both women came to understand the lives of *kijich'on* sex workers by talking to them in the VD clinics and trying to befriend them on a casual basis. They tried to offer Bible study classes as well. The CM organizers also have had coalitional ties to women's church groups. In May 1988, women's organizations from seven different denominations in Korea wrote a protest letter to KQED TV, a station catering to Korean immigrants in Los Angeles, against its misinformed characterization of Korean "comfort women" in one of their programs. They claimed their position not only as "proud daughters of the Korean nation" but also as "Christian women who proclaim Jesus Christ as our savior."[21]

The early leaders of both movements shared ideological views as well, namely, that patriarchy, imperialism, and militarism were responsible for creating systems of militarized sex work. As Prof. Yun Chŏng Ok argued,

"So long as there is no change in the sexual consciousness both of men, who do not realise that they are being controlled by using women's sex, or of women, who have internalised the 'ideal of chastity' imposed upon them, there will be no end to the danger of sex being used again as an expedient means of control."[22] Shin Hei Soo, another prominent leader of the CM, argued in her 1991 Ph.D. dissertation that Korea's economic "miracle" developed in tandem with and partly owing to the sex industry in which Korean businesses and government encouraged male employees to indulge. She viewed this sociological phenomenon as a function of South Korea's dependent status in the world economy.[23] Some leaders of the KM also have blamed U.S. imperialism and U.S.-led capitalism for the plight and abuse of the *kijich'on* women. In their view, South Korea is a colony of the United States, and the plight of the women represents the oppressed plight of the Korean people.[24]

The feminism and antimilitarism of the leaders of both groups were also linked to their understanding of nationalism—that the suffering and abuse inflicted on Korean women by foreigners is a manifestation of Korea's weakness or lack of sovereignty. Nationalism serves as the CM's key instrument of mobilization and publicity inside Korea. In terms of organizational alliances, the Korean Association of Pacific War Victims and Bereaved Families, a group specifically seeking personal war damages and official Japanese accountability, increasingly has become a main coalition partner. It is not a self-identified human rights organization and is not mobilized for the specific purpose of promoting women's rights and issues.

Moreover, the CM leaders themselves share the anti-Japanese resentment harbored by many other Koreans. In spring 1992, when I visited the office of the Korean Council, one of the board members, a longtime Christian activist, exclaimed in Korean, "Do you know what I pray for each day? That Japan be destroyed!" The two founders and main leaders of the movement, Yun Chong Ok and Yi Hyo Chae, come from a generation that experienced the colonial oppressions of the past, and they are similar in age to most *chŏngsindae* survivors. Yi and Yun have both pointed out that they could have been victims, too, generating empathy for the survivors and universalizing these women's experiences as a victimization that could have happened to an entire generation of Korean women. Yi has stated unequivocally that the *chŏngsindae* system "can only be defined as a crime of genocide against the Korean people."[25] In this light, the survivors represent not only the degradation of the Korean people but also the collective wish to reclaim national sovereignty and integrity.

In one of their first declarations on the Korean government's responsibility in this matter, the CM's leaders in May 1990 questioned the rationale for then-President Roh Tae Woo's visit to Japan scheduled for later that month and charged him with the task of getting the movement's demands met. In this public letter, the cosigners framed their grievance and call for redress in purely nationalistic terms, reminding readers of Japan's past imperialistic abuses in Korea and its current "unprincipled foreign policy behavior." Although the purpose of the statement was to pressure the Korean leader to become an advocate for the former victims, the reference to the *chŏngsindae* survivors appears only toward the end of the document, after the grievances about colonial rule, lack of real Korean sovereignty, and discrimination against Korean minorities living in Japan.[26]

Similarly, some leaders in the KM have viewed the historical presence of foreign troops as an affront to Korean sovereignty and therefore have opposed the permanent presence of U.S. forces. They have criticized the Status of Forces Agreement between the two countries as an unequal treaty and have advocated revisions to enable the South Korean government to exercise more sovereignty, especially in terms of legal jurisdiction over crimes committed by U.S. military personnel (toward women) on Korean soil. After the brutal murder of Yun Kŭmi, the KM helped establish the National Campaign for the Eradication of Crimes by U.S. Troops in Korea in 1993. In fact, a former leading staff member at My Sister's Place became one of the founding leaders of this organization. Despite these commonalities, what began with the possibility of cooperation and mutual support on behalf of women's dignity, welfare, and governmental accountability quickly soured. Shortly after the initial meetings to forge the CM, Yu and Moon broke away from the CM leaders because the latter were generally not willing to accept *kijich'on* women's needs and interests as legitimate.[27] Why were the two groups unable to become coalitional partners?

Differences in Ideology, Leadership, and Organization

The parting ways reflects significant ideological differences regarding sexual norms, nationalism, and political activism between the two groups. First, despite Yun Chong Ok's call in the starting phase of the CM for Koreans to "completely change the social conceptions of women's sexuality" in order to stop the marginalization of "fallen women," the CM retained a traditional understanding of acceptable female sexual behavior. Many of the leaders and survivors emphasized that the former "comfort women" were innocent victims whereas *kijich'on* women were not. *Chŏngsindae* survivors were insistent that their cause not be linked to that of *kijich'on* women,[28] emphasizing that their identities as sex slaves were not to be equated with those of "willing whores." In the CM's view, the *chŏngsindae* survivors represent in body and mind the most humiliating, degrading, and painful colonial oppressions that were *imposed* on Korean people, not voluntary adventures into the world of sex. On the other hand, the KM leaders have viewed the situation of the majority of *kijich'on* women as the outcome of economic coercion (in addition to physical coercion for some) and therefore not a matter of exercising one's own free will. Yu Pong Nim told me in a conversation in the winter of 1991 that when she addresses audiences in order to raise their awareness of *kijich'on* women's lives, she poses out loud, "Did any of you ever dream you would become a *kijich'on* prostitute when you were little? Do you think the *kijich'on* women did?"[29] The inability to agree on who constitutes a rightful victim of militarized sexual abuse was the major cause of the KM leaders' initial dissociation with the CM.

This difference might also pose other practical problems for the camptown sex workers themselves. If there are *chŏngsindae* survivors who also are *kijich'on* survivors, they would not be in a position to step forth and demand justice and compensation for the first identity and existence because the second would compromise their moral legitimacy. The conflict over who constitutes a "legitimate victim," then, involves a conflict over identities. The public discourse on the *chŏngsindae* has tended to identify all the victims and survivors as a group, including non-Koreans. It has emphasized their innocence and enslaved status, although there are differences among them, including time spent in bondage, the value that the Japanese placed on their race or ethnicity, and their exposure to the dangers of battle. But because their suffering was so great both during and after the war and because one cannot and should not quantify the amount of suffering from rape and abuse in order to legitimate people's claim to moral and legal redress, those who seek accountability focus on the institutions and authorities that created and supported the *chŏngsindae* as a system. But in regard to the camptown sex workers, the common inclination is to overlook or ignore the system of sexual labor, debt bondage, violence, and human degradation and rather focus on the question of the camptown woman's "choice." I would argue here that although there are women who walked into the camptowns without having been kidnapped or otherwise physically coerced, and also those who were sexually curious about the goings-on with American soldiers, this does not mean that they agreed to debt bondage, beatings, and murder. Regardless of the individual causes of entry into sexual labor, those who oversee and regulate the system must be held morally and legally accountable for violating basic human rights.

Nationalism provides another source of conflict. The CM takes a traditional anticolonial stance. Its goal is to reveal and right the wrongs of the past. Its moral basis stems from victimization by an aggressor and the fact that the entire nation, not only a portion of the population, had been subjugated. Social movement theorists note that such movements are constructed actively by their leaders, participants, and target groups through communication, interaction with countergroups, and consciousness raising.[30] They particularly emphasize the importance of the social and ideological context in which the "frame alignment"[31] of social movements takes place, particularly the "nature of the belief system held by potential participants" and the "extent to which the framing effort resonates within the 'life world' of potential participants."[32] In this light, the CM's appeal to nationalism within South Korea rather than women's human rights makes sense. With the newly found impetus for democratization coming only in the late 1980s and the first civilian president in over thirty years assuming office in 1993—about the same time that the CM was picking up speed—South Korean society lacked the legal, institutional, and discursive infrastructure to address human rights in general and women's human rights in particular. Moreover, the kind of human rights violations that Koreans were familiar with were those involving state repression of basic civil liberties and the imprisonment or torture of dissidents. But all Koreans, young and old, were familiar with the history of Japanese colonialism. When I asked a leader of the CM in 1992 why the causes of the *chŏngsindae* women and *kijich'on* women were not being linked and a larger women's human rights movement was not being forged, she candidly replied that there was not "enough anti-Americanism" to fuel such a joint movement, whereas for the former alone there was enough "anti-Japanism."[33]

Relatedly, there is a significant difference in the symbolic value of the two groups of women. Whereas *chŏngsindae* women symbolize the loss of Korean sovereignty and therefore a nation's powerlessness, the *kijich'on* women represent active attempts by the Korean government since the end of the Korean War to protect its national security by helping to institutionalize and regulate *kijich'on* prostitution.³⁴ If the moral and legal burden of the *chŏngsindae* system falls on the Japanese people and government, then the moral and legal burden of the *kijich'on* system falls on Koreans, the Korean government, and the U.S. military.

Owing partly to these differences, the KM's understanding of nationalism is more complicated. For the KM leaders and staffers, it is not only a foreign government (or, in this case, military) that serves as the oppressor of women but also that Korean government, especially the former military regimes, that sought U.S. protection and tutelage. Whereas the CM's criticism of the Korean government has been limited to its relative inaction on their behalf, the *kijich'on* activists have characterized the Korean government as a pimp because it has facilitated the sale of women to U.S. soldier–clients who historically have brought with them valuable foreign exchange and military commitment. Antigovernment sentiments have been part and parcel of the KM's version of nationalism. Moreover, whereas anti-Americanism rose since the Kwangju Massacre of 1980 (and the belief by many Koreans that the United States allowed it to happen) and the radicalization of the student movement in that decade, the majority of Koreans still support the maintenance of U.S. forces, especially in light of the nuclear weapons development North Korea has undertaken in the 1990s. Although it is difficult to quantify how much antiforeign sentiment is required for a nationalist movement to pick up speed, it seems that the KM faces a shortage in that area.

The difference between the two movements in terms of nationalist ideology and political views in general also is a result of the different activist careers of the two movement's leaders. The CM leaders generally are middle aged or older; the two cofounders, Yun Chong Ok and Lee Hyo Chae, are both in their seventies. Many of the CM leaders can be characterized as middle class and moderate in political views as compared to the KM leaders. They tend to be academics, as Yun and Lee have been (at the elite women's university, Ewha, in Seoul) as well as two other leaders, Shin Hei Soo and Chong Chin Song. For the most part, the CM leaders were not outspoken political activists during the heated antigovernment protest era of the 1980s. In contrast, almost all of the early leaders of the KM came of political age through their participation in the street protests and battles with the police during the 1980s. Most were in their late teens or early twenties when they became involved and still maintain close affiliation with college students, who regularly come to serve as teachers and assistants at the *kijich'on* counseling centers. Several of them have served time in prison for their antigovernment beliefs and actions. In general, they can be characterized as more militant and radical in political ideology and activism than their counterparts in the CM. Moreover, their socioeconomic status is more diverse; they come from less recognized colleges and universities, as well as elite institutions like Ewha, whereas Ewha graduates have occupied a critical mass of the *chŏngsindae* leadership since the beginning. One of the most outspoken *kijich'on* activists is Kim Yon Ja, a former sex worker and madam of twenty-five years, whereas no *chŏngsindae* survivor has risen to leadership status in the CM. These differences help explain the lack of cooperation between the two movements' leadership and the difficulty of the KM in gaining general public support.

Last, the difference in the two movements' organizational purpose and activities helps account for the difference in the visibility and publicization between the two causes. The CM began as a movement to document past abuses and demand legal and historical redress, through education, on behalf of the survivors, whereas the KM began as an effort to aid and counsel sex workers. Accordingly, one of the first organizational actions that the CM leaders took was to establish a research committee in Seoul, initially under the auspices of the Church and Society Committee of Korea Church Women United (July 1988) and then independently as the Research Committee on the Chŏngsindae (July 1990).[35] In comparison, the KM organizers rented a small room in the shantytown of Songsan in Uijŏngbu (home of the U.S. I Corps Group) and opened their doors to any *kijich'on* woman seeking shelter, companionship, a meal, or English lessons. They called this gathering "My Sister's Place." These organizational choices make sense given that the CM began as a movement in search of victims and evidence of abuse and that the KM faced a situation where tens of thousands of women visibly walked the streets, used their broken English to hustle drinks, and often suffered physical beatings by their bar owners and clients. Digging out information and past victims was crucial to the survival of the CM, while offering physical and emotional aid to those in need was immediately relevant to the KM.

The academic aspect of the CM—research and documentation—has become one of its biggest assets because it has offered credibility to the movement's claims and helped outsiders to evaluate facts as well as the movement's ideological and emotional motivations. Moreover, the research has helped generate interest among academics, both domestically and internationally, to conduct their own research about Japan's World War II past.[36] Their findings in turn have helped strengthen the cause of the CM. In comparison, the KM has been weak in the area of research and documentation. Besides the different emphasis in mission—aiding sex workers in their current situation—the *kijich'on* activists and civilian researchers in general (even if they are U.S. citizens) lack access to policy papers, reports, and other documents in the U.S. military establishment's possession that might offer proof of institutional and governmental responsibility for some aspects of the military prostitution system in Korea. Without documentation, it is difficult to prove who is responsible for what kinds of abusive or exploitive outcomes in these women's lives and therefore who could be held legally, financially, and morally accountable.

Contemporary Developments in Civil Society

Scholarship on civil society in South Korea highlights the proliferation of interest groups and civic movements and the decline of leftist-oriented and militant activism since the late 1980s.[37] These developments apply to the women's movement as well.

First, women's issues and organization have proliferated in the last decade—growing beyond the two recurring issues that have been the focus since the 1970s, labor rights and revision of the Family Law—to include, among others, nondiscrimination in college entrance examinations, domestic violence, equal employment opportunities, ratification of the United Nations (UN) Convention on the Elimination of Discrimination against Women, and the changing of citizenship requirements from patrilineage to bilineage. Within the KM itself, activists have splintered off to create new groups, owing to leadership conflicts, different perceptions of the problem, and the fact that it is relatively easy to start a civic group in the 1990s as compared to the years under authoritarianism. Although Yu Pong Nim and Faye Moon were the only activists to set up a counseling center and begin to educate the larger population about *kijich'on* life back in 1986, numerous local churches and nongovernmental organizations (NGOs) have since begun to minister to the women, often in conflict with secular groups. For some, "saving" these women from sin is key; for others, kicking U.S. troops out of Korea is the only real solution. Still others tend to the needs of Amerasian children in the camptowns. There is dissension here as well, with some believing that what is best for the children is to get them adopted by Americans or Europeans (so that they can leave behind the social stigma they face in Korea) and others believing that changing Korean mentality regarding race, sex, and class will ultimately be in the children's best interest. Saewoomtuh, another counseling and advocacy center, was formed after its founders were unable to reconcile differences over organizational leadership styles and goals with the heads of the original center in Tongduch'on, My Sister's Place. The CM, by contrast, has remained centralized and intact, with the Korean Council serving as the authority on and clearinghouse for movement activities. The lesson seems to be that while the democratization of civic movements introduces new civic actors into political life and helps generate different perspectives and possible solutions to particular social concerns, it creates problems for the development and growth of fledgling causes if it happens too early because consolidation of personnel, resources, and goals cannot occur.

Second, the decline of radical activism in Korea means that radical groups no longer have a powerful platform of protest and resistance and must increasingly go it alone or appeal to more mainstream organizations and audiences. The KM appears to be in this transitional state: in December 1996, movement leaders organized the first "cultural festival" around the *kijich'on* issue and invited musicians, documentary filmmakers, critics, and a diverse audience to the two-day affair. Given the general democratization in artistic and cultural life in the past decade, such programs might help advance the recognition of *kijich'on* issues more widely. The festival indeed attracted individuals who were not directly connected or concerned with the *kijich'on* issue but who walked away with increased awareness and sympathy for the movement.[38]

There is another aspect in the development of contemporary civil society that is less studied but is certain to influence significantly the success or failure of civic movements in the future: the international connection. The CM's early move to identify itself as a movement for women's human rights and lobby the UN and international NGOs to take up their cause is directly responsible for its successes. The Korean Council tirelessly persuaded the UN Commission on Human Rights to address the issue of war crimes and official Japanese reparation. The commission's 1996 *Report of the Special Rapporteur* unequivocally identified the *chŏngsindae* system as a war crime and a crime against humanity and echoed the council's demands for Japanese apology, compensation, and historical documentation.[39]

Elisabeth Friedman has noted that "women's human rights activists have come to recognize the power of [the] international human rights framework, which lends legitimacy to political demands, since it is already accepted by most governments and brings with it established protocols."[40] Charlotte Bunch, a longtime leader of the international women's human rights movement and director of the Center for Women's Global Leadership at Rutgers University, has stated that "the international pressure has made the Tokyo government come as far as it has."[41] I believe that without such international structures and discourse intent upon protecting and promoting women's human rights, the CM, despite its diligent organizing efforts and moral fervor, would have remained a national or regional movement for war reparations.

In contrast, the KM never inserted itself within the official UN machinery but relied mostly on those individuals and NGOs from abroad that expressed some interest in understanding and publicizing the issue. As a result, the international contacts and activities of the KM have remained mostly regional and under the purview of a loose coalition of antimilitarism activists. In addition, the KM lost a vital international partner in its cause after the 1992 closing of U.S. naval bases in the Philippines. Until then, Filipino women's groups had been some of the most active protesters against U.S. bases and militarized prostitution.

Conclusion

Not only have the CM and the KM found little room for cooperation, but, also, they have essentially lost the opportunity to promote an expanded understanding of human rights that incorporates issues around human trafficking and sexual exploitation and violence into the mainstream of the women's movement in Korea. The CM, as the more visible and internationally recognized organization, has in the short run overshadowed, rather than shed light on, the *kijich'on* problem. In February 1997, An Ilsun, activist and author of a recent novel on *kijich'on* life, stated, "There is hardly any interest in Korea regarding this *kijich'on* issue."[42] The staff members of Saewoomtuh regretfully stated that the CM has had no positive influence on the KM.[43] They pointed out that, for example, no official support from the CM had been expressed when the *kijich'on* women's advocates mobilized Koreans both in and outside the camptowns to protest the brutal murder of Yun Kŭmi in 1993.

In an article by Soh, she emphasized that Japanese "'ethnonationalism' . . . augur[s] ill for a pro-human rights verdict on the pending 'comfort women' lawsuits."[44] But it should be stressed here that South Koreans' own version of ethnonationalism, which emphasizes "innocence" (moral chastity) as a requirement for claiming women's human rights, also bodes ill for the promotion of pro–human rights ideology and institutional frameworks within their country. For an individual to keep alive the notion that she is not morally tainted because she did not willingly have sex with foreign soldiers and because she had been "innocent" about sex prior to *chŏngsindae* sex work may be psychologically empowering. However, the CM's and society's promotion of the cause based on the notion that *chŏngsindae* survivors can demand reparations, claim their honor, and command the respect of the nation because they were virgin victims of war crimes forges a tenuous ground for women's human rights. After all, social norms about the appropriate age (and marriage status) for sexual activity change. Moreover, the emphasis on sexual innocence sets too high a threshold for the public's understanding and advocacy of women's human rights by tending to count only the most egregious and extreme abuses as legitimate cases for redress. In turn, an exclusive, rather than inclusive, interpretation of human rights may develop. *Kijich'on* activists have been facing this challenge. They support the CM's goals and have full sympathy for the *chŏngsindae* "grandmothers" but cannot ride on the CM's coattails, since those very survivors and leaders dissociate themselves from the *kijich'on* people.

At a conference on "Men, Women, and War" held in March 1997 in Londonderry, Northern Ireland, I asked Professor Yun if the Korean Council has any plans for the future direction of the CM-*cum*-human rights movement if and when the Japanese government meets their demands. She replied, "Well, that's a difficult question"—and shook her head sideways. Understandably, the focus is on getting Japan to respond favorably. But there was no sense of what might or should come after. What comes after, though, is a pressing question, given the momentum of attention to women's human rights issues and the voicing, after generations of silence, of women's victimization through militarization. Ron Eyerman and Andrew Jamison note that the "cognitive praxis of social movements is an important source of new societal images and the transformation of societal identities."[45] The CM has indeed pried open the doors of opportunity for expanding and advancing new "societal images and identities" that can inform women's human rights; the loss would be in not building upon the movement's efforts and standing by for another few decades for the lives and cause of *kijich'on* women to be unearthed and shaped anew. We should not ask then why history repeats itself.

Notes

1. For example, Chungmoo Choi, ed., *The Comfort Women: Colonialism, War, and Sex*, a special issue of *positions: east asia cultures critique* 5, no. 1 (1997): 219–53; and Nora Okja Keller, *Comfort Woman* (New York: Viking-Penguin, 1997). See also Pyon Yongju, *Murmuring*, 16mm filmstrip, 98 min. (Seoul: Docu-Factory Vista, 1995); and Noriko Sekiguchi, *Sensô Daughters: Daughters of War*, video, 54 min. (New York: First Run Icarus, 1990).

2. See Catherine Durand, "Les ´femmes de réconfort[a] ont réussi a brisé le silence: prostituées de force pendant la guerre, niées par l'histoire officielle, elles ont témoigné devant le Tribunal international des crimes de guerre" (The "comfort women" have successfully broken the silence: prostituted by force during the war, denied by official history, they have given witness before an international war crimes court), *Marie Claire* (Paris), March 2001, 264–66.

3. The Report of the United Nations Special Rapporteur includes the official positions of the South and North Korean governments. The South Korean Ministry of Justice stated that it is very "difficult to determine whether the Government of Japan actually had a legal responsibility to compensate for crimes committed 50 years ago." This stance is in opposition to that of the Korean Council for the Women Drafted for Military Sexual Slavery by Japan (hereafter the Korean Council), the North Korean government, the Special Rapporteur, the International Commission of Jurists, and such nongovernmental organizations as International Education Development. See Radhika Coomaraswamy, *Report on the Mission to the Democratic People's Republic of Korea, the Republic of Korea, and Japan on the Issue of Military Sexual Slavery in Wartime: Addendum: Report of the Special Rapporteur on Violence against Women* (New York: UN Commission on Human Rights, Sub-Commission on Prevention of Discrimination and Protection of Minorities, Working Group on Contemporary Forms of Slavery, 1996).

4. Korea Church Women United (KCWU), *Kisaeng Tourism: A Nation-Wide Survey Report on Conditions in Four Areas: Seoul, Pusan, Cheju, Kyongju*, Research Issue Material, no. 3 (Seoul: KCWU, 1984).

5. See KCWU, *Women and Tourism, International Seminar Report* (Seoul: KCWU, 1988).

6. Chunghee Sarah Soh, "The Korean 'Comfort Women': Movement for Redress," *Asian Survey* 36, no. 12 (1996): 1238.

7. Keith Howard, ed., *True Stories of the Korean Comfort Women* (London: Cassell, 1995), 24.

8. J. T. Takagi and Hye Jung Park, *The Women Outside*, video, 60 min. (New York: Third World Newsreel, 1995). The subject of this documentary film is U.S.-Korea military prostitution.

9. These observations and those below of "Bakery Auntie" come from my field research conducted in Korea during 1991 and 1992.

10. See Katharine H. S. Moon, "The Role of Women in the Clean-Up Campaign: 'Personal Ambassadors'" and "The International Is Personal: Effects of the Clean-Up Campaign on Kijich'on Women," in *Sex among Allies: Military Prostitution in U.S.-Korea Relations* (New York: Columbia University Press, 1997), 84–103, 127–48.

11. *Rainbow Center Newsletter*, Flushing, N.Y., no. 3 (January 1994).

12. Chungmoo Choi, "Korean Women in a Culture of Inequality," in *Korea Briefing*, ed. Donald Clark (Boulder, Colo.: Westview Press, 1992), 104.

13. Moon, *Sex among Allies*, 17–47.

14. See Saundra Sturdevant and Brenda Stolzfus, ed., *Let the Good Times Roll: Prostitution and the U.S. Military in Asia* (New York: New Press, 1993) for the personal accounts of camptown life, including the debt system, by former U.S. camptown sex workers in Asia.

15. See Diana S. Lee and Grace Yoonkyung Lee, *Camp Arirang*, video, 28 min. (New York: Third World Newsreel, 1995), a documentary film on U.S.-Korea military prostitution.

16. *Mal Magazine* 26 (August 1988): 108.

17. Soh, "The Korean 'Comfort Women,'" 1238.

18. Moon, *Sex among Allies*, 14–47, 127–48.

19. Ibid., 127–48.

20. Ibid., 99–100.

21. Korean Council, "Protest Letter regarding KQED-TV's May 5, 1988, Depiction of the Chŏngsindae Issue in the Broadcast of *The World in War*" (in Korean), reprinted in *Chŏngsindae munje charyojip* (Resources on the chŏngsindae issue, I), ed. Korean Council (Seoul: Korean Council, 1991), 47.

22. George Hicks, *The Comfort Women: Japan's Brutal Regime of Enforced Prostitution in the Second World War* (New York: W.W. Norton & Co., 1994), 174.

23. Hei Soo Shin, "Women's Sexual Services and Economic Development: The Political Economy of the Entertainment Industry and South Korean Dependent Development" (Ph.D. dissertation, Rutgers University, 1991).

24. My Sister's Place, *Kijichon ui choguk* (The homeland of camptowns) (Tongduch'on, Korea: My Sister's Place, 1991), 4–6.

25. K. Connie Kang, "Bitter Page of History Koreatown Library Opens to Serve as Memorial to 'Comfort Women' Taken by Japan in WWII," *Los Angeles Times*, November 23, 1994, 1.

26. KCWU, Korean Women's Associations United, and Council of Representatives of Female University Students, *Statement: Women's Position on President Roh Tae Woo's Visit to Japan* (in Korean), Seoul, May 18, 1990, reprinted in *Chŏngsindae munje charyojip*, 48–49.

27. Yu Pok Nim, interview with the author, Tongduch'on, December 1991.

28. *Choson Daily News* reporter, interview with the author, Boston, July 1994.

29. Yu Pok Nim interview.

30. Bert Klandermans, "The Social Construction of Protest and Multiorganizational Fields," in *Frontiers in Social Movement Theory*, ed. Aldon Morris and Carol Mueller (New Haven, Conn.: Yale University Press, 1992), 86.

31. David Snow, E. Burke Rochford, Jr., Steven K. Worden, and Robert D. Benford, "Frame Alignment Processes, Micro-Mobilization and Movement Participation," *American Sociological Review* 51, no. 4 (1986): 464–81.

32. Klandermans, "Social Construction of Protest," 80.

33. CM leader, interview with the author, Seoul, winter 1992.

34. The public discourse in Korea on the *chŏngsindae* emphasizes Koreans' helpless and unwitting sacrifice of young women to Japanese colonizers. However, Youn-ok Song points out that the practice of trafficking in girls and women for prostitution outside Korea was already well established in Korea during the 1920s, such that "to be a victim of this trafficking became an ordinary misfortune." See Youn-ok Song, "Japanese Colonial Rule and State-Managed Prostitution: Korea's Licensed Prostitutes," in *The Comfort Women: Colonialism, War, and Sex*, 202.

35. Korean Council, *Chŏngsindae munje charyojip*, 42.

36. For example, see Yuki Tanaka, *Hidden Horrors: Japanese War Crimes in World War Two* (Boulder, Colo.: Westview Press, 1996).

37. For example, see Sunhyuk Kim's two articles, "Civil Society in South Korea: From Grand Democracy Movements to Petty Interest Groups?" *Journal of Northeast Asian Studies* 15, no. 2 (1996): 81–97; and "State and Civil Society in South Korea's Democratic Consolidation: Is the Battle Really Over?" *Asian Survey* 37, no. 12 (1997): 1135–44.

38. *Saewoomtuh Newsletter*, no. 3, February 15, 1997.

39. See Coomaraswamy, *Report on the Mission*.

40. Elisabeth Friedman, "Women's Human Rights: The Emergence of a Movement," in *Women's Rights, Human Rights: International Feminist Perspectives*, ed. Julie Peters and Andrea Wolper (New York: Routledge, 1995), 19.

41. Kang, "Bitter Page of History."

42. An Ilsun is the author of *Ppaetbŏl* (Seoul: Konggan Media Publishing Co., 1995), telephone conversation, February 1997.

43. Saewoomtuh staff members, facsimile communication to author, February 18, 1997.
44. Soh, "The Korean 'Comfort Women,'" 1240.
45. Ron Eyerman and Andrew Jamison, *Social Movements: A Cognitive Approach* (University Park: Pennsylvania State University Press, 1991), 166.

7

Uncomfortable Fatigues

Chamorro Soldiers, Gendered Identities,
and the Question of Decolonization in Guam

Keith L. Camacho and Laurel A. Monnig

> Let me tell you something about Chamorros . . . they are one of the most decorated, motivated, sophisticated soldiers in the world, man. When they join any of the armed forces, they are there to prove themselves . . . so when we go into the military we tend to be the best of the best. And I hear this from everybody else . . . from generals, sergeant majors.
>
> —Olympio I. Magofña, U.S. Army recruiter

> I could balance the two, I could never be confused. Like a lot of the people, a lot of my peers who served with me in the military cannot understand the dichotomy that on the one hand there is this warrior, a highly American soldier, right? And then, on the other hand, he is also an advocate for indigenous rights. They cannot balance that. But with me, I could balance the two of them.
>
> —John Benavente, U.S. Army veteran and activist

First Sergeant Olympio I. Magofña, a Chamorro recruiter in the U.S. Army, extols in the opening epigraph the virtues of Chamorros in U.S. military uniform—that is, *male* Chamorro soldierhood. As with every military around the globe, soldiering in colonial Guam is predominantly a male and an overtly masculine occupation. In the second quote above, John Benavente, a Chamorro man in his sixties, reflects on his life in fatigues as a retired U.S. Army enlisted soldier.[1] He is also a contemporary Chamorro rights activist, a path certainly not pursued by all Chamorro soldiers. Benavente shares his views in an interview about Guam's political status as an unincorporated territory of the United States, as well as his activism in Chamorro decolonization movements.² These movements have struggled with the motives and consequences of U.S. military rule on Guam since the turn of the twentieth century. Calls for recognizing and legitimizing Chamorro land rights, Chamorro language programs, and Chamorro self-determination are some of the concerns voiced by these movements in their quest to decolonize the island and its indigenous Chamorro people.

Yet, Benavente is conscious of how militarist and masculine narratives garnered from his experiences in the U.S. military inform his ideas regarding Chamorro decolonization. Indeed, he peppers his conversations about the decolonization of Guam with "militarized" acronyms, metaphors, and terminology. Like some Chamorro activists, for example, Benavente now sees himself as a "warrior" of indigenous cultural, economic, and political rights. He finds no contradiction between his history of U.S. military service and indigenous activism, which both shape his conceptions of identity today. In his narrative of life experiences, Benavente thus does not recount any conflict in being a veteran of a colonial army *and* an advocate for indigenous rights in Guam. He could, as he puts it, "balance the two of them."

Not all Chamorro male military personnel or veterans of the U.S. Armed Forces have such ease in reflecting on the problems inherent in U.S. militarization. After all, their participation in the U.S. military demands their loyalty. In fact, the stated goal of military service is to foster, upon command, discipline, obedience, and violence among individuals and collectivities; ambivalence is not deliberately cultivated. Further, critical thinking and questioning of the process of military indoctrination are not actively promoted by and among U.S. military personnel. But what about the life story of John Benavente? What does his story, and others like his, offer in terms of a gendered analysis of U.S. militarization and masculinity in Asia and the Pacific? What strategies for resistance do indigenous experiences in the U.S. military present activists and scholars concerned with the increased rise in U.S. militarization at home and abroad?³

In this chapter, we explore the interrelated processes of militarization and masculinization among Guam's Chamorro men in the U.S. Armed Forces and the implications these processes have for the decolonization of Guam. By decolonization, we mean it in the broadest sense of individual and collective acts of self-determination, especially as framed in response to these processes of U.S. colonial militarization and masculinization.⁴

While a fuller account of gender relations considers women as well, the scope of this chapter is conceptually restricted to issues of masculinity. However, as other scholars[5] have found, our analytical attention to masculinity can speak to other issues of gender. In fact, the gendered roles assigned to and represented by Chamorro men and women inform each other through a "dialectic process of change."[6] In this respect, we ground our discussion in the interconnected cultural constructions of "masculinity" and "femininity." Therefore we focus on the processes of militarization and masculinization that sometimes produce the conditions for Chamorro *men* to interrogate critically and self-reflexively U.S. militarist policies, practices, and prejudices.

The Question of Decolonization

Based on our fieldwork performed in Guam from 1998 to 2004, we take stock in Cynthia Enloe's call for more innovative studies on the relationships between colonized indigenous peoples and the various processes of militarization and masculinization.[7] As Enloe observes, "We know little about how men from the colonized societies experienced the militarized standards of manhood or how their experiences shaped postwar nationalist movements and the relations between local men and women and between imperial and colonized men."[8] What Enloe implicitly underscores is the critical awareness of where race and gender collide in the making of marginalized masculinities in relation to the U.S. military's construction of dominant, white masculinity. We, too, are interested in the ways in which colonized peoples, such as the Chamorros of Guam, use their experiences in the U.S. military to negotiate their racialized, militarized, and masculinized identities, especially in regards to the question of decolonization.

In examining the processes of militarization and masculinization among Chamorro soldiers, we contend that the "question of decolonization" in Guam need not be asked only in the conventional sense, that is, in terms set and standardized by the United Nations (UN), indigenous nationalist and secessionist movements, European and U.S. notions of democracy, or international laws and treaties.[9] In large part, these decolonization processes and social movements, observes Geoff Bertram, have "been dominated by constitutional lawyers and their categories of analysis."[10] Indeed, decolonization processes and movements differ from one setting to another, from the use of violence and armed conflicts to the use of educational programs and electoral voting. In keeping with this understanding that decolonization may take a variety of forms, this chapter probes some of the diverse processes that may stimulate the formulation of decolonization movements in the Pacific Islands and elsewhere.

In Guam, processes of decolonization have developed despite, and some argue *because of*, the intense militarization of the island. Since the U.S. colonial acquisition of Guam in 1898, Chamorro scholar Laura Souder-Jaffrey asserts that the island's economic, political, and social relationship with the United States has been predominantly and consistently framed in militarist terms. Referring to the history of U.S. federal and military governance in Guam, Souder-Jaffrey explains that a "military mentality has persisted, as the framework for governing the Territory of Guam, in varying degrees to the present day."[11] "It is critical to recognize," she continues, "that this hierarchical, military rule, i.e. from the top downwards, defined the federal-territorial relationship at the onset."[12] As a result, U.S. federal and military interests and policies remain paramount in Guam. Possibilities for alternative and indigenous-sanctioned forms of citizenship, economic development, and political status options, among others, are thus weakened by the primacy of U.S. federalism and militarism from the turn of the twentieth century to today.

Nevertheless, indigenous Chamorro movements pushed for an end to military rule and called for recognition of civil rights as early as 1901 in the form of a petition signed by a group of Chamorro political elites.[13] During the first half of the twentieth century, Chamorro leaders often formulated petitions to stop military rule, to grant Chamorros U.S. citizenship, and to expand human and civil rights for Chamorros. Prior to World War II, Chamorro leaders unfortunately saw no success in their petitions for political recognition and representation due to the totalitarian nature of Guam's former naval government.[14] With the signing of the Organic act of 1950, after half a century of U.S. colonialism, Chamorros were granted civilian rule and a limited form of U.S. citizenship. Yet, the military and its needs continued to shape the administrative decisions and governmental ethos of the civilian administration of Guam.

By the late 1960s, Chamorro decolonization efforts took on a variety of forms as debates on Guam's political status increased. Organizations for Chamorro language rights, conventions for the drafting of constitutions, groups for the return of Chamorro ancestral lands, and campaigns for the revision of limitations within the civil administration demonstrated that more Chamorros were engaged in the political language of decolonization.[15] In 1970, for example, the island's indigenous and local population elected their first governor, reflecting a heightened sense of political autonomy and agency on the part of Guam's residents. Prior to these local elections, the U.S. president appointed military or civilian governors to the island—a practice consistent with colonial governance policies of the twentieth century. And by the 1980s and 1990s, tensions grew within decolonization movements—such as between those who supported closer ties to the United States and those who desired separation from the United States—that reflected the competing political interests and diversity of opinions on the part of Guam's Chamorro and local populations.

Indeed, the potentiality of what a decolonized Guam would look like was shaped in part by the UN's options for dependent territories.[16] In the struggle to negotiate decolonization, the local government of Guam conducted several plebiscites with the goal of establishing a clear, majority favorite for the population on Guam. At the moment, three possible political-status options are available to Guam and are slated to be voted on in a plebiscite some time in the future: Statehood (or integration), Free Association, and Independence.[17] In brief, Statehood would incorporate Guam into the United States, while the political status of Free Association would allow for more political control while still retaining ties to the United States. Independence would grant Guam international sovereignty. The people of Guam, especially the indigenous Chamorros, are now wrestling with the implications of these political statuses as future options.

Yet, Guam is not entirely a special case with respect to the question of decolonization; it is one among other instances of U.S. territorial expansion and acquisition in Asia, the Caribbean, North America, and the Pacific. The United States has a history of conveying ambivalent positions on its theories and policies regarding the decolonization of territories. In some respects, the United States has supported decolonization efforts in Asia, South America, and Europe, or wherever the need to justify and protect U.S. economic or political interests arose.[18] On the other hand, in past centuries, the United States has taken "decolonization" of European-claimed lands in the continental United States as a "transitional step to annexation by the United States."[19] During the U.S. colonization of California, Oregon, and Cuba in the nineteenth century, for example, Walter LaFeber notes that U.S. foreign policy viewed decolonization as "less an act of altruism . . . than an integral and successful part of the nation's most aggressive self-interest."[20] Despite its anticolonial origins, the United States' political, social, and military treatment of Native Americans exemplifies the most tragic, visible, and problematic example of its contradictory policies on decolonization.[21]

With regards to the Pacific Islands, Donald D. Johnson writes that "the United States in recent years has hardly been the leader of decolonization in the Pacific."[22] Given the United States' ambivalent history of decolonization, it comes as no surprise that the decolonization of its territories in the Pacific has been "slow and irregular."[23] In Guam, as Laura Souder-Jaffrey argues, the "unbalanced and constant vacillation of federal policy and action towards Guam has created instability and lack of direction and purpose at the local government level."[24] Furthermore, the United States continues to see the geographical area called Micronesia, with Guam as one of its many islands, as a vital "buffer zone" to protect the westernmost coast of the continental United States from perceived threats in Asia.[25]

Whether through the sanction of the UN, through the initiative of Chamorro leaders, or through the limited support of the United States, it remains evident that processes of decolonization in Guam and the Pacific are frequently understood in the conventional sense. Western laws and indigenous Pacific Islander appropriations of Western laws lie at the center of many discussions on decolonization; contested concepts like "citizenship," "constitution," "democracy," "human rights," and "private property" are now part of the political vocabulary of decolonization movements throughout the Pacific Islands region.[26] But, as Bertram notes, these conventional processes and concepts of decolonization reflect "a set of priorities which seem far removed from the nature of Island societies or the social and economic processes at work there."[27] Within a broader context, Kathyrn Manuelito similarly argues that "prescriptions and descriptions of self-determination are one-sided from the dominant society. Assumptions that indigenous people agree with the dominant society's definitions of self-determination continue to prevent progress toward self-determination by indigenous people."[28] Thus, as Timothy J. Gaffaney reveals, the "importance of alternative explanations for decolonization become all the more important."[29]

How, then, can the question of decolonization be asked without "being far removed" from indigenous worldviews? How can decolonization be achieved by indigenous people in the Pacific and elsewhere? We hope to show that even in the most militarized and masculinized of spaces, such as the U.S. Armed Forces, some indigenous Chamorro men are already asking questions of profound implications for the decolonization of Guam. The question of decolonization stirs, as Vicente M. Diaz asserts, in the very "materiality of things and ideas that are non-Chamorro in origin," such as the U.S. military and its notion of manhood.[30] In thinking about their subjectivities as colonized subjects, ethnic minorities, and indigenous men in the U.S. military, some Chamorro soldiers have begun to ask: what *is* decolonization?[31] As men in U.S. camouflage fatigues, they are coming to terms with the ways in which their identities are gendered, racialized, politicized, militarized, and decolonized.

Intersections of Militarization and Gender in the Pacific

Militarization is a complex and contested process wherever it is active, but its mechanisms are often visible in places such as the Pacific.[32] We define "militarization," in part, by referring to Catherine Lutz's notion of militarization as "a discursive process, involving a shift in general societal beliefs and values in ways necessary to legitimate the use of force, the organization of large armies and their leaders, and the higher taxes or tribute used to pay for them."[33] Militarization can be read as a discursive process based on the representation and exchange of ideas, values, and images, or it can be understood as a material process in its production of violence and violent forms via technological, electronic, or nuclear means.[34] For the purpose of this chapter, we emphasize the discursive but also address the material elements of militarization.[35]

Since the end of World War II, numerous indigenous societies in the Pacific have experienced some degree of material and/or discursive militarization. In large part, however, a majority of Pacific Islanders dwell in areas not directly affected by militarist policies and practices. For colonial powers, nevertheless, the Pacific remains a critical area for the implementation of various military agendas. As Owen Wilkes and Sitiveni Ratuva assert, the Pacific represents "a highly militarised part of the world."[36] They state that the region has been militarized in four general ways. Often dictated by the needs of colonial metropolitan powers, these forms of militarization include (1) preparing for a global nuclear war; (2) defending the continental boundaries of colonial powers, such as the western coastline of the United States; (3) anticipating a military confrontation between Asia and North

America; and (4) supporting local or indigenous military activities in the interest of Pacific island or colonial nation-states.[37]

The U.S. and Allied use of Pacific Islands as "staging grounds" for the invasion of Japan in World War II, the establishment of segregated military brothels in Honolulu, Oahu, in the 1940s, and the French nuclear testing of bombs in the atolls of French Polynesia during the 1990s are all examples that illustrate material forms of colonial militarization in the Pacific.[38] Indigenous material militarization also exists in the shape of national armed forces in Fiji, Papua New Guinea, Tonga, and Vanuatu—armed forces that are developed and maintained in the interests of ceremonial gatherings, civil defense, internal security, and national defense.[39] These forms of material militarization have impacted Pacific Island societies in numerous ways, raising tremendous implications for the study of intercultural relations, environmental and nuclear waste, indigenous soldiering, regional coalition building, and international law.[40]

But to suggest that material and discursive forms of militarization are totalizing, distinctly separate processes is misleading. In the Pacific, histories of colonial and even indigenous militarization frequently overlap, informed by older *gendered* literary, scientific, and religious representations of the "primitive."[41] As Stuart Hall argues, European and U.S. missionaries, traders, novelists, scientists, and explorers have often produced racialized and gendered images of non-Europeans, such as Pacific Islanders, as either the "noble savage" or the "ignoble savage."[42] These images are usually "associated with the contradistinctions between Polynesian/Melanesians, light-skinned/dark-skinned, and civilized/uncivilized."[43] These alternate views, Ty Kāwika Tengan notes, "have historically structured the ways in which indigenous Pacific Islanders have been viewed by outsiders."[44] For example, racist stereotypes of the "strong," "light-skinned" Polynesian male or the "warlike," "dark-skinned" Melanesian male abound in the scientific, ethnographic, and missionary literature of the Pacific.[45] Up to today, these racist perceptions of Pacific Islander men continue, especially in athletic sports such as New Zealand rugby[46] and U.S. football.[47] Some of these images are even perpetuated by Pacific Islander men themselves where, as in the case of the Māori of New Zealand, their talents "are seen as raw materials to be captured, brought under Pākehā (white) control, and molded into a commodity."[48]

Comparably, Americans and Europeans have frequently represented Pacific Islander women as "feminine," or as "pleasure-oriented and easily subordinated to Western desires."[49] Depictions of Pacific Islander women dating from the eighteenth century onward have often portrayed indigenous women as having the "propensity for sexual excess," if not licentious behavior.[50] The tourism industries of Guam, Hawai'i, New Caledonia, and Tahiti draw from this Euro-American record of erotic and exotic images of the indigenous people and landscape of the Pacific. In the case of Hawai'i, for example, foreign sojourners, tourists, and settlers have generally viewed Hawai'i as "a welcoming feminine place, waiting with open arms to embrace those who come to penetrate, protect, mold, and develop."[51]

In a variety of ways, the discursive militarization of the Pacific has occurred, and still occurs, through the use of metaphors, rhetoric, and images that portray the diversity of this region in "feminine" or "masculine" terms—terms that are malleable to militarist, economic, and political objectives. Colonial militaries, for example, often describe their relationships with Pacific Island societies in paternal, patronizing, and patriarchal ways, attempting to justify the "protection" of feminized or emasculated sexes and identities.[52] As Brendan Hokowhitu asserts, this discursive, gendered record of the Pacific "underscored the white man's humanistic 'burden' to conquer the world, civilize it, and then provide enlightened leadership into the future."[53] "It was believed," Hokowhitu continues, "that only the white man possessed the mental fortitude to tackle such a burden."[54]

The U.S. Militarization of Guam and Chamorro Enlistment in the U.S. Military

In Guam, the "burden" of imparting Western civilization upon the Chamorro population began with Spanish colonial, military, and religious activities in the seventeenth century.[55] With the Spanish–American War of 1898, the United States then assumed control over Guam and its approximately ten thousand Chamorro inhabitants. Like the Spanish before them, the United States constructed military harbors, outposts, and facilities. To this effect, the island served as a coaling station for U.S. naval ships traveling throughout the Pacific region, as well as a venue for early twentieth-century U.S. colonialism. The U.S. Navy, the U.S. entity of authority in Guam, implemented a government with an intense military ethos with vast power over the Chamorro population.[56] The autocratic authority of this type of administration was concentrated in the person of the naval governor, appointed by the president of the United States. Lou Leon Guerrero, an elderly Chamorro woman, recalls life on Guam during this pre–World War II period, stating that the island "was run by the military . . . and [that] the authorities were mostly Americans."[57] U.S. military descriptions of Guam also coded the island as "feminine," an amalgam of tropes that feminized Chamorros as "child-like," "hospitable," and "peaceful." As Anne Perez Hattori explains, Guam was feminized as "a space available for the colonial penetration of a masculinized naval establishment."[58]

For the Chamorros of Guam, their history of enlistment in the U.S. military began in the 1930s. During the depression, the first Chamorros enlisted into the U.S. military, encouraged by the island's naval governor, George Alexander. In his way of thinking, enlistment offered some Chamorros, especially young men, supplementary forms of income, "'which in turn would assist in bringing the island closer to the point of becoming self-supporting.'"[59] From the beginning, on the part of the U.S. military regime on Guam, Chamorro military enlistment was rhetorically tied to perceived economic independence. In this vein, the naval governor's recruitment program of Chamorro men was deemed "a success." From the beginning of the depression era program until the start of World War II, 625 Chamorro men enlisted into the U.S. military as mess attendants.[60]

The case of Chamorro enlistment in the U.S. military and its implications on gender is unique in detail but not in process. Rather, Chamorro experiences in the U.S. military represent continuity in the colonial conscription of marginal ethnic groups as laborers, mercenaries, military soldiers, and police officers. For example, in the modern era, various European countries conscripted the military service of minorities, such as Irish, Poles, Scots, and Swedes; elsewhere, the Fulani and Nupe kingdoms of Africa, for example, recruited "slaves" to serve their armies, whereas the British colonial government in South Asia enlisted the military labor of Indians.[61] In the case of Spanish military and labor forces of the seventeenth century, the Spanish sent *indios* and mestizos, under the direction of Jesuits, to take possession of the Mariana Islands; this group constituted indigenous peoples from Spain's expansive empire, such as the Pampangos, Tagalogs, and Visayans of the Philippines.[62] Likewise, in other areas of the Pacific Islands, the British colonial governments of Aotearoa and Fiji enlisted the Māori and Fijians, respectively, to serve in World War I.

In the United States, indigenous and minority groups also participated in various American wars of expansion and conquest; African Americans, Chamorros, Filipinos, Hawaiians, Japanese Americans, Latinos, Native

Americans, and Sāmoans comprise some of these cultural groups.[63] The Choctaw, Navajo, and Yaqui, for example, served in World War II as key communication specialists in the European and Pacific theaters of the war.[64] As these and other examples demonstrate, marginal ethnic groups, such as indigenous peoples, outcasts, and slaves, have historically contributed to the colonial expansion of territories, the development of civil conflicts, and the defense of national borders.[65] In many cases, these different groups of people enlisted in these militaries to acquire greater forms of economic, political, and social mobility; some sought citizenship, or a sense of "belonging" in the polity; others saw military service as honorable and prestigious. On the other hand, various colonial states often recruited the military labor of these peoples because they possess so-called "martial traditions." Furthermore, as Cynthia H. Enloe argues, colonial states conscripted the labor of minority ethnic groups because "bringing those particular groups into a direct relationship with a state agency will preserve the social ordering that underpins that state."[66]

In this respect, Chamorro service in the military did not guarantee them greater political and economic autonomy as individuals, as a collective cultural unit, or as an island society. For example, male Chamorros could *only* enlist as mess attendants prior to World War II, forbidden to pursue higher paying ranks occupied by white military personnel.[67] "I will admit that it was hard to be the best," recalled former navy steward Adrian C. Sanchez, "when you are down there looking up."[68] Yet more Chamorro men entered the military after World War II primarily because of cultural reasons of obligation. This sense of obligation stems from Chamorro responses to the brutality of the Japanese colonial project in wartime Guam (from 1941 to 1944) and to the return of Americans as "liberators" of Japanese colonialism in 1944. Thus, Chamorro men saw enlistment as one way to reciprocate—to give *chenchule'*, or a form of labor based on reciprocal relations—to "Uncle Sam" for "liberating" them from Japanese military occupation during World War II.[69] In 1950, only a few years after the war, Congress passed an Organic Act for Guam, which replaced the island's naval government in favor of a local government premised on U.S. federalism and constitutionalism. The passing of this act granted Chamorros a limited form of citizenship and increased opportunities for enlistment in the U.S. military. By 1971, approximately 3,270[70] men of Guam (not exclusively Chamorro) were then enlisted in the U.S. military.[71] Immigration into Guam was substantial at this juncture of the island's history; Chamorros accounted for about half of the population. Recruitment demographics reflect the change in Guam's demographics. Yet, Chamorro enlistment numbers remained disproportionately high.

From a material aspect, though, it was the military itself that created an economic environment that forced young Chamorros into the military. Explained as necessary to maintain security in the region, the military closed Guam to "all foreign and domestic U.S. sea and air commercial carriers without permission of the US Navy" from 1945 to 1962, an action that stifled any nonmilitary economic growth.[72] In addition, the military acquired, through condemnation or "lease," nearly two thirds of the private property on Guam.[73] Military personnel and foreign contract labor, consisting of such groups as Filipinos, Hawaiians, Koreans, and Palauans, migrated to the island for postwar reconstruction and militarization projects, augmenting growing staffing needs.

The weak economy due to the security closure compounded the alienation of family lands. This loss of land combined with intense in-migration altered Chamorro traditional forms of agricultural development and sustainability, casting them into only a few realistic options for work, namely military service or civil government work.[74] The military continues to be one of the top employers of young men on Guam, with the Iraq War deterring few. In a recent newspaper article, Petty Officer First Class Rey Awa reflects, "There are no layoffs in the military, and it pays for college, too."[75] On Guam, "in the private sector" where "job security can be volatile," Awa continues, as opposed to low paying, entry-level jobs in restaurant and service industries, the military provided him a relatively "good" living at a young age.

The fact that the U.S. military continues to occupy a third of the island, only 30 miles long and 214 square miles in area, attests to the pervasive presence of militarism. For example, Andersen Air Force Base in the village of Yigo and Naval Station in the village of Sumay are severed from the rest of the island by a "seemingly endless" array of fences.[76] In reference to cultural perceptions of these fences, Chamorro writer C. T. Perez states, "I learned quickly that my success in life would be measured by how well I could emulate 'inside' [of the fence] attributes and suppress 'outside' [of the fence] characteristics."[77] Life on the outside of the fences is often judged and compared to that on the inside—or the "American, white, middle-class" life that the military displays and represents.

Similarly, former U.S. Congressional Representative for Guam Robert Underwood comments on the naturalization of military fences in Guam. He says, "You drive around Guam and you see the military fences. And you ask people, 'Does that fence bother you?' or 'Does it just seem like the coconut tree, is it part of your reality?' Most people would say, 'Oh, it's part of my reality.' Well, if the fence doesn't bother you, the fence is designed to keep who away from who, to keep you away from them. And what's your response, 'Gosh, I wish I can join the military to get inside.' And if that's your response . . . then it doesn't look like an intrusion, [but] like a natural order."[78]

Like Hawai'i, another U.S. colonial possession in the Pacific, the U.S. military in Guam has engrained "itself through accumulated familiarity into the everyday ways of life that produce what we experience as normal."[79] Thus, embracing the U.S. military presence on the island supports the military economy and naturalizes the idea that the military remains integral to the island's livelihood. This further enhances an ethos of fear on Guam over the withdrawal of U.S. military facilities and employment opportunities. These processes of militarization continue to occur in Guam despite the rise in antibase sentiment and activism in East Asia and the Pacific (see the chapters by Wesley Ueunten and Katharine Moon, chapters 5 and 6, respectively).[80]

Engendering Masculinity: Chamorro Soldiers in the U.S. Military

Historically, the reciprocal relationship that exists between the processes of militarization and masculinization has enabled various colonial powers to maintain possession and control over their respective territories. [81] As John Hopton observes, political and military leaders "have used ideologies of idealized masculinity that valorize the notion of strong active males collectively risking their personal safety for the greater good of the wider community."[82] "If the reciprocal relationship between masculinity and militarism is weakened," Hopton continues, "so too is the power of the state to manipulate public support for its right to use violence to pursue policies at home and abroad."[83] States thus have a "vested interest in maintaining strong ideological links between militarism and masculinity."[84]

With respect to the U.S. military, notions of "masculinity" simply do not exist in some homogenous, reified stasis. The inroads made by women, the critiques made by gays and lesbians, and the analyses made about peacekeepers all demonstrate that notions of masculinity are dynamic and contextual.[85] However, the "cult of the warrior" continues to influence and dominate the ways in which men are viewed as U.S. soldiers. As Cynthia Enloe argues, the U.S. military is coded as a hypermasculine space; soldiers embody the notion of heterosexual "manhood" and exhibit the most demonstrable "masculinity" in terms of physical prowess, stoic presence, and "justifiable" violence.[86] In the case of soldiers from colonized populations or ethnic groups, these men bring their own notions of masculinity and manhood with them to soldiering in the U.S. military. In many respects, Chamorro men are engendered by the U.S. military in ways similar to military and state engenderings of men in the past. One case in point is Spanish colonialism in the Pacific.

Given the history of Spanish efforts to suppress Chamorro political organization and power, Chamorro men have come to see the U.S. military as spaces to remasculinize their emasculated images. As evidenced in oral traditions, Chamorro men prior to the onset of Spanish colonialism were often represented as intelligent and physically robust with supernatural, corporeal qualities. The legends of Gadao of Guam or Taga of Tinian reflected "the spirit of Chamorros who prided themselves on extraordinary strength and other superhuman abilities."[87] In these legends, Chamorro men, young and old, jumped across islands, outmaneuvered foes, uprooted coconut trees, and escaped bodily harm. Even some Spanish accounts depicted Chamorro men as hard workers and skilled warriors, positions the Spaniards held with admiration and respect, but also with anger and contempt.[88] In terms of traditional Chamorro warfare, some Spanish accounts portrayed Chamorro conflicts along the lines of "fanfare" rather than "ferocity."[89] As Scott Russell notes, Chamorros had short-lived battles among themselves or against the Spaniards; in many instances Chamorros sought to avoid "excessive loss of life."[90]

While little is known about older, gendered traditions of Chamorro men, notions of Chamorro masculinity have been radically transformed by the onset of U.S. colonialism in 1898. Nearly three centuries of Spanish colonialism had taken its toll on Chamorro perceptions of masculinity, and these notions of the emasculated Chamorro man were adopted and adapted by the U.S. colonial administration. The once-proud and idealized image of the Chamorro male had changed into the image of a "trickster" called "Juan Malo." As Robert Tenorio Torres states, Juan Malo represents a "symbol of resistance and an example of the Chamorro who can no longer battle physically, must defeat his [colonial] conquerors by outwitting them."[91] Today, Juan Malo is a composite character who speaks to how Chamorro men have been emasculated within Western forms of colonialism; he is a figure of sarcasm and ridicule and somebody who must resort to alternative and indirect means of confrontation and resistance.

In part, the U.S. military now offers a space for Chamorro men, as perceived "warriors," to counter a Spanish colonial history of gendered subjugation. Like Pacific Islanders elsewhere in colonial militaries, Chamorro men have come to understand the U.S. military as one of the few options available to "achieve a masculinity based on notions of family, leadership, providing, [and] strength."[92] When asked why Chamorro men join the services, for example, Army Recruiter Olympio I. Magofña replies that Chamorro men enlist because of their presumed gender roles assigned to them since antiquity. "Our ancestors believe," he states, that the "man has to go out there and do the manly job and provide for the family. And the women have to stay home and take care of the kids and the house."[93]

By fulfilling the role of provider, asserts Magofña, Chamorro men in the military support their families, seek various forms of education, enhance their physical capabilities, and continue the tradition of male warriors. In particular, he observes that many Chamorro men are proud of their military service, especially those "we call 'combat arms,' which is military occupation skills." He states that through the service of combat arms one can receive immediate recognition and, in turn, increase one's rank and status in the military. These sentiments echo across the western Pacific region, he adds, demonstrating increased levels of enlistment by Pacific Islanders in the U.S. military.[94]

Compared to recruitment efforts in the continental United States, Olympio I. Magofña remarks that "our geographical areas are promilitary . . . it's nothing compared to the states. In the stateside now [because of September 11 and the Iraq War], it's very, very hard to recruit, but compared to our geographical area in the Pacific, everybody wants to go into the army."[95] According to Magofña, this area includes American Sāmoa, the Commonwealth of the Northern Mariana Islands, the Federated States of Micronesia, Guam, Japan, the Republic of Palau, the Republic of the Marshall Islands, and South Korea. In his view, Army recruitment numbers in Guam are particularly high, averaging forty to fifty enlistees a month whereas other U.S. continental recruitment offices are struggling even to make their quotas. The army recruiting station in Guam has a quota of thirty enlistees per month.

Similarly, Eddie Dueñas, a general of the Guam National Guard and an activist advocating statehood, was another of many who commented on Guam being a "recruiter's heaven": "The story in Guam, there never was any need for a draft. It has always been voluntary . . . Even up till now. In fact, Guam is a recruiter's heaven. If you want to be top recruiter, put Guam in your area, and you got it. No really. So this all tells you about these people [Chamorros], you know . . . So you can see for example how they are handling themselves, and they are taking that step and they are competing."[96] This process of remasculinization via joining the U.S. military is likewise alluded to by Jose Ulloa Garrido, a retired military veteran and a longtime Chamorro rights activist. Linking Chamorro volunteerism in the military with gendered and biological notions of masculinity, Garrido comments, "Well I did volunteer. Us Chamorros, we're intrigued by volunteering [for the military]. We like to experience something like that . . . Maybe it's [in] our blood to be born fighters, you know. And we like to go to battle. That's why you see a lot of Chamorros volunteering for any place that has a war."[97] To no surprise, these are all masculine qualities that attract young Chamorro men into the U.S. Armed Services, representing continuity among the different generations. Military veteran Angel Santos, in the following quote, describes a funeral he attended with his family as a young boy. Recollecting the funeral for a Chamorro soldier who died in Vietnam, Santos evokes notions of the cult of the warrior: "Here I was looking down at this young soldier, who was only twenty-two years old when he was killed and I asked myself 'Why did he have to die so young, what did he sacrifice his life for?' And when my parents told me that he died for my freedom, and for the democracy for all people throughout the world, I made [a] promise to myself, and to that soldier, to that warrior, never mind soldier, that I want to be like him. I, too, if called upon, will spill my own blood and die just like him."[98] As reflected in the remarks by Magofña, Dueñas, Garrido, and Santos, Chamorro male reasons for joining the military are couched in the gendered rhetoric of cultural obligation, educational advancement, economic opportunity, and political loyalty.

All of these combined motivations for Chamorro men to work for the U.S. military translate into disproportionately high numbers of Chamorro enlistees. Chamorros, both men and women, enlist in greater numbers than any other American ethnic group in the United States or its territories.[99] And Chamorro casualty rates have been considerably higher in every U.S. war since the Korean War, including the most recent war in Iraq.[100] Chamorro enlistment in the colonial U.S. military is about the economic deprivation of Guam's job market, about educational opportunities, and most certainly about the militarized environment within which Chamorro "boys" grow to "manhood." After all, as one Chamorro stated, "joining the Armed Forces was a guaranteed ticket off the island. For many of our young Guamanian men, the military served as a rite of passage into adulthood."[101]

As these examples illustrate, Chamorro men negotiate masculinity and manhood in the U.S. military through varying means. Furthermore, Chamorros redefine their emasculated images by grafting some aspect of Pacific "savagery" and "warriorhood" into their military service. These are extremely problematic endeavors, as they reinforce long-standing racialized tropes of Pacific Islander men and women as either the "noble savage" or the "ignoble savage." However, Chamorro men can gain a measured form of respect by excelling—"being the best of the best"—within the racist and colonial landscape of the military, and maybe can even defeat the colonizer in *his* own game.[102] In other words, Chamorro men have the opportunity to legitimize their manhood by reshaping their bodies and masculinities through the same military activities as their American counterparts in the military. Chamorro males, like other colonized Pacific Islander men, can recoup a sense of "legitimate" masculinity through joining the military and tapping into potent images of warriorhood.

Chamorro Soldiering and the Decolonization of Guam

But it is precisely this appearance of achievement in the military—or the naturalization of military order—that supports the conditions through which Chamorro male soldiers can think critically about their gendered, militarized, and colonized subjectivities. For not all Chamorro male experiences in the U.S. military are as uniformly celebratory and unproblematic as they may seem. As much as the U.S. military engenders male soldiers as "warriors," it also engenders men, especially racially and politically marginal men of the state, in ways contrary to the assumed roles of the white, heterosexual, obedient, and stoic warrior. The military, through its structures of domination, inherently—although usually not intentionally—fosters ambivalence.[103] As Chamorro male soldiers come to the realization that their remasculinized selves are concomitantly being emasculated by the U.S. military, questions of decolonization arise with more force, meaning, and irony. As Yen Lê Espiritu asserts, Asian American men and other men of color "have been largely excluded from white-based cultural notions of the masculine."[104] At the same time, colonial militaries have long expressed ambivalence and uncertainty about the precise roles of marginal, indigenous, or outcaste soldiers, emasculating further even those who have "sacrificed" their lives for the states of these militaries.[105]

For some Chamorro men, the seeming enthusiasm for the U.S. military and all it supposedly represents for their manhood is fraught with discomfort, tension, and ambivalence; in other words, maybe the fatigues do not fit so well. Ed L. G. Benavente, a longtime Chamorro rights activist, eloquently expresses these tensions in his reflections on Chamorro military veterans who later became decolonization activists. He specifically highlights the ways in which these Chamorro veterans came to terms with their contradictory experiences in the U.S. military. Benavente observes that many Chamorro men enter the military "to spread democracy and the precepts of life, liberty, and the pursuit of happiness for other nations as well and not just the United States [especially] in opposition to communism." [106] He continues,

> After coming back from wars, knowing that they're [Chamorro men] fighting for those same precepts, they found out as soon as they land [in Guam] that their lands were condemned since the 1940s. So when they see that contradiction, the veterans found out that after coming home from a battlefield, that they in reality were dispossessed. They are now renters in homes, apartments, and so forth, knowing full well that the United States military holds their entire properties.
> ... So, they [veteran Chamorros] awoke themselves to the reality, "Why am I fighting a war for liberty of peoples in foreign places, when [all I have to do] is come to Guam because I can face the reality that I have been dispossessed from my lands for military purposes? ... You [Uncle Sam] make me fight those foreign wars and then when I come back you treat me like that." ... So it's a total contradiction in terms of America and its beliefs ... That's the sad history about our people, those are the sad histories of our people and our experiences as a people—that is, that you don't need to go

to foreign wars when injustice and inequality exists even in a place called America.[107]

Like many colonized or marginalized soldiers in colonial armies, these Chamorro male soldier–activists, who Ed Benavente describes, are to some extent "mimic men."[108] As Homi Bhabha portrays, they are contradictory figures who at once bolster colonial authority by their willing participation in the military *and* challenge and agitate it because of their ambivalence and questioning. As we contend, their ambivalence is directly related to their experiences in the U.S. military.

Eloy Hara, a military "lifer," described how extremely upset he was with the U.S. military for denying him a promotion based on "racism," a promotion he believed he well deserved after years of steadfast service.[109] This experience very well could be echoed by other men of color in the military:

> I was victimized because of my race [in the military]. Even when my performance was outstanding . . . But that's why I said that it's isolated because of over twenty years in the military, most of my superiors were good, honest officers. It so happened that I ran into two rednecks that didn't appreciate that I know so much more than they do. I am lower rank than they are, and I am of a different race, but yet I can out-smart the two of them put together . . . They tried to ruin me, [and] they did prevent me from going up in rank. And even when I brought it up to my highest authority, you know, that I was being prejudiced, it fell on deaf ears. Even to the point that I told the admiral, "Admiral, you can take your navy and jam it up you ass, sir!" . . . But then I found out later on, they did blackball my record in Washington. This is back in the 60s and 70s, before equal opportunity really came into being. No matter how hard I tried to move up in rank or get an officer commission, I even went as far as go to college to getting my degree, my bachelor's, working on my master's degree, sustain superior performance . . . I said, "Your fucking navy, sir, is screwing me up." Pardon my French, but you know.[110]

Despite his negative experiences, he served out his obligations to the military to the bitter end. Making the best of his remaining time in the service, he contends he made the military work for him; he "used the navy to train me better" by taking "every opportunity that I could and be trained," even going on for a master's degree. Like many others, he rationalized how the benefits of U.S. democracy far outweigh the negative aspects of being "associated with the United States." For some Chamorros, like this man, due to the cyclical nature of *chenchule'* (reciprocity), Chamorro loyalty and military service deserved payment from the United States in the form of U.S. citizenship, decolonization, and "political advancement"—that is, closer ties to the United States, or statehood.[111]

For others, usually those who desire more independence from the United States, it was injustice that they either experienced or witnessed in the military that accentuated their critiques of the U.S. military and the wider colonial landscape on Guam. The scenarios varied considerably. Some were discriminated against because they were assumed to be African American by their white superiors. Others, like Antonio Artero Sablan, another U.S. veteran, were "shocked" by the treatment of other nonwhites in their military units. Sablan stated,

> But when I was in the military, sometimes I wonder why does a black person get punished more? Gets hit. When I say hit, we have an inspection, and they pick on him because he's black, and they let go of people, or the violation on another white man. I find sometimes to my surprise that I would have . . . you know, when I was in the military, we had about maybe seven or eight black guys out of a total, within our own company, of about seventy people. We find that all the black guys were sent back. None of them made it all the way. And when you are sent back, meaning when you're up to seven weeks, right, and boot camp, I mean it is hell . . . You're looking to getting yourself out of that hellhole. And I'm using terminology of the military type. In other words, punishment and suffering that's in there because they punish you, and they make you work, they make you get up real early, they make you go to bed real late. It's just totally a displacement of what you're used to in civilian life. And you know, you were seven weeks into the program and then all of a sudden these guys were brought back. And then the next company they fall into is the newest company . . . that are starting. So sometimes, they go back to week number three. So that means they are a month, a month and half, back from where they were. And I said something, [so] I'm wondering, what are the violations?

Why are these guys being treated that way? To me, I was not a fighter back then. I was more of a "yes, sir" type of person.[112]

Sablan described how these experiences made him question discrimination in the form of the colonization of Guam: "But those are the things that make you over the years . . . It's just that if you sit back and you question, why was I a participant in that process? Why did I play in that role? Because I didn't know any better, and I wasn't as sensitive. The thing that made me become sensitive [was] when I saw black guys being sent back, and I couldn't understand why." John Benavente reflected after having served as a member of the riot police in a "race riot" in California involving "a bunch of hippies" protesting the end of the Vietnam war. Jose Ulloa Garrido, stationed on Guam and working as a military mechanic, was livid after his military superior would not allow his fellow Chamorro mechanics and himself to speak Chamorro on the job. Whether in the jungles of Vietnam or in military barracks in Germany, Chamorro male soldiers began to question why they sacrifice their lives for a U.S. government that continues to impose its colonial policies and practices among Chamorros in Guam.

It is an all too common narrative heard on Guam among male Chamorro activists—this connection between military soldiering and decolonization. These men wrestle with the formation of resistant narratives, although through possibly indirect means and intentions; as Bhaba explains, "Resistance is not necessarily an oppositional act of political intention, nor is it the simple negation or exclusion of the 'content' of another culture . . . It is the effect of ambivalence produced within the rules of recognition of dominating discourses as they articulate the signs of cultural difference and re-implicate them within the deferential relations of colonial power—hierarchy, normalization, marginalization, and so forth."[113] The Chamorro male soldiers we highlight are undergoing an ambivalent coming-to-terms with their militarized and masculinized subjectivities, which then become part of the possibilities of resistant discursive strategies.

Many Chamorro male activists often preface their critique of the United States by stating that they had served in the military, giving them the perceived right to speak out against the military. In other words, many Chamorro men in decolonization movements often cite their military service and "patriotism" as legitimate grounds for critiquing U.S. colonialism. For example, Jose Ulloa Garrido stated that "I proved my loyalty to the U.S." through his participation in the U.S. Army and National Guard. With his "loyalty" established, he continued to explain that the quest for Chamorro self-determination is not about being "anti-American"; a struggle often misjudged by other Chamorros and non-Chamorros.[114] Rather, it is "very American to dissent," it is part of being "American."

In a colonial situation such as Guam where U.S. citizenship is circumscribed, this strategy of Chamorro soldiers–decolonization activists whereby they preface their critique of the U.S. by establishing their U.S. military service—up front and explicit—emphasizes their claim to a more substantial citizenship. Through their "American" militarized connections, they hope to demonstrate an elevated sense of U.S. citizenship that in turn legitimizes their voices of dissent against the colonizer. Cynthia Enloe exposes a similar discursive turn when she discusses how gay and lesbian groups protest the military policies on homosexuality.[115] They ground their resistance in the language of militarization by embracing, rather than critiquing, the notion that to be a soldier in the U.S. military is to be a more valuable U.S. citizen—a citizen worthy of more than the average citizen. In other words, these protesters try to expose the irrationality of the U.S. military's policies by highlighting their exemplary military service as some form of "higher" citizenship. Enloe contends that militarism is advanced because "many gay and lesbian citizens join together with their heterosexual compatriots in believing that soldiering is good citizenship writ large, or epitomizes public service, or amounts to laying down one's life for one's country."[116] Male Chamorro decolonization activists may be articulating similar militarized narratives on Guam, but, as mentioned previously, our concern is not how Chamorro soldiers are demilitarizing Guam or their individual lives as much as how male Chamorro soldiers use their military experiences to shape their narratives on resistance. These decolonizing narratives will eventually lead to demilitarizing narratives because colonialism and militarism are so interlinked on Guam.

Uncomfortable Fatigues: Conclusion

On August 1, 1998, Guam celebrated the commemoration of the Organic Act in the Plaza De España, a small, picturesque plaza built during the Spanish colonial period.[117] The Organic Act of 1950, an act that replaced the island's naval administration with a civil one, is the document believed by some to be a major step toward Chamorro self-determination. Former veteran, politician, and activist Carlos Taitano was a featured speaker at the event. At the height of his political career, he was instrumental in pushing the United States to implement the Organic Act. Indeed, he was the *only* Chamorro individual, among U.S. congressional officials, present at the signing of the Organic Act.

In his speech, the handsome, elderly Taitano recalled a phrase spoken by President Roosevelt. During World War II, he heard the president say that part of the U.S. wartime mission was to "decolonize the world."[118] Because of these comments, Taitano joined the U.S. military. Like many young Chamorro male soldiers of his generation, he was "happy to do it," enlisting with the presumption that the president's words would also apply to Guam. Taitano professes that he took those words from the president as "as a promise to me" about a potentially "decolonized" Guam. His words at this commemorative event crystallized the critical relationships between the processes of militarization and masculinization in Guam and among Chamorro men and the implications these processes have for the question of decolonization in Guam.

At the same event, another respected Chamorro leader, then speaker of the Guam legislature, Antonio Unpingco, also gave a speech rooted in the intersection of militarization, masculinization, and decolonization.[119] He told the audience how his father joined the military in 1917 but was only permitted to enlist as a military steward: "Anything else was out of the question," the speaker somberly remarked. Unpingco's father, along with his fellow stewards, hoped for more from the military, but not all of their hopes were fulfilled. It was people like his father, the Chamorro military men of the early twentieth century, who pushed for individual advancement so their children and others may not have to endure the sting of Guam's naval military discrimination. Expressing similar themes to Carlos Taitano, Unpingco's speech utilized military service, that institution of Chamorro masculinity, to comment on the continuing need to decolonize Guam.

But defining decolonization movements in Guam and elsewhere in the Pacific in the midst of pervasive militarization is exceedingly difficult. It is not surprising that the UN General Assembly declared in 1960 that "military bases and installations in colonial territories could constitute a major obstacle to the implementation" of decolonization processes.[120] Despite the efforts of some energetic leaders and spurts of productive political activity, decolonization efforts in Guam often seem to suffer from a type of collective fatigue from the processes of a militarized island. In fact, the United States remains ambivalent of and, at times, oppositional toward the decolonization of its colonies in the Pacific.[121] Further, as Donald D. Johnson explains, the "absence of any clear-cut program or goal of political autonomy has left feelings of frustration among local political leaders."[122] Taken in the conventional sense, though, these efforts at decolonization speak more to international laws and treaties than to the experiences and views of indigenous peoples themselves.

In our interactions with Chamorro male soldiers and veterans, we found that at some point in our conversations they revealed a level of discomfort about their various experiences in the U.S. military as colonized men, ethnic minorities, and indigenous soldiers. What many of these male Chamorro soldiers had disclosed was the fact that their fatigues never fit so snugly in the first place—a discomfort that has helped some of them to think about the contradictions and problems of militarism. At the time of their military service, many of these Chamorros had begun to ask what decolonization means and, more importantly, had begun to think about the political implications of their gendered, militarized, and colonized subjectivities.

Notes

This chapter was presented at conferences sponsored by the American Ethnological Association, the Association for Asian American Studies, and the Society for the Anthropology of North America. We would like to thank everybody for their feedback and support. *Un dangkolo na si yu'us ma'ase* to Vicente M. Diaz, Janet D. Keller, Martin Manalansan, Jocelyn Pacleb, Theresa Cenidoza Suarez, Ty Kāwika Tengan, Arlene Torres, and Geoffrey M. White.

1. The opening epigraphs come, respectively, from two interviews: Olympio I. Magofña, interview by Keith L. Camacho, Hagåtña, Guam, August 2004; and John Benavente, interview by Laurel A. Monnig, Hagåtña, Guam, November 2000.

2. As Christina Duffy Burnett and Burke Marshall note, the term "unincorporated territory" stems from the *Insular Cases*, a series of legal decisions in 1901 that legalized the U.S. colonization of Spanish lands lost in the Spanish–American War of 1898, specifically the Philippines, Guam, and Puerto Rico (1). They state that unincorporated territories belong to, but are "not a part of," the United States, with each territory establishing different political relationships with the United States (1). For more on the subject of territorial affairs in the United States, see

their article, "Between the Foreign and the Domestic: The Doctrine of Territorial Incorporation, Invented and Reinvented," in *Foreign in a Domestic Sense: Puerto Rico, American Expansion, and the Constitution*, ed. Christina Duffy Burnett and Burke Marshall (Durham, N.C.: Duke University Press, 2001), 1–36.

3. U.S. military domestic and international reorganization efforts are underway in response to the September 11 attacks on the World Trade Center and the Pentagon. As Laura Hein notes, the United States is "back on track to become a permanently militarized state with national security—defined in terms of guns and espionage—as the unquestionable highest priority" (101). See her article, "Citizens, Foreigners, and the State: U.S. and Japan in the Wake of 9/11," in *Crossed Memories: Perspectives on 9/11 and American Power*, ed. Laura Hein and Daizaburo Yui (Tokyo: Center for Pacific and American Studies Graduate School of Arts and Sciences, The University of Tokyo, 2003), 94–116.

4. Norman Meller, "Indigenous Self-Determination and Its Implementation," *Pacific Studies* 23, no. 1–2 (2000): 9.

5. Cynthia Enloe, *The Morning After: Sexual Politics and the End of the Cold War* (Berkeley: University of California Press, 1993), 20.

6. Laura M. Torres Souder, "Unveiling Herstory: Chamorro Women in Historical Perspective," in *Pacific History: Papers from the 8th Pacific History Association Conference*, ed. Donald H. Rubinstein (Mangilao, Guam: University of Guam Press and Micronesian Area Research Center, 1992), 159.

7. Laurel A. Monnig, an anthropologist from the continental United States, conducted ethnographic fieldwork on Guam during two separate periods: the summer of 1998, and the years 2000 and 2001. Keith L. Camacho, a Chamorro historian, conducted ethnographic and archival research in Guam and the Northern Mariana Islands during the summers of 2002 and 2004.

8. Enloe, *The Morning After*, 81.

9. Stewart Firth, "The Rise and Fall of Decolonization in the Pacific," in *Emerging from Empire? Decolonization in the Pacific*, ed. Donald Denoon (Canberra, Australia: Division of Pacific and Asian History, Research School of Pacific and Asian Studies, Australian National University, 1997), 11.

10. Geoff Bertram, "The Political Economy of Decolonisation and Nationhood in Small Pacific Societies," in *Class and Culture in the South Pacific*, ed. Antony Hooper, Steve Britton, Ron Crocombe, Judith Huntsman, and Cluny Macpherson (Auckland, New Zealand: Centre for Pacific Studies, University of Auckland, 1987), 17.

11. Laura Souder-Jaffrey, "A Not So Perfect Union: Federal-Territorial Relations Between the United States and Guam," in *Chamorro Self-Determination: The Right of a People/I Derechon I Taotao*, ed. Laura Souder-Jaffrey and Robert A. Underwood (Mangilao, Guam: Chamorro Studies Association and Micronesian Area Research Center, University of Guam, 1987), 11.

12. Ibid., 13.

13. Joseph F. Ada with Leland Bettis, "The Quest for Commonweath, the Quest for Change," in *Kinalamten pulitikåt: siñenten i chamorro* (Issues in Guam's political development: the Chamorro perspective) (Agaña, Guam: The Political Status Education Coordinating Commission, 1996), 125–203.

14. Souder-Jaffrey, "A Not So Perfect Union," 10.

15. Ada with Bettis, "The Quest for Commonweath," 132.

16. It should be noted that the people of the northern Mariana Islands, former mandated territories of Japan, voted to decolonize in 1975. A majority of Chamorros and Carolinians, the legally defined indigenous populations of the northern Marianas, chose to integrate into the United States, opting for a "commonwealth" status with the United States. The polity of the northern Mariana Islands, with Guam being the southernmost island of this archipelago, is now called the Commonwealth of the Northern Mariana Islands. For more on this subject, see Arnold H. Leibowitz, *Defining Status: A Comprehensive Analysis of United States Territorial Relations* (Dordrecht, Netherlands: Martinus Nijhoff Publishers, 1989).

17. Since these political-status options are also the names of Chamorro organizations on Guam, we want to maintain the capitalization of these terms.

18. Michael H. Hunt, "Conclusions: The Decolonization Puzzle in US Policy—Promise versus Performance," in *The United States and Decolonization: Power and Freedom*, ed. David Ryan and Victor Pungong (London: Macmillan Press, Ltd, 2000), 220.

19. Walter LaFeber, "The American View of Decolonization, 1776–1920: An Ironic Legacy," in *The United States and Decolonization: Power and Freedom*, ed. David Ryan and Victor Pungong (London: Macmillan Press, Ltd, 2000), 29.

20. Ibid.

21. The U.S. Constitution plays a vital role in the mediation of the federal relations between Native Americans and the United States, then and now. For more on this subject, see Vine Deloria, Jr.'s article, "The Application of the Constitution of American Indians," in *Exiled in the Land of the Free: Democracy, Indian Nations, and the U.S. Constitution*, ed. Oren Lyons, John Mohawk, Vine Deloria, Jr., Laurence Hauptman, Howard Berman, Donald Grinde, Jr., Curtis Berkey, and Robert Venables (Santa Fe, N.Mex.: Clear Light Publishers, 1992), 282–315.

22. Donald D. Johnson, "American Impact on the Pacific Islands Since World War II," in *Oceania and Beyond: Essays on the Pacific Since 1945*, ed. F. P. King (Westport, Conn.: Greenwood Press, 1976), 239.

23. Ibid., 240.

24. Souder-Jaffrey, "A Not So Perfect Union," 21.

25. Johnson, "American Impact," 240.

26. Uetabo Neemia, "Decolonization and Democracy in the South Pacific," in *Culture and Democracy in the South Pacific*, ed. Ron Crocombe, Uentabo Neemia,

Asesela Ravuvu, and Werner Vom Busch (Suva, Fiji: Institute of Pacific Studies, University of the South Pacific, 1992), 8.

27. Bertram, "The Political Economy of Decolonisation," 17.

28. Kathryn Manuelito, "An Indigenous Perspective on Self-Determination," in *Decolonizing Research in Cross-Cultural Contexts*, ed. Kagendo Mutua and Beth Blue Swadener (Albany, N.Y.: State University of New York Press, 2004), 236.

29. Timothy J. Gaffaney, "Linking Colonization and Decolonization: The Case of Micronesia," *Pacific Studies* 18, no. 2 (1995): 49.

30. Vicente M. Diaz, "Simply Chamorro: Telling Tales of Demise and Survival in Guam," *The Contemporary Pacific* 6, no. 1 (1994): 53.

31. Understandably, the term "soldier" often refers to military personnel in the U.S. Army or Marines. Yet not all marines identify themselves as "soldiers"; they prefer the title "marines." Still, since most of our interviewees are former soldiers, that is to say combat personnel, we will use the term "soldier" throughout the chapter to describe Chamorro male military experiences. At the same time, we are wary of its masculine connotations, as well as the fact that Chamorro experiences are not historically or contemporaneously limited to the role of soldiers.

32. For an extensive discussion of World War II in the Pacific Islands, see Geoffrey M. White and Lamont Lindstrom, ed., *The Pacific Theater: Island Representations of World War II* (Honolulu: University of Hawai'i Press, 1989); also, on the issue of nuclear testing in French Polynesia, see Bengt Danielsson and Marie-Thérèse Danielsson, *Poisoned Reign: French Nuclear Colonialism in the Pacific* (Victoria, Australia: Penguin Books, 1986); and, finally, for more on the role of the American military in Hawai'i, see Kathy E. Ferguson and Phyllis Turnbull, *Oh, Say, Can You See? The Semiotics of the Military in Hawai'i* (Minneapolis: University of Minnesota Press, 1999).

33. Catherine Lutz, "Making War at Home in the United States: Militarization and the Current Crisis," *American Anthropologist* 104, no. 3 (2002): 723.

34. John Gillis, "Introduction," in *The Militarization of the Western World*, ed. John R. Gillis (New Brunswick, N.J.: Rutgers University Press, 1989), 1.

35. "Militarism" originally connoted, as Gillis reveals, "the dominance of the military over civilian authority," whereas "militarization" did not initially imply the formal dominance of military ideologies over a society (1). Given the popular academic usage of "militarization" since the 1970s, however, both terms have come to overlap in numerous studies, causing much blurring in the meanings of these terms. Ibid.

36. Owen Wilkes and Sitiveni Ratuva, "Militarism in the Pacific and the Case of Fiji," in *Tu Galala: Social Change in the Pacific*, ed. David Robie (Wellington, New Zealand: Bridget Williams Books Limited, 1992), 53.

37. Ibid., 54.

38. See, for example, Beth Bailey and David Farber, *The First Strange Place: Race and Sex in World War II Hawaii* (Baltimore, Md.: The John Hopkins University Press, 1992).

39. Teresia K. Teaiwa, "Militarism, Tourism and the Native: Articulations in Oceania" (Ph.D. dissertation, University of California, Santa Cruz, 2001), 94.

40. In severe cases, the results of colonial militarization have been culturally, medically, and politically devastating for indigenous people. One example concerns the history of U.S. nuclear bomb testing in the Marshall Islands from 1946 to 1958. Since that period, some Marshallese have experienced a disproportionately high rate of medical problems, such as certain types of cancer. Although the Marshallese have attained some measure of political autonomy, having formed the Republic of the Marshall Islands in 1979, the United States still uses the Marshalls, specifically Kwajalein Atoll, as a "strategic site" for missile testing. For more on Marshallese testimonials regarding the effects of American nuclear radiation, see Zohl dé Ishtar, *Daughters of the Pacific* (North Melbourne, Australia: Spinifex Press, 1994).

41. David Hanlon and Geoffrey M. White, "Introduction," in *Voyaging through the Contemporary Pacific*, ed. David Hanlon and Geoffrey M. White (Lanham, Md.: Rowman & Littlefield, 2000), 2.

42. Stuart Hall, "The West and the Rest: Discourse and Power," in *Modernity: An Introduction to Modern Societies*, ed. Stuart Hall, David Held, Don Hubert, and Kenneth Thompson (Malden, Mass.: Blackwell Publishers, 1996), 184–227.

43. Ty Kāwika Tengan, "(En)gendering Colonialism: Masculinities in Hawai'i and Aotearoa," *Cultural Values* 6, no. 3 (2002): 241.

44. Ibid.

45. Ibid.

46. Brendan Hokowhitu, "Tackling Māori Masculinity: A Colonial Genealogy of Savagery and Sport," *The Contemporary Pacific* 16, no. 2 (2004): 272; Tengan, "(En)gendering Colonialism," 246.

47. Vicente M. Diaz, "'Fight Boys, 'til the Last . . .': Islandstyle Football and the Remasculinization of Indigeneity in the Militarized American Pacific Islands," in *Pacific Diaspora: Island Peoples in the United States and Across the Pacific*, ed. Paul Spickard, Joanne L. Rondilla, and Debbie Hippolite Wright (Honolulu: University of Hawai'i Press, 2002), 169–94.

48. Hokowhitu, "Tackling Māori Masculinity," 272.

49. Hanlon and White, "Introduction," 2.

50. Margaret Jolly and Lenore Manderson, "Introduction," in *Sites of Desire/Economies of Pleasure in Asia and the Pacific*, ed. Lenore Manderson and Margaret Jolly (Chicago: University of Chicago Press, 1997), 8.

51. Ferguson and Turnbull, *Oh, Say, Can You See?*, 6.

52. Tengan, "(En)gendering Colonialism," 243.

53. Hokowhitu, "Tackling Māori Masculinity," 265.

54. Ibid.

55. For example, the Spanish *reducción*, or reduction, sought to convert all Chamorros in the Marianas archipelago and to relocate them to Guam under direct Spanish colonial control during the late 1600s. This was perhaps the most militarist and violent of practices among the Spanish colonial authorities, many of whom were Jesuit priests. For more on the subject of Spanish colonization in the Marianas, see Francis X. Hezel, *From Conquest to Colonization: Spain in the Mariana Islands, 1690 to 1740* (Saipan, CNMI: Commonwealth of the Northern Mariana Islands Historic Preservation, 2000).

56. Robert Underwood, "Excursions into Inauthenticity: the Chamorro Migrant Stream" (paper presented at the Symposium on Mobility, Identity, and Policy in the Island Pacific, Dunedin, New Zealand, February 1983), 12.

57. Lou Leon Guerrero, interview by Laurel A. Monnig, Hagåtña, Guam, February 2001.

58. Anne Hattori, *Colonial Dis-Ease: US Navy Health Policies and the Chamorros of Guam 1898–1941* (Honolulu: University of Hawai'i Press, 2004), 92–93.

59. Robert Underwood, "Excursions into Inauthenticity," 10; quoting the Annual Report of the Governor of Guam (Agaña, Guam: Naval Government of Guam, 1935), 45.

60. In 1940, the Chamorro population of Guam was 20,177 individuals (91 percent), with 2,113 non-Chamorros (9 percent), for a total of 22,290 people on Guam. See Robert F. Rogers, *Destiny's Landfall: A History of Guam* (Honolulu: University of Hawai'i Press, 1995), 273, citing U.S. Bureau of Census Reports.

61. Warren L. Young, *Minorities and the Military: A Cross-National Study in World Perspective* (Westport, Conn.: Greenwood Press, 1982), 8–9.

62. Augusto V. De Viana, *In the Far Islands: The Role of Natives from the Philippines in the Conquest, Colonization and Repopulation of the Mariana Islands, 1668–1903* (España, Manila: University of Santo Tomas Publishing House, 2004), 192.

63. Yen Lê Espiritu, *Home Bound: Filipino American Lives across Cultures, Communities and Countries* (Berkeley, Calif.: Berkeley University Press, 2003), 28–33.

64. Bruce White, "The American Army and the Indian," in *Ethnic Armies: Polyethnic Armed Forces from the Time of the Habsburgs to the Age of the Superpowers*, ed. N. F. Dreisziger (Ontario, Canada: Wilfrid Laurier University Press, 1990), 80. On Native Americans in the U.S. military during World War II, see Alison R. Bernstein, *American Indians and World War II: Toward a New Era in Indian Affairs* (Norman, Okla.: University of Oklahoma Press, 1991).

65. At the same time, modern countries like colonial Japan did not actively pursue the conscription of minority groups: Koreans and the outcast Burakumin, for example, were excluded from military service until labor shortages necessitated

their use at the close of World War II. White, "The American Army and the Indian," 79. See also Takashi Fujitani, "Right to Kill, Right to Make Live: Koreans as Japanese and Japanese as Americans During WWII," *Representations* 99, no. 1 (2007): 13–39.

66. Cynthia H. Enloe, "Ethnicity in the Evolution of Asia's Armed Bureaucracies," in *Ethnicity and the Military in Asia*, ed. DeWitt C. Ellinwood and Cynthia H. Enloe (New Brunswick, N.J.: Transaction Books, 1981), 6.

67. Larry Mayo, "The Militarization of Guamanian Society," in *Social Change in the Pacific Islands*, ed. Albert B. Robillard (New York: Kegan Paul International, 1992), 115. Rogers, *Destiny's Landfall*, 130–34.

68. Adrian C. Sanchez, *The Chamorro Brown Steward* (Tamuning, Guam: Star Press, 1990), 14.

69. Vicente M. Diaz, "Deliberating 'Liberation Day': Identity, History, Memory and War in Guam," in *Perilous Memories: The Asia-Pacific War(s)*, ed. Takashi Fujitani, Geoffrey M. White, and Lisa Yoneyama (Durham, N.C.: Duke University Press, 1998), 8; Laura M. Torres Souder, "Psyche Under Siege: Uncle Sam, Look What You've Done to Us" (paper presented at the Ninth Annual Conference of the Guam Association of Social Workers, Guam, March 1989), 1.

70. In 1960, there were 34,762 Chamorros (52 percent) and 32,282 non-Chamorros (48 percent), with a total of 67,044 people on Guam. In 1980, there were 47,845 Chamorros (45 percent) and 58,134 non-Chamorros (55 percent), with a total of 105,979. In 1990, Chamorros comprised 57,648 individuals (43 percent) and non-Chamorros 75,504 individuals (57 percent), for a total of 133,152. See Rogers, *Destiny's Landfall*, 273.

71. Robert A. Underwood, "Excursions into Authenticity: The Chamorros of Guam," *Pacific Viewpoint* 26, no. 1 (1985): 167.

72. Rogers, *Destiny's Landfall*, 230. In 1962, the naval security closure was lifted on Guam. Tourism became the new development strategy, one that has remained erratic through the years.

73. Anne Perez Hattori, "Guardians of Our Soil: Indigenous Responses to Post-World War II Military Land Appropriation on Guam" in *Farms, Firms, and Runways: Perspectives on U.S. Military Bases in the Western Pacific*, ed. L. Eve Armentrout Ma (Chicago: Imprint Publications, 2001), 186–202.

74. Underwood, "Excursions into Inauthenticity"; Mayo, "The Militarization of Guamanian Society."

75. Gaynor Dumat-ol Daleno, "580 Guam jobs gone," *Pacific Daily News*, August 11, 2005, 3.

76. C. T. Perez, "Inside Out" in *Indigenous Women: The Right to a Voice*, ed. Diana Vinding (Copenhagen: International Work Group for Indigenous Affairs, 1998), 86–88.

77. Ibid.

78. Robert A. Underwood, interview conducted by Keith L. Camacho, Mangilao, Guam, August 2004.

79. Ferguson and Turnbull, *Oh, Say, Can You See?*, xiv.

80. Catherine Lutz, "U.S. Military Bases: The Edge, Essence, and Eviction of Empire" (paper presented at the American Anthropological Association conference, Chicago, Ill., November 2003), 6.

81. John Hopton, "The State and Military Masculinity," in *Military Masculinities: Identity and the State*, ed. Paul R. Higate (Westport, Conn.: Praeger, 2003), 113.

82. Ibid.

83. Ibid., 115.

84. Ibid.

85. Samantha Regan de Bere, "Masculinity in Work and Family Lives: Implications for Military Service and Resettlement," in *Military Masculinities: Identity and the State*, ed. Paul R. Higate (Westport, Conn.: Praeger, 2003), 94. See also Enloe, *The Morning After*, who asks in chapter 1, "Are UN Peacekeepers Real Men?"

86. Cynthia Enloe, *Maneuvers: The International Politics of Militarizing Women's Lives* (Berkeley: University of California Press, 2000).

87. Robert Tenorio Torres, "Pre-Contact Marianas Folklore, Legends and Literature: A Critical Commentary," *Micronesian: Journal of the Humanities and Social Sciences* 2, no. 1–2 (2003): 10.

88. Juan Pobre, *The Account of Fray Juan Pobre's Residence in the Marianas, 1602*, trans. Marjorie G. Driver (Mangilao, Guam: Micronesian Area Research Center, 1993), 19.

89. Scott Russell, *Tiempon i manmofo'na: Ancient Chamorro Culture and History of the Northern Mariana Islands* (Saipan, CNMI: Commonwealth of the Northern Mariana Islands Division of Historic Preservation, 1998), 213.

90. Ibid.

91. Robert Tenorio Torres, "Colonial and Conquest Lore of the Marianas: A Critical Commentary," *Micronesian: Journal of the Humanities and Social Sciences* 2, no. 1–2 (2003): 26.

92. Tengan, "(En)gendering Colonialism," 248.

93. Olympio I. Magofña, interview by Keith L. Camacho, Hagåtña, Guam, August 2004. At the time of this interview, First Sergeant Magofña was the detachment commander of Guam's U.S. Army Recruiting Office.

94. James Brooke, "On Farthest U.S. Shores, Iraq Is a Way to a Dream," *The New York Times*, July 31, 2005, http://www.nytimes.com/2005/07/31/national/31recruit.html?hp=&pagewanted=print (accessed November 11, 2009). See also Giff Johnson, with reporting by Frank Rosario, Jason Aubuchon, and Nancy Chism, "Micronesia's Iraq Death Toll Rises," *Pacific Magazine*, November 2004, 14–15.

95. Olympio I. Magofña, interview by Keith L. Camacho, Hagåtña, Guam, August 2004.

96. Eddie Dueñas, interview by Laurel A. Monnig, Hagatña, Guam, November 2000.

97. Joe Garrido, interview by Laurel A. Monnig, Mangilao, Guam, January 2000.

98. Angel Leon Guerrero Santos, interview by Laurel A. Monnig, Hagatña, Guam, February 2001. Santos, a veteran of the U.S. military, was a charismatic Chamorro leader for Chamorro rights, especially land struggles with the U.S. military. In the late 1980s, he became emblematic of indigenous struggles through a Chamorro nationalism, which articulated questions of race, class, and environmental destruction of lands in novel ways. He later became a senator in the Guam Legislature. He passed away in July of 2003.

99. Mayo, "The Militarization of Guamanian Society," 238; and Underwood, "Excursions into Inauthenticity," 10.

100. Katie Worth, "Casualty Rate from War Higher For Area," *Pacific Daily News*, October 5, 2004, A1; also see Giff Johnson with reporting by Frank Rosario, Jason Aubuchon, and Nancy Chism, "Micronesia's Iraq Death Toll Rises," *Pacific Magazine*, November 2004, 14–15.

101. Cecille Dodge, "Views From Both Sides of A Fence: Attitudes that Promote Disharmony Between The Civilian and Military Communities in Guam," in *Uncle Sam in Micronesia: Social Benefits, Social Costs*, ed. Donald H. Rubinstein and Vivian L. Damas (Mangilao, Guam: Micronesian Area Research Center, 1991), 25.

102. Hokowhitu, "Tackling Māori Masculinity," 269–70.

103. Homi Bhabha, "Of Mimicry and Men: The Ambivalence of Colonial Discourse," *October* 28 (1984): 125–33.

104. Espiritu, *Home Bound*, 128.

105. See T. Fujitani, "Go for Broke, the Movie: Japanese American Soldiers in U.S. National, Military, and Racial Discourses," in *Perilous Memories: The Asia-Pacific War(s)*, ed. Takashi Fujitani, Geoffrey M. White, and Lisa Yoneyama (Durham, N.C.: Duke University Press, 1998), 239–66.

106. Ed Leon Guerrero Benavente, interview by Keith L. Camacho, Mangilao, Guam, March 2002.

107. Ibid.

108. Bhabha, "Of Mimicry and Men."

109. Eloy Hara, interview by Laurel A. Monnig, Hagatña, Guam, July 1998.

110. Ibid.

111. Robert Underwood cited in Diaz, "Deliberating 'Liberation Day,'" 13–14.

112. Antonio Artero Sablan, interview by Laurel A. Monnig, Sinajaña, Guam, November 2000.

113. Homi Bhabha, "Signs Taken for Wonders: Questions of Ambivalence and Authority Under a Tree Outside Delhi," *Critical Inquiry* 12 (1985): 149.

114. Jose Ulloa Garrido, interview by Laurel A. Monnig, Mangilao, Guam, July 1998.
115. Enloe, *Maneuvers*, 14–32.
116. Ibid., 24.
117. As recorded in the field notes of Laurel Monnig, August 1, 1998, during the Commemoration of the Organic Act, Plaza de España, Hagatña, Guam.
118. Speech given by Carlos Taitano, ibid.
119. Speech given by Antonio Unpingco, ibid.
120. "UN General Assembly Resolution 1514 (XV) of December 14, 1960," in *Basic Facts About the United Nations* (New York: United Nations Publications, 1998), 276–80.
121. Stephen Henningham, *The Pacific Island States: Security and Sovereignty in the Post-Cold War World* (New York: Macmillan Press, Ltd., 1995), 61.
122. Johnson, "American Impact," 241.

8

Militarized Filipino Masculinity and the Language of Citizenship in San Diego

Theresa Cenidoza Suarez

This chapter focuses on the co-construction of masculinity and manhood among Filipino navy men and their families in San Diego, California, since the mid-1940s.[1] This multigenerational study is primarily based on original recorded interview data of approximately twenty Filipino navy families residing in San Diego, of which three members of each family (the male enlistee, the spouse, and an adult child) were interviewed, for a total of sixty participants whose affiliation with the U.S. Navy spans approximately fifty years. I examine the conditions of labor for Filipino navy men, how the work available to them is made to be undignified to reflect their devaluation as workers, and to institutionalize their nonman status in relationship to white hegemonic masculinity. In particular, I illustrate how Filipino men *nevertheless* find meaning in such work to secure a sense of Filipino masculinity and manhood through the roles of "family provider" and fatherhood. Moreover, I examine the contingency of these roles and how they rely not only on Filipino navy men but also on the expectations of their spouses (or former spouses, in some cases), children, and, to an extent, transnational family networks. I conclude with a discussion of Filipino masculinity in relationship to the United States, and how the U.S. Navy makes available to them the rhetorical language of citizenship in terms of "patriotic duty," regardless of legal and social citizenship, and its various meanings for Filipino navy men and their families.

Neferti Tadiar described in "Sexual Economies in the Asia-Pacific Community" that sexuality and ideals of masculinity and femininity undergird large-scale international relations, especially between the Philippines and the United States.[2] In light of Tadiar's analysis, I illustrate how

181

Filipino manhood is constructed on an ideal of heteronormative masculinity in the U.S. Navy. Roderick Ferguson explains in "The Nightmares of the Heteronormative" how heteronormative masculinity is a construct premised on the Weberian notion of rationality, which has historically formed the basis of legal citizenship and rights in the United States—an ideology of inclusion made possible through the exclusion of subjects deemed irrational, such as women, homosexuals, and nonwhite groups (with a focus on African Americans).[3] In particular, Ferguson notes how the legal institution of marriage functions in society to regulate sexual expression and identify rational citizen–subjects, as well as to conform them to the institutional and ideological makeup of liberal capitalist societies.[4] Thus, building upon Ferguson's analysis, I investigate how heteronormative masculinity is co-constructed among Filipino navy men and their families; the function of heterosexuality and marriage in constituting and producing militarized and gendered Filipino citizen–subjects out of imperial domination; and the role of the patriarchal economy and military in the production of intimate, reciprocal, and contradictory relations out of conditions of imperial plunder and subdued labor.[5] The feminization of work made available to Filipino stewards in the U.S. Navy institutionalized the devaluation of their masculinity. The demasculinization of colonized men was indeed integral to the consolidation of white hegemonic U.S. imperial authority in the Philippines.[6]

Yet, Filipino masculinity is a necessary and tenuous co-construction among Filipino navy families as well and not exclusively a male-gendered or male-gendering project. In the field of Asian American studies, David Eng, in *Racial Castration*, underscores that Asian American male subjectivity is constituted and sustained by the psychic valences and material dimensions of gender, sexuality, and sexual difference as constitutive of contemporary racial formation.[7] I contend that heteronormative Filipino manhood is constituted through the co-constructions of heteronormative womanhood and childhood as well. All of these roles are imagined and lived within a transnational domestic sphere inescapably militarized and domesticated within the contexts of U.S. military culture and U.S. imperialism. The inversion of masculine and feminine roles on U.S. ship decks, in admiral quarters, and in mess halls—the militarized spaces where Filipino men have historically performed feminized domestic work as navy stewards and other less-esteemed labor—heightened efforts among Filipino navy families to establish heteronormative gender relations among kin even as these families effectively stretched the normative boundaries of Filipino manhood, womanhood, and childhood.[8]

Arguably, Filipino navy families invest the notion of Filipino manhood with expectations of heteronormative masculinity in order that these historically colonized and militarized communities may *nearly* fulfill painfully idealized expectations of normative gender roles—roles that are not only promoted in U.S. military culture and society but also rewarded. Yet, the everyday lives of Filipino navy families also reveal the limits of the normative nuclear family trope idealized by the military, political pundits, the media, and in some cases, *even among the families themselves.*[9] Based on David Eng and Alice Hom's analysis in *Q & A: Queer in Asian America*, I *queer* the construction of Filipino navy families as a "political practice based on transgressions of the normal or normativity rather than a straight/gay binary of heterosexual/homosexual identity."[10] In other words, the construction of Filipino U.S. Navy families may be considered a *transgression* of normativity created out of the unauthorized yet made-to-be-normalized circumstances of U.S. imperial dependency and demise. Indeed, given the historical specificities of U.S. domination in the Philippines, Filipino masculinity is constituted on *different* terms than that of other U.S. military servicemen.

The Militarization of San Diego

San Diego serves as a relevant site to study Filipino navy families due to the history of naval recruitment in the Philippines, the expansive military-industrial complex in San Diego, and the large population of Filipinos in the area. Statistics from the year 2000 indicate that there were 121,147 Filipino residents in San Diego County.[11] Although Filipinos comprised only 4 percent of the county's general population, they constitute more than 50 percent of the Asian American population.[12] As a historical "navy town," San Diego is a prominent area of settlement for many Filipino navy men and their families. For the majority of Filipino navy men, San Diego was their first U.S. destination—the former home of the Naval Training Center where many received their basic training.[13]

The military–industrial complex in San Diego has provided training for the U.S. Pacific Fleet since the early twentieth century. According to Mike Davis in *Under the Perfect Sun: The San Diego Tourists Never See*, geopolitical tensions in the Pacific (especially the rise in U.S.–Japan rivalry between

1906 and 1913) contributed to the creation of a Pacific Fleet base in San Diego by progressives concerned about protecting California from the "yellow peril."[14] Thus, the recruitment of Filipino men from the Philippines for the U.S. Pacific Fleet may present a curious paradox to purported fears of Asian encroachment; arguably, their "inclusion" in the U.S. Navy is based on their domesticated role in the U.S. military.

Despite some restructuring and downsizing of domestic military bases in recent years, the U.S. Navy and the U.S. Marine Corps in San Diego remain ubiquitous to the economic and cultural landscape of San Diego.[15] As Davis explains, "The Navy was an ideal industry: to most eyes its handsome warships and soaring carrier planes beautified rather than disfigured the environment. Each cruiser or carrier, moreover, added to the economy the purchasing power of a small- or medium-sized factory."[16] Over 10 percent of the total land in the San Diego metropolitan area, about 52.5 square miles, has been used by the U.S. Navy over the years, indicating the kind of economic and political influence the defense industry has on the region.[17] The influence of the military–industrial complex also engenders a climate of conservative republicanism in San Diego, stemming from early twentieth-century white-supremacist attitudes that cater to the needs of military and political elite.[18] Ordinary enlisted men, including Filipino enlistees, have faced the challenges of affordable housing and low wages.[19] Among nonwhite enlisted men generally, racial discrimination would affect their treatment and acceptance in the San Diego social milieu, especially when not in uniform.

Racialized Domestics in the U.S. Navy

Race played an integral role in the modernization of the U.S. Navy. The U.S. military was among the earliest institutions of the United States that relied on a racially integrated labor force. African Americans began enlisting in large numbers following the Civil War and were allowed to serve in several ratings—at least initially.[20] However, the Jim Crow era of "separate but equal" policies at the turn of the twentieth century effectively led to segregated messing and berthing.[21] Eventually, the ratings available to African Americans were restricted to the less desirable engine-room ratings and the steward branch due, in part, to fear that African Americans may advance to military positions of authority ahead of whites.[22] Other racial and ethnic groups (including American Indians,

Chamorros, Chinese, Filipinos, Hawaiians, Japanese, Puerto Ricans, and Sāmoan) were inducted into the navy prior to World War II in relatively fewer numbers than African Americans (see chapters 3 and 7).[23] Concern about the legal citizenship status of these groups, and the ability to enforce racially restrictive policies, limited their recruitment; yet, more than half of these groups were colonized subjects of the United States without any legal recourse to dispute the navy's policies. Furthermore, their status as noncitizens justified their automatic exclusion from ratings requiring access to information deemed "classified" and ensured their institutionalization as nonclassified, feminized labor. Thus, the work made available to nonwhite men in the U.S. Navy, including Filipino enlistees, *institutionalized* the devaluation of their masculinity by safeguarding white supremacy and heteronormative masculinity from work made less dignified.

Among Filipino men in particular, their legal status as U.S. colonial subjects and as "U.S. Nationals" facilitated their recruitment in the navy, and in time, they exceeded the number of African American stewards.[24] U.S. militarization and colonization of the Philippines led to the establishment of primary base installations, such as Clark Air Base and Subic Bay Naval Base, along with other military stations located throughout the Philippines, such as Sangley Point in Cavite and Camp John Hayes in Baguio. These recruiting stations served as institutional mechanisms facilitating the recruitment of Filipino men into the U.S. Armed Forces.[25] Growing dissatisfaction with black mess attendants led to the racialization of Filipino men as superior servants, not unlike their Chinese and Japanese predecessors, based on Orientalist presumptions of the Filipino temperament as agreeable and of Filipinos' less intimidating stature that was also suitable to stoop labor (i.e., cleaning floors, washing clothes, cooking, etc.).[26] Yen Espiritu argues that Filipino men were subject to practices of differential inclusion and were integrated into the U.S. Navy, and the nation, only and precisely because of their subordinate standing.[27] In other words, as official policy, the U.S. Navy enlisted Filipino men in the Philippines only as subordinate domestic workers whose feminized labor was absolutely integral to the everyday functioning of the U.S. Navy. Their subordinate standing was intended to guard against any nonwhite enlisted man from advancing ahead of white men in all ranks and rates. Thus, white privilege (like access to promotions) and masculinity (through work perceived as more dignified, like positions of military authority) have been institutionalized and protected in the U.S. Navy throughout much of the twentieth century.

Fluctuations in the enlistment of Filipino men reflected shifts in geopolitical relations in the Pacific. Indeed, practices of differential inclusion are evidenced in the timely recruitment of Chamorro men in 1937 as navy stewards, who moderated uncertain relations with the Philippines up to World War II, after which the colonial status of the Philippines (and the Philippines' ability to provide "superior servants") became clear. The Tydings-McDuffie Act of 1934 set in motion the processes for Philippine independence from U.S. colonial rule and was formalized in 1947; however, only after meeting contingencies set in the Military Bases Agreement, which guaranteed the U.S. extraterritorial rights in the Philippines, were the operations of U.S. military bases and the recruitment of Filipino men as stewards in the U.S. Navy continued there. Needless to say, this begs the question as to whether or not the Philippines *truly* was ever liberated from U.S. colonial rule.[28]

Devalued Filipino Masculinity

Several of the study participants, however, found unofficial ways to maneuver through the ratings system and describe how asserting themselves as Filipino men demanded "resourcefulness" that they alone were uniquely positioned to execute in order to bring more dignity to their work.[29] Mr. Camatcho, who enlisted in 1946, described how he was able to change an undesirable relocation order. He felt that his reputation as a trusted personal steward to an admiral with powerful influence could be harnessed with an unsettling mix of male flattery and self-effacement: "All I do is call [the admiral] up at the Pentagon, where I was also working at the time . . . I tell him my orders . . . and where I *prefer* to go . . . and he said he will look into it, and it happened."[30] Mr. Camatcho's face brightened with a wide, knowing smile as he expressed his self-perceived knack for finding a way to manage the military's arbitrary assignments for stewards. In this unusual case, his assignment was changed because of a paternalistic relationship with a white admiral whose power Mr. Camatcho knew how to access temporarily for his own personal advantage. He, too, had gained powerful insight as a personal steward to the admiral and knew intimately how and when the admiral ate, slept, dressed, and spent his in-between hours. Such feminized labor

Mr. Camatcho described as "easy enough," but more significant was the insight he gained from access to such power from *inside* the ship's hull at its *most* vulnerable. Mr. de la Rosa, who enlisted in 1961, explains, "Some stewards were treated badly but the admiral helped me a lot, even when I did something wrong."[31] Mr. de la Rosa relied on the benign intervention and rescue of the admiral, who patiently guided him on domestic etiquette (like learning proper table settings and preparing meals on time) even when Mr. de la Rosa "messed up" and did not get it right the first time. He added, "If they are good to you, then you do good things not only for them, but the next one [admiral] you work for."[32] While cordial relationships were not uncommon, they were certainly not the norm. However, Mr. de la Rosa revealed how controlling the quality output of his work—however domestic—was a way to reaffirm his personal dignity as a Filipino man by his *own* authority. These examples illustrate the complex trajectory of U.S. empire and militarism in everyday life: how some Filipino navy men believed they could maneuver, if not steer, militarized circumstances in better ways, on their terms, even when "proper" masculine authority and feminized labor would remain institutionalized as respectively white and nonwhite.

There was a range of less popular ratings and duty stations that Filipino navy men were permitted to enter into upon initial enlistment as a steward, such as engine-room boiler tenders, storekeepers, or disbursing clerks. These were positions considered necessary—even *vital* to daily operations—but clearly devalued. Mr. Castillo, who enlisted in 1960, worked in a deafening engine room as a boiler tender without protective gear (which was not required then), and he suffered moderate hearing loss as a result. Mr. Magbuhat, who enlisted in 1956 and passed away during the course of this research, worked as a boiler tender and handled steaming hot water that was absolutely vital to the ship's ability to sail—but without protective gear, as well.

In one poignant example, Mr. Fedalizo, who enlisted in 1945, had additional domestic duties besides his primary responsibilities as a steward. He worked as a member of a decontamination unit, cleaning radioactive residue from bomber airplanes, which resulted from atomic bomb tests off Bikini Atoll, Marshall Islands, in the mid-1950s.[33] In recalling his painstaking work in Bikini Atoll, Mr. Fedalizo remembers the violence of American wartime nuclearism in Japan as well:

What we do, was when the airplane landed, we go over there on the landing strip and decontaminate that plane—because when the bomb explodes, it forms a mushroom cloud, and the airplanes go through that cloud. Naturally, they are contaminated with radiation, and so, when they land, those planes have to be decontaminated in order to be able to be used again. So that was our job . . . we all go in there, and more or less wash up the planes . . . fifteen or twenty times, because after you finish one washing, you have to measure . . . the amount of radiation . . . And [in Japan] the thing that made an impression on me so much was that there's a silhouette . . . everything was black, but this space—this area of cement—was an outline of a body . . . Maybe the person got hit by the bomb and fell right there, and while the radiation was working, it burned the body of that person—man or woman—and shielded the concrete so it left that impression.[34]

Silence spaced his words upon unexpectedly describing to me the buried memories of the black silhouettes of the dead he saw in Nagasaki City, Japan, following the second atomic bomb devastation that punctuated the final phase of World War II. In that moment, I hoped that my own respectful silence and soft gaze conveyed the compassion I felt he was seeking from me. Even as this anecdote illustrated a physical "casualty" of war, Mr. Fedalizo expressed the psychic valence of indignity that shadowed him daily, that is, of knowing he had served an institution that condoned indiscriminate violence against innocent civilians. What was his culpability in the needless deaths of civilian men, women, and children? At what cost are the quotidian demands of Filipino masculinity and manhood met? Mr. Fedalizo chose to highlight, in the seconds following, the moments when relief from degraded labor might offer an all-too-brief respite, such as cookouts on the beach with fellow servicemen in Bikini Atoll and "nights on the town" with Filipino and African American enlisted men in downtown San Diego. Still unresolved, however, is the complicated notion of "casualties of war" and the indelible traces of the ideological and cultural violence of U.S. imperial rule, which inhabit mind and body due to the latent violence of the "benevolent" war that resulted in the colonization of the Philippines and the recruitment of Filipino men into the U.S. Navy *in the first place*. Vicente M. Diaz described how memories of the Japanese occupation of Guam and the stories told him by his parents who survived the war in the Philippines haunt him still: "To this day the war rages, even when I wake up with my heart racing and my body and bed drenched."[35] The violence of war is indirectly experienced through collective memory in these examples and is certainly anything but subtle.[36]

Mr. Fedalizo and other participants assumed perilous positions in the U.S. imperial military and, perhaps unwittingly, participated in the direct decimation of their Pacific home. The Pacific was exploited for such reckless military experimentation, as the geopolitical context of the cold war era ushered in an unprecedented arms race between the United States (the purported leader of democracy and the "free world") and the former Soviet Union (deemed communist foe). The bold demonstration of sovereign domain by the U.S. military to perform such deadly oceanic exercises without regard to the ramifications on the vitality of the Pacific, and for indigenous peoples' ways of life, further burdened the region by such "nuclear colonialism" imposed by the industrialized world (as chapter 2 also describes).[37] Certainly implicated are the colonial subjects, whose inclusion in the imperial military would validate the violence.

The U.S. Navy officially opened the ratings system and modified enlistment test procedures that were scrutinized by the early 1970s. Recruitment from the Philippines exclusively for stewards was modified in 1971 by a U.S. State Department agreement with the Philippine government to allow Filipinos to enter any enlisted rating they were considered qualified for by means of education, prior experience, and security qualifications: this included small numbers of enlisted Filipino women. However, the Bureau of Naval Personnel would emphasize how "the actual needs of the unit to which they are attached will influence the actual rating that they can pursue."[38] The steward rating was discontinued in late 1974 and was replaced by the Mess Management Specialist rating, which covered most of the responsibilities of the former rating except in the area of providing routine housekeeping and cleaning services for officers.

Reauthorized Filipino Manhood

Despite changes in official U.S. military policy, the following example illustrates its limits in everyday life through what I term the militarized reauthorization of Filipino masculinity. Mr. Ancho recalled these words exchanged with his former commanding officer, whom he met unexpectedly on a family vacation in Oahu in the early 1980s. Mr. Ancho was retired from military service for twenty years by this time, casually called his former admiral who lived there (he obtained the phone number through the local phone book), and was invited to the former admiral's lavish home. After exchanging small talk about retirement, Mr. Ancho was struck by how his former admiral addressed him by his name:

> ANCHO: Sir, throughout my years in the service, you never called me by my name . . . you called me "boy."
> ADMIRAL: Well, you're a man, now, Ancho . . . you served in the U.S. military.[39]

After twenty years of preparing the admiral numerous meals (including the admiral's favorite, chop suey), Mr. Ancho was bestowed by military authority as finally being a *real* man, identifiable by given name, instead of as a "boy." He laughed out loud with a mix of disbelief and humor in recalling this conversation. I respected his cues and listened attentively, trying to maintain my own composure. Apparently, the admiral was so taken by reminiscing on their days as admiral and personal steward that he offered Mr. Ancho and his wife jobs on the spot as domestic house servants, complete with personal quarters and a car. Interestingly, Mr. Ancho considered the offer quite appealing, as it was free room and board in Hawai'i with a free car, and lamented his wife's firm response that she and the children already had their own lives in San Diego. The admiral's paternalistic *reauthorization* of Mr. Ancho's manhood presupposed that Mr. Ancho should sacrifice his masculinity and personhood by daily performing feminized domestic labor for white officers (and their families) who did not care about it and refused to do it for themselves. Indeed, this example illustrates how Filipino men were still considered "boys," as domesticated natives, and *not* real men. Moreover, Mr. Ancho's response revealed a curious and complicated relationship of masculine affection and attachment that he imagined between them *as men*, which I found personally unsettling, for rate and duty station do not *make the man*.

Militarized Filipino Fatherhood

What *does* appear, though, to "make the man" is fatherhood. The ability of Filipino enlistees as fathers and husbands to provide for their own families was not only desirable but also, eventually, rewarded by the military as honorable and respectable. Through the Philippines Enlistment Program, bachelorhood was an institutionalized requirement of Filipino enlistees, one that made unlawful the making and supporting of families of their own. An expressed requirement for Filipino enlistment was certification of their dependency status to verify that "applicants be single and have no one solely or partially dependent upon them for support," including a spouse, other dependents, and even parents.[40] Several of the participants chuckled when I reminded them of the "bachelorhood" requirement and explained offhandedly how difficult that was for the navy to enforce. How could they *not* meet expectations of them *as Filipino men* to support their loved ones left behind in the Philippines? In fact, one participant was married when he joined the navy and later sought permission from the military to be properly "remarried" (so to speak) in order to legalize the arrangement.[41] On the downside, several participants met with marital tension in the United States when they tried to fulfill transpacific expectations of Filipino masculinity to provide for loved ones in the Philippines.

In a poignant example, Mr. Fedalizo shared this memory of how fatherhood was rewarded under the watchful eyes of the U.S. military: "[That was] the very first time in my life I've ever seen that happen—a full captain of the United States Navy handed *me* a cup of coffee. He says, 'Congratulations' . . . [and] hands me a radiogram. It said, 'Baby Bernadette born March 18. Mother and daughter doing fine.' Captain said congratulations again, 'Sit down and drink your coffee, and after you finish your coffee, go down and get me a box of cigars.'"[42] Though it was an early Sunday morning, and the ship's store was closed, Mr. Fedalizo was advised to wake the storekeeper and reward the captain for sharing the good news. He laughed in dismissing the inconvenience, simply happy to hear any word about his family in San Diego. In this example, Mr. Fedalizo's new role as a father not only authorized this "special audience" with the captain but also rewarded his paternal role as a new father. Indeed, under the captain's watch are the colonial prerogatives of proper masculinity and domestication of the native fulfilled. The captain's response was at the least rude and at best the only way perhaps he had to express his compliments; either way, it did not change how creating and raising a family somehow would mean, for Mr. Fedalizo, meeting expectations of being his *own* man.

Still, militarized Filipino fatherhood meant that Filipino men could not always provide particularly well for their own families, which created ongoing tensions for several participants. Mr. Fedalizo described how military life created hardships for enlisted families like his to make ends meet: "When we just moved into this house, we extended ourselves financially. What I used to do is, I send her my paychecks... But the problem is, the check *does not* travel if you're not in port! [So]... there's a Jack-in-the-Box over here. She tells me she used to get eleven hamburgers for a dollar... sometimes they eat hamburger eight days a week—twice on Sunday! If they don't buy hamburgers, she would feed the kids pancakes... She used to tell the kids *how to do*, [since] we don't have too much money. They got along, [but] those were the difficult times for me."[43] Mr. Fedalizo recalled these memories to me with pride for his late wife's resourcefulness and leadership, since his own masculinized expectations of being an effective provider was precarious without her support. As Mr. de la Rosa echoed confidently, "They underestimated the steward, but I was proud because that [job] is the one that fed my family."[44] Given the humble family backgrounds of the participants (many came from families with poor to modest means) and the feminized, degraded labor made available to them as stewards, it is no wonder that the ability to feed their own families was so highly regarded as a small way to reconstitute Filipino masculinity on their *own* terms. In another example, Mr. Franco, who enlisted in 1963, reconstituted Filipino masculinity through his own son, whom he instructed as an eight year old to *provide* (note the masculinist phrasing) a safe home for himself, his younger brother, and their mother each night by checking that the doors and windows were locked—since sadly, his father had to leave the family "unprotected" due to overseas deployment.[45]

Thus, the notion of *family* has served as motivation among these participants to reinvent, if not to subvert, institutionalized efforts to devalue their labor and personhood. Historically, U.S. immigration policies and labor-recruitment practices in the Philippines have recruited a gendered labor force of color, which effectively outlawed the formation of Filipino families on the U.S. continent in the early twentieth century, perceived as they were as distractions to worker efficiency and exploitability. As Rhacel Parreñas argued, Filipino male migrants in the 1920s and 1930s were largely recruited as manual laborers for California's agribusiness and were "subjected and disciplined through the maximization of their bodies as machines."[46] That is, Filipino men were only considered working bodies and not reproductive or desirable bodies. Philip Vera Cruz, a prominent labor organizer with the United Farm Workers Union, described in his biography how "this cruel situation denied us the right to live a normal, respectable life.

As men without families in the U.S., it was hard then, and even now, to just get together among ourselves as though we were a family."[47] Nevertheless, non-normative formations of family among Filipino and Asian groups flourished during this early period of "bachelor societies" in California.[48]

Filipino fatherhood is characterized by a desire (if not the ability) *to provide for* their families and may be decidedly disassociated from the unauthorized conquest of the Philippines and the differential inclusion of Filipino men into the U.S. Navy. Furthermore, Filipino manhood is framed in terms of "duty" obligations on both sides of the Pacific for families caught in the imperial crossfire. Yet, as Mr. Villa aptly stated, "You can buy anything you want for your family, but the Americans don't give you the due respect."[49] In other words, even though the consumption of consumer goods would provide immediate gratification, such status markers would not fundamentally alter the status quo. In the Philippines, however, Mr. Fune, who enlisted in 1945, explained how possessing U.S. consumer goods conferred much sought-after respect: "We look up to [the navy people] because, my God, they have a nice house they can afford . . . and a Coleman lantern . . . that thing is so bright when you pass by their house . . . we were used to candles or the kerosene lamp."[50]

The lack of desirable opportunities for sustainable livelihoods in the Philippines—ravaged by U.S. militarization, foreign capitalist interests, environmental degradation, and political corruption—engendered a desire for "made-*it*-in-the-U.S.A." legitimacy and status in order to fulfill *familiar* and *familial* conceptions of heteronormative masculinity. These were gained (and commonly shared among family residing abroad via *balikbayan* parcel services that might ensure reliable delivery) through the conspicuous consumption of familiar U.S. name-brand goods, such as Lee brand jeans, Spam luncheon meat, Colgate toothpaste, Covergirl makeup, Hershey's chocolates, and other common U.S. household items, like multivitamins. Yet such mundane consumerism, the bane of the elite and the mainstay of the poor and working class, merely gestures at their subjective meanings.[51] Some participants were haunted by an inability to reconcile the relative privileges of living in the United States against the despair of the beloved who remain in the Philippines. Other participants quite simply desired the imagined status afforded them and their families by U.S.-made products and high-end luxury goods.

Yet, the effort to provide for the family reflects the contingency and limitation of their positions in the U.S. Navy, as well as the family labor necessary for the "provider role" to be actualized. Indeed, Filipino masculinity is characterized by not only the ability of these men to provide for their own and for extended families, but also the ability to co-provide with spouses, and at times, *not at all*. In fact, the management of household finances was a source of conflict among a few participants. For example, Mrs. Magbuhat held the "family purse" in her early years of marriage, which concerned Mr. Magbuhat's parents, who did not expect a simple, uneducated woman to manage their son's income.[52] Providing financially for family in the Philippines helped to maintain familial connections in concrete ways, such as by facilitating transnational marriages and attendant celebrations, which were difficult for many of the participants to manage on their own. For example, Mr. Cordivin's parents played a key role in shaping his role as a husband and father, despite how his everyday duties as a navy steward kept him overseas for long periods of time. They arranged a marriage for him with a friend of the family and also helped care for his new wife and their children in the Philippines until Mr. Cordivin was ready to send for them.[53] Mrs. Cordivin explained, "I stayed with my parents until he came back, and then we move to Cavite and have our own house. He's a good man. He's a good provider."[54] An arranged marriage allowed Mr. and Mrs. Cordivin to fulfill expectations of Filipino manhood and womanhood, even if military duties separated them in their early years of marriage. The Villa family, for example, lived apart for eight years, but Mrs. Villa recalled that living with her family in the Philippines provided her with support in raising their children—support that was missed when they migrated to the United States.[55]

Several participants used military leave to return to the Philippines to reunite with school classmates or village peers, to marry, and to start families of their own before returning abroad.[56] Mr. Fune explained this phenomenon with a simple question: "Can you imagine a sailor with a middle-school education [marrying] a professional?"[57] Mr. Fune described the prestige that affiliation with the U.S. Navy afforded uneducated Filipino sailors, who were highly regarded among professional women in the Philippines for the prospect of accompanying them to the United States. Mr. Magbuhat echoed this sentiment about the enhanced perception of Filipino U.S. servicemen in the Philippines when he said, "Everyone looked down at the navy in the U.S., but you are looked [at] as something in the Philippines."[58] These perspectives suggest that some participants found, through marriages celebrated with kin in the Philippines, the reauthorization of their masculinity, despite the feminized work required of them in the U.S. Navy. Thus, physical distance from family in the Philippines (and elsewhere), a difficult aspect of the military and migration experience, did not necessarily render familial ties less influential.[59] These ties were taut with the desire to construct an idealized masculinity *on all sides* of the Pacific, outlined by imperial uniforms that, Mr. Fedalizo exclaims, "were about four inches too long" and, even when tailored, arguably never fit quite right.

The Language of Citizenship and Patriotic Duty

The cycles of economic expansion and contraction that have impacted immigration flows throughout U.S. history are reflected in the ways in which U.S. Navy Filipino enlistees were intermittently offered legal citizenship. Lengthy legal haggling about granting citizenship rights to all members of the U.S. Armed Forces reveals how citizenship as a legal and political category challenged long-standing legal investments in maintaining white male privileges in all areas of life and property despite liberal claims of universal inclusion *for all*. The legal investment in guarding whiteness is also revealed in broader Asian immigration history, for Asians were legally forbidden, as "aliens ineligible for citizenship," from owning land and from participating in the primary labor force and in the court cases that upheld these laws.[60] Filipinos, as the only colonial "nationals" of the U.S. empire in the U.S. Armed Forces, would occupy a long-standing ambivalent and curious position, as reflected in this brief legal history.

Yet despite this, the U.S. Navy made available to Filipino enlistees the *language* of citizenship and masculinity in terms of *patriotic* patriarchal duty regardless of legal and social citizenship. From the outset, Mr. Fune, who enlisted in 1945, described his attraction for the U.S. military: "We want to be Americanized. In the Philippines, you go to the movies in Manila and [they] are all American films. Golly, I wish I can drive a car like that. Someday, I will be driving a car like that. We really embrace the Western culture. It's happening in Manila right now . . . we are completely Americanized. We're completely 'pro-Western' now."[61] Feminized work as stewards was made tolerable for the status gained by working in the U.S. Navy and *possible* inclusion in the nation, including the implicit gender power associated with the U.S. military as a masculine paragon of white privilege.[62] In this case, the promise of Filipino masculinity and manhood was imagined through the rewards of an "American" manhood, symbolized as the freedom associated with driving a fast, American-made muscle car. Yet, in describing his experiences of fatherhood, Mr. Fune reflects on the limits of his masculinized role: "As I am looking back, my kids can't speak Tagalog at all . . . I should have insisted to teach them myself . . . They completely forgot that they're Filipino . . . All my girls are all married to American[s] . . . If I put fish and vegetables there, they say 'yuck!' My kids completely forgot the language, everything."[63] Mr. Fune revealed in this statement a melancholy sentiment echoed by other participants. That is, reconstituting Filipino manhood and masculinity is *never completely accomplished*, despite any trappings and rewards of being loyal to the U.S. Navy and living in the United States. Children, in particular, serve to remind them of the mix of joy and sorrow that accompanies unmet expectations of raising young Filipino men and women in their adopted homeland. In fact, several participants revealed a stunning desire to show me tangible evidence of belonging *still* and "making it" as Americans. Mr. Fune's home displayed a "signed" mass-produced portrait of former President George W. Bush, with a dedication of gratitude for his patriotism and financial campaign contributions. Mr. Ancho drew my attention to a similar mass-produced framed portrait of former President Bill Clinton and Hillary Clinton that sits prominently in the family room, congratulating the Anchos on their golden wedding anniversary.[64] Mr. de la Rosa proudly showed me an official portrait taken with former President Nixon alongside a sizable group of other Filipino stewards.[65] Inderpal Grewal states, "America was important to so many across the world because its power enabled the American nation-state to disseminate the promise of democratic citizenship and belonging through consumer practices as well as disciplinary technologies."[66] Thus, these examples show how the domestic space is always overseen, authorized, and enabled *every* day by U.S. authority—regardless of how and whether these Filipino men identify, cope with, and resolve their expectations of themselves as men through the language of citizenship.[67]

In closing, Filipino masculinity is domesticated, indeed *made legible*, through militarized authorization and reproduced in and through liberal humanist military institutions, discourses, and practices where the condition of possibility of human self-possession as Filipino navy men is doubly compounded by the logic of U.S. imperialism in the Philippines. As

Lisa Lowe explains, such violence is "not only carried out in the humanist languages of liberty, equality, reason, progress, and human rights—almost without exception, they must be translated into the political and juridical spaces of this tradition."[68] Thus, their devotion to "providing," "family," and "fatherhood" illustrates Filipino navy men's interpretations of "humanist logic" in the imperial center, which, as the basis of enlightenment tradition in U.S. history, implicates absolutely *all* U.S. inhabitants to deal with the limitations and constraints posed through such "tradition" in contemporary life.[68] As such, I contend that Filipino masculinity and manhood is co-constructed by Filipino navy families in San Diego in dynamic, quotidian ways to cope with the idiosyncrasies that their historical trajectories entail from within the U.S. imperial center.

Notes

I wish to thank Dr. Yen Lê Espiritu, Dr. Lisa Sun-Hee Park, Dr. Thuy Vo Dang, Dr. Nina Ha, Dr. Setsu Shigematsu, Dr. Keith L. Camacho, and Danniel M. Suarez for their helpful comments on this chapter, as well as the numerous participants in San Diego who made this research possible. The research was funded and supported by the Pacific Rim Research Program of the University of California (UC) Office of the President, the California Cultures Research Center of UC San Diego, the Fletcher Jones Dissertation Fellowship of the UC Office of the President, and a Brython Davis Scholarship.

1. In this study, I define "Filipino navy men" as male citizens of the Philippines who enlisted in the U.S. Navy in the Philippines between the 1940s and the early 1970s. The term "Filipino navy families" is generally defined here as familial networks of kin as recognized by the participants themselves. Most of the participants identified as "Filipino" men and women. One non-Filipino spouse interviewed in this study regarded her family as "Filipino."

2. Neferti Tadiar, "Sexual Economies in the Asia-Pacific Community," in *What Is in a Rim?: Critical Perspectives on the Pacific Region Idea*, ed. Arif Dirlik (Lanham, Md.: Rowman & Littlefield, 1998), 219–48.

3. Roderick Ferguson, "The Nightmares of the Heteronormative," *Cultural Values* 4, no. 4 (2000): 419–44.

4. See Ferguson, "The Nightmares of the Heteronormative." See also Nayan Shah, "Adjudicating Intimacies on U.S. Frontiers," in *Haunted by Empire: Geographies of Intimacy in North American History*, ed. Ann Laura Stoler (Durham, N.C.: Duke University Press, 2006), 116–39. For a critical discussion of the Asian

American family trope, see also Robert G. Lee, *Orientals: Asian Americans in Popular Culture* (Philadelphia: Temple University Press, 1999).

5. Ann McClintock, *Imperial Leather: Race, Gender, and Sexuality in the Colonial Contest* (New York: Routledge, 1995).

6. Ann L. Stoler, "Carnal Knowledge and Imperial Power: Gender, Race, and Morality in Colonial Asia," in *Gender at the Crossroads of Knowledge: Feminist Anthropology in the Postmodern Era*, ed. Micaela di Leonardo (Berkeley: University of California Press, 1991), 51–101.

7. David Eng, *Racial Castration: Managing Masculinity in Asian America* (Durham, N.C.: Duke University Press, 2001).

8. Nazli Kibria, *Family Tightrope: The Changing Lives of Vietnamese Americans* (Princeton, N.J.: Princeton University Press, 1993).

9. Stephanie Coontz, *The Way We Never Were: American Families and the Nostalgia Trap* (New York: Basic Books, 1992).

10. David Eng and Alice Hom, ed., *Q & A: Queer in Asian America* (Philadelphia: Temple University Press, 1998), 1.

11. Yen Espiritu, *Homebound: Filipino American Lives across Cultures, Communities, and Countries* (Berkeley: University of California Press, 2003), 17.

12. Ibid.

13. Ibid.

14. Mike Davis, Kelly Mayhew, and Jim Miller, *Under the Perfect Sun: The San Diego Tourists Never See* (New York: New York Press, 2003), 43–44.

15. Examples include the presence of several military vessels, like the USS *Midway* museum, in the San Diego harbor; military hospitals and base shopping facilities frequented by veterans and their families; the business partnerships between the U.S. military and San Diego–based civilian contractors; the extensive media coverage of jubilant family reunions following military deployments; the annual Miramar Air Show, which draws thousands of Southern California civilian residents to the Marine Corps Air Station (MCAS) Miramar military base; holiday parades honoring servicemen and women, which may involve exposing the public to military vehicles (such as tanks); and even the daily roar of military planes and helicopters traveling overhead.

16. Davis et al., *Under the Perfect Sun*, 47.

17. Roger Showley, *San Diego: Perfecting Paradise* (Carlsbad, Calif.: Heritage Media Corporation, 1999).

18. Davis et al., *Under the Perfect Sun*, 48.

19. Ibid., 48.

20. Frederick S. Harrod, *Manning the New Navy: The Development of a Modern Naval Enlisted Force, 1899–1940* (Westport, Conn.: Greenwood Press, 1978), 57.

21. Ibid., 57. See also Richard E. Miller, *The Messman Chronicles: African Americans in the U.S. Navy 1932–1943* (Annapolis, Md.: Naval Institute Press, 2004).

22. Harrod, *Manning the New Navy*, 58–59.
23. Ibid., 183–84.
24. See Miller, *The Messman Chronicles*.
25. L. Eve Ammentrout Ma, ed., *Farms, Firms, and Runways: Perspectives on U.S. Military Bases in the Western Pacific* (Chicago: Imprint Publications, 2001), 124–85.
26. Harrod, *Manning the New Navy*, 60–61. See also Gary Okihiro, "When and Where I Enter," in *Asian American Studies: A Reader*, ed. Jean Yu-wen Shen Wu and Min Song (New Brunswick, N.J.: Rutgers University Press, 2000), 3–20.
27. See Espiritu, *Homebound*. See also Catherine C. Choy, *Empire of Care: Nursing and Migration in Filipino American History* (Durham, N.C.: Duke University Press, 2003).
28. See Harrod, *Manning the New Navy*. On July 1, 1937, Guam was assigned a monthly quota of ten mess attendants, third class, and later increased the number to fifteen (61).
29. Ibid.
30. Mr. Camatcho, interview with the author, tape recording, July 2004.
31. Mr. de la Rosa, interview with the author, tape recording, January 2004.
32. Ibid.
33. Bikini Atoll and Midway Island are militarized U.S. territories in the Pacific Ocean.
34. Mr. Fedalizo, interview with the author, tape recording, July 2004.
35. Vicente M. Diaz, "Deliberating 'Liberation Day': Identity, History, Memory, and War in Guam," in *Perilous Memories*, ed. T. Fujitani, Geoffrey M. White, and Lisa Yoneyama (Durham, N.C.: Duke University Press, 2001), 155.
36. Avery F. Gordon, *Ghostly Matters: Haunting and the Sociological Imagination* (Minneapolis: University of Minnesota Press, 1997).
37. Other countries participated in the bombing of the Pacific. See also Bengt Danielsson and Marie-Thérèse Danielsson, *Poisoned Reign: French Nuclear Colonialism in the Pacific* (New York: Penguin Books, 1986).
38. E. S. Briggs, *Navy Recruiting Manual (Enlisted): COMNAVCRUITCOM Instruction 1130.8B (CRUITMAN-ENL)* (Arlington, Va.: Navy Recruiting Command, 1976). This photocopy of the *Navy Recruiting Manual* was provided by librarians at the Naval Historical Center in Washington, D.C., in July 2003.
39. Mr. Ancho, interview with the author, tape recording, September 2003.
40. Briggs, *Navy Recruiting Manual*.
41. Mr. Villa, interview with the author, tape recording, February 2004.
42. Mr. Fedalizo interview.
43. Ibid.
44. Mr. de la Rosa interview.
45. Mr. and Mrs. Franco, interview with the author, tape recording, July 2004.

46. Rhacel Parreñas, "'White Trash' Meets the 'Little Brown Monkeys': The Taxi Dance Hall as a Site of Interracial and Gender Alliances between White Working Class Women and Filipino Immigrant Men in the 1920s and 30s," *Amerasia Journal* 24 (1998): 115–34.

47. Craig Scharlin and Lilia V. Villanueva, *Philip Vera Cruz: A Personal History of Filipino Immigrants and the Farmworkers Movement* (Los Angeles: University of California–Los Angeles [UCLA] Labor Center, Institute of Industrial Relations and UCLA Asian American Studies Center, 1992).

48. Nayan Shah, *Contagious Divides: Epidemics and Race in San Francisco's Chinatown* (Berkeley: University of California Press, 2001).

49. Mr. Villa interview.

50. Mr. Fune, interview with the author, tape recording, July 2004.

51. Viviana Zelizer, *The Social Meaning of Money* (New York: Basic Books, 1994).

52. Mrs. Magbuhat, interview with the author, tape recording, December 2003.

53. Mr. and Mrs. Cordivin, interview with the author, tape recording, July 2004.

54. Ibid.

55. Mr.Villa interview.

56. For a contemporary analysis of gendered expectations of marriage through the lens of masculinity, see also Hung Cam Thai, *For Better or For Worse: Vietnamese International Marriages in the New Global Economy* (New Brunswick, N.J.: Rutgers University Press, 2008).

57. Mr. Fune interview.

58. Mr. Magbuhat, interview with the author, tape recording, December 2003.

59. Martin Manalansan, *Global Divas* (Durham, N.C.: Duke University Press, 2003).

60. Espiritu, *Homebound*.

61. Mr. Fune interview.

62. George Lipsitz, *The Possessive Investment in Whiteness* (Philadelphia: Temple University Press, 1998).

63. Mr. Fune interview.

64. Mr. Ancho interview.

65. Mr. de la Rosa interview.

66. Inderpal Grewal, *Transnational America: Feminisms, Diaspora* (Durham, N.C.: Duke University Press, 2005), 2.

67. For further discussion of the meanings of citizenship among Filipino veterans of Philippine and U.S. military units, see also Theodore Gonzalves, "'We hold a neatly folded hope': Filipino Veterans of World War II on Citizenship and Political Obligation," *Amerasia Journal* 21, no. 3 (1995/1996): 155–74.

68. Lisa Lowe, "The Intimacies of Four Continents" in *Haunted by Empire: Geographies of Intimacy in North American History*, ed. Ann Laura Stoler (Durham, N.C.: Duke University Press, 2006), 208.

69. For another perspective, see E. San Juan Jr., *After Postcolonialism: Remapping Philippines-United States Confrontations* (Lanham, Md.: Rowman and Littlefield, 2000), 11. San Juan states, "The narrative of the United States as a multiracial and multinational polity is still in the process of being fought through in everyday life, in the interstices of lived collective experience. In the racializing politics of that narrative, we are all implicated as protagonists (together with other people of color) interrogating the hegemonic definition of 'American' as centered in a patriarchal, white-supremacist discourse opposed to the actualization of a democratic, just, egalitarian order" (11).

III

Hetero/Homo-sexualized Militaries

9

On Romantic Love and Military Violence

Transpacific Imperialism and U.S.–Japan Complicity

Naoki Sakai

From the perspective of colonialism, the international encounter between individuals is first brought about by the presence of the colonizing military. It is normally expected that the relationship between the dominating and the dominated ought to be governed by military administration and technology. In the twentieth century, colonial governance required new systems of administration, and the contact between individuals brought about by colonial rule occurred more and more within a militaristic administration, as the sphere of the military has become increasingly multilateral. That is to say that the system of total war was implemented into all spheres of citizens' lives concomitant with the expansion of the military.

In regimes in which militaristic dominance is put into practice, contact between soldiers of the colonizing military and residents of the colonized territory is most frequently symbolized by the model of sexual encounter. Social relations between the colonial military and the local population are, in due course, administered through the increasingly rationalized management of sexual encounters. The military comfort station system[1] introduced by the Japanese Navy and Army can be seen as an instance of this kind of rationality carried to its natural conclusion. Under this administrative system, an extensive structure of hygiene and welfare management was installed in order to control the points of contact between natives and soldiers, and organized efforts were made to ensure that the lives of the soldiers were nurtured and controlled. In other words, the military system of the colonized territories, too, was integrated into the totalitarianism of the suzerain state via biopolitics. This is why the issue of comfort women cannot be thought of as particular to Japanese imperial nationalism. In view of the fact that the comfort station system survived, albeit in a more privatized and voluntaristic form, after the demise of the Japanese Empire, one cannot overlook the regimes of the trans-Pacific security rule that lie at the foundation of the neocolonial relationships between the United States and countries like Japan, the Philippines, and South Korea in post–World War II East Asia. As is more and more widely known, many aspects of the Japanese comfort station system were adopted and conserved in the U.S. military's management in Asia. I suspect that, as Chalmers Johnson recently observed,[2] the U.S. international strategy is supported by a network of military bases, not only in East Asia, but also on a worldwide scale; and that the U.S. military's dominance inherited many aspects of the system of colonial dominance from the Japanese Empire. Evidently, Japanese imperialism was grafted onto American imperialism, and we will remain enslaved to the legacies of past colonialisms in East Asia unless we are fully aware of the continuity between Japanese and the U.S. colonialisms and the complicity of the postwar Japanese particularism and American universalism.[3]

It is best, almost without exception, to consider the plot of commercial movies that portray international love affairs between characters of differing nationalities, ethnicities, or races as allegories of diplomacy or international politics, and undoubtedly this truism derives its legitimacy from the actuality of U.S. postwar military dominance. Parallel to the scenario of commercial films that portray international love and romance is the dramaturgy that unfolds within the sex industry, which is intertwined with various military facilities, and the "intimate" relationships consummated there between individuals.

Perhaps it is more precise to say that, within the overt framework of man as the dominating and woman as the dominated, an international relationship of domination and subordination acquires an extremely intensive symbolization through the trope of romantic love because the latent scenario that is conveyed is the confirmation of the explicit supermasculinity of the colonizing man, on the one hand, and of the implicit demasculinization of the colonized man, on the other. Furthermore, the fact that we rarely encounter a reverse framework in which a woman dominates and a man is dominated suggests that, normally, nationalism does not put up with such an arrangement of gender roles. It follows that, in respect to the forms of desire, nationalism inevitably presents itself as an ideology of homosociality.

In the general scenario of romantic love, the woman plays the phallic role that supports the ethnic, racial, or national identity of the male, or the dominator. In this respect, the conventional scenario of romantic love never contradicts heterosexual normalcy. Right away, two corollaries are drawn in connection with power relations in what Ann Stoler referred to as "the politics of intimacy"[4]: first, the fate of a nation is narrated on the stage of international theater, in relation to other nations, ethnicity, or races, as a heterosexual affair involving characters allegorizing the social groups at issue. Even if, in the first instance, the nation is identified in terms of the nonracial or nonethnic category of citizenship, the concretization of international politics in the domain of intimacy necessarily determines characters involved in conflicts in racial or ethnic terms. While playing the essential role in giving rise to what John Stuart Mill famously called "the sentiment of nationality,"[5] the general scenario of romantic love necessarily brings back the racial and ethnic strategies of nationalism. This is because, even though the idea of a national belonging could officially be indifferent to the identity of race or ethnicity, the actualization of it in aestheticizing instances—the depiction of an international romantic love affair is indeed one such instance—can never evade its racialization or the initiation of what Étienne Balibar called "fictive ethnicity" precisely because the racialized sentiment of "we, the people" is conjured up when the primordial camaraderie of the nation emerges.[6] To the extent that "the sentiment of nationality" is fundamental, or even foundational, to the aesthetic formation of the nation, the national belonging cannot bypass the questions of ethnic and racial identity.

Second, nationalism is not incompatible with colonialism that consists of a fantasy of dominating an "other" nation, ethnicity, or race. It is true that nationalism finds its legitimacy in an anticolonial aspiration toward the independence of a nation from any dominating outside rule or force, but insofar as the autonomy of the nation is understood as the maintenance of masculinity according to the agenda of this heterosexual normalcy, nationalism rather affirms the nation becoming increasingly dominant and influential in the international arena. As long as we are in accord with heterosexual normalcy, therefore, the subordination of an outside territory, minority ethnic group, or race is perceived as a symptom indicating the fulfillment of the nation's craving for independence.

Characteristically, the colonial power relation is articulated to the sexual relation in double registers. The domination of one group of men by another group of men is reinscribed in the domination of women by men. The domination of a woman by a man can always be interpreted according to the scheme of homosociality with women being deprived of their active agency and reduced to an item of gift exchange. Thereupon, the woman would cease to be an interactive personality; she would instead be a property and reregistered as that which can only be owned.

Let us not forget that, at the same time, it is always possible that the colonial power relation can be expressed in the trope of rape, and this possibility always exists as the antonym to romantic love. In colonial situations, romantic love is always a disjunctive alternative to rape; the alternative is disjunctive in the sense of formal logic: if it is romantic love, then it cannot be rape; or inversely if it is rape, it cannot be a romantic love affair. Hence, it is usually presumed by colonizing men that the depiction of a romantic love affair is already a testimony to the absence of rape. Generally speaking, rape can be committed by men against men or even by women against men. But, in what is at stake in the depiction of romantic love in colonial situations, it is primarily violence exerted by men against women that inversely structures romantic love in heterosexual tropics. First of all, rape is the violation of a woman's will, but it can also be understood as an infringement upon the property right of a man—father, brother, husband, or the nation of men—who is supposed to own her. One must never lose sight of the fact that, in colonial situations, there are always two moments of power relations operating in the nationalistic story of romantic love: the domination of woman by man, and that of one group of men over another group of men.

Rape transpires precisely because the dominant figure fails to create a *power* relation with the dominated, namely a relationship in which the dominated agrees to the reality of subjugation, where the fact of domination is normalized or regularized. While rape is a forced violation of the will of the dominated, a romantic love affair assumes an agreement of some kind between the dominating and the dominated.

Regardless of whether or not this sequence reflects the actual series of events, in the initial stage of colonization, the very roles of the dominant and the dominated, of the colonizer and the colonized, are established through struggle, that is, by means of military violence. Rape, then, would be a continuation of the same sort of struggle, which can only end with a coercive subjugation marked by the naked exercise of violence and the absence of a *power* relation. Let us keep in mind that, in the colonial situation normally and in its initial stages especially, the colonizers are usually a numerical minority and, in due course, suffer from the anxiety of "insecurity." It is particularly significant that, from the perspective of the colonizer, a power relation with the colonized must never be depicted in terms of rape but rather in terms of romantic love: it must be a relationship that derives from the *consent* of the colonized—despite the fact that it is clearly a relationship between the dominating and the dominated—and in which the colonized holds affection toward the colonizer. It is suggested that the colonizer typically seeks proof of the affection of the colonized. The colonizer wants "to be loved" by the colonized, to be "desired by her." In other words, the colonizer wants the colonized to want to be the object of the colonizer's desire. This is because the former wants to dominate the latter in a certain *power* relation without appealing to the naked use of military violence in which, paradoxical though it may seem, the colonizer and the colonized are equals.

I must hasten to add that, as is evident in the current occupation of Iraq by the United States and Britain, the conquest by means of military violence cannot necessarily guarantee the continuation of domination between the conqueror and the conquered. Even at the expense of his or her own death, the conquered is able to refuse the order of the conqueror. Violence alone can never establish a *power* relation; something in addition to physical enforcement is necessary in order to establish a power relation capable of reproducing itself.

At this stage of my argument, two preliminary remarks are necessary. First, I am *not* saying that power is so pervasive that even the cinematic presentation of romantic love ought to be interpreted as an integral component of the workings of power. If power were everywhere, it would be unnecessary for us to be specifically concerned with how romantic love has been presented in the twentieth century cinematically, for it would be neither more nor less pertinent to the logic of politics than any other aspect of everyday life. If power is everywhere, then it will not be a special matter for politics.

Second, and as a supplement to the first point, the cinematic narration of a romantic love affair in the colonial situation cannot rid itself of a *constitutive contradiction*, but for which a love affair would be reduced to a rape. This narration must secure the factual subjugation of a woman, who allegorically represents the status of the colonized, but this subjugation must be established as a consequence of her willingness; she must be willing to give up or sacrifice her freedom and autonomy because she loves a man who symbolizes the colonizer. At a certain point in a sequence of utterances, actions, and incidents between a man and a woman, the woman must indicate her agreement to the man in words, or by some gesture: "I want you, so I am willing to change myself and to be what I have never been hitherto." Unless this condensed moment of intensive decision is presented or hinted at, the story would not be one of a romantic love affair. Logically, however, it is equally possible for a man of the colonizing side to say to a woman of the colonized side, "I want you, so I am willing to change myself and to be what I have never been hitherto." However fleetingly the state of equality may last, only when the man and woman are free and in a state of equality in spite of colonial hierarchy—that is, they are exposed to one another for self-transformation—can their relationship be called romantic love.

Nevertheless, a few exceptions notwithstanding, the overwhelming majority of cinematic love affairs in colonial situations only depict stories leading to the subjugation of women according to the framework of colonial domination; they show how women capitulate to an inferior status and are willing to surrender their freedom for men's affection. How many stories portray men of courage becoming turncoats for women's love? We can scarcely find romantic love stories in which men invent new identities to obtain women's affection. In this respect, the cinematic depiction of romantic love conforms to the economy of homosociality in which women are deprived of the potentiality of *subjectification* even though it is they, not men, who are to change and produce a new field of experience as a result of their involvement in love affairs.[7] Despite all these cases, the fact remains that the primordial equality of a man and a woman must be acknowledged in order to ascertain the subjugation of the woman as well as of the colonized. It is for this reason that the cinematic representation of romantic love cannot evade such a constitutive contradiction as found in the utterance "Do you understand?" Pointing out the paradoxical logic of politics, Jacques Rancière argues, "In ordinary social usage, an expression like 'Do you understand?' is a false interrogative whose positive content is as follows: 'There is nothing for you to understand, you don't need to understand' and even, possibly, 'It's not up to you to understand; all you have to do is obey.' 'Do you understand?' is an expression that tells us precisely that 'to understand' means two different, if not contrary, things: to understand a problem and to understand an order."[8]

Freedom is innate in every human being, and power can operate only upon free human beings. Power is not in opposition to freedom. In order for the relationship of domination to continue, therefore, there must be some form of agreement between the conqueror and the conquered. Only by acknowledging the freedom of the conquered and seducing him or her into validating the relation of domination can the conqueror establish the authority of the dominant and continue to hold that power.

Thus, romantic love as an allegory for diplomatic relations takes this fundamental form: *the colonizer pilfers the desire of the colonized*. Various conflicts between nations or between ethnicities are often narrated in this form and through the trope of sexual relations. Precisely because the conqueror and the conquered are in a strategic situation is there a power relation between them. A scenario of romantic love can be mobilized to allegorize a power relation between them for the very reason that any solution to conflicts necessitates the acknowledgment of freedom as well as the agreement of the dominated to forgo it. I borrow the idiom "power relation" from Michel Foucault's lecture series *Society Must Be Defended*, *The Birth of Biopolitics*, and other essays, in order to stress its *historical nature*:[9] "Once we begin to talk about power relations, we are not talking about right, and we are not talking about sovereignty; we are talking about domination, about an infinitely dense and multiple domination that never comes to an end. There is no escape from domination, and there is therefore no escape from history."[10] Far from being a symbol of the resolution of incessant discord between domination and rebellion, the romantic love affair insinuates the state of war behind the appearance of the happy ending in colonial situations. Yet, just like the peculiar interrogative "Do you understand?" the agreement supposedly reached in the story of romantic love harbors a paradoxical dispute about what is agreed upon. Hence, it is equally possible to describe a failure to establish a power relation in terms of the trope of war and violent coercion. As a matter of fact, it is absolutely necessary to comprehend the cinematic depiction of romantic love without assuming the reign of sovereignty; the international love affair must be apprehended within a historical analysis premised on *all against all*, in which historical need for rebellion is always inscribed, rather than within a narrative in which such a need is erased.

One prominent example is the Rape of Nanjing: the 1937 massacre of Chinese local citizens by the Japanese army was registered as an imposition of coercive force with no attention paid to the freedom of the local residents. It implies that the invader was rejected by the dominated and had to appeal to naked violence to gain control. Furthermore, whether it is represented either as rape or as a romantic relationship is of decisive importance for the identitarian desire of the colonizer as well as for the justification of invasion. It is therefore no coincidence that, three years after the Rape of Nanjing, the Japanese film *China Night*, depicting a love affair between a Japanese man and a Chinese woman in Shanghai, was distributed throughout East Asia, including parts of China that were under Japanese occupation.

The cinematic presentations of romantic love displace the type of violent coercion that may well be expressed as rape and, at the same time, fulfill male narcissism, thereby providing a fantastic solution to international contradictions and conflicts through the mediation of the female.

Here, two disclaimers are needed. First, it is not possible to postulate either an occurrence of a love affair or rape independently of the various utterances concerning it. Of particular significance is the fact that the very distinction of a love affair, as a symbolic speech act instituting agreement, from rape, as a performance indicating an absence thereof, cannot be determined in and of itself or by tracing back to the original happening. Stripped of all social meanings, coitus is neither a love affair nor a rape. Neither of these exists outside discourse. We cannot evade the intertwining of an act and a testimony—one form of locution or another—about that act as soon as we try to determine whether the act was based on agreement or coercion. In this respect, both love affair and rape are of discourse in nature. It depends on how it is reported, disputed, evaluated, or fantasized as to whether an incident is determined as either love affair or rape.

Second, it is misleading to assume that the positionality of either the colonizer or the colonized is a given. As Ann Laura Stoler cautioned in her study of the politics of sexuality in colonial modernity,[11] the formal membership of the colonizer nation does not ensure that a foot soldier of the occupying force, a construction engineer in the colonial administration, or a migrant worker from a depressed region in the colonizing country can always occupy the positionality of the colonizer in the microphysics of colonial rule. Their identity as a colonizer needs to be repeatedly affirmed in the *fantasized* situations of colonial encounter. However, since, as an imagery scenario, the fantasized positionality of the colonizer is frequently not deployed in a specific locale of microphysics, the pertinence of fantastic identification is not limited to the place where a colonial encounter actually takes place. On the contrary, the cinematic image of romantic love is consumed as a universal trope for a generalized audience seeking its identity in the configuration of characters in the story of romantic love. In this sense, the cinematic image of romantic love serves to project a category specific to the locale of microphysics onto the plane of generality. It serves to generalize the colonial relationship, as if it were independent of the locale of colonial subjugation. Thus, positionalities pertinent to specific power relations, such as those of colonizer, native, white, colored, Westerner, and so forth, appear as general categories in the taxonomy of humanity and as if independent of local power relations in which they are embedded.

Here, one might as well delve into the semantics of why the military sex-slavery institution was officially called "the military comfort station (*jûgun iansho*)." Besides the denotation of "the place that offers sexual gratification to soldiers," there must be some connotation that conjures up the "comforting" aspect in the initial design of this place. Let us note that the Japanese military had to establish chains of comfort stations in a systematic manner, mainly in response to a large number of rapes committed by Japanese soldiers in their occupied territories. Local commanders of the Japanese troops controlling occupied territories in China repeatedly reported to the headquarters that rapes committed by the occupying soldiers provoked insidious and violent resistance by the local populace. It is evident that, for the Japanese colonial administration, it was first and foremost a matter of political domination, or of how to rule the colonized population, before it was a moral and criminal question, just as the recurring rapes committed by American soldiers in many parts of East Asia—the Philippines, Okinawa, and South Korea—are perceived, first of all, as a severe hindrance to the legitimacy of the U.S. military presence in the regions. For soldiers exposed to the constant hostility of the colonized, therefore, "comfort" must have connoted relief from insecurity in occupied lands or freedom from colonial anxiety.

It is also for this reason that, in the very plots featuring love relationships involving the consensus of the dominated, we must detect another layer: violent domination that hints at the potentiality of rape. The "intimate" relation between individuals as an allegory of international politics does not mean that the sexual love relationship established therein is exceptional; on the contrary, it is through the representation of the love relation that the inter*national* relationship is rendered emotively and affectively apprehensible. *As long as the relation between individuals is understood exclusively as a relationship between nations, ethnicities, or races, the allegorical trope of romantic love is inevitable as a negation of rape.* It follows that, to the extent that one wants to evade seeing one's relation to the local to be equivalent to rape, one would want to see it through the trope of romantic love. It seems to me that, for nationalists, love relations between individuals of different nationalities, ethnicities, or races cannot evade this economy of allegory. Thus the American soldier who wishes to identify with the role of the conqueror in this relationship, and the Korean, Filipina, or Japanese sex workers who are used to playing, or are required to play, the role of the subjugated have come to symbolize and represent the colonial relationships between the United States and the peoples of these countries. Therefore, it is no accident that the sex workers who worked in the areas surrounding U.S. bases in the Philippines, Japan, and Korea have often been referred to as "diplomats" who "represent" each of these colonized nations.

Katharine H. S. Moon brilliantly analyzed the processes by which Korean prostitutes serving the U.S. soldiers were hailed as "personal ambassadors" by government officials of South Korea. However, it is not necessarily unreasonable to see prostitution in the areas around U.S. military bases as "contributing to international understanding" and to emphasize its diplomatic aspects,[12] for "[the women's] relationship with foreign soldiers *personify and define*, not only underlie, relations between governments"[13]; neither is it contradictory to the American, Japanese, or Korean patriotic spirit. According to Moon, the Blue House Political Secretary who oversaw the Base Community Clean-Up Committee emphasized that the Korean prostitutes "should imitate the spirit of Japanese prostitutes who sold their bodies to the post-1945 U. S. occupation forces."[14] In her interview with him, he recalled that he admonished camptown prostitutes by saying, "The patriotism of the Japanese prostitute spread to the rest of the society to develop Japan."[15] We cannot overlook the structural complicity between American imperial nationalism and the nationalisms of its satellite states in East Asia, and between the multiethnic universalism of the United States and the ethnic particularism of Japan, Taiwan, and South Korea. As long as patriotism is premised upon male domination of women, the contribution of sex workers working around U.S. military bases would have to be rationalized in this way: these women are presented as tributes and offered as signs of goodwill to American soldiers, on the one hand, and as patriots volunteering to sacrifice themselves for their nation, on the other.

The Korean War–era film *Love Is a Many-Splendored Thing*, nominated for eight Academy Awards, tells the love story of an American special correspondent and a female doctor of mixed European and Chinese blood in Hong Kong. The film won a Golden Globe Award for its contribution to international understanding ("Best Film Promoting International Understanding")—at a point in time, 1955, when people not only of East Asia but also throughout the world could not avoid the encroachment of the cold war as a framework for the international environment. It is clear that the story of *Love Is a Many-Splendored Thing* does not contradict the logic of desire in the imperialist policies of the United States. It is worth emphasizing the following two points with regard to American nationalism and the context of "international understanding": first, despite its militaristic nature, American military presence could not be spoken of in terms of the trope of rape, and second, it was absolutely imperative that American domination be based on the consent of people in East Asia. The aspect of consensus in this international understanding was perhaps further highlighted by the fact that the film was based on the novel by a Eurasian writer, Han Suyin, who was played by a white actress, Jennifer Jones.

Via a militaristic system, many U.S. soldiers, military-employed civilians, and diplomatic attachés were introduced to Japan, Korea, the Philippines, Vietnam, Thailand, and so forth. From their perspective, experiences of living in Japan, Korea, and Vietnam had to be *intensively* expressed through their contact with the sex workers with whom they interacted; that is, they experienced exotic Asia through their interaction with sex workers there.

The above examination of the representation of romantic love is devised as more of a response to the issues that have been at stake in the production of the areas—that is, of the ethnographic regions cartographically mapped onto geographic extensions—that fall on the other side of the colonial difference of the West and the rest. Among the many moments of colonial difference, what I want to draw attention to is the distribution of "universalism" and "particularism" in this configuration.[16] In the area studies of Japan in the United States—and in the institutions of Japanese national history and literature in Japan as well—after World War II, it has been almost always taken for granted that, for cultural, historical, or religious reasons, the Japanese were incapable of freeing themselves from the tradition of particularism, while the Americans were somewhat destined to embrace universalistic values; the Japanese Empire could never advocate universalism for the integration of multiple ethnicities because it belonged to the "other side."

Strictly censored during the period of the Allied occupation of Japan were comparative inquiries about the U.S. and Japanese imperialisms, which could have disclosed the astonishing parallels of their respective imperialist strategies and colonialist rhetoric. However, the assumption of Japanese particularism effectively allowed area specialists to overlook the strikingly similar features of imperialistic strategies that the United States and Japan employed during the war. It was imperative for U.S. policy makers to transform the Japanese intellectual world into one of cultural particularism through a number of tactics, including a selective distribution of commercial films. Thanks to this assumption, the Japanese intellectuals were exempted from the painful task of reflecting upon their own imperialism, colonialism, and the universalistic mode of wartime self-justification. Rather than oppressing ethnic particularism in its annexed territories, until its defeat, the Japanese state advocated the rhetoric of universal integration under the mask of a racial hierarchy, to which many "progressive" intellectuals contributed. Consequently, as the issues of the comfort women and the prime minister's visit to the Yasukuni Shrine have amply demonstrated in recent years, it is still difficult for many in Japan to discard the posture of being the most advanced and modernized among the countries of Asia, in other words, of being the honorary "whites" of Asia.

Therefore, the particularistic and less-universalistic tendencies that Japan's social formation may appear to exhibit today have a lot to do with the configuration of hegemony in post–World War II East Asia. We cannot assume that particularistic traits are manifest in many aspects of everyday life in today's Japan precisely because the Japanese state has been innately or traditionally incapable of integrating minority populations, while, comparatively, the United States is a multicultural society whose culture is inherently open to integrationist policies and universalistic values. It is not because Japan belongs to the "other side" that Japan seems exclusionary and to adhere to particularistic values. On the contrary, if I may put it simply, it is because the Japanese state could not afford to continue to advocate an imperial nationalism. Japan was defeated, and, as a result, its state had to withdraw from direct justification of the colonial administration. Prior to the demise of the Japanese Empire and since Japan's defeat, an imperialism without universalism was and still is an oxymoron.[17] Colonial domination requires the kind of universalism that was advocated by universalistic thinkers such as Tanabe Hajime, Miki Kiyoshi, and Takata Yasuma in Imperial Japan and was formulated in the American Modernization Theory after the war.[18] But the transpacific complicity of U.S. universalism and Japanese particularism has obfuscated the fact of the postwar international arrangement in East Asia. Under the U.S. collective security system, a hegemonic arrangement was cultivated in which universalism and particularism were distributed to the United States and Japan, respectively. It was a trans-Pacific arrangement marked by the *complicity* of the United States and Japan that effectively disavowed and continues to disavow the past of colonial atrocities; without this, the two countries would not have the relationship as they do today.

Clearly, the conditions brought about by the colonialisms of the latenineteenth century and the first half of the twentieth century are beginning to be invisible except around the extraterritorial regions of U.S. military bases. However, among the people of the countries that have reaped the benefits of colonialism—the United States, countries in Western Europe, Japan, Australia, and others (the so-called First World)—a regressive movement toward the self-serving history of the nation and the narcissistic collective sentimentalism nurtured by the colonial fantasies of a glorified past have also been gaining momentum. There seems less and less resistance against the collective craving to disavow the past that testifies to the ugly sides of the nation. The disavowal in Japan of the issues concerning the comfort women is perhaps the best expression of a regressive movement of this kind. Yet, at the same time, an increasing number of people in Japan are relieved from the restrictive fantasies of gender stereotypes.

We must understand how certain representations of sexual relations are appropriated by international politics and employed to consolidate power relations in colonial domination. For international, interracial, or interethnic sexuality is *not immediately* a relation of the victor and the vanquished; it becomes so only when it is *mediated* by the regimes of fantasy and national identification. It seems that we are now called upon to reelaborate the strategies of decolonization in consideration of the politics of cultural representation. Accordingly, an examination of a history depicting romantic love and rape, which of course must include the issues of the comfort women and military prostitution, is urgently called for. Does not the recent collapse of self-confidence in Japanese masculinity, in the implied postulation of the "Japanese as Asia's white people," parallel the processes of the last few decades in which social struggles have been waged about the racial and national fantasies of "whiteness" and "American" masculinity? Can we not compare the withdrawal sometimes noted in European men to the increasing introversion of Japanese males? Today it seems very important to link what we have often referred to as neoracism in Western Europe together with the surge of anti–North Korean sentiment propelling regressive movements in Japan toward the racist exclusion of resident Koreans. Above all, processes of decolonization will reconfigure the *complicity* of the U.S. "universalism" and Japanese "particularism," a hegemonic arrangement of the postwar period under which so many remnants of British, Japanese, and American colonial violence have been obfuscated. The colonial remnants have been consistently disavowed, and, for this reason, they continue to haunt us.

Notes

1. Among the more extensive historical studies of the Comfort Station system in English, see Yoshiaki Yoshimi, *Comfort Women*, trans. Suzanne O'Brien (New York: Columbia University Press, 2000); and Yuki Tanaka, *Japan's Comfort Women: The Military and Involuntary Prostitution During War and Occupation* (London: Routledge, 2002).

2. Chalmers Johnson, *Blowback* (New York: Times Warner, 2002); *The Sorrows of Empire—Militarism, Secrecy, and the End of the Republic* (New York: Metropolitan Books, 2004).

3. See footnote 18.

4. Ann Laura Stoler, *Carnal Knowledge and Imperial Power* (Berkeley: University of California Press, 2002), see chapters 2 and 3 in particular. It goes without saying that, in Foucauldian terminology, "intimacy" is correlative with the regimes of biopower, but in the twentieth century it is around what Foucault calls "population" that biopolitics, in which individualization by subjection is acquired through the production of an internal, secret, and hidden truth, is deployed. See Michel Foucault, *Security, Territory, Population—Lectures at the Collège de France 1977–1978*, trans. Graham Burchell (New York: Palgrave, 2007), 163–90. Biopolitics cannot be understood in other than the general framework of governmentality called "liberalism." "The self-limitation of governmental practice by liberal reason was accompanied by the split between international objectives

and the emergence of unlimited objectives in imperialism." Michel Foucault, *The Birth of Biopolitics—Lectures at the Collège de France 1978-1979*, trans. Graham Burchell (New York: Palgrave, 2008), 21.

5. See John Stuart Mill, "Considerations of Representative Government," in *John Stuart Mill*, ed. H. B. Acton (1861; repr.; London: Everyman's Library, 1972), 187-428.

6. Étienne Balibar, "Fichte and the Internal Border," in *Masses, Classes, Ideas—Studies on Politics and Philosophy Before and After Marx*, trans. James Swenson (New York: Routledge, 1994). Étienne Balibar argues in reference to Fichte's *Addresses to the German Nation*: "In what makes a people *a people* there is indeed an essential link to something originary, but this something originary is not the empirical *being* of the people; it is only the *effect* of its practical relation to the linguistic origin" (77). What gives rise to the internality of the nation, marked by the internal borders that represent "the nonrepresentable limit of every border, as it would be seen 'from within' its lines" (63) is the movement of continuous formation, of speaking as one acts and acting as one speaks (79). "The originary, authentic language is not only the language of action, it is moral action in language; it is not a language that has a history, but a 'live speech' that makes history, and that must be seized in the moment of its making"(79). Fictive ethnicity emerges in this "live speech" insofar as the figure of fictive ethnicity accompanies the primordial sense of being together with people whom the live speech is addressed to and shared with. The racialized sentiment of "we, the people" need not be grounded on the empirical being—physiological, historical, or genealogical—of the people. Fictive ethnicity begins with the internal border.

7. Here, I follow Jacques Rancière's notion of subjectification: "By *subjectification* I mean the production through a series of actions of a body and a capacity for enunciation not previously identifiable within a given field of experience, whose identification is thus part of the reconfiguration of the field of experience" (italics in the original). *Disagreement*, trans. Julie Ross (Minneapolis: University of Minnesota Press, 1999), 35. Subjectification implies "the production of a new field of experience" and flight from given identities (35).

8. Ibid., 44-45.

9. Michel Foucault, *Society Must Be Defended—Lectures at the Collège de France 1975-1976*, trans. David Macey (New York: Picador 2003), and essays such as "'Omnes et singulatim': Toward a Critique of Political Reason" and "The Subject and Power," in *Essential Works of Foucault 1954-1984*, vol. 3, *Power*, ed. James D. Faubion (New York: The New Press, 2000), 298-325, 326-48.

10. Foucault, Society Must Be Defended, 111.

11. Stoler, *Carnal Knowledge and Imperial Power*.

12. In their campaign to deal with racial discrimination among camptown prostitutes against black servicemen and the spread of venereal diseases, the U.S.

military demanded of the Korean government that Korean sex workers should be given "patriotic" education so as to be more aware of their diplomatic function between South Korea and the United States. See Katharine H. S. Moon, *Sex among Allies: Military Prostitution in U.S.-Korean Relations* (New York: Columbia University Press, 1997).

13. Ibid., 12, emphasis mine. Also significant is a video installation about sex workers in camptowns entitled *The Women Outside* (1996) by Hye Jung Park, displayed during the international show "The American Effects: Global Perspective on the United States 1900-2003" at the Whitney Museum of American Art in 2003 in New York City.

14. Moon, *Sex among Allies*, 102-3.

15. Ibid., 103.

16. The dichotomy of "universalism" and "particularism" was most frequently utilized in so-called Modernization Theory. It is important to note, however, that I have never endorsed their conceptions of universality and particularity simply because there are too many theoretical defects in them.

17. Furthermore, let us not forget that every nationalism is necessarily a universalism within the membership of the established nation. Without this universalism, a nation cannot project the sense of camaraderie. See my articles, "Modernity and Its Critique: The Problem of Universalism and Particularism," *The South Atlantic Quarterly, Postmodernism and Japan* 87, no. 3 (1988): 475-504; "'You Asians': On the Historical Role of the West and Asia Binary," *The South Atlantic Quarterly* 99, no. 4 (2000): 789-817.

18. In the 1920s and 1930s, political doctrines with a particularistic orientation were viewed with increasing suspicion by Japanese state authorities. With a few exceptions—such as Watsuji Tetsurô, who believed in the racial purity of the Japanese against Chinese, Koreans, and other heterogeneous ethnicities in the empire—Japanese intellectuals generally succumbed to universalistic rhetoric emphasizing the integration of national society. By national society, of course, they meant the territory of the Japanese Empire including the Korean Peninsula, Taiwan, Sakhalin, the Pacific Islands, certain parts of today's China, and Manchuria. Some particularistic ideologies, such as ethnic nationalism (*minzokushugi*), were targeted by state censorship, and their ideologues were often imprisoned. The Japanese were expected to celebrate the integration of ethnic, class, regional, and gender diversities into the national unity. So as to consolidate this universalistic ideal of the Japanese Empire, a number of theoretical projects were launched to undermine and critique the reification of racial, ethnic, and cultural identities. In this respect, Tanabe Hajime (1885-1962), Miki Kiyoshi (1897-1945), and Takata Yasuma (1883-1972) were representative figures and responsible for some of the theoretical schemes for the Japanese Empire. Tanabe taught philosophy at the Kyoto Imperial University and constructed the social ontology of universalistic

individualism (the Logic of the Species). Miki taught philosophy and served as the leader of the governmental think tank called the Showa Research Association (Showa Kenkyûkai) and outlined the philosophical foundation of the East Asian Community. Takata Yasuma was the leading sociologist teaching at the Kyoto Imperial University and attempted the theory of plastic ethnicity. The theme that was common among these three thinkers was the historical and philosophical analysis of reified ethnicity or nationality; they were critical of the substantialization of ethnic identity, and they tried to offer the sociological and philosophical theories of national subjectivity. They were critical of fascist particularism, but they were not at all guarded against imperial nationalism. (Japanese names above follow the convention of surname followed by given name.)

10

Masculinity and Male-on-Male Sexual Violence in the Military

Focusing on the Absence of the Issue

Insook Kwon

Translated by Daisy Y. Kim

According to the 2004 National Human Rights Commission of Korea (NHRCK) investigative report on male-on-male sexual violence in the military, 15.4 percent of those surveyed responded affirmatively to having suffered from sexual violence, while 7.2 percent admitted to having inflicted sexual harm on someone else.[1] For more than fifty-five years, Korea's conscription law has sustained an armed forces of more than six hundred thousand, and if we consider that male-on-male sexual violence in the military is not a recent occurrence, this means that an extraordinary number of men have continually been exposed to and have experienced sexual violence. Why is it, then, that male sexual violence has never been raised as a genuine problem until now?

In July 2003,[2] male-on-male sexual violence in the military first raised public interest in earnest after the suicide of an enlisted recruit, known as Private Kim, overlapped with a successive string of male-on-male sexual violence cases.[3] The public articulated a range of reactions, including surprise that "men are sexually harassing men";[4] expressions of worry that the current situation is a result of "military discipline becoming too slack";[5] sympathy from those who believe this is to be expected "when you force hot-blooded boys into a confined place"; and even disgust in a response stating that "male on male sexual behavior is an abnormality that only occurs between homosexuals."[6] Responses were forthcoming not only from the media but also from military authorities. Among these responses, the most common recommendation was to improve living quarters and to individualize sleeping arrangements.[7] Furthermore, the chief of staff of the Korean Army prescribed "sexual violence" as "a sex-related military discipline incident" and implemented the "Supplement for the Redemption and Systemic Prevention of Sex-Related Military Discipline Violations," where the first proscription was "On the Regulation of Enlisting Sexually Handicapped [homosexual, etc.] Persons."

Surprise at the plausibility of sexual violence—the perception that such actions are the behavior of homosexuals, or "sympathetic" discussions that condone the uncontrollable sexual desires of young men—reflects some of the problems in the present condition of Korea's perception of male-on-male sexual violence in the military. First, disbelief reflects a lack of basic awareness about the problematic implications of this issue. To this day in Korea, the lack of prior research dealing with the actual circumstances and causes of male-on-male sexual violence in the military is another factor that adds to the sense of unfamiliarity and lack of association with the problem.[8] Of course, as mentioned before, this kind of unfamiliarity is not a natural response. That countless men directly and indirectly experienced sexual violence, but never revealed their experiences to the rest of society, indicates the urgent need to explain the sources of the silence.

Moreover, we cannot ignore the problems that arise because of the general absence of victims' testimonies and their interpretations of such experiences. It is easy for military authorities to regard the issue as a symptom of deteriorating military discipline and to bury the matter for the sake of preserving the hierarchical organizational structure and overall strength of the military rather than to focus on the individual human rights of the victim. The difficulty of publicizing the issue also resides within the army's tendency to categorize all "abnormal behavior," including consensual sex and nonconsensual male-on-male sexual violence as a result of slackening discipline.[9] By framing any sexual behavior among men as repugnant, "abnormal sexual behavior" associated with sodomy, male-on-male sexual violence has been seen by the public as a matter of military discipline rather than as rape.[10] Regarding sexual behavior among males as disgraceful and as homosexual conduct can obscure the distinction between one's sexual orientation and the criminality associated with sexual violence. Furthermore, the sympathetic perspective strengthens Korean society's acceptance of young men as incapable of restraining their sexual desires and produces an ambiguous relationship between accountability and sexual violence.[11]

The fact that male-on-male sexual violence has never become a social issue or has never been publicized presents a great limitation for understanding sexual violence. In the present movement against sexual violence, which often views the man as harasser and the woman as victim, the issue of how to interpret the male victim remains problematic. More importantly, in a society with a universal conscription requirement—and where great numbers of men have experienced sexual violence, committed it, or both—the frequency and the causes of those occurrences are necessarily related. Also, the Korean Army is a place that young men call a second school. Because a majority of Korean men go to the army for a set time period, it is an institution that seeks to produce a homogeneous masculinity.[12] It is important to examine the nature of the relationship between sexual violence and the military because the military has a significant influence in shaping masculinity—a notion defined in opposition to femininity—and is a place where men frequently experience and witness both direct and indirect forms of sexual violence.[13]

Currently, not only is Korean society's knowledge about male-on-male sexual violence in the military negligible but its knowledge about male-on-male sexual violence in general is also rather low. Even as the movement against sexual violence has progressed, the notion that men—who are often regarded as the assaulter—could be the victim has not been recognized as a topic of public interest. Significant numbers of women and child victims have received much attention from the public, but the only publicly known male victims of sexual violence have been male children. Since male victims almost never came forth, the lack of awareness can be attributed to the difficulty of organizing a group of sympathizers. The practice of defining rape as "the forced penetration of the female organ by the male organ" (heterosexual rape), which is reflected in society's accepted social norms and legal institutions, as well as the tendency to perceive sexual violence among men as a type of abnormal sexual behavior among homosexuals[14] are both factors that have played roles in the public's disinterest. Such restricted standards have rendered it difficult to assert the right of men to be protected legally and socially and to acknowledge men as potential victims of sexual violence.

Yet, according to the 2004 annual report by the NHRCK, 63.2 percent of sexual violence within the military occurs in a public or partially public setting. There is a dire need for an explanation as to why some members of society react in disbelief even though such incidents occur publicly. Despite the active public engagement with military issues, there has been a complete lack of discussion about sexual violence in the military for more than several decades.

Thus, this chapter investigates why sexual violence within the military has never become public discourse. I closely examine the source of this public silence and the causes of sexual violence within the context of the military.[15] The reasons for this silence lie not just in the particularities of male-on-male sexual violence but also in the hierarchical character of the military where the order of rank and masculine behavior are both emphasized.

The research method is based on a literature review and in-depth personal interviews. With aggressors, interviews were conducted with eight men out of the eleven who were detained for male-on-male sexual violence misconduct. It was a daunting task to secure interviews with victims of sexual violence: from a cohort that had been discharged from the army in the past three years, only three could be interviewed. To supplement the interviews, I incorporated in this study the relevant sections from consultation records of six victims of male-on-male sexual violence from the Korean Sexual Violence Consultation Clinic. As to the details of interpersonal relations, since only the relationship of rank seemed to matter at the time of the incident, the details of age, education, and position within the unit have not been revealed.

In order to supplement the limitations of a small sample size and establish a measure of generality, much of the study relied on incorporating research from existing literature regarding the causes and the public silence surrounding the issue. In many cases, American and British research on male sexual violence was utilized. Although the justification for relying on such research was due to the absence of studies in Korea, it was also because cultural differences do not factor so significantly when analyzing male-on-male sexual violence. The results of research across various societies do not center on cultural differences as the main cause of male-on-male sexual violence because of the commonalities that exist across societies as possible factors for the cause of sexual violence such as (a) the power difference between men and women that exists in any patriarchal society, (b) male-centered sexual desire, (c) the double standard for men and women regarding sex, and (d) an aversion to homosexuality. Of course, differences exist in the pattern of injury and assault. This is because the frequency of incidents or rate of reporting by victims and perpetrators alike are affected depending on the legal or institutional framework and the institutionalization of sexual education. Even though research that compares the legal institutions relating to sexual violence is currently taking place, there is no research that is based purely on a cultural difference approach.[16]

In particular, research related to the military supersedes the unique characteristics of various respective societies. In each and every society, the military has a special role and a unique character. Of course, the facts that Korea has a universal conscription requirement and that most men have directly or indirectly experienced sexual violence while in the military have made the seriousness of the problem rather widespread; thus, the effect of sexual violence is that much greater. Due to the lack of existing research, however, it was realistically difficult to include what is particular to Korea. Instead, the focus has been placed on the psychocultural traits general to the spatial organization referred to as the Korean military.[17]

Underpublicized Male-on-Male Sexual Violence

Male-on-male sexual violence is a widespread phenomenon that occurs regardless of nationality or ethnicity. Examples of wartime male-on-male sexual violence, such as the incidents of male rape, collective harassment, and homicide that occurred as racial tensions escalated inside a collapsing Soviet Union Federation Army in 1990; the various forms of sexual attacks experienced by three thousand to five thousand soldiers during the war in Bosnia; and the rape of retreating government officials and resistance forces during Iraq's invasion of Kuwait in 1990 indicate that rape or sex-related aggression often functions as a form of retaliation during times of ethnic–racial conflict and war.[18]

However, even without the aggravation of war or civil conflict, male-on-male sexual violence still occurs. According to a 1995 report released by the U.S. Department of Defense's Department of Human Resources, approximately 35 percent of men (and 70 percent of women) experienced unwanted sexual jokes, stories, whistles, or gazes. About 15 percent of men experienced behavior or comments that were sexually discriminatory. The study also revealed that 8 percent of men (as well as 41 percent of women) experienced unsolicited sexual touching or caressing, kisses, or behavior aimed at initiating sexual relations (such as receiving requests for a date or for a drink, despite repeated refusal). Two percent of men (as well as 13 percent of women) experienced demands for sexual favors in exchange for a job-related promotion or as an act of revenge. Regarding rape and attempted rape, 1 percent of men and 6 percent of women responded in the affirmative. Such acts mostly took place during regular work hours.[19] Recently, the Department of Defense reported that of 2,012 victims, 9 percent were male, but 99 percent of aggressors were male.[20]

When we examine the U.S. Department of Defense and the NHRCK report that indicates that more than 14 percent of enlisted men experienced sexual harassment in Korea, it is undeniable that the rate of occurrence is significant. But research on male-on-male sexual violence in the military is scarce in Great Britain and in the United States and almost nonexistent in South Korea. As mentioned before, awareness about this problem only began to appear with the extreme case of one recruit's suicide. Why is it that even the plain facts are not known to the public?

Sexual Violence as Injury to Masculinity

The most important reason sexual harassment has not been publicized is that, for men, to be identified as a "victim" is identical to denigrating masculinity. For the sake of confidentiality, throughout this study I use the terms "victim" and "aggressor," although it is also the case that, at times, the victim can, in another context, become the aggressor. In an environment that regards acquiring and maintaining genuine masculinity as important as life itself, let us examine why sexual violence, a process that denies masculinity, occurs and how victims interpret the injury to their masculinity and subsequently decide to resort to silence.

Rank and Masculinity

The military is a place designated as a "second school" for men and a place where "boys become men." It is a place where boys are reborn as men and a place where men are educated and acquire a masculinity that a male adult should possess. (The complex relationship between militarization, masculinity, and colonization is a common theme across the chapters by Michael Lujan Bevacqua [chapter 3], Keith L. Camacho and Laurel A. Monnig [chapter 7], and Theresa Cenidoza Suarez [chapter 8] in this volume.)

This notion dictates the army as a place where masculinities compete: "An individual's worth is measured by a standard of masculinity; what is not becoming of a man is not becoming of a soldier and hence renders a person incompetent. Therefore, a soldier who cannot meet this standard feels insecure and must make an effort to hide or overcome his insecurity."[21] Concerning masculinity within the army, Kim Hyun-yong commented that "those who have difficulty adjusting to military life or have expressed discontent receive severe reproach from men who have already served in the military such as 'you are not even a man (you are a woman),' and they must accept the injurious meaning of comments such as 'It is behavior not appropriate for a man.'"[22] A cultural code that dictates manly behavior as a worthy code of conduct and unmanly behavior as deserving reproach or severe punishment is internalized and practiced in the military—practices that trace their origin to colonial conscription in Japan's imperial army. The hierarchical culture of the military came directly from the Japanese imperial army during the history of Korea's colonization.

The standard of masculinity is realized vis-à-vis rank: "New recruits are considered 'pre-male beings' and the corporals are those who have secured a domineering masculinity by passing through all the stages of manhood,"[23] says Kim, which reflects her interpretation of the relationship between rank and masculinity. The fact that those who are not favored are compared to girls can be confirmed in how others address them—for example, by adding the term of address *nyon* (bitch).[24] According to the testimony of Victim 1, "Curse words, such as *ssiballyon* (fucking bitch) or *chotkat'un nyona* (fucking whore)" are terms used to belittle these men as women.[25]

Such tactics ensure that masculinity functions to secure a hierarchical order and is also employed as one method of training: "Winning the competition of masculinities is an efficient method for a commissioned officer to deal with a subordinate, a superior to deal with his inferior; for that reason, masculinity is exaggerated."[26] Male soldiers in the military feel anxious and daunted while caught in between the exaggerated standard of masculinity and their inability to measure up. Such psychological anxiety that accompanies the competition of masculinities enables men to affirm their masculinity by punishing those who are unable to meet the standard and by feminizing other men to obtain a superior, and thus masculine, position.

Sexual Violence in Order to Protect Masculinity

A report on sexual violence by the Korea Institute of Criminology stated that "those men who have encountered sexual harassment no longer exist as male, but as an object of femininity." Thus, it concluded that "to be the object of attack is to transform the male who is only male in body into a female in every other sense."[27] In the military's view, the feminizing of the other male occurs most drastically in the act of sexual violence. Sexual violence feminizes the receiver of violence in two senses. First, it feminizes the victim by reducing the victim to a sexual object, a position that women generally hold in Korean society. Second, it feminizes by labeling him as a weak person unable to defend himself. In the end, the one who suffers sexual violence becomes a being who has lost or injured his masculinity. Within this context, a group mentality that confirms hierarchical order and each individual's masculine aggression is put into operation, a fact that is demonstrated in the testimony of an interviewee who indicated that the reason for his aggression was because he considered his inferior as "close," "cute," or "naïve," or one who is able to be approached and reduced to a status of sexual object more easily. An interviewee who had repeatedly demanded an inferior to engage in oral intercourse said the following:

> AGGRESSOR 2: I had about five or six inferiors. To put it bluntly, there were those who had had some sexual experiences with women; to put it badly, there were those who had caused a lot of problems before, like those who drank, who would have taken the demand from me as a joke, but in my opinion, that kid was innocent . . . he did not talk much, and looked young. In fact, he is young. When you look at him, he looks like a good person.

The treatment of the victim as a youth or child is understood in a context of hierarchical relationships.

> AGGRESSOR 6: I am assaulted often by those who are older. For example, men with coarse mustaches come to me and say, "Come here, let's see how big your thing [penis] is," and they rub their prickly faces on it.
>
> KWON: Within the regiment or in society?

AGGRESSOR 6: In the regiment. Yes, it might be because I am young in age or because those who have led military lives for twenty or twenty-five years find someone like me cute.

Among the victims of sexual violence, the only thing common to all was that their rank was low. Because their rank was low, domination was easy, and they were not treated like fully grown men but like young children or women.

The importance of confirming masculinity, hierarchical order, and sexual violence appears in the culture of similarly organized groups. In dealing with groups composed only or mostly of males, Michael Scarce claims that in the military, prisons, athletic departments of high schools, and college fraternities where women's membership is banned, sexual harassment and the competition of masculinities is typically employed as a means of control. Actions include stripping naked, sometimes including the touching of the genitals, and using sexual harassment as a tool for orienting new members. At one American high school, new members of an athletic team were forced to masturbate; at another school, older teammates of a wrestling team raped a younger teammate by anally penetrating him with a stick as a punishment for missing practice. These teammates left the victim naked on a practice mat with his eyes and arms bound.

At yet another high school, on a soccer team, a member was dragged from the shower and his naked body displayed to the passersby with his penis taped to a towel rack. Such examples reveal how sexual violence is a tool for men to mete out discipline and establish hierarchical order, a process that is made possible by creating a feminized victim.[28]

The U.S. Human Rights Watch revealed from its research on prisoners that victims of sexual harassment are labeled as bisexual, gay, pretty boy, small boy, and queen. Once oral sex and penetration occurs, the victim bears the labels of a queer and a coward.[29]

Sexual violence affirms the victim's feminized position and tells him what he has lost and what he must reacquire. In Scarce's book *Male on Male Rape: The Hidden Toll of Stigma and Shame*, "At one fraternity at a large midwestern university, for example, the rush participants were sexually assaulted in a number of ways by gangs of their soon-to-be upperclass 'brothers.' The attacks included verbal abuse of the victims, referring to them as 'little women,' 'girls,' and 'wusses,' and occurred frequently over a period of a week or so. During this time, there were expected to act out in exaggerated female stereotypes. After the series of attacks, they were told to go 'do to women what we did to you to get your manhood back.'"[30] The feminization and sexual harassment of lower-ranking recruits in the military and new members of fraternities are used to make them "authentic men" and to obtain a degree of homogeneity in the group's masculinity.

Sexual Violence: An Injury to Masculinity

In the military, a group mentality is created through a publicly open disciplinary process aimed at molding a "real" man. Hence, within this context of competing masculinities, the process of examining and revealing a sexually injured self would be considered a vital injury to a victim's manhood. In other words, it is the equivalent of proclaiming that "I am a homosexual," or "I am no different from a woman." Even beyond the military, men find it hard to regard themselves as victims. On this subject, John M. Preble and Nicolas Groth explain,

> In the development of males in our society, role expectations place a premium on self-sufficiency and independence. Males are not expected to be vulnerable. In the face of adversity they are expected to "fight their own battles" and not turn to others for help or assistance. Therefore, if a boy is taken advantage of sexually, he may perceive this as evidence of failure on his part to be invincible, and that to report this would expose his personal defect to others. To turn to others for help would only further testify to his inability to take care of himself and take charge of this life. Attributing such psychological meaning to the event would inhibit him from reporting himself to be a victim.[31]

In short, even in civilian society, declaring oneself as victim has a level of meaning equal to giving up one's manhood. Inside the military, such connotations are more exaggerated.

One victim who experienced rape even suspected his own manhood:

> VICTIM 8: I wonder whether I am qualified to be a boyfriend to my girlfriend . . . My girlfriend has faith in me, but why it is that other girlfriends believe that their boyfriends should be dependable and thus, "manly"? Honestly, after that incident, I

have trouble having sexual relations with my girlfriend, and I avoid them.

Those interviewees who experienced sexual violence claimed that they would never reveal the fact that they had been violated:

> VICTIM 1: At the time, I thought what a strange person. Because I thought this way, I acted as if it were nothing, since he would soon be discharged and I just had to endure for a little bit longer. Let's just endure; let's not make a big deal out of this. If people know about this, I will be seen as a disgrace. Especially since it is wise to stay out of sight from others' critical gazes.
> VICTIM 2: When most men come back from the military, they cannot speak of such things. For the most part, men lie about their experiences in the military. I experienced hardship. Who would ever admit to having to provide his arm as a pillow for another man?
> KWON: *You think it is shameful?*
> VICTIM 2: Yes.

Also, according to Sylvia D. Broussard and William G. Wagner's research, male students create a criticizing and punitive environment, and, instead of giving assistance to the male victim, they tend to view the incident as trifling.[32] One victim criticized soldiers who had made sexual harassment an issue:

> VICTIM 1: Customarily when such incidents happen and if they suspect that you were the victim, they justify it by framing it as your fault by saying things like, "It is because you already had problems and conducted yourself like that, that is why they [the higher ranks] bothered you."

Because the emphasis on hierarchical order is great, there is a strong chance that the victim will be punished if he makes the matter public:

> VICTIM 2: But at that time, I had no choice. Really. If I had spoken about this, sexual harassment in that particular regiment

might have declined, but only I would suffer, while other people reaped the benefits. If the higher-ups knew about the harassment, some things might have improved, but my immediate superiors would have alienated me.

Equating the victim as a weak person means that to become a victim is to be positioned low on the vertical hierarchy that governs relationships among men. In particular, by becoming a victim of sexual assault, seen as the equivalent to giving up one's manhood, one becomes a disgrace for other men and a subject who needs to be retrained as a man.

Sexual Violence as "Everyday" and as a Sign of Intimacy

The problem with male sexual violence lies in justifying sexual violence as a sign of intimacy or of becoming closer with another. The rationalization of male-on-male sexual harassment, such as touching the sexual organ as a form of joke or as a natural behavior, is a prominent trend in Korea.[33] According to the 2004 NHRCK investigative report, 64 percent responded that they did not report a case of sexual harassment because "it is not a problem since such things occur ordinarily."[34] During the in-depth interviews with the aggressors, the most frequently cited reason for sexual harassment was because it was merely a prank and an expression of friendliness:

> AGGRESSOR 6: It was not something where I single-handedly approached the soldiers and forced them, as they struggled to fend me off; as I passed by, I held them like this [demonstration] . . . as a joke. And the deposition states that I once kissed him and stuck my tongue in his mouth, or put my tongue to his lips and licked him, but I never did that . . . All I did was to touch his lips with my tongue as a practical joke.
> AGGRESSOR 2: There are superiors who play such pranks and those who do not . . . making you suck their penises and different body parts like the butt . . . I thought that all was just a joke, but the more such jokes were played, the acts became more serious.

Chumminess was cited as the number one reason for playing such pranks:

AGGRESSOR 4: Those who commit minor acts of harassment do it to inferiors that they are close to or take particularly good care of.
AGGRESSOR 6: I regarded kissing my inferiors on the lips as a playful, mischievous way of showing my affection for them.
AGGRESSOR 8: Actually for someone like me, I would not have been able to pull such pranks on inferiors who I did not consider close to me. I thought that because we were close, we were on frank terms without any barriers . . . Because I acted without restraint, I guess the degree became excessive.

Initially, the victims tried to state that they also viewed sexual violence as a way of expressing mischief or affection, expressing the same viewpoint of the perpetrators:

VICTIM 3: First, it's a sign of intimacy. I mean since we are in the same regiment, it's not that I don't like him. If they don't like you, they don't even look at you, don't do anything to you, really.
VICTIM 1: When I was a second- and first-year conscript, as a joke, the superiors would feel my bottom while we were sleeping, and it was weird, but I thought to myself that it was all because the superiors liked me.

These men are opposed to the interpretation that what happened to them was sexual violence. However, the justification of friendliness and prank is often a learned reaction acquired within the context of power and rank. One victim claims that he accepted the harassment as a joke because the leader of the regiment, a sergeant, characterized it as such:

VICTIM 2: The sergeant who was really close to me and treated me affectionately, taught me. He taught me how to take the clothes off a woman (by taking off my clothes) and *even though I thought it was strange to myself*, I did not consider it a big deal. While the sergeant was showing me, we were caught by the staff sergeant. And at the time, both the staff sergeant and sergeant said, "It's just a joke," so I just left it at that.

Although in the beginning of the interview, the victims justified the incidents as a customary thing, they later revealed individual discomfort and feelings of injury during their testimonies. Even in the previous example, the fact that the interviewee thought differently to himself indicates that he did not just regard the matter as mere mischief or affection:

> VICTIM 2: That conscript [another conscript who was caught for sexual harassment] was like a real pervert, but our superior merely touched my bottom, *even though I did not like it*, or did such things like touching my breast, or just asked me to provide my arm as a pillow. Or touched my nipples or penis, and during work hours, would tell me erotic stories.
>
> VICTIM 3: He would hug the inferiors for no good reason, or, since it was just between guys, would touch their penises during bath time . . . or tapped their butts, and no one disliked it. Though I felt a *little uncomfortable when it was done to me*, none of other guys really disliked it.
>
> VICTIM 1: Well, the chief sergeant, often came to my bedside and touched me all over. When I pushed him away, it did not happen again.
>
> KWON: *Didn't that action influence how you were treated afterward?*
>
> VICTIM 1: I never do things like that. I always just say it. I think by seeing things like that, you learn to fix your own mistakes. From my perspective and principles, I knew it wasn't right.

Such inconsistent reactions reveal that people have grown accustomed to conceptualizing sexual violence in the language of the wrongdoer. Even though they may feel anger or pain, by rationalizing the deed as acceptable, the logic of intimacy and prank as a norm is justified.

Sexual Violence that Has Become Thoroughly Hierarchical

Such logic centered on mischief makes it impossible to imagine a reverse situation in which an inferior sexually harasses a superior. Out of those who were interviewed, all the aggressors inflicted harm on inferiors, while the victims were all victimized by superiors. Moreover, both aggressors and victims knew that resistance would not be easy.

> VICTIM 3 (who later becomes an aggressor): Well, the inferior was a private [second year] who was four years younger than me. At

first, I felt his buttocks and then, his penis. But he did not like this . . . You know how it shows on your face when you don't like something even though you maintain a smile. [Laughter] When asked, "When older brother was a college student, how old were you?" he was only a high school student. "Then can I touch your thing? Or not?"

KWON: As I said before, such occurrences take place because the military is a place where you cannot refuse a superior even though he orders things like making you tell erotic stories, and the environment is such that the inferior cannot ask, "Why are you doing this?" even though he does not like what is happening to him.

VICTIM 3: Of course, you cannot ask such things. If you said, "Why are you doing this?" you would be beaten. As the saying goes, in the military, the sergeant is king. If you become a sergeant, you can do anything you want.

For the aggressor and victim who insist on it being a prank and a sign of intimacy, sexual violence is also something that is not possible among conscripts of the same rank.

AGGRESSOR 5: Among rank-mates, they really dislike it. Usually, they don't do such things. It is because we know each other so well; when I have difficulty with something, my rank-mates help me out and when they can't do something, then I help them out.

KWON: Is this because you are able to express your discomfort or because of the hierarchical positioning? So it is just the inferiors who get picked on and cannot say anything about it?

AGGRESSOR 5: Yes, that is why it is mostly the inferiors.

KWON: In any case, is it accurate to say that such actions are acts of sexual violence? Due to power struggles?

AGGRESSOR 5: Yes. If I weren't wearing a military uniform, do you think that the inferior would remain quiet? Honestly, even if you are close, anywhere else, you would not be able engage in such actions.

In short, why is it that male-on-male sexual violence in the military has become hierarchical? Terri S. Nelson, who for a long time has given psychological treatment to both aggressors and victims of male–male and male–female sexual violence within the military, interprets the frequent occurrence as stemming from the desire to exercise power.[35]

Scarce, who has long researched male-on-male rape, has the same opinions about sexual violence in the military: "Just like in prison, in the military, the superiority of the male emerges from within a widespread territory and internal power conflict in order to establish authority."[36] That desire for power and control is a central factor in the cause of sexual violence, a point that various researchers have agreed upon. The reason the rank relationship in the military attracts greater interest is due to the fact that the military is a space where rank and order, dictated by the command structure, is exaggerated. In a space where position and submission are important organizing principles, the internalized nature of sexual violence lacking a buffer can become that much stronger.

When we turn to the example of the prison, an area that has been isolated from the rest of society, the close relationship between the desire for control and power and sexual violence can be discerned. Convicts interviewed by the U.S. Human Rights Watch pointed to power, control, and revenge as the most important reasons behind the violence.[37] According to this report, rather than being deprived of the opportunity to engage in sexual relations as the reason for male-on-male violence, the stated reason was that the aggressor felt powerless and deprived of the ability to make his own decisions. The convicts in the prison were unable to make decisions about the most basic parts of their lives: what to eat, what to wear, what time to wake up, where and who to live with. Such psychological powerlessness incites a strong desire to reinforce one's self-worth in relation to someone else.

For some men, the desire to become a person with power, a person in control of something, erupts as sexual violence because sexual violence such as rape is seen as controlling another's body and as an opportunity to affirm their masculine power by relegating the other to an object of sex (i.e., by feminizing the other). It can be proven indirectly that a strong relationship between such an exercise of power and desire for control and sexual violence exists in the military, where strict discipline and oppression are pervasive more so than in the prison example in the United States. If we were to relate this to the military, for a long period of two or three years in an environment entirely different from what they had been used to since childhood, conscripts must begin anew from the bottom rank and be incorporated into an entirely new hierarchical order.

Regarding the organizational structure of the army, the 2002 NHRCK report explained the following:

> From an organizational perspective, robust order is necessary in order to maintain organization and discipline in a large homogeneous structure, such as the military. Moreover, the maintaining of discipline rests on the foundation of rank and the necessity of sustaining such vertical relationships. From a psychological perspective, the members of the military organization must have unity, belief in an "ideology of national interest," as well as the demand for "the highest degree of patriotism and loyalty" in order to function as a unit under any circumstances. But the uniqueness of the military is that the soldier, especially one who is recruited as matter of civic duty, has his individual independence severely restricted, something that is completely different from the society he had lived in before entering the military.[38]

The restraint on self-control begins at a very basic level. The military is a place where each and every part of daily life, such as what to eat, what to wear, and where to sleep, becomes a means of control. While the degree of control may not be the same, the military and the prison share many similar qualities, such as being subject to discipline and having one's existence dependent on membership in a collective body. In contrast to civilian society, in the military, because one has been deprived of power and control over one's own self in many ways, the desire to compensate for the loss only grows inversely. One victim talked of his dissatisfaction:

> VICTIM 1: Usually, when the sergeant is nice to him, because the private now feels comfortable, many times he acts however he wants. But for the other privates, even though he is offensive, they can't really report anything to the sergeant, so they just harass the private. During this time, they hit him a lot and when hitting isn't sufficient, they resort to sexual methods, which can be seen as an expression of dissatisfaction since they are unable to fulfill their needs.

In reality, aggressors say that they sexually harassed those inferiors who were "cute" (Aggressor 3) or "naïve and innocent" (Aggressor 2). This means that based on their rank, they acted according to their will to control by picking an opposite who they wanted to possess or who was easily able to be possessed. As nearly all perpetrators and victims have said, being intimate was possible with someone who was more easily subjugated, and they picked subjects who were unlikely to resist. There were also instances when a more direct desire for control persisted:

> AGGRESSOR 1: After coming to the army, when you are from a wealthy family and are well educated, you see that these superiors have nothing going for them except that they entered the army before you. You are nice to the ones who seem intimidating and make no effort toward those who appear to yield easily. You can't hit them, so you begin to search for ways in which to legitimately harass them . . .
>
> VICTIM 1: I think most incidents of sexual harassment occur because superiors can get away with it, unlike in ordinary society, where they can't do things like that. Since they are the top of the crop, this entitles them to do anything to the inferiors.

The desire for control can be found in acts such as genital touching, which often happens in cases of male sexual harassment. According to the NHRCK report, 12.9 percent of victims had been subject to genital touching, while 22.5 percent witnessed such action.[39] For these men, the penis is not only a tool for sexual behavior but also a symbol of power and strength. One interviewee talked of the penis as a symbol of power rather than a sexual organ used for performing a reproductive function:

> VICTIM 3 (who later becomes an aggressor): In my case, I resisted embracing . . . since I don't like men. Since embracing is intimate physical contact, I don't do it. I prefer touching the penis instead. Most people think the same way.

The male sexual organ's symbolic meaning can be the cause of even greater resistance:

VICTIM 1: When we were children, we would touch [each other's] penises, and because we were young, it didn't really matter. But when you are older, it is considered shameful conduct. Since I don't look like much, since I appear simple . . . It seems like most people who get harassed feel the same way. No matter how minor, it will come as a disgraceful feeling. That is why I made a bit of a stance to resist.

Regardless of how the inferior feels about having his genitals touched, in the military, where rank is everything, it is as if it is the superiors' right to touch:

VICTIM 3 (who later becomes an aggressor): The inferior was a private and four years younger than me. At first, I felt his buttocks. Then I held his penis . . .

AGGRESSOR 2: Whether it is touching each other's penises, there are superiors who are like that. When they pulled pranks like that, I just accepted it as a joke, and I thought that if I felt any shame, I would have hated it, and they would not have done it . . . so I thought that my inferior would just "consider it a prank" . . . That is why I felt his penis.

Such examples reflect an amalgamation of trivializing, rationalizing intimacy, and a desire for control and domination, made possible because of the two characteristics unique to the military: (1) although it is a place where one must give up many privileges in life because the nation demands it, it is an institution wherein one has no power from within because of rank; and (2) it is also a place where, depending on the individual, an even greater power can be exercised via sexual means. Furthermore, such a hierarchical institution controls how sexual violence is viewed by rationalizing and trivializing it in the form of intimacy.

Violence that Accompanies Sexual Violence

Along with the fact that rank dictates the fabrication of the intimacy or prank logic, the close connection between cruel behavior and sexual violence reveals that this interpretation is one that is centered on the aggressor. According to the results of a report by the NHRCK regarding physical violence at the time of harassment, 21.4 percent responded that physical violence accompanied sexual conduct. The results of an investigation into the realities of military life revealed that 60.32 percent of soldiers said that some sort of physical beating takes place in the military and 65.69 percent responded that there was cruel behavior.[40] Even though the results emphasize rank, and I acknowledge the group-centered trait that aims to use collective violence effectively, the results ultimately show that the military is a place where violent and cruel acts occur frequently among members of its community. The research results about violence in general and sexual violence from the Korean Institute of Criminology reveal evidence that allows us to understand this violence in the military. The results indicate that violent behavior toward others and sexual violence are closely related.

It was reported that "not only is there a meaningful relationship between assault on females and sexual violence, but there is also a relationship between assault toward males and sexual violence. If a male had an experience assaulting others, he had more experiences with rape, serious sexual abuse, and minor acts of sexual violence. In fact, about half of the men who had assaulted others also had experiences of committing minor sexual violence."[41] Of course, the sexual violence mentioned here refers to men abusing women. Nevertheless, the close relationship between the two different kinds of abuse shows a common impetus in the desire to dominate and control others. Thus, the military is a place conducive to sexual violence where rank is strongly emphasized and violence is commonly practiced. As mentioned above, like the case of prisons, greater oppression correlates to a higher frequency of violence. The interview results coincide with such analysis:

> AGGRESSOR 2: Because the spaces were so tight, one inferior always slept next to me. Before we went to bed and even while he was asleep . . . since we were not on such good terms, and I really did not like the way he carried out his duties . . . as one who had been endowed with the power to discipline, I played the part of the villain in order to establish discipline.

The previous situation of a squad leader of an internal unit who had inflicted sexual violence upon an inferior reveals how sexual violence that is disguised as trivial and mischief is in reality one kind of physical abuse. In addition, it tells of the internal limitations of a body that is disciplined by hierarchical rank and order with the aim of achieving victory in wartime.

The Fear and Stigma of Being Branded a Homosexual

Terri Nelson, who had long consulted with military sexual violence victims, insisted that a strong fear of being labeled a homosexual persisted commonly for all victims of male-on-male sexual violence. He also suggested that such psychological burdens were the main reason for low rates of reporting.[42] Clinical psychologists John Preble and Nicolas Groth indicated that when victims of male sexual violence began their psychological treatment the most basic questions were "What kind of influence does the incident have on my sexual orientation?"; "Am I gay?"; and "Am I now going to become homosexual?" All these questions revealed a certain fear and burden.[43] For the conventional male who had suffered sexual harassment, not only did he believe that he would start to exhibit homosexual behavior afterward but also, as Emmanuel Reynaud stated, a victimized male is seen as one who had essentially become a female-like man, or a man who is no different from a woman.[44] Because those men who have experienced sexual violence question their sexual orientation on their own, it is even more difficult for them to overcome the fear that they will be publicly stigmatized as homosexuals. The internalized fear about homosexuality appeared prominently in the personal interviews. Both perpetrator and victim claimed that they were not homosexuals, and many insisted that not only were they not homosexuals but they, in fact, disliked homosexuals. One interviewee (Aggressor 8) expressed his strong denial of being associated with homosexuality: "Even if someone came to me and said, 'I will forgive your sins if you admit that you are homosexual,' I would not do it. I'd rather receive the punishment rather than admit that I am homosexual." Regardless of whether they were aggressor or victim, everyone harbored a fear of being categorized as homosexual. Moreover, the denial and phobia is exaggerated in the military setting because being a homosexual is grounds for exclusion from conscription and consensual same-sex relations warrant punishments for sodomy and other misdemeanors.

From Victim to Aggressor

Another reason why male-on-male sexual violence in the army has not been publicized is because the rate of turnover between victim and aggressor is rather high. Out of the eight aggressors interviewed, four had experience as victims, and out of the three victims, two had been aggressors. Moreover, the NHRCK report indicates that 83 percent of aggressors had victim experience.[45] In short, a victim can easily become an aggressor in the military, and since the correlation between the victim–aggressor role and rank is high, rather than resolving the issue by publicizing the incident, there is an instilled belief that all problems will disappear with a change of rank.

> VICTIM 1: In my case, for exactly six months, superiors, really high-up superiors, who had only a few days left until their discharges, sexually harassed me. After those six months, as I was a cook, two inferiors entered the unit and as my work load decreased, life became more comfortable. At that point, the superiors could not mistreat me. As everyone's rank increases, if the highest superiors bother the subordinates right below them, there is concern about whether the even lower inferiors will treat those midlevel subordinates with respect.

The fact that the role of victim and aggressor reverses as rank changes should be examined from women's perspectives. The victim–aggressor relationship that arises from the rank-dictated superior–inferior relationship is also likely to manifest in ordinary society in a similar fashion upon the women who are designated as the weaker counterparts. In short, in a society where men and women are differentiated by power relations based on sex, the oppression and harm that occurs because of rank and power produces the possibility of shifting men's experience from that of aggressors to victims. Not only is there a need to overcome the negative characterizations of femininity or of becoming feminine in society but also to reexamine the military where sexual violence is overlooked. In such a society, it must be realized that the military experience can easily perpetuate and make more commonplace the male-centered focus socially, economically, and culturally. In reality, most research shows that male sexual violence on women is not sexual desire, but the manipulation of sex to fulfill a desire for domination through violent behavior.[46]

For men who are collectively trained in how to exercise power or to demand control in the military, the standard male-centered culture and male-dominant hierarchical order in some ways very naturally regard sexual violence toward women as frequent and ordinary. Intimacy, which is often used to justify cases of sexual harassment in the workplace, has already been studied. In a reality where sexual violence cannot contradict rank, and a female inferior cannot sexually harass a male superior, it is evident that an aggressor-centered language and awareness dominates. In order to show more clearly that male-on-male violence in the military is one direct cause for male violence against women in Korean society, further investigation and research needs to be pursued. Furthermore, there needs to be more research on the relationships that connect Korean militarization to Japanese colonialism and U.S. neocolonialism. It is reasonable to assume, however, that there is a clear and definite connection between the occurrence of male sexual violence in the military and high rates of sexual violence in society and in the home, reflecting the psychological and cultural roots of existing attitudes toward sexually discriminatory habits.

Conclusion

The problem of male-on-male sexual violence in the military has arisen from the following myriad factors. First, sexual violence has been incorporated as a tool for giving birth to the "genuine male" as an outgrowth from competing militarized masculinities. Second, sexual violence, which is related to ordinary violence and cruel behavior in general, can become a more serious problem within a nontransparent space. Third, the difficulty of identifying oneself as a victim and the aggressor-centered logic of euphemizing sexual violence by calling it mischief and intimacy become more deeply ingrained in a military society where strict hierarchy persists. Fourth, based on the living conditions within a large military unit, the additional injury to the victim from peer pressure makes it difficult for him to report the incident. Fifth, the victim becomes silent within a space where he is easily categorized as homosexual and where homosexuals are prohibited by martial law.

Such male-on-male sexual violence in the military is a serious problem from a women's perspective as well. One can only worry about the harmful influence that perpetrators of sexual violence will have on women, who make up the underprivileged and powerless of Korean society at large. Also worrisome is the feminization of the object of violence and of subjugation. For men who have completed such military training, the task of changing the perception toward femininity and instilling respect for women becomes that much more challenging.

The present reality makes us realize once again that the conscription law is a law that demands much greater public interest in order not only to resolve the issue of an individual conscript's human rights but also to address the sexual violence taking place in Korean society and to resolve the persistence of a sexually discriminatory culture.

Notes

1. NHRCK, *Report for Sexual Violence in the Military* (Seoul: NHRCK, 2004).

2. On July 13, 2003, *Hankyoreh* newspaper reported the suicide of army conscript "Kim," and the topic became the talk of the town when other newspapers published articles concerning male-on-male sexual violence the following day.

3. In this chapter, instead of using the terminology sexual violence among "homosexuals," the term "male-on-male" is used. Male-on-male sexual violence, which acts as a means of espousing a domineering masculinity and contains a punitive element toward male homosexuality, is a phenomenon unique to men. On July 14, 2003, the *Donga ilbo* newspaper reported that a lieutenant colonel of a certain regiment was arrested and kept in custody for sexually harassing an on-duty officer more than ten times. News of this incident appeared around the same time as Kim's suicide. On the 29th of the same month, a corporal accused of sexually harassing a female captain while she was sleeping in her tent was taken into custody. Yet, the very same female captain, who in fact conducted the criminal investigation, was booked for cruel behavior, and a controversy arose over whether the captain should be treated as a victim or an aggressor.

4. "A Man Sexually Harassed Another Man?" is the title of an in-depth investigative report published by the magazine *Weekly Chosun* in the aftermath of Kim's suicide (*Weekly Chosun*, July 31, 2003, Issue 1764). *Hankyoreh 21* depicted the shocked public sentiment with questions as "How is it possible that men are sexually harassing men in the military?" (*Hankyoreh 21*, July 24, 2003, Issue 469).

5. A July 29, 2003, issue of the *Munhwa ilbo* newspaper concluded that the unfolding sexual harassment controversy was a "phenomenon resulting entirely from disorder in military discipline." *Kyunghyang* newspaper also reported on July 31, 2003, that "the lifeline of the army, law and order, had collapsed."

6. In *Kookmin ilbo*, a July 14, 2003, publication established male-on-male sexual violence as male-on-male sexual behavior and insisted on the following: "Homosexual sexual violence not only goes against a God-given natural order but also contradicts the nature of man. Especially in the barracks, which is a strictly ranked society, the character and the conduct of sexual violence cannot be uttered. As homosexual be-

havior is considered the principal cause of the AIDS contagion, sexual violence among homosexuals cannot be tolerated from a health hygiene viewpoint." Readers made comments such as "I am dumbstruck that such a thing can happen" and lamented the following: "How can such a thing happen among soldiers for whom discipline is everything?" and "It is possible that the number of homosexuals in the barracks are increasing without our knowledge." (*Dae-han Maeil*, July 14, 2003)

7. In response to the sexual violence cases, military authorities have invested in improving living quarters and introducing beds. "For improving the environment in the barracks 500 billion won was invested, and old-fashioned consolidated barracks in 103 squadrons were changed to separate beds. *Defense Journal* January 2004, http://www.dema.mil.kr/jour/jour01/html (site now discontinued). "By 2020, 6.97 trillion won will be spent on changing 1,150 barracks into bed-style facilities." (*Hankyoreh*, November 2003)

8. The only investigative reports have taken place in 2000, when National Assembly representative Dae-chul Chung submitted a simple numerical value of 11 percent as having experienced or having heard of bodily caressing, narration of sex stories, masturbation, or touching of the genitals within the military, and one chapter in a 2002 NHRCK report titled, "Basic Research on Devising a Scheme to Improve the Human Rights Reality within the Military." According to this report, 9.1 percent of respondents had experienced sexual contact since serving in the army. NHRCK, *Basic Research for the Reality and Solution for Human Rights in the Military* (Seoul: NHRCK, 2002). Hyun-yong Kim's master's thesis, "Military Duty and the Sex Politics of a Militarized Nation," is seen as the only the only interview-based research relating to homosexual sexual violence. But even in this study, male-on-male sexual violence, as a subtopic, covers only a small portion, and, thus, it is difficult to gather sufficient information on the actual conditions. Hyun-yong Kim, "Military Duty and the Sex Politics of a Militarized Nation" (master's thesis, Ewha Women's University, 2002).

9. See chapter 5 of Brownmiller, "An Investigation on the Reality of Sexual Violence in the Army," in *Against Our Will* (New York: Simon & Schuster, 1975), which deals specifically with the laws, policies, and knowledge pertaining to male sexual violence in the military.

10. Korean Ministry of National Defense, *A Guide to Preventing the Violation of Sex-related Military Discipline* (Seoul, Korea: Ministry of National Defense, 2001).

11. Hyun-yong Kim takes the very existence of this generally accepted idea as the problem. Kim argues against the notion of soldiers regarding homosexual sexual abuse as taking place "since there is no way to release sexual desire among men" and perceives sexual abuse as a joke. Instead Kim claims that it has to do with the meaning of masculinity within the military. Kim, "Military Duty and the Sex Politics of a Militarized Nation," 82.

12. Seung-sook Cho, "Military Culture and Masculinity," in *Masculinity and Korean Society* (Seoul, Korea: Society and Culture Research Institute, Research Committee on Women and Korean Society, 1997), 155–85; Dong-heun Lee, "Male-centeredness of Military Culture and Gender-Equal Education" (master's thesis, Yonsei University, 2001); Kim, "Military Duty and the Sex Politics of a Militarized Nation."

13. The 2004 NHRCK report states that 24.7 percent of soldiers had seen or heard of male-on-male sexual violence in the military (47).

14. According to Korean criminal law 297, the current regulation on rape law, rape is categorized as "one who rapes a woman with violence or threat." Young-hui Shim criticized the many problems of this legal document, which is based on thinking centered on sexual organs and differentiates between specific sexes and, in relation to women, does not recognize the rape of wives as rape. Young-hui Shim, *Dangerous Society and Sexual Violence* (Seoul, Korea: Nanam Press, 1998).

15. Other examples of such public silence are noted, in chapter 11 of this volume, in relation to the thousands of Korean men who were conscripted into the Japanese imperial army, and, in chapter 12, in terms of the militarized sexual relations between U.S. occupying troops and Korean women.

16. Regarding the Korean example, Young-hui Shim's book, *Dangerous Society and Sexual Violence*, is based on the perspective of social history, where sexual violence is characterized as a product of modernity. As a product of industrialization and modernization, sexual violence can be seen to possess traits similar across many societies, but Korea's accelerated speed of and approach to modernization are also unique characteristics under which sexual violence in Korea has occurred.

17. This point is definitely a limitation arising from the lack of preexisting research. It is hoped that research on the traits singular to Korean society continues.

18. Michael Scarce, *Male on Male Rape* (Cambridge, Mass.: Perseus Publishing, 1997).

19. Lisa D. Bastian, Anita R. Lancaster, and Heidi E. Reyst, *Sexual Harassment Survey* (Washington, D.C.: U.S. Department of Defense, 1996).

20. U.S. Department of Defense, *Armed Forces 2002 Sexual Harassment Survey* (Washington, D.C.: Defense Manpower Data Center, 2004).

21. Lee, "Male-centeredness of Military Culture and Gender-Equal Education," 30.

22. Kim, "Military Duty and the Sex Politics of a Militarized Nation," ii.

23. Ibid.

24. This word has many levels of meaning and is generally a derogatory term of address to women. Depending on the context, *nyon* can mean "wench," "hussy," "slut," "bitch," and so on. [Translator's note: Romanization of Korean terms follows the McCune-Reischauer system, the most widely used romanization system in academic literature.]

25. *Ssibal* is a universal curse with the English equivalent of "fuck." *Ssiballyon* can be translated as "fucking bitch." [Translator's note: *Chot* literally refers to the male sexual organ. In colloquial terms, *chotkat'un nyon* closely resembles "slut" or "whore."]

26. Lee, "Male-centeredness of Military Culture and Gender-Equal Education."

27. Korea Institute of Criminology, "Research on the Actual Conditions and the Causes of Sexual Violence, Part II" (Seoul, Korea: Korean Institute of Criminology, 1998), 37.

28. Scarce, *Male on Male Rape*.

29. Human Rights Watch, "Chapter V. Rape Scenarios," *No Escape: Male Rape in U.S. Prisons*, http://www.hrw.org/reports/2001/prison/report5.html#_1_31 (accessed December 2, 2003).

30. Scarce, *Male on Male Rape*, 54.

31. John M. Preble and Nicholas Groth, *Male Victims of Same-Sex Abuse: Addressing Their Sexual Response* (Baltimore, Md.: Sidran Press, 2002), 4.

32. S. D. Broussard and W. G. Wagner, "Child Sexual Abuse: Who is to Blame?" *Child Abuse and Neglect* 12 (1998): 563–69.

33. Kim, "Military Duty and the Sex Politics of a Militarized Nation."

34. NHRCK, *Report for Sexual Violence in the Military*.

35. Terri S. Nelson, *For the Love of Country: Confronting Rape and Sexual Harassment in the U.S. Military* (New York: Haworth Maltreatment and Trauma Press, 2002).

36. Scarce, *Male on Male Rape*, 47.

37. Human Rights Watch, "Chapter V. Rape Scenarios."

38. NHRCK, Basic Research, 28–29.

39. Emmanuel Reynaud, *Holy Virility: The Social Construction of Masculinity* (London: Pluto Press, 1983); NHRCK, *Report for Sexual Violence in the Military*.

40. NHRCK, *Report for Sexual Violence in the Military*, no page numbers listed.

41. Korean Institute of Criminology, "Research on the Actual Conditions and the Causes of Sexual Violence, Part II," 207–8.

42. Nelson, *For the Love of Country*.

43. Preble and Groth, *Male Victims of Same-Sex Abuse*, 39.

44. Reynaud, *Holy Virility*.

45. NHRCK, *Report for Sexual Violence in the Military*.

46. Shim, *Dangerous Society and Sexual Violence*; Korean Institute of Criminology, "Research on the Actual Conditions and the Causes of Sexual Violence, Part II"; Nelson, *For the Love of Country*.

11

Why Have the Japanese Self-Defense Forces Included Women?

The State's "Nonfeminist Reasons"

Fumika Sato

This chapter analyzes why and how the Japanese Self-Defense Forces (SDF) have included women over the past five decades. Although a large number of studies have examined the relationship between women and the military by feminist scholars around the world, little is known about the relationship between women and the SDF.[1] This is part of my larger research on the shifting gendered formations of the SDF.[2]

Several Japanese feminists have made tremendous scholarly contributions to illuminate and critique women's past roles in militarizing the Japanese Empire.[3] The Japanese Empire drafted 143,000 Taiwanese and Korean men since 1943, but they never conscripted Japanese women into the Imperial Japanese Army. Japanese feminist scholars, such as Kano Mikiyo, have rigorously examined Japanese women's responsibility for World War II. Kano's work demonstrates the strong and consistent reproduction of a binary gender norm, which promoted male ascendancy.[4] We can observe this regulated gender norm not only in the principle of conscription but also in the principle of suffrage. While the Japanese Empire extended suffrage to Taiwanese and Korean men inside the country in 1925, it was not until after World War II that Japanese women acquired franchise.

However, when the Japanese government signed the San Francisco Peace Treaty in 1951 and officially ended its state of war with the United States and forty-seven other countries, Taiwanese and Korean men inside the country lost their citizenship. The Japanese government refused to give these men any opportunities to choose their citizenship and regarded

251

them as foreigners.⁵ As for Japanese women, they got suffrage in 1945 as a part of the democratization process. Can we consider suffrage as a proof of a new gender norm in post–World War II Japan? Can we understand the "feminization" of the post–World War II Japanese military as evidence of a new gender norm?

What remains lacking are critical feminist analyses about the relationship between women and the military in post–World War II Japan. It is within this context that I situate my work as an extension of a longer legacy of Japanese feminist scholarly work. In what follows, I demonstrate how women have played an important role in militarizing postwar Japan. Furthermore, I want to emphasize (particularly to non-feminist scholars) how the "feminization" of the SDF has been caused by "statist reasons" rather than "feminist reasons." For Japanese feminists to resist recent accelerating militarization, feminist investigations and scholarship on the gendered and heteronormative formation of SDF is an emergent field of inquiry.

Historical Background of the SDF

The history of the SDF must be understood in the context of Japan's defeat in World War II and its subsequent formal demilitarization. After World War II and under the U.S.-led occupation, Japan was totally demilitarized. Article Nine of Japan's new constitution promulgated in 1946 prohibited Japan from maintaining military forces and from using war to settle international disputes.⁶

With the onset of the cold war, the policy regarding demilitarization underwent a reverse course. Foreign policy makers in Washington, out of anxiety fueled by their war in Korea, began to envision a rearmed Japan as a potential Pacific ally in its new global war against communism. In the early 1950s, the general headquarters (GHQ) of the Allied forces pressed Japan to remilitarize.⁷ On July 8, 1950, General Douglas MacArthur sent then Prime Minister Yoshida Shigeru a memorandum on the reinforcement of the Japanese police forces.⁸ When the Korean War broke out in 1950, the new Japanese postwar, postsurrender military force started as the National Police Reserve. Initially the new organization was designed simply to reinforce police power. Japanese government officials, well aware of the newly instituted constitution's Article Nine prohibition, defined it as a police force whose duty was only to pacify domestic incidents.

In 1952, the Japanese government, again with Washington's support, even urging,[9] renamed and reorganized the fledgling Police Reserve as the Security Corps. The end of the U.S. occupation of Japan was marked formally by the coming into force of the San Francisco Peace Treaty.[10] Simultaneously, the Japanese government removed the original purpose of domestic policing from the newly named Security Corps' mandate. These policy changes served to strengthen the militaristic character of the Security Corps, despite official reassurances that it conformed to the memorandum and spirit of the "Peace Constitution."

In 1954, the Japanese government concluded the Mutual Security Act (MSA) with the United States and, subsequently, the Security Corps was renamed the Japanese Self-Defense Forces, the title by which today's Japanese military is still known.[11]

Among Japanese citizens there have been continuing debates over the character, structure, and purpose of the SDF since it was established in 1954: Is it or is it not a "military"? If it is a "military," does its very existence violate the conditions of Article Nine of the constitution? This is more than a narrow debate about legal terms. Many Japanese, especially liberal or left-wing Japanese and many Japanese feminists as well, derive their identities as post-Imperial, postwar Japanese citizens from their personal identification with the "Peace Constitution."

Article Nine of the Japanese Constitution asserts that "the right of belligerency of the state will not be recognized." Various elected officials of Japanese governments (not only of the long-dominant Liberal Democratic Party, the country's leading conservative party founded in 1955, but also most of the Democratic Party of Japan, the fledgling ruling party since 2009) have tried to legitimate the SDF within the terms of Article Nine. They claim that Japan can make use of the minimum force necessary for self-defense and that the use of such force is quite different from exercising the right of belligerency. Therefore some people who want to say that there are no constitutional problems surrounding the SDF often argue that the SDF is *not a military* but a self-defense force.[12]

It remains an unsettled question whether the SDF is a "military." However, there are several points that need to be clarified. First, by the early twenty-first century, the budget of the SDF in 2002 reached a level that placed it within the top four in the world.[13] Second, the SDF has become a large organization with a uniformed, professional "manpower" of 228,536 (including 11,167 women) members in fiscal year 2008. Third, the SDF is equipped with some of the contemporary era's most sophisticated weaponry—F-15 jet fighters, Aegis warships, HAWK (abbreviation for "Homing All the Way Killer") air-defense guided missiles, though it explicitly eschews any nuclear weaponry and any research on nuclear weaponry. Fourth, since the 1990s, the SDF has had more and more opportunities to deploy overseas and carry on regular joint maneuvers with other states' militaries, specifically with the U.S. military. Thus the SDF today has the capacity, if not the authority or the mission, to wield significant military force. All of this amounts to saying that one must analytically treat the SDF as a military.

From January 2004 to September 2006, the Japanese government dispatched more than five thousand Ground Self-Defense Force (GSDF) members to Iraq. This was a remarkable historical event because it was the first time the SDF was sent to a "combat area," which the Japanese government did not admit as such. Domestically, this refueled the current debate about Article Nine of the constitution; thus, the government upgraded the Defense Agency to the Defense Ministry in 2007. Internationally, while the mission in Iraq strengthened the ties between Japan and the United States, it evoked the anxiety of Asian people about Japanese remilitarization.

Some Japanese, especially conservative or right-wing and antifeminist Japanese, consider remilitarization as "normalization." Sabine Frühstück, who observed the SDF members' lives and examined the "uneasiness" regarding their roles, respectability, masculinities, and identities, warned that the SDF had aimed at "normalization" of the armed forces by maneuvering gender, memory, and popular culture.[14] In order to pay attention to "normalization" of the SDF, this chapter clarifies several statist nonfeminist reasons for introducing women into the SDF.

Women in the SDF and Feminist Questions

In her comparative study of militarization in Asia, Eastern Europe, Africa, the Middle East, and the United States, Cynthia Enloe has found that there are "statist non-feminist reasons" for officials deciding to increase the numbers and roles of women soldiers.[15] Enloe has demonstrated how many "non-feminist reasons" operate when policy makers try to recruit the sorts of personnel they believe are most desirable for their national militaries. For example, senior proapartheid policy makers of the South African military came to rely more on women in the 1980s when the white elite began to realize they were running out of "reliable" men. Similarly, in Russia, the percentages of women rose from less than 1 percent of the 1980s Soviet army to 12 percent of the post-Communist Russian armed forces by 2002, in part because Russian women as mothers had so effectively organized in the 1990s to resist the conscription of their sons. The U.S. military in the 1970s and 1980s likewise increased women's numbers and roles after the U.S. Congress ended male conscription in 1973 and launched instead an all-volunteer force. Many governments thus have long relied on an increasing, if small, percentage of women to serve inside their still-masculinized state militaries.

My research suggests that we should add the post–World War II Japanese government to the list of governments that have broken seemingly patriarchal social codes in order to meet their own military's "manpower" needs. By 2008, the total number of women in the SDF reached eleven thousand, which comprises 4.9 percent of the total force.[16] Since the Japanese government decided to send the SDF to help rebuild war-ravaged Iraq in 2004, about ten female members have been included in each troop. We miss the point if we regard these facts merely as the results of "pro-feminist policies."

Some women's movements in the United States, Canada, Australia, and postapartheid South Africa have pressured their own governments to increase the percentages, jobs, and promotional chances for women in their militaries. As a result of her research on the relationship between gender and citizenship, Nira Yuval-Davis points out that defending one's fellow citizens and country has been seen by many liberal feminists as the duty of all citizens—both men and women—to die (as well as to kill) for the sake of the homeland or the nation.[17] This concept of soldiering has persuaded some feminists to fight for the inclusion of women in the military; they argue that without sharing this ultimate civic duty with men, they would not be able to get equal citizenship rights to those of men.[18]

On the other hand, many other feminists, including many American, Canadian, Australian, and South African feminists, have come to the realization that more women in the military would only militarize those women and legitimize the military. These latter feminists' analyses of women in the military are similar to that of most contemporary Japanese feminists. Since the Persian Gulf War broke out, the controversy surrounding female soldiers has arisen among Japanese feminists. Except for a few, most feminists in Japan criticized the National Organization for Women's (NOW) demand for the right of female soldiers to fight.[19] Instead of falling into the trap of seeking "equal opportunity" within the military, Japanese feminists have questioned the idea of opportunity within the military, asking, "The opportunity to do *what*?"[20] Another question now arises: Are there also nonfeminist reasons in post–World War II history for the inclusion of women in the Japanese military?

I will examine the history of women in the Japanese military by analyzing the government's personnel policies shaping the SDF. In the SDF's over fifty-year mediated development to date, the policy context and content have gone through four analytically distinct stages.

The First Stage (1950–1966): Only Nursing Jobs

In the first stage (1950–1966), Japanese policy makers opened only SDF nursing jobs to women, all of whom (like the SDF's male enlistees) were volunteers. The Police Reserve (as it was then named) consisted exclusively of men in uniform. However, despite nursing jobs being on the margins of this small, fledgling organization, officials thought it necessary to recruit women as nurses. These female nurses did not wear a Police Reserve uniform because they were categorized by government planners as civilian nurses. However, in 1952, when the government created an Army Nursing Corps, these nurses were more fully integrated into the main force and, thus, since then have worn military uniforms. The gradual militarization (and organizational integration) of women as nurses to soldiers follows a common pattern that one can see in the U.S., British, and Russian militaries.[21]

The Army Nursing Corps admitted only those women who were qualified nurses. They were assigned to work in the hospitals of GSDF and in the dispensaries of local units. In 1952, about one thousand women applied, sixty-two were accepted, and fifty-seven entered the military.[22]

Mady Wechsler Segal, researching women's military roles cross-nationally and chronologically, states that "when gender segregation is extremely high, the military must rely on women to perform military functions that are dominated by women in the civilian workplaces."[23] Nursing is such a job, and it "has often been the first military job to open to women in substantial numbers."[24] Segal's observation applies to post-1950 Japanese military history.

It appears that male officials crafting the still-nascent SDF believed that they could safely include women as "feminine" military nurses. Even though they offered nurses weapons training with the rifle, they could do it without the fear of undermining the masculinity of the new military. According to Karl L. Wiegand, who had a twenty-six-year career in the U.S. Air Force and served in Tokyo as the air attaché at the U.S. Embassy, GSDF officers stressed that the purpose of the weapons training was "for familiarization only," and there was "no intent to use women in combat."[25]

Due to the fact that there were many war nurses during World War II, there was no resistance from men in uniform at this time to women serving as nurses.[26] Rather, the SDF gave them a warm welcome. For example, the National Security Board, predecessor of the Defense Agency, implored the former chief nurse of the army hospital to enter this nascent Army Nursing Corps.[27]

The Second Stage (1967–1985): Opening Military Support Jobs to Women

In the second stage (1967–1985), the gendered formation of the SDF changed significantly. The Japanese government's military planners seemed to have launched in 1967 an unacknowledged second stage in their crafting of a gendered strategy for recruiting and deploying women in the military when they decided to significantly expand the numbers and types of jobs SDF women could perform.

In 1967, the GSDF's new policy of using women in so-called supporting jobs set the stage for launching the Women's Army Corps (WAC) the following year. The male officials' reasoning seems to have been a desire to more "efficiently" use male SDF soldiers, that is, to use men to do what these officials considered to be "manly" jobs. One civilian official, Kaibara Osamu, who was director general of the Secretariat of the Minister of State for Defense from 1965 to 1966, recollected the experience that affected his own change of policy consciousness: "One day, I went to the [SDF] magazine [production office] in Saitama Prefecture . . . I saw many men arranging things in the magazine. What a waste! This is not a man's job but a woman's job, I thought, women are good at organizing, you know? Think about World War II. The women voluntary corps were very successful, weren't they? So I thought that men should run with machine guns while women take care of storing them. Such a division of labor would be best, I thought."[28] This statement exemplifies how this senior male official is attempting to (re)craft a military personnel policy that guarantees that *only* male soldiers will have to perform and execute, and thereby "secure," the masculinized integrity and character of their militarized professions.

However, even if women were to be treated as second-class soldiers, that is, not essential to the SDF's "core" tasks, there was still a resistance to including women as soldiers.

According to Kaibara, all of the military elites of the GSDF in the late 1960s opposed the idea of creating the WAC and thus expanding women's roles in the SDF.[29] However, a senior civilian official sent an elite military officer to the United States on a tour of inspection specifically to learn how the Pentagon was using women, even though women comprised a mere 2 percent of the U.S. military in the late 1960s (the Vietnam War era). Another Japanese defense official, who had lived in the United States as an ambassador and had known the U.S. WAC well, persuaded this visiting official to approve the idea of a Japanese WAC. Kaibara used the expression "brainwash" to describe how this U.S.-based Japanese official persuaded his visiting colleague of the wisdom of making greater use of women inside the SDF.[30]

What made the SDF's senior male policy makers decide to admit women as soldiers in spite of this intramilitary male resistance? We could say that it had little to do with their commitment to women's advancement in Japanese society. Instead, there is ample evidence to show that their decision was motivated by a "statist non-feminist reason" to make up for the shortfalls of young male recruits.[31]

During the late 1960s to the early 1970s, Japan's civilian job market was highly favorable for young Japanese men. These were the early years of what was to become Japan's remarkably successful "economic boom." It was consequently very difficult for the SDF to attract qualified young men. During this period, the SDF's applicants were only about twice as many as the quotas set by the SDF planners for replenishing its male soldiers. One civilian official stated in 1999 that the number of applicants the Defense Agency obtains should be at least three times as many as the quotas to get qualified personnel. However, at this time, the number of young Japanese men who expressed an interest in enlisting in the SDF was below their projected aims. According to this official, the SDF recruiters went downtown and enlisted young men who did not have jobs. However, there were many disciplinary problems caused by these newly recruited soldiers, and the resignation rate was very high.[32]

It was difficult in this context to recruit appropriate men, and so the SDF discovered a new pool of talented recruits: young women. The SDF implemented quotas for women and was able to attract excellent female recruits.³³ At the same time they were successful in filling their recruiting quotas for young women, they were unable to successfully recruit enough young men. Thus women made up for this lack of male recruits, supplementing the ranks.

Moreover, there was another reason SDF officials chose to include more women as soldiers: they aimed to make women "wise" mothers who could understand the needs of national security. Though this is an important factor in other countries, it is especially important in Japan where there has been much controversy surrounding the legitimacy of the SDF.

In the Japanese legislative body, the Diet, it has been noted that women are not interested in the SDF. In 1985, at the end of this second stage, one of the most interesting Diet arguments was spelled out by Santo Akiko, one of a mere handful of female Diet members from the ruling Liberal Democratic Party.³⁴ She told her mostly male legislative colleagues, "Though women take care of their homes, they don't care about their state. However they should understand they can't live happy lives without a peaceful state. Women should have the strong will to defend their state."³⁵ This same rationale was used to persuade men to end their resistance to considering a SDF career during the second-stage changes within the SDF. According to the WAC's research on the past, present, and future of the WAC, one male officer of the Ground Staff Office persuaded his subordinates who did not accept the idea of WAC as follows: "If the SDF admits women, we could get more supporters. This is because if one girl decides to become a SDF member, she would have to persuade everyone in her home. Moreover, such a woman with a healthy spirit would bear children who would become soldiers."³⁶ What the passage makes clear at once is that this male official's apparent aim was for women, as retired military personnel, to become "wise mothers" who could understand the needs of national security. Thus, the very fact that women are generally not interested in the SDF led some officials to think that women's way of thinking would be crucial to change both the current and future public opinion about the SDF.

The Third Stage (1986–1991): Quantitative and Qualitative Expansion

In the third stage (1986–1991), there was a quantitative and qualitative expansion for women in the military to make up for recruiting shortfalls in the number of male soldiers. From the late 1980s to the beginning of the

1990s, the civilian job market was highly favorable for young men. If a military lacks access to a system of compulsory male conscription, especially when the civilian job market is good for young men, it is common that there is a shortfall in military recruiters. Therefore, policy makers turned to women, who had been excluded by the masculinized private sector from enjoying the benefits of a good job market. Gender discrimination in the private sector thus contributed to the gendered formation of the SDF.

There is evidence to suggest that SDF officials thought of women as compensation for the shortfalls in male soldiers during what Japanese now call "the Bubble Economy." The number of women in 1991 (7,680, or 3.2 percent) doubled compared with the figures in 1986 (4,232, or 1.7 percent).

The third stage may sound the same as stage two. However, in the second stage, male officials limited women's jobs to only supporting jobs such as personnel, administration, accounting, and communication. What distinguishes this stage from the previous stage is the fact that women's jobs exceeded those explicitly gender-segregated supporting jobs.

In addition to the previously mentioned economic factors that pressured male officials to utilize women, during this third stage an additional factor influenced their decisions. This new external factor was the civilian government officials' 1985 ratification of the Convention on the Elimination of All Forms of Discrimination against Women (CEDAW), the United Nations treaty designed to commit member states to end gender discrimination in their own countries.

To implement CEDAW's provisions, the Japanese government created the "Law on Securing, etc., of Equal Opportunity and Treatment between Men and Women in Employment." Mady Wechsler Segal has stated that "a driving force toward increasing women's representation in the military has been laws prohibiting discrimination based on gender."[37] In Japan, this law became such "a driving force." In 1986, when this law was brought into force, civilian and military officials of the Defense Agency again decided to significantly expand the numbers and types of jobs SDF women could perform. This "reform" led to a rapid increase in the number of women in the SDF working in previously "masculinized" jobs, including engineering, artillery, and air defense control.[38]

Though CEDAW was the trigger for these changes, it does not follow that these were caused by feminists' efforts. The point I wish to emphasize is that there have not been any Japanese feminist campaigns pushing for these "reforms." Wiegand conducted interviews with the Prime Minister's Office and the Labor Ministry in 1979, when CEDAW was adopted, and pointed out that officials are pushing for greater opportunity for women "because they want Japan to be viewed as a progressive modern nation among the industrialized countries of the world."[39] That is to say, their decision was motivated by another "non-feminist reason": to appear "modern" and "democratic" in the eyes of the state's principal international allies.

In spite of these "reforms," it is also a mistake to think that female SDF members have been totally integrated. Those officials have not forgotten to add some limitations, including "combat exclusion." Therefore, women cannot join regiments such as infantry and armor and are not permitted to fly F-15 jet fighters; neither can they embark on escort vessels and submarines. Also, the percentage of female officers (which is still less than 2 percent throughout this stage) is much less than that of female soldiers (which rose from 4 percent at the second stage to 8 percent at the third stage). The rank in which the number of women increased most rapidly was the lowest one, "*shi*," which has a limited term of contract.

There are other things to note. Women were utilized for creating the image of the SDF. In fact, we can also observe this role in the previous stage. For example, when the sovereignty of Okinawa was transferred from the United States to Japan in 1972, the SDF deployed a female official to the recruitment division of Okinawa. This was apparently their strategy to appease Okinawan antipathy against the SDF. The SDF not only utilized women in the recruitment division but also frequently made women participate in local beauty contests. One of these women, who won first prize as "Miss Kochi" (Kochi is the name of one of the prefectures in Japan), worked to serve on a publicity campaign for the SDF. There is much evidence to prove that women have been playing a more important role in the SDF's image making.

Figure 11.1 shows the ratio of recruitment posters at each stage by gender of its models. We can see that the rate of male-only posters is decreasing and the rate of female-only posters is increasing. These recruitment posters were selected by the SDF's own recruiting strategists. Although female models have appeared since 1965, between 1950 and 2008, the SDF advertising designers began to overrepresent women in their posters intended to appeal to young Japanese.

Figure 11.2 is a 2003 SDF recruiting poster. Although this is from the fourth stage, the representation shows the common gender formation of

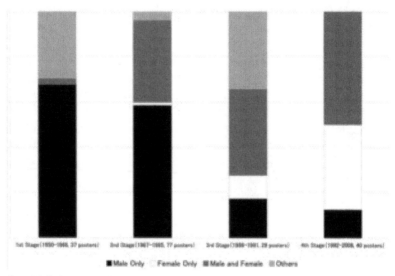

Figure 11.1. Gender representation in recruitment posters used by the Japanese SDF, shown in four stages. The rate of male-only posters is decreasing, and the rate of female-only posters is increasing.

this stage. These girls comprise one of the famous Japanese idol groups, named "Morning Musume [daughters]" and most of their fans are young boys. The Chinese characters written in blue ink on the left corner means "SDF Recruit." The message—"How cool it is that you work hard! GO! GO! PEACE!"—is written in red ink. Neither tanks, submarines, nor fighters appear in this poster. The girls do not even wear SDF uniforms. As this poster indicates, Japanese women have played an important role in the creation of the nonmilitaristic image of the SDF. The image created by female-only posters such as Figure 11.2 was totally different from the one created by male-only posters during the first two stages.

The next posters, for example, contrast: one is from the first stage and the other is from the third stage. We should notice the difference; Figure 11.3 is a painting and Figure 11.4 is a photograph.[40] However the composition of each is the same; in each, three soldiers are in line, one is from the GSDF, one is from the Maritime Self-Defense Force (MSDF), and the last is from the Air Self-Defense Force (ASDF).

Let us now look at these posters in a new light. We can find that the SDF designers' deliberate presentation of the gender of the models in each poster is different. While in Figure 11.3, the three men do not

Figure 11.2. Fourth-stage SDF recruiting poster, 2003, depicting the famous Japanese idol group and featuring the message "How cool it is that you work hard! GO! GO! PEACE"

smile but rather tighten their mouths, the three women all smile, showing their white teeth in Figure 11.4. Moreover, in Figure 11.3, the text is only "GSDF/MSDF/ASDF/Recruit." In Figure 11.4, there is a catchphrase written: "We love your vitality." Actually, "love" is a word that often appears in posters that include female models. Figure 11.5 is another poster from the third stage that includes the word "love." This poster consists of a girl and a male SDF official, and there is a catchphrase written "I love a reliable man!"

The question now arises: who loves whom? As for Figure 11.5, what this phrase at once makes clear is that this female model loves this male model because he is a reliable SDF member. There may be two interpretations for Figure 11.4, however. On the one hand, we can think the audience loves the female models' vitality because they are vital SDF members. On the other hand, we can interpret that the female models love the applicants' vitality because they are applying for the SDF. In either interpretation, a heterosexist logic operates.

As a result of her cross-national study of North American and Western European twentieth-century efforts by male state officials to mobilize both

Figure 11.3. First-stage SDF recruiting poster, 1954, depicting tight-lipped men and featuring only the message "GSDF/MSDF/ASDF/Recruit"

Figure 11.4. Third-stage SDF recruiting poster, 1989, depicting smiling girls and featuring the message "We love your vitality."

Figure 11.5. Third-stage SDF recruiting poster, 1987, featuring the message "I love a reliable man!"

the ideas of femininity and women themselves to serve patriarchal war-waging agendas, Jean Bethke Elshtain writes, "The historic representation that invigorates women's collective self-recognition as essentially caring, concerned, nonviolent beings who can, however, be mobilized as wartime civic cheerleaders and home-front helpmeets—'Women of Britain Say—GO!' was the most famous and effective First World War recruitment poster—is the Just Warrior's better half, the Beautiful Soul."[41] Women in the SDF are an important part of the military. That is, they are more than simply supporters on the sidelines cheering their men onward. However, I would like to expand Elshtain's "beautiful soul" metaphor to women in the representation of the SDF because they are tenderly smiling at and cheering potential applicants and are thus projected as heterosexual women. The message of the female models in the representation of the SDF at peacetime—exemplified in 11.2, "GO! GO! PEACE!"—is reminiscent of the British recruitment poster. In this case, the "Women of Japan Say—GO!" to borrow Elshtain's phrase, the role of women in the representation of the SDF seems to be this "Beautiful Soul."

The Fourth Stage (1992–): Female Elites as Cadets

The new policy decision that marks the beginning of the most recent (and continuing) stage in the SDF is the 1992 decision to admit women as cadets into the National Defense Academy (NDA). This decision was meant to give more women the opportunity to eventually gain promotion to the ranks of senior officers. Thus, since this stage, the possibilities that women will become officers and that women will become decision makers have become much more likely than in the three earlier policy stages.

There was a long debate before the birth of the idea of female cadets. It was in the Diet's Budget Committee in 1979 that the issue on the admission of women to the NDA was first discussed. At this time, Yamashita Motonori, minister of state for defense, answered that the NDA is the school where senior commanders are trained, and it was not appropriate for women. However he promised that they would examine this matter.[42]

At this time, the Defense Agency; the Ground, Maritime, and Air Staff Offices; and the NDA were opposed to Yamashita. They thought women could not endure the training of the NDA, and that the environment of the NDA would never be suitable for women. They thought that the "efficiency of the military is much more important than gender equality," and it was reported in the newspaper, *Nikkei shimbun*, that some military officials were afraid that "unqualified male cadets would have a sense of inferiority by 'Amazon troops' and that it would affect their morale."[43]

The CEDAW is again the key to understanding the changes during this stage. The Prime Minister's Office had to prepare for the ratification of the CEDAW, and, thus, officials in the Prime Minister's Office thought that the NDA should be open to women according to the principle of gender equality. Consequently, a long series of battles between the Prime Minister's Office and the Defense Agency ensued for over a decade.

However, it is a fallacy to assume that those officials and Diet legislators who tried to open the door for women tried to argue that women's potential as military personnel was equal to that of men's. For instance, they made introductory remarks such as "I do not mean women can command male soldiers, but there are many other positions" and "Generally speaking, women are not suitable for such military duties, . . . but there are some staff positions which don't require physical strength."[44] From these remarks, one general point becomes very clear:

statist "non-feminist reasoning" oiled and propelled the incorporation of women in the SDF. They opened the door for women, not because they thought women should be treated the same as men, like some liberal feminists argue, nor because they thought women could reform the military as a masculinist institution, like some pacifist feminists contend. They did it because they were concerned about the image of Japan in the eyes of the state's principal international allies and about the image of the public sector compared to, or from the perspective of, the domestic private sector.

Let us for the moment consider another controversy. In 1992, the Defense Agency announced that they would start to review women's job limitations, including "combat exclusion." Again, male military officers argued strongly against lifting this exclusion, making statements such as the following: "Supposing war broke out, I would hesitate to order female soldiers to fight," "Why don't you discuss Japanese women's instincts for motherhood and Japanese men's view of womanhood," and "It is not desirable for women who give birth to engage in combat jobs."[45] These comments show how essentialist notions about women as mothers are invoked in order to oppose the gender integration in the military.

On the other hand, some civilian male officials were enthusiastic about this reform. For example, one official said, "We want to create the most open workplace for women all over the world."[46] Here we can again see their concern about the image of Japan in the eyes of the state's principal international allies.

However, this same official also stated that the "apparent differences between men and women in physical strength will naturally establish women's job limitation."[47] We can find the same ambivalence in one retired general's remark: "The SDF must be a gender equal workplace, but the feminization of the SDF would be troublesome."[48] The notion of "feminization" of the military shows their desire to keep the SDF a male, heterosexist sphere. In addition, as we saw previously, the SDF promoted heteronormative "feminization" as a strategy for their marketing purposes so that they could create the safe and nonmilitaristic image of the SDF. We can interpret this ambivalence around the "feminization" of their images in contrast to the reality of the legacy of the history of the Japanese Empire and the U.S. military occupation. The SDF has struggled to shed the negative legacy of the Imperial Japanese Army and to gain legitimacy since its establishment.

Let us now return to the personnel policies. By the revision of women's job limitations in 1993, the percentage of MOS (Military Occupational Specialty) in the GSDF open to women reached 93 percent, from 71 percent.[49] However, as we saw previously, officials have never forgotten to claim that they should consider gender differences in terms of physical strength. Thus, they left some limitations using the protection-of-motherhood and privacy rationales. Therefore, women still cannot fly F-15 jet fighters, nor can they embark on submarines.[50] It is a rather contradictory predicament that women can join regiments such as infantry and armor, but they cannot join a squadron in battlefront. It may be worth asking who can go to the battlefront given that Article Nine of the Japanese Constitution prohibits "the right of belligerency."

Ironically, when the Japanese government judged Samawa, the southern Iraqi city, as a noncombat area and decided to dispatch the SDF there, eleven female officials were included in the first troop without any controversy. The SDF strategist included female officials in the troop so that they could persuade skeptical Japanese people to regard Samawa as a noncombat area and the Iraq mission as a benevolent peace operation. If Samawa is a dangerous combat area and the Iraq mission is to wage war, who would send women there?

Judging from this evidence, even in this fourth stage in which male officials decided to admit some women as elite cadets into the NDA and to admit some women to combat and noncombat jobs, we can still observe "non-feminist reasons" to incorporate women in the SDF.

Conclusion

As argued previously, there are many "non-feminist reasons" for a movement toward feminization of the SDF: to allow men exclusively to undertake the more aggressive or militaristic "masculine" aspects of their professions; to make up for the lack of male recruits; to inspire in women's consciousness the idea of national security; to appear "modern" and "democratic" in the eyes of Japan's principal international allies; to create the image of the SDF as a safe and benevolent peace-keeper; and even to camouflage a combat area in the so-called war on terror.

It is noteworthy that during all four of these policy stages—from 1950 to the present—there were no Japanese feminist campaigns pushing for gender equality in the SDF. This makes the Japanese postwar women's movement seem quite distinct from the liberal feminist wing of several other countries' postwar women's movements. Here one gets a glimpse of the unique background of Japanese feminists: the post–World War II Japanese military has been a volunteer force from the beginning. This change points toward the international trend to abandon the draft system.[51]

Additionally, in Japan, in order to be considered a first-class citizen, it is not necessary for anyone to become a SDF member. We may note, in passing, that many SDF members envy the presumed privileges of first-class citizenship associated with soldiers in other nations, especially the United States. In fact, whereas soldiering has been a primary means for the hoped attainment of U.S. citizenship, in contrast, citizenship was not an attainment but a prerequisite to soldiering in Japan. We should remember this prerequisite has excluded *Zainichi* Koreans (Koreans residing in Japan) and Taiwanese from the SDF and could be interpreted as ethnic discrimination that bars former colonial subjects from certain occupational opportunities. Unlike suffrage and pension, however, this exclusion has not, by and large, been recognized as ethnic discrimination. One may say that the SDF has held little appeal for minorities living in Japan.[52]

And this is also the reason few Japanese feminists have fought for the inclusion of women in the SDF. Instead, they have been deeply concerned about the threat of resurgent militarism in Japan that adopts the soldiering-as-first-class-citizenship model. The fact that some liberal feminists fight for the inclusion of women in the military and argue that women's entry into and promotion within that military can be interpreted as steps toward all women gaining "first-class citizenship" seems to keep this relationship active.[53] But even in the United States, the correlation between "being soldiers and being first-class citizens" has been challenged since 1973 when the United States launched the all-volunteer forces.[54] Furthermore, Figure 11.6 serves as evidence that contradicts the soldiering-as-first-class-citizenship argument.

As this figure indicates, the ratio of female soldiers in the military is not strongly correlated to GEM.[55] Like the SDF, NATO countries' armed forces tend to integrate more women in order to appear "modern" and "democratic" in the eyes of their international allies. However, we should not conflate how women join the military with how women participate in the decision-making process in the public sphere.[56] The question we have to ask is: who has gained the most by assigning a superior worth to one

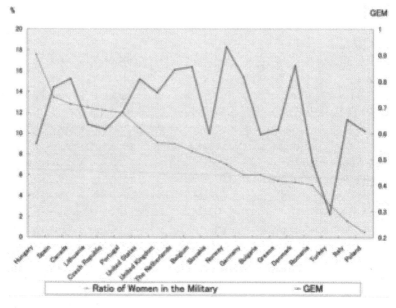

Figure 11.6. Percentages of female soldiers in NATO countries' armed forces and the gender empowerment measurement (GEM)

being a soldier? We can safely state that it is not feminists, but militaries, producing a more militarized state and feminized military.

Finally, it ought to be stated that, although Japanese feminists may have avoided falling into a trap of the soldiering-as-first-class-citizenship, Japanese feminists have nurtured an analytical deficiency; they seemed to fear the results of gender equality in the military too much to pay attention to the women in the SDF and the shifting gender politics and new feminized formation of the SDF. It is useful to quote from Enloe, who observed that the process of militarization needs divisions among women: "the processes of militarization frequently were oiled by the failures of women activists to create cross-sector alliances, to lower those barriers separating women."[57] Viewed in this light, we might say that Japanese feminists' inattention to and ignorance of women's roles in the SDF has failed to create alliances of women that cut across both the inside and outside of the military to resist militarizing post–World War II Japan.[58]

Notes

I am indebted to Dr. Cynthia Enloe of Clark University for making me more aware of the implications of my findings. I also wish to express my gratitude to the editor of this anthology, Dr. Setsu Shigematsu. This chapter owes much to her thoughtful and helpful comments. This chapter was translated from the Japanese by Fumika Sato with Setsu Shigematsu.

1. Many anthologies or symposiums have been published since the 1980s. See Wendy Chapkis, ed., *Loaded Questions: Women in the Military* (Amsterdam: The Transnational Institute, 1981); Eva Isaksson, ed., *Women and the Military System* (New York: St. Martin's Press, 1988); Lois Ann Lorentzen and Jennifer Turpin, ed., *The Women and War Reader* (New York: New York University Press, 1998); Jean Bethke Elshtain and Sheila Tobias, ed., *Women, Militarism and War: Essays in History, Politics, and Social Theory* (Savage, Md.: Rowman & Littlefield, 1990); Constance R. Sutton, ed., *Feminism, Nationalism and Militarism* (Arlington, Va.: The Association for Feminist Anthropology/American Anthropological Association in collaboration with the International Women's Anthropology Conference, 1995). As a recent comparative study of women in the militaries of the North Atlantic Treaty Organization (NATO) countries, see Helena Carreiras, *Gender and the Military: Women in the Armed Forces of Western Democracies* (London: Routledge, 2006). Except for a groundbreaking work of Sabine Frühstück, *Uneasy Warriors: Gender, Memory, and Popular Culture in the Japanese Army* (Berkeley: University of California Press, 2007), I only found Karl L. Wiegand, "Japan: Cautious Utilization," in *Female Soldiers—Combatants or Noncombatants?: Historical and Contemporary Perspectives*, ed. Nancy Loring Goldman (Westport, Conn.: Greenwood Press, 1982), 179–88, as English-language literature dealing with women in the Self-Defense Forces.

2. Japanese names are written following the convention of surname followed by given name. Sato Fumika, *Gunjisoshiki to jendâ: jieitai no joseitachi* (Gender and the military: women in the Japanese Self-Defense Forces) (Tokyo: Keio University Press, 2004), which is a revised and renamed version of my doctoral dissertation.

3. See Suzuki Yuko, *Feminizumu to sensô: fujin undôka no sensô kyôryoku* (Feminism and war: the war collaboration of feminist activists) (Tokyo: Maruju sha, 1997), which deals with the relationship between war and prominent leaders of Japanese women's movements, and Kano Mikiyo, *Onnatachi no "jûgo"* (Women's homefront) (Tokyo: Impact Shuppankai, 1995), which investigates Japanese women's lives on the home front.

4. Kano Mikiyo, "'Okuninotame' ni shinukoto to umukoto to" (Dying or giving birth 'for the sake of our nation'), in *"Nihon" kokka to onna* (The "Japanese" state and women), ed. Igeta Midori (Tokyo: Seikyusha, 2000), 95. This volume collects several feminists' work on women's role in the Japanese Empire.

5. In 1991, the Japanese government defined them and their descendants as special permanent residents. This status improved their social situation, but they still cannot gain suffrage without naturalization.

6. Article Nine is stated as follows: "Aspiring sincerely to an international peace based on justice and order, the Japanese people forever renounce war as a sovereign right of the nation and the threat or use of force as means of settling international disputes. In order to accomplish the aim of the preceding paragraph, land, sea, and air forces, as well as other war potential, will never be maintained. The right of belligerency of the state will not be recognized."

7. It was not the first time for the United States to think of remilitarization of Japan. According to Masuda Hiroshi, who examined the process of rearmament of Japan, some officials of the Department of State and the War Office had begun to maneuver for remilitarization of Japan since 1948. However, MacArthur himself firmly opposed their idea. Here we can see that the state is not always monolithic; there was conflict around the issue of Japan's rearmament within the occupier, the U.S. government. See Masuda, *Jieitai no tanjô: nihon no saigunbi to amerika* (The birth of Japanese Self-Defense Forces: Japan's remilitarization and the United States) (Tokyo: Chuko Shinsho, 2004), 5–9.

8. Bôeichô (Japanese Defense Agency), *Jieitai jûnenshi* (Publication to commemorate the tenth year of Japanese Self-Defense Forces) (Tokyo: Boeicho, 1961), 19.

9. On September 8, 1951, Japan concluded the Security Treaty with the United States. The terms of the treaty allowed for the presence of U.S. Armed Forces in Japan while it expected Japan to take on more responsibility for its own defense.

10. This treaty, the Multilateral Treaty of Peace with Japan, was concluded on September 8, 1951, in San Francisco, California, at the same time Japan and the United States concluded the Security Treaty.

11. The MSA required that the Japanese government develop the Security Corps. Article Eight of the MSA says, "The Government of Japan . . . will make . . . the full contribution . . . to the development and maintenance of its own defensive strength and the defensive strength of the free world, take all reasonable measures which may be needed to develop its defense capacities, and take appropriate steps to ensure the effective utilization of any assistance provided by the Government of the United States of America." As for the full text of MSA, see the WGBH Educational Foundation, "U.S. and Japan Mutual Defense Assistance Agreement," http://www.learner.org/channel/workshops/primarysources/coldwar/docs/usjapan.html (accessed March 14, 2005).

12. However, in the early twenty-first century, the political situation is changing. More and more people insist that there are indeed constitutional problems surrounding the SDF and that it is time to amend the constitution. These people argue that the SDF is clearly a military. On the other hand, at the beginning of the

new century, some people, including many Japanese feminists, who want to protect the "Peace Constitution" tend to argue that the SDF should *not* be military but should be strictly a self-defense force.

13. As it is well known, though the defense allocation's share of Japan's total GDP is very low (about 1 percent), the absolute expenditures for the national defense were very high. According to the International Institute for Strategic Studies, the only other three contemporary state militaries with higher budgets were the United States, China, and Russia in 2002 ($329.6 billion in the United States, $48.4 billion in China, $48.0 billion in Russia, and $37.1 billion in Japan). See the International Institute for Strategic Studies, *Military Balance 2003/2004* (London: Institute for Strategic Studies, 2003), 335–40. As of 2009, Japan now ranks seventh in the world in military expenditures according to the Stockholm International Peace Research Institute, *SIPRI 2009 Yearbook: Armaments, Disarmaments and International Security* (Oxford: Oxford University Press, 2009).

14. Frühstück, *Uneasy Warriors*, 185.

15. Cynthia Enloe, *Maneuvers: The International Politics of Militarizing Women's Lives* (Berkeley: University of California Press, 2000), 280. By using the term "statist non-feminist reasons," Enloe insists that we should pay attention to the fact that patriarchal governments have their own reasons for introducing women into their militaries and for expanding the numbers and roles of women as soldiers.

16. Bôeishô (Japanese Ministry of Defense), *Nippon no bôei: heisei 21 nendoban* (Defense of Japan 2009) (Tokyo: Bôeishô, 2009), 387. This, as well as all subsequent percentages, has been calculated from data of the Japanese Defense Agency or Ministry of Defense by the author.

17. Nira Yuval-Davis, "Women, Citizenship and Difference," *Feminist Review* 57 (1997): 20.

18. Ibid.

19. Aiuchi Mako and Kondo Keiko, who were feminist activists in Sapporo, introduced and supported the National Organization for Women's (NOW) Resolution on Women in Combat. In the 1990s, Japanese feminists debated the issue of (U.S.) female soldiers. See Kano Mikiyo, "Saikô feminizumu to guntai" (Rethinking feminism and the military), *Impaction* 115 (1999): 106–20.

20. Jennifer Tiffany, "The Equal Opportunity Trap," in *Loaded Questions: Women in the Military*, ed. Wendy Chapkis (Amsterdam: The Transnational Institute, 1981), 39. As for Japanese feminists' debates, see Kano, "Saikô feminizumu to guntai" for more details.

21. See Enloe, chapter 6, "Nursing the Military: The Imperfect Management of Respectability," in *Maneuvers*.

22. "15 bai mo ôbo: yobitai kangofu no saiyô shiken" (Fifteen times as many as nurses took an employment examination for the Police Reserve), *Asahi shimbun*,

August 27, 1952, evening edition, 3; "Josei no tôyô, sekkyokuteki ni" (In order to positively assign women), *Asagumo*, June 21, 2001, 1.

23. Mady Wechsler Segal, "Women's Military Roles Cross-Nationally: Past, Present, and Future," *Gender & Society* 9, no. 6 (1995): 767.

24. Ibid.

25. See Wiegand, "Japan: Cautious Utilization," 185.

26. I gratefully acknowledge a discussion with Dr. Keiko Tamura, a visiting fellow at the Australian National University, on this point, on February 24, 2005 in Kyoto.

27. "Onna no hoantaiin 62 mei ga nyûtai" (62 women entered the Security Corps), *Asahi shimbun*, November 19, 1952, evening edition, 3; and "Fujin shôsa hoantai e" (A female major entered the Security Corps), *Asahi shimbun*, November 22, 1952, morning edition.

28. Center of Excellence (COE) Oral Policy Research Project, *Kaibara Osamu ôraru hisutori jôkan* (Oral history of Kaibara Osamu, volume one) (Tokyo: Seisaku Kenkyu Daigakuin Daigaku, 2001), 258–59. This, as well as all subsequent direct quotations from interviews with Japanese officials, have been translated into English by the author.

29. COE Oral Policy Research Project, *Kaibara Osamu ôraru hisutori jôkan*, 259.

30. Ibid.

31. See Enloe, *Maneuvers*, 280.

32. Interview with the author, Tokyo, October 29, 1999. These disciplinary problems included, for example, committing crimes, being heavily in debt, and fighting with other men.

33. Though the percentage differs among courses, it ranges from 6.9 to 8.9 in fiscal year 2004. Currently, the only course excluding women is a cadet school, which boys can enter after the age of fifteen. See Sato, *Gunjisoshiki to jendâ*, 221.

34. At the time, women comprised less than 4 percent of the entire Diet.

35. Japanese Congressional Record, 102nd House of Councilors, 8th Budget Committee, March 16, 1985. The speaker was Santo Akiko, who was a female member of the Liberal Democratic Party.

36. Fujin jieikan kyôikutai (The GSDF WAC training unit), *Fujin jieikan no seido oyobi kyôikutai no arubekisugata* (The Institution of WAC and what our training unit should be) (n.p., 1998), 106.

37. Segal, "Women's Military Roles Cross-Nationally," 769.

38. According to a civilian official, as a result of this SDF "reform," the percentage of SDF jobs open to women reached 75 percent (from 39 percent). See the Japanese Congressional Record, 107th House of Representatives, 4th Governmental Committee, October 28, 1986.

39. The phrase that I quoted comes from their private conversations. Officials whom Wiegand interviewed also told him in private conversations that

"the women's movement in Japan is principally a top-down effort," and Wiegand concluded that "women's emancipation in Japan has been achieved principally by constitutional proviso and by international pressure, not by an aggressive internal pressure from organized women's groups fighting for that emancipation." Although it might be an error to assume that all of Japanese women's movements were top-down efforts, I agree with him in thinking that there have not been any women's campaigns pushing for gender equality in the SDF. See Wiegand, "Japan: Cautious Utilization," 186–87.

40. Photographic posters have appeared since 1964.

41. Jean Bethke Elshtain, *Women and War* (New York: Basic Books, 1987), 140.

42. Japanese Congressional Record, the 87th House of Councilors, the 13th Budget Committee, March 23, 1979. The speaker was Shimura Aiko, who was a female member of the Liberal Democratic Party.

43. "Bôdai ni onna ga hairu hi wa" (When can women enter the NDA?), *Nikkei shimbun* (Japan economic times newspaper), April 5, 1979, evening edition, 2. The original term is "*Amazonesu gundan,*" which is equivalent to "Amazon troops."

44. Japanese Congressional Record, 102nd House of Councilors, 16th Foreign Affairs Committee, June 6, 1985. The former speaker was Kuroyanagi Akira, who was a male member of the Komeito Party, and the latter one was Eiko Nukiyama, who was a female member of Minshato Party.

45. "Josei jieikan no 'sentô' haichi ni nayamu, seigen teppai o kento" (The Defense Agency are troubled by 'combat' deployments of female SDF members, examination of women's job limitations), *Mainichi shimbun*, January 16, 1993, evening edition, 1; and "Kûji kekkyoku miokuri, josei no sentôki tôjô" (The ASDF finally concludes to maintain the exclusion of women from fighter pilots), *Asahi shimbun*, March 9, 1993, morning edition, 26.

46. "Josei jieikan no 'sentô' haichi ni nayamu," *Mainichi shimbun*, 1.

47. Ibid.

48. Shikata Toshiyuki, "Otsukaresama dêsu!: jieitai to sekuhara mondai" (Thanks for all your hard work!: the SDF and the problem of sexual harassment), *Securitarian*, August 1998, 37. I am grateful to Dr. Frühstück of University of California, Santa Barbara for sharing information of this article with me. *Securitarian* is a monthly public relations magazine, published from April 1992 to September 2006 in cooperation with the Defense Agency. Shikata's comment is similar to Stephanie Gutmann's outspoken criticisms of gender integration in the U.S. military. See Stephanie Gutmann, *The Kinder, Gentler Military: Can America's Gender-Neutral Fighting Force Still Win Wars?* (New York: Scribner, 2000).

49. "Sentô shokushu no WAC shikô junchô" (A pilot case of WAC members in combat jobs is going well), *Asagumo*, August 22, 1996, 1. *Asagumo* is a weekly newspaper that deals with defense information, and most of SDF officials subscribe to it.

50. As a result of the revisions to women's job limitations in 2007, some positions, including escort vessels and minesweepers, are being opened in 2009.

51. For example, Spain and France ended the draft system in 2001, and Portugal and Italy in 2004. See the Ministry of Foreign Affairs of Japan, "Regional Affairs," http://www.mofa.go.jp/mofaj/area/ (accessed March 14, 2005).

52. Considering the SDF has attracted men and women from underprivileged socioeconomic backgrounds, there is room for argument on this point.

53. Enloe has pointed out that the very success of connecting citizenship with military service has urged many feminists to press for women's "right" to serve in the nation's military. See Enloe, *Maneuvers*, 245.

54. Yuval-Davis pointed out that "in modern warfare, fighting is often no longer a citizen's duty." She refers to the fact that all the soldiers of the multinational force who fought in the Persian Gulf War did it not as part of national service but as their professional career. See Yuval-Davis, "Women, Citizenship and Difference," 20.

55. GEM is an index that shows the degree to which women are active and participate in the decision-making process in business and politics. The basis for the measurement is the ratio of women's earned income; the ratio of women professionals appointed to expert, technical, and managerial positions; and the ratio of women among parliamentarians.

56. Carreiras's empirical analysis of correlation coefficients shows the same result: there is no significant relation between GEM and the percentages of women in the military. She points out, however, that there is a significant correlation between GEM and her own index of gender inclusiveness, which measures women's *qualified* presence beyond women's *simple presence*. It would be better to say that the relationship in the military and GEM calls for further investigation. See Carreiras, *Gender and the Military*, 125–27.

57. See Enloe, *Maneuvers*, 295.

58. In May 2007, one SDF servicewoman took a sexual harassment case to court. This was the first suit brought by an active member. The SDF refused to renew her contract, so she was terminated from her workplace in March 2009. In contrast to her situation, the perpetrator continued working after a sixty-day suspension from duty. Setting aside the question of this unfair result, it is noteworthy that this suit has bridged women both inside and outside the SDF. See Sato Fumika, "Jieitai wa 21 seiki no guntai tariuruka?: sekuhara saiban kara mietekuru mono" (Can the SDF become an appropriate twenty-first century military?: a consideration of a sexual harassment case), *Mita Hyôron* (Mita Review) 1123 (2009): 60–63 for more details.

12

Genealogies of Unbelonging

Amerasians and Transnational Adoptees as Legacies of U.S. Militarism in South Korea

Patti Duncan

> *When peace comes, there are going to be massive casualties.*
>
> —Yeshua Moser-Puangsuwan

"Which is better, Korea or America?" a woman asks a group of children. They respond in unison, "America! America!" The Amerasian children sit around a table in the True Love Mission, an alternative educational center run by Yon Ja Kim in South Korea, and represented in the documentary film *Camp Arirang*. Kim is a former military camptown prostitute, and the children are primarily the mixed-race sons and daughters of current camptown women and U.S. soldiers.[1] Because discrimination against mixed-race people prevents them from attending public schools, Kim founded the True Love Mission, which she runs out of her home. Here, the children learn English from student volunteers, spend the night when their mothers work late at the clubs, and are taught that, although born and raised in South Korea, they belong in the United States with their birth fathers, many of whom have presumably abandoned the children and their mothers. In this representation, Amerasian subjects internalize the message not only that they belong in the United States—a message that is compounded, no doubt, by consistent social messages from other Koreans that they do *not* belong in Korea—but also that the United States is superior to Korea. Such a belief is one byproduct of the long-term occupation of South Korea by U.S. military personnel, as well as social–historical conflicts between the United States and Korea. Paradoxically, this belief that the United States is superior to Korea exists alongside the stigmatization of Amerasian subjects.

Korean women who associate with U.S. military personnel are often viewed with suspicion and contempt. The documentary highlights the complex relationship between the United States and countries like Korea in which U.S. militarism has played a profound role in shaping national economies. Also, the Amerasian subjects featured in *Camp Arirang* represent another rarely discussed byproduct of the U.S. military occupation of South Korea.

In this chapter, I seek to intervene into assumptions that "war" and "peace" are binarily opposed and mutually exclusive, and I argue that U.S. militarism (and military occupation), neocolonialism, and unequal global economic policies continue to disrupt the lives of people in South Korea. I am concerned with the lingering impact of the Korean War and the subsequent U.S. military presence in South Korea and, in particular, the ways in which certain bodies are not only subjected to practices of militarism and war but also constituted by these very practices.[2] While it could be argued that all bodies are in fact constituted by such processes, I focus on the production of certain groups of women and children in South Korea as militarized (non)citizen–subjects. I ask, what are the long-term consequences of war in South Korea, and what or who constitutes the legacies of war that continue long after "peace" has been established?

Many authors have documented the ways in which war and militarism continue to negatively impact local communities around the globe, and some researchers have documented the specific ways in which such processes affect women and constructions of gender.[3] War and its correlative processes (militarization, violence, and displacement) affect women in myriad ways. As mothers, wives, and daughters of soldiers, as soldiers themselves, as casualties and victims of violence, including sexual violence, as militarized prostitutes, as war refugees and displaced peoples, as wartime production workers, and as resisters to war, women experience war in multiple, complex ways that may also be shaped by additional factors including race, ethnicity, culture, class, national belonging, sexual identity, age, and ability.[4] While women's participation in and experience of war have often been overlooked, and conventional international assumptions about war suggest that it is the purview of men, it is becoming increasingly clear that women experience the effects of war, suffer from war, and, in some cases, benefit from war as much as men do and in distinct, *gendered* ways. Yet even while some researchers highlight the many ways in which women experience war and militarism, few writers have considered the racialized constitution of gender that shapes such experiences.

For local populations, consequences of U.S. militarism include increased poverty and the creation of a global sex economy, what Anna Agathangelou and L. H. M. Ling refer to as "desire industries," in which local women and U.S. male soldiers experience unequal power relations. Such relations are rife with economic disparities, language and cultural barriers, and increased violence against women. Emerging from such relations in the South Korean postwar period are (1) a higher rate of (unidirectional) transnational adoption and (2) a larger number of mixed-race, "Amerasian" children who are subsequently stigmatized because of their presumed association with both prostitution and U.S. occupation of the homeland.[5] In this chapter, I argue for a deeper analysis of the ways in which the two (sometimes overlapping) groups are represented, exploring the meanings attached to both groups as well as possible linkages between the experiences of adoptees and Amerasians. Parts of my argument are informed by conversations I had with mixed-race Koreans and adoptees in South Korea, as well as members of women's and feminist organizations and feminist scholars in late 2004. One of my goals is to disentangle the complex, interwoven, yet distinct, legacies of U.S. militarism for Amerasians and adoptees. In both cases, interactions between U.S. military personnel and Korean civilians underscore the ways in which militarized relations are also colonialist relations and, as such, are always already gendered, sexualized, and racialized forms of contact. In fact, it is this process of militarization–racialization–sexualization that produces bodies–subjects that are subsequently stigmatized, abjected, or unilaterally transported (via adoption) transnationally.

Discursive Constructions of Militarism

I use the terms "militarism" and "militarization" somewhat interchangeably and in the broadest possible sense, invoking definitions by Cynthia Enloe, Gwyn Kirk and Margo Okazawa-Rey, H. Patricia Hynes, and Jean Bethke Elshstain and Sheila Tobias. Hynes defines militarism as "the encroachment of military institutions and ends into politics and society."[6] Elshtain and Tobias employ the term to account for a "deep and wide infrastructure that sustains a war-like peace."[7] In positing militarism as a context that is both "war-like" and all encompassing, these authors suggest deep and long-lasting consequences. Enloe refers to militarization as an institution, an ideology, and a process.[8] She writes, "Militarization can be defined as a process with both a material and an ideological dimension. In the material sense it encompasses the gradual encroachment of the military institution into the civilian arena—for example, if a textiles plant becomes dependent on military contracts for survival, then its workers have become militarized, ultimately dependent on the military for their livelihoods."[9] Likewise, Gwyn Kirk and Margo Okazawa-Rey define militarism as "a system and worldview based on the objectification of 'others' as enemies, a culture that celebrates war and killing . . . [operating] through specific military institutions and actions."[10] They argue that militarism actively produces and sustains a culture of violence, including violence against women.[11] In each of these definitions, militarism emerges as a set of discourses and practices, neither reified nor absolute.

Fiona Ngo suggests that militarization as a practice "seeks to create gendered, racialized, and sexualized subjects who can then reproduce the system of militarization through both biological reproduction and labor on military bases."[12] For many Amerasians born in Korean camptowns, for example, sex work may provide one of the few options for economic survival. This idea has been substantiated through numerous conversations with South Korean camptown activists and former *kijich'on* women. Militarization, then, operates through ideologies that objectify and dehumanize and through institutions that sustain violence and economic injustice. Militarization may be overt, or it may take subtle, covert forms. I use the term in a broader sense than referring strictly to the effects military forces of sovereign nations have on a country, recognizing the ways in which United Nations peacekeeping missions also bring with them the accompanying effects of militarization.[13] Militarization produces subjects, creating and sustaining notions of gender, race, class, and culture.

Militarization is supported by a global militarized economy that requires the use of certain (national, social–political, and individual) bodies for the enrichment of others. Based on capitalist patriarchal assumptions about which bodies matter, U.S. militarization often relies on the bodies of young women all over Asia and the Pacific to produce and sustain a heterosexual militarized masculinity. Militarized prostitution has a long history, and has been well documented in Asia and the Pacific. In Korea, Japan, the Philippines, Vietnam, Hawai'i, and Cambodia, militarism has increased poverty among women and the introduction of U.S. military troops has produced particular forms of prostitution that are condoned and regulated by military forces and local governments who collude in the regulation of and control over women's bodies and sexualities.[14]

For male soldiers stationed in Asia and the Pacific, stereotypes about Asian and Pacific Islander women shape and are shaped by the global militarized economy. Kamala Kempadoo asks readers to consider how the experience (for Western, mostly white male soldiers) of being stationed in a foreign country in which first contact with women of that country occurs through commodified sex may influence the ways in which Western, mostly white militarized men relate to women of color in other settings. How do such ideologies shape discourse about women of color, prostitution and sex work, and interracial sexual encounters, and how do the subsequent discourses about racialized sex and sexualized race reconstitute notions of prostitution?[15] How do such ideologies sustain transnational dynamics of sexism, classism, and racism within a system where consumers and providers of sex occupy distinct gender, class, and racial positions in the larger (neocolonialist) international context? And how do such ideologies contribute to a cultural context in which acts of violence, including sexual violence, against local women increase exponentially during times of war and militarization and continue to occur even in times of "peace" that follow?

Militarized Prostitution in South Korea: *Kijich'on* Women

After thirty-five years of Japanese colonialism in which Korean people collectively suffered brutal violence and loss of culture and language, the nation was split along the thirty-eighth parallel in 1945, with the Soviet Union gaining control over the north and the United States over the south. In 1950, North Korean forces invaded South Korea, and the subsequent war (from 1950 to 1953) devastated the nation. Every major city was destroyed during the war, along with more than 10 percent of the population. There were over two million civilian casualties. Ten million people were displaced from their homes and separated from family members by the division, and the majority of the surviving population was homeless.[16] Both the Korean War and the partition of Korea continue to haunt the Korean peninsula and its diasporic population. As Grace Cho suggests, the Korean War is not over in geopolitical terms, as a peace treaty was never signed. As a result, there are currently nearly twenty-nine thousand U.S.

troops in South Korea, stationed at military bases throughout the country. And every major U.S. base has a camptown outside its gates.[17]

Social interactions within these camptowns highlight extreme disparities between local civilian populations and U.S. military personnel. One camptown worker in Uijongbu, Ms. Pak, explains, "We Koreans are still poor and many go hungry. But Americans come here and they can eat whatever they want; they can do whatever they want; they can buy whatever they want . . . When you go to the U.S. Army base, everything is automatic. They can use as much electricity or water as they need. Meanwhile, the government tells us to save electricity and water. It's a world apart."[18] The U.S. military occupation of South Korea involves a complex dynamic of national, gender, racial, and class inequalities. Some scholars argue that the most constant and common form of U.S.–Korean relations between 1945 and the present is the continuous subordination of Korean women to the sexual servicing of American men.[19] Since the Korean War, more than one million Korean women have worked as prostitutes for the U.S. military.[20] As Katharine Moon has shown, militarized prostitution in Korea is highly systematized, sponsored, and regulated by both the Korean government and the U.S. military. Military camptown prostitution has been viewed as "functional for national security and economic growth."[21] In fact, the South Korean government actually "negotiated militarized prostitution as a foreign policy enticement to keep U.S. troops on the peninsula."[22] Thus, the system of militarized prostitution is condoned and bolstered by both the U.S. and Korean governments, and the Status of Forces Agreement signed by South Korea and the United States in 1966 gives the U.S. military wide latitude in Korea, including the free use of land for military activities (and for the establishment of over one hundred military bases and installations in the country).[23] Since the 1950s, women working as prostitutes have been central to the U.S. military occupation of South Korea.[24]

Furthermore, according to Bruce Cumings, "The social construction of every Korean female as a potential object of pleasure for Americans . . . is the most important aspect of the whole relationship and the primary memory of Korea for generations of young American men who have served there."[25] Similarly, Thomas Kelly, a former officer in the U.S. forces in Korea, states, "[U.S. soldiers] said, 'Korea is filled with prostitutes. Most of the women are prostitutes in this country.' Because they never knew any that weren't."[26] In fact, in many cases *kijich'on* women may be the only

Koreans that U.S. military personnel interact with on a regular daily basis, and such limited contact has contributed to widespread stereotypes regarding Korean women's sexuality.[27] In Korea, as Moon's and Sakai's chapters remind us, the history of the *chŏngsindae* (euphemistically referred to as "comfort women") haunts the national landscape, reminding citizens of the forced prostitution—or mass militarized and institutionalized rape—of nearly two hundred thousand young (mostly Korean) women and girls by the Japanese military under Japanese colonial society.[28] Within such a historical context, and within a society that prides itself on racial and cultural homogeneity, Korean women's contemporary association with U.S. military is severely stigmatized.[29]

Korean women who work in military camptowns (*kijich'on*) continue to be denigrated and referred to in Korean as *yanggongju* ("Western princess") and *yanggalbo* ("Western whore"). As Cho points out, *yanggongju* can also be translated to mean "Yankee whore," "G.I. [general infantry] bride," or "UN [United Nations] lady," signifying the shifting and contradictory social positions occupied by Korean women who work as sexual laborers for U.S. military personnel, as well as women who may date or marry American men.[30] *Kijich'on* women live and work within a system of debt bondage, and their proximity to U.S. military bases increases their risk for exploitation by military personnel, employers, customers, and potential partners. Furthermore, they (and others living on or near U.S. military bases in South Korea) are subject to multiple forms of violence, which support and intensify the social, cultural, and economic subjugation they experience. In the documentary film, *Camp Arirang*, Jin Soo, a *kijich'on* woman, describes the U.S. soldier she has been dating: "One night Charlie came home and beat the hell out of me. I tried to fight, but he came after me with a knife. I still have the scars. The police asked for witnesses, but of course no one would talk. Who would take my word against an American GI?"[31] Because the Status of Forces Agreement legitimates an unequal relationship between U.S. military personnel and local South Korean civilians, U.S. soldiers are rarely held accountable for crimes against Korean people. According to the National Campaign for the Eradication of Crimes Against Civilians by U.S. Troops in Korea, a human rights organization formed in 1993 to document and investigate crimes committed by U.S. soldiers, there have been over one hundred thousand cases of criminal acts (or about two crimes each day) committed by U.S. personnel against the local population. Much of this violence has targeted *kijich'on* women and has included sexual harassment, rape, and murder.³²

Typically, since the 1950s, Korean women who have entered prostitution have done so as a means to escape extreme poverty. Coming from poor, rural families with little access to education, women working as prostitutes in U.S. military camptowns often experienced the death of one or both parents, divorce, sexual abuse or rape (and subsequent rejection by one's family), or human trafficking.³³ Some women and girls have entered *kijich'on* life because, as mixed-race daughters of other *kijich'on* women, they realize they have few options for economic survival within Korean society. At the same time, U.S. military prostitution and tourism contribute significant revenue to the national economy, contributing to South Korean economic development.³⁴ On the flip side, for young American male soldiers from poor and working-class backgrounds, military camptowns in South Korea represent sites in which access to women's bodies is readily available and accessible, sites in which "'privileges' which were formerly restricted by class, race and gender are now available to everybody; there is no need to be rich to exploit women in very poor countries."³⁵

Margo Okazawa-Rey describes two types of contact between the U.S servicemen and *kijich'on* women: first, the impersonal selling of sexual services for money, and, two, an intimate live-in relationship, in which there may be promise of a longer term commitment, including marriage. Between 1951 and 1964, more than twenty-eight thousand Korean women entered the United States as wives of military personnel.³⁶ For *kijich'on* women, marriage to a U.S. soldier represents one strategy for obtaining what is often considered a "normal" life as a wife and mother, two attributes deemed necessary for Korean womanhood.³⁷ In some cases, Korean women do marry U.S. military personnel, and immigrate to the United States.³⁸ Once in the United States, these women—referred to by Ji-Yeon Yuh as "military brides"—and their Amerasian children face stigma and discrimination from other Koreans both within Korea and the United States, who view them as social pariahs to be avoided.³⁹ Seen as traitors, they are often viewed with suspicion and subjected to racist stereotypes, pity, and hostility: "The fact that they have mingled flesh and blood with foreigners . . . in a society that has been racially and culturally homogeneous for thousands of years makes them pariahs, a disgrace to themselves and their people, Korean by birth but no longer Korean in body and spirit."[40] Even second-generation Koreans in the United States often ignore or look down upon them.[41]

Moon suggests another reason these women have been rendered invisible and nearly written out of Korean and Korean American history: "Koreans have not wanted reminders of the war lurking around them and the insecurity that their newfound wealth and international power have been built on."[42] *Kijich'on* women and Korean military brides are living symbols of the devastation of the Korean War and partition, and their children are physical reminders of poverty, political instability, separation from family, war, and the consequent dependence on the United States. Also, they and their children signify the unequal neoimperialist relationship between the United States and Korea. The prostitution of South Korean women in service of U.S. military personnel is "striking evidence of their nation's compromised sovereignty."[43] *Kijich'on* women, then, are simultaneously denigrated, praised for their "sacrifice" to the nation-state, and pitied for what Korean feminists and activists are beginning to perceive as their victimization by U.S. imperialism and militarism.[44]

In most cases, however, *kijich'on* women do not marry the American soldiers who purchase their sexual services. U.S. military personnel in Korea are on "noncommand-sponsored" status, meaning that the U.S. military will not pay for their families to accompany them. Because a tour of duty in Korea is considered a "hardship tour," U.S. soldiers stationed in South Korea tend to be young, transient, and living outside of the United States for the first time in their lives.[45] Presumably, for many of them, this is their first contact with Koreans, Korean culture, and Korean women. When *kijich'on* women become pregnant, they are typically abandoned by the U.S. soldiers they had hoped would marry them.[46] The Amerasian children born to camptown women experience little to no sense of belonging within Korean society. Since many *kijich'on* women are removed from their family registries, both they and their children are treated as noncitizens, and the children in such cases can claim no legal Korean citizenship.[47] To claim U.S. citizenship, Amerasians in Korea require documentation from their biological fathers, the majority of whom abandoned their mothers when their tours of duty ended. Thus, Amerasian children often experience extreme stigma and discrimination within their home countries, while hoping to someday find their American fathers and live in the United States. Many Amerasians in Korea are, in effect, stateless.

Amerasians in South Korea: Physical Reminders of War and U.S. Militarism

To be clear about my own stakes in this multilayered discourse, I write as a mixed-race ("Amerasian") Korean American woman, the daughter of a Korean immigrant woman and a former U.S. Army sergeant of European descent. My experiences growing up in a biracial, bicultural military household were shaped by U.S. policies structured to reproduce military families in the service of "the nation." They were also shaped by the discrimination I witnessed against my mother, not only from white U.S. citizens (including members of my extended family) but also from Korean nationals and Korean Americans who looked down on her association with the U.S. military and the racial discrimination and hostility I myself have experienced in the United States and South Korea. This discrimination has taken significantly different forms, and in South Korea it has always performed a double-gesture that simultaneously privileges U.S. status, citizenship, and access to English language and stigmatizes the women and children associated with U.S. military personnel.

Amerasians in Korea, also referred to as people of "mixed blood," experience insults, name calling, negative stereotypes, mistreatment from both peers and adults, hostility from teachers, high rates of dropping out of school, physical and sexual abuse, and extreme poverty. In a society in which public schools teach students to be proud of their "racial purity," mixed-race Koreans are the most disparaged social class and suffer the highest school drop-out rates in the country (more than 25 percent, as opposed to the 1.1 percent drop-out rate for other Korean students).[48] Like their mothers, Amerasians in Korea are subjected to discrimination, contempt, and a host of derogatory terms, including *t'wigi* and *kkamundung'i*, two extremely derisive terms for racially mixed people that distinguish between those with white fathers and those with black fathers. While both groups experience discrimination and harassment, those with black fathers are often racialized and sexualized in more extreme ways, encountering greater hostility.[49] Amerasians in South Korea confront extreme difficulties finding employment and until recently were banned from military conscription, rendering them ineligible for government jobs and benefits and for fulfilling cultural roles for both South Korean masculinity and citizenship.[50] Amerasians in other parts of Asia are often treated similarly. For example, between twelve thousand and fifteen thousand Amerasian children fathered by U.S. soldiers were left in Vietnam after the war, negatively referred to as *bui doi* ("dust of life") and *my lai* ("American half-breed") and subjected to extreme hardship, according to Linda Trinh Vo.[51] In Okinawa, Amerasian children are severely stigmatized, socially marginalized, and often "forced into a system of prostitution around U.S. bases."[52] In the Philippines, Vietnam, Okinawa, and South Korea, most Amerasians are raised in poverty, experience severe harassment and intimidation from peers, and have few opportunities for education.[53]

Amerasians in each of these contexts are most visible within military camptown settings and are associated with U.S. military occupation. In fact, their presence is "a direct outcome of the massive U.S. military presence,"[54] and Amerasians are often associated with wartime and military prostitution. Because of the massive U.S. military presence in South Korea, viewed by many people as "unwanted, intrusive, and/or cultural contaminants,"[55] and because Amerasian people represent, even embody, such tensions, they are perceived as constant physical reminders of the domination of Korea by the United States and are subsequently severely discriminated against. Young Ja, a *kijich'on* woman interviewed in the documentary film *Camp Arirang*, discusses her Amerasian child: "Whenever my family visits, they make fun of my son because he is American. So I don't let them visit . . . I tell them, is he your son? Why do you come to ridicule him? Don't come!" On the topic of her son's future, she explains, "There will come a day when I must give him up and send him to America. Once he goes, all I want him to know is that he was born in Korea, his mother is Korean, and she is dead. It will be easier for him that way."[56]

Similarly, Susan Soon-Keum Cox, an Amerasian adoptee, offers the following explanation for her adoption: "There was no possibility for me to really have a good life in Korea given the circumstances that my mother was Korean and my father was not, and that simple fact would have followed me always. It was the stigma of orphan as well as the stigma of mixed race."[57] And Tony Koehn, an Amerasian whose biological father was African American, discusses the thirteen years he spent growing up in South Korea with his mother: "I used to get beat up by other kids," he says, noting, "Korea has one race really." Explaining how he and his mother were stared at and treated badly, he states, "I think she felt a little bit ashamed . . . When I was thirteen, we decided that adoption was the way to go and I entered an orphanage."[58]

In her discussion of Vietnamese mixed-race identity, Fiona Ngo argues that the presumption that often follows Amerasian identity is that "the

Amerasian child is the product of sexual contact between an American man, who is undoubtedly a serviceman, and a Vietnamese woman, who is undoubtedly a prostitute. The progeny of this illicit pairing bears the marks of the mother's supposed immorality, particularly if the child is a woman. The mixed-race individual, then, is sexualized and demonized."[59] The history and multiple meanings of a particular war are embodied and physically signified by Amerasians. Hence, mixed-race girls and women are particularly sexualized, marked by association to militarized prostitution. The specific processes through which Amerasian girls and women are racialized and sexualized remain unfixed; however, the meanings of their racialized sexualization (and sexualized racialization) occur within a transnational, historical, and social context in which biracial and mixed-race groups of people have long been stigmatized in accordance with orientalist perspectives that both exoticize and fetishize Asian women and men as part of a strategy of domination.

The combined forces of U.S. militarism and occupation of South Korea, constructions of heterosexual U.S. militarized masculinity, stereotypes about Asian women's sexuality, and unequal power relations between the United States and South Korea merge with the collusion of both governments to produce a highly regulated system of militarized prostitution in South Korea in which military prostitutes are simultaneously praised for their contributions to the national economy and stigmatized for their association with both prostitution and U.S. military. Their children, the mixed-race offspring of U.S. military personnel and South Korean *kijich'on* women, are the physical embodiment of these complex associations and tensions, are regarded as the dregs of society in Korea, and are rendered stateless. Under heavy political pressure, the U.S. government recognized Amerasians in South Korea and included them in the Amerasian Immigration Act of 1982, which allowed Amerasians born between 1950 and 1982 to emigrate to the United States. However, the guidelines to this act are extremely strict: Amerasians attempting to emigrate must provide evidence of paternity by a U.S. citizen, and they must find a U.S. citizen willing to sponsor them, which would entail assuming financial responsibility for at least five years.[60] To date, there are a handful of organizations working to improve the situation for Amerasians in South Korea, including the Pearl S. Buck Foundation, the Korean Amerasian Association, and the Amerasian Children's Association on U.S. military bases, which provides special one-time events and parties for Amerasian children. However, without adequate support and resources, Amerasians in Korea continue to experience severe hardship.

Viewing the military as an institution, and *kijich'on* women's work as crucial to the maintenance and economy of U.S. military camptowns, Okazawa-Rey concludes that "the problem of U.S. militarism in East Asia is, at root, a problem for people in the United States."[61] To create a "counter-process," she states that U.S. feminists must act as allies to women in South Korea, supporting their right to self-determination and demanding full accountability for the actions of the U.S. military personnel in Korea. "More fundamentally, we must mount an anti-militarist campaign calling for the removal of all U.S. bases and military personnel from the region and for de-militarization in general."[62] Such a counterprocess should involve critiques of both external and internal forces in order to challenge colonialist processes of U.S. military occupation in South Korea *and* the regulation of women's bodies within global and local contexts. Thus, it necessitates a critical evaluation of gender norms and the racialized processes associated with gender systems. Constructing and sustaining forms of masculinity that are not directly linked to heterosexual, patriarchal, imperialist militarism, including the domination and commodification of South Korean women, could enable men (both U.S. military personnel and Korean citizens) to experience manhood detached from misogyny, racism, and violence against women. Constructions of femininity that are not inextricably tied to traditional norms of female chastity, "pure" homogeneous race–ethnicity, and motherhood only within marriage could potentially lessen the stigma experienced by *kijich'on* women and mixed-race people in South Korea.

Unidirectional Transnational Adoption

At present, however, such critical reconstructions occur infrequently and usually only within progressive social movements, and the majority of South Korean society continues to view *kijich'on* women as "fallen women" and as unfit mothers. In South Korea, Vietnam, the Philippines, Cambodia, and other Asian countries in which war and an increased U.S. military presence have resulted in extremely high rates of poverty, militarized prostitution, and large number of Amerasian children, transnational adoption has a history. In these and other contexts affected by political and economic interventions, many women have placed their children for adoption in the

United States and other Western countries due to their lack of economic resources or a fear that their children will be persecuted. For example, "Operation Babylift," a 1975 U.S. government program signed by President Gerald Ford, resulted in the transfer of more than four thousand Vietnamese children being flown to the United States, Canada, Europe, and Australia for adoption. It is estimated that at least half of these children were Amerasian children who had been orphaned or whose mothers feared for their safety in a society that stigmatizes mixed-race Vietnamese.[63] In the Philippines, similar processes have occurred. Quoting Maria Socorro Diokno about Amerasians in the Philippines, de Schmidt writes, "Every day one Amerasian 'souvenir' baby is born. Every day some of these babies are abandoned or sold."[64] She goes on to address the subsequent prostitution of many Amerasian children. However, Sturdevant and Stoltzfus suggest that the existence of Amerasian children has been particularly problematic in homogeneous cultural contexts like South Korea, in which "a child fathered by a U.S. serviceman is living evidence of what a woman's work is or has been," making it extremely difficult for women working as camptown prostitutes to leave the work and often resulting in placing the children for adoption.[65] While there are similarities in transnational adoption histories within various militarized contexts, it is also important to distinguish among such contexts and to clarify specific time periods under consideration.

Transnational adoption has a complex history in relation to wars and Western empire building, especially situations in which mixed-race children were fathered by U.S. or UN soldiers as part of the large-scale sexual exploitation or militarized prostitution of local women. However, the history of transnational adoption is complex and not linked solely to women's experiences with military camptowns or the birth of Amerasian children. According to Toby Alice Volkman, the origins of transnational adoption can be traced to the aftermath of World War II and the Korean War, resulting in an "almost unidirectional movement of young children from poor nations to the more affluent West."[66] The history of transnational adoption from South Korea originated as a rescue mission focused on mixed-race children born to Korean women and U.S. military personnel. Harry and Bertha Holt, born-again Christians from rural Oregon, adopted eight children from Korea in 1955, and later established Holt's Adoption Agency (now Holt International Children's Services), making South

Korea "the country with the longest continuous foreign adoption program in the world."[67]

The Korean War and U.S. military occupation of South Korea continue to play a large role in shaping social conditions that lead to children's loss of parents; to limited options for women, who may subsequently abandon, relinquish custody of, or be induced to surrender their children; and to the inequalities and state policies that constitute certain children as "adoptable." However, other factors influencing adoption include gender relations and norms and global economic restructuring. According to Eleana Kim, children were sometimes given up because of the "staunchly patrilineal 'Confucian' society that place[s] primal importance on consanguineous relations, especially on the status that comes with bearing sons."[68] She also refers to the deeply embedded patriarchal ideologies that render it nearly impossible for a woman to survive as a single mother in South Korea.[69] And as Tobias Hubinette argues, some children have been taken without the consent of their birth parents or through extreme coercion, often driven by economic vulnerability.

The first wave of adoptees from Korea arrived between 1955 and 1965 and consisted mainly of mixed-race children fathered by U.S. soldiers.[70] They were followed by "full-blood" Korean orphans, or children of unmarried women of impoverished families. While children in the earlier period were more likely to be Amerasian and associated with U.S. military personnel, the experiences of those adopted in subsequent periods tended to be structured by global economic disparity and gender norms. For example, Hubinette cites the modernization process that took place between 1961 and 1987 under authoritarian regimes as a period during which children of young, impoverished, urban factory workers replaced "war orphans."[71] Transnational adoption operated alternately as a strategy of population control, a child welfare practice, and a "goodwill strategy to develop political ties to and trade relations with important Western allies."[72] During the 1980s, it is estimated that more than eight thousand children were placed for adoption from South Korea each year.

Increasingly, Korean transnational adoption has become linked to South Korea's modernization process. As such, many Koreans have come to perceive the extremely high rates of South Korean transnational adoption as humiliating. This shame was induced in part by the negative press from U.S. journalists following the 1988 Summer Olympics in Seoul, who claimed that Korea was "exporting its 'greatest natural resource,' its children."[73]

However, it is also tied to the economic aspect of transnational adoption, which reportedly introduced between US$15 and 20 million each year into the South Korean economy. By the 1980s, transnational adoption had become a thriving and profitable consumer-oriented industry, characterized by what Barbara Yngvesson refers to as "commodity thinking" in which children are differentially valued as commodities in a global export market.[74] During that period, the majority of children adopted from Korea were born to middle-class high school or college students and subsequently classified as illegitimate, and therefore they were available for international adoption.[75]

Since the late 1980s, the adoption rates from South Korea have been steadily declining, though it remains one of the world's predominant sending nations.[76] In all, South Korea has exported more children for international adoption than any other nation in the world, as approximately two hundred thousand South Korean children have been sent to countries in the west for adoption since 1953, the majority of them (75 percent) adopted to American families.[77] The United States is the predominant receiving country of internationally adopted children, accounting for 40 to 53 percent of the annual transnational movement of children during the 1980s.[78] Currently, more than two thousand Korean children are transnationally adopted each year.[79] The United States continues to be the primary receiving nation of all internationally adopted children, accounting for approximately 50 percent.[80] Today, there are approximately one hundred thousand adult adoptees from Korea living in North America, Western Europe, and Australia, adopted between the late 1960s and the early 1980s. According to Kim, women tend to outnumber men by two to one.[81]

The politics of transnational adoption highlight extreme power differences between nations and require a critical interrogation of a global militarized economy that enables the flow of children from disempowered, occupied nations like South Korea to wealthy, dominant, Western nations like the United States. U.S. militarization is maintained through neoliberalism, free trade agreements, and processes of globalization that promote the movement of goods (and some people) across national borders. Immigration policies are hotly contested in U.S. discourse, but transnational adoption relies on narratives of rescue to enable the "most privileged form of immigration in the world today; with the stroke of a pen a 'needy object' is transformed into a 'treasured subject,' worthy of economic protection, political rights, and social recognition."[82] Narratives of transnational adoption, according to David Eng, are also narratives of "salvation—from poverty, disease, and the barbarism of the Third World" that "displace global and local histories of colonialism, military intervention, capitalist exploitation, racism, and gender discrimination."[83] While U.S. representations of transnational adoption often focus on rescuing "innocent" children from poverty and neglect, Laura Briggs highlights the ways in which such processes are "invested with colonial legacies and can be allied with U.S. state power and other kinds of violence."[84] Karen Dubinsky characterizes the "rescue" narrative of transnational adoption: "First you destroy our country, and then you rescue our children."[85] In Latin America, for example, transnational adoption with the United States is often characterized as an extension of U.S. military and economic power—an allegory for U.S. foreign policy. As such, transnational adoption operates much like U.S. foreign policy, through a process of "strategic forgetting."[86]

This erasure includes not only forgetting histories of localized violence, colonialism, war, and militarization but also forgetting language, culture, and place. It presumes the lack of significance of birth mothers and fathers and centers the experiences and desires of adoptive parents as citizen-consumers in a global economy. "We came as children, we came as babies," says Susan Soon Keum Cox, a mixed-race Korean American adoptee and vice president of Holt International Children's Services. "It was the deliberate choice of our parents to bring us. And so we didn't immigrate here because we wanted to come; we immigrated because adults wanted to bring us here."[87] Likewise, Hubinette argues that adoptees "are brought over only to satisfy the needs and desires of their well-to-do acquirers."[88] He refers to Korean adoptees as members of a victim diaspora, defined by Robin Cohen as part of "an involuntary dispersal caused by catastrophic and traumatic events such as mass poverty, labour mobilisation, forced transportation, severe persecution and refugee movement."[89] These adoptions, according to some authors, are often driven by the rescue mentality of Western (often U.S.) militarist ideologies, as well as the neocolonialist belief that children, no matter where they originate, always benefit from being raised by (white) Western parents and from exposure to Western ideals and civilization. Hubinette characterizes contemporary transnational adoption as the involuntary movement of (predominantly) people of color to the households of (predominantly) white Westerners, part of a system that is increasingly profit driven and motivated by consumer demand, involving the loss of family, culture, and language.[90]

Recently, more scholarship has addressed the particular experiences of Korean adoptees in relation to identity formation, race and racism, gender, and a desire to return to Korea.[91] Yngvesson refers to the complex "in-between" space occupied by transnational adoptees, often characterized by ambiguities of belonging.[92] Kim describes the return to Korea that is increasingly an expected part of the experience of transnational adoption for Korean adult adoptees. She suggests that "overseas Koreans" returning to Korea often engender complex, ambivalent responses from Korean nationals. As both "family" and "foreigners," Korean adoptees returning to Korea highlight processes of globalization and mobility in which notions of kinship continue to be regulated, managed, and legislated by state power.[93] David Eng discusses the gendered aspects of transnational adoption in relation to more explicit gendered migration (of migrant workers, military wives, mail-order brides, etc.). He writes, "Scholarship in postcolonial and transnational feminism links the historical emergence of war brides and mail-order brides to foundations of military prostitution and the commodification of Third World female bodies for First World male consumption and pleasure. From this perspective, we might say that the historical phenomena of war brides and mail-order brides make explicit what is often only implicit or absent in traditional analyses of transnational adoption (the majority of adoptees being baby girls)."[94]

Referring to transnational adoption as a recent form of gendered commodification shaped by an international gendered division of labor, Eng asks what kind of gendered, racialized "labor" the transnational adoptee performs for the (adoptive) family and the (U.S.) nation.[95] In fact, he suggests, she performs an ideological labor: "the shoring up of an idealized notion of kinship, the making good of the white heterosexual nuclear family."[96] Hence, the process of transnational adoption raises crucial questions of kinship and of motherhood. One means of connecting the discussion of transnational adoption to that of mixed-race Koreans is through acknowledgment of the ways in which stigma of mixed-race Koreans opened the door to the first wave of Korean adoptees to the United States. While, today, *kijich'on* women and Korean birth mothers are not necessarily overlapping populations, consideration of the origins of Korean international adoption benefits from an interrogation of the construction of Korean *kijich'on* women as "unfit mothers," a designation often attached to women of color and Third World women as well as those associated with other aspects of the global sex industry.

Moon and others have documented the pervasive and long-term control over Korean women's bodies enacted by various means throughout the long history of military camptowns in South Korea, including the "Clean-Up Campaign" to curtail the spread of sexually transmitted infection and diseases.[97] (See chapter 6 in this volume.) While publicly expressing a desire to protect families (and national security), it has become increasingly clear that such developments have primarily served the interests and emphasized the protection of U.S. military servicemen (and their American families) rather than Korean women or their children, including Amerasian children. Programs such as the Korean Clean-Up Campaign and current "VD [venereal disease] checks" in the Philippines and elsewhere serve as forms of racial–gender surveillance, objectifying and policing the bodies of Asian women and blaming them for sexually transmitted infections. Thus, U.S. servicemen and their American families are seen as needing to be protected from *kijich'on* women and Amerasian children, both associated with deviant, racialized sexuality and viewed as cultural contaminants. At the same time, media in both the United States and Korea have depicted Korean children placed for transnational adoption (particularly full-blood and able-bodied Korean infants) as simultaneously "innocent" children and as victims of Korean consumer-oriented culture and U.S. neoimperalism. These processes highlight differential strategies of forging and fracturing family relations and kinship ties. Transnational adoption, then, may be seen as part of a "disciplining method of regulating and controlling women's bodies and reproduction in the name of social engineering and development"[98] and also as a process that imagines certain social–cultural–familial bonds while simultaneously rupturing others.

Conclusion: A Transnational Feminist Approach

To date, scholars have documented a long history of U.S. military violence against women and girls in numerous Asian countries, including sexual violence, forced prostitution, reproductive health abuses, and murder. In South Korea, U.S. militarization has had devastating effects on local economies, social systems, and gender relations. In this chapter, I have been particularly concerned not only with the ways in which U.S. militarism results in larger numbers of Amerasian children born to women in military camptowns and increased transnational adoption but also with the subsequent meanings attached to both groups, produced as they are through an association with multiple processes including U.S. military and economic policies and globalization. The stigmatization of both groups highlights women's relationship to motherhood, and both suggest that processes related to U.S. militarism in South Korea negatively impact women's experiences of motherhood and children's identities. The stigma, sense of displacement, exile, and social ostracism associated with Amerasian identity and transnational adoption also signify the "genealogies of unbelonging" referred to in my title.[99] Such genealogies mark not only the lack of a sense of belonging experienced by these two groups but also the historical processes that make it difficult to name what has happened to them (us) and how their (our) relationship to both Korea and the United States has been constructed.

Both "genealogies of unbelonging" and the strategic forgetting mentioned previously, which enables the fracturing of certain kinship ties, are linked to what Yngvesson refers to as "erasures of belonging"—those disavowals of the social, cultural, and political connections adoptees and mixed-race Koreans must continually negotiate within both Korea and the United States.[100] While transnational adoptees have historically been perceived as "innocent" children in need of rescue (albeit the offspring of "bad" women or "unfit" mothers), mixed-race Koreans continue to be stigmatized for their (our) presumed association with U.S. military and prostitution. In both cases, Korean women who place children for adoption or raise mixed-race children may be marked as sexually deviant or "unfit." The production of racialized-sexualized subjects through militarized sexual–economic–power relations results in a form of "extra-American nuclear" family, operating alongside increasingly gendered forms of migration. I argue that such developments illustrate the ways in which effects of war are deeply felt long after conflicts have officially ended and are intensified within highly militarized societies such as South Korea. In the context of South Korea–U.S. relations, what does it mean that "stateless" subjects are alternately produced, disavowed, "forgotten," "rescued," and ultimately rationalized as the collateral excess bioproduct of "military necessity"?[101] How are *kijich'on* women gendered and racialized? In what ways do Amerasians and transnational adoptees also experience constructions of subjectivity that are intrinsically tied to specific forms of racialized sexuality that legitimize certain attitudes and behaviors regarding both groups?

Women in South Korea and in other parts of Asia resist effects of war and militarism, as Moon's and Ueunten's chapters in this volume have also documented. In Okinawa, for example, a group called Okinawa Women Act against Military Violence (OWAAMV) resists the global militarized economy by critiquing the human rights violations enacted not only by the U.S. military but also by the Japanese military. Fukumura and Matsuoka discuss the U.S. military presence in Okinawa as a nexus of oppression and violence, documenting both the numerous recorded cases of violence against local women and children by U.S. military personnel and the wide-scale mobilization of local resistance to U.S. military presence. In its report to the International Conference on Violence against Women in War and Armed Conflict Situations, OWAAMV argues that even in times of "peace," long-term military presence results in violence against local women and that such violence is always directly related to the economic and political relationships between the country deploying the military and the country receiving the military presence.[102] Fukumura and Matsuoka cite Yayori Matsui, suggesting that the military presence (ostensibly for national "security") must be critically examined to ask whose security is protected when U.S. military presence places local women and children at risk.

The ways in which women respond to militarism in Asia "cannot be reduced to the familiar terms of the women's movement in the United States and Europe."[103] A sustained transnational feminist response to these effects of war and militarism in South Korea must first recognize at least two important elements: first, as mentioned earlier, that this is also a U.S. issue and problem, as the U.S. government and military colludes with the local South Korean government to control and regulate the bodies of women and children; and second, that the specific experiences of women and children in South Korea must be adequately contextualized within a framework that recognizes intersecting categories of identity, oppression, and resistance.

A sustained transnational feminist approach to militarism in South Korea would mean exploring not only the experiences of women during and after periods of conflict but also gender relations, racialized constructions of gender, femininity and masculinity, processes that shape motherhood and fatherhood, and notions of citizenship. It means, as Enloe suggests, interrogating the distinct ways in which local and international politics affect men and women, exploring the connections "between international debt, foreign investment, and militarism on the one hand, and violence against women, and domestic work, on the other."[104] It means asking how power operates not only within societies but also *between* societies. Doing so enables us to recognize and analyze power differences and ways in which every aspect of culture, including labor, migration, family and parenting, relationships to institutions, and whether or not one experiences a sense of belonging may be gendered and racialized within specific national contexts. Understanding these processes will allow us to better comprehend the multiple and complex ways women and men experience and respond to war and militarism. Hence, I am calling for greater and more explicit analytical links to understand how the U.S. military occupation of South Korea and subsequent militarized-sexualized relations result in the production of stateless and displaced populations and to consider the experiences of people who are systematically devalued by both Confucian and militarized neocolonial ideologies that enable the mixed-race children referred to in my opening paragraph to cry out for "America."

Notes

I gratefully acknowledge the support of a Faculty Enhancement Grant from Portland State University, which allowed me to conduct the research for this chapter. I would also like to thank Setsu Shigematsu, Keith L. Camacho, Elaine H. Kim, Margo Okazawa-Rey, Eleana Kim, Ji-Young Shin, Christina Vidlund, Patricia Schechter, Erin McKee, the members of Sahngoksoo (a Korean American study group in Seattle, Washington), and the many people who offered questions and suggestions at presentations of earlier versions of this chapter at the National Women's Studies Association and the Association for Asian American Studies conferences in 2006 and 2007. The phrase "genealogies of unbelonging" comes from Laura Hyun Yi Kang's 2002 book, *Compositional Subjects: Enfiguring Asian/American Women* (Durham, N.C.: Duke University Press), 146. I invoke her argument here to suggest the ways in which notions of kinship and genealogy are complicated by processes associated with U.S. militarism in South Korea, Korean women's association with U.S. military personnel, the existence of mixed-race people in Korea, the politics of transnational adoption, and the global economy. The epigraph by Yeshua Moser-Puangsuwan is cited in the documentary film *Disarm*, produced and directed by Mary Wareham, Next Step Productions, Washington, D.C., 2004.

    1. *Camp Arirang*, a documentary film by Diana S. Lee and Grace Yoon Kyung Lee, distributed by NAATA, San Francisco, Calif., 1995. Please note that I use the terms "prostitute" and "militarized prostitution" throughout this chapter. At times, I also use the terms "sex work," "sex labor," "sex industry," and "desire industries."

While I recognize that each of these terms is problematic, for various reasons, I choose to employ the terms "prostitute," "prostituted women," and "prostitution" most frequently in association with militarism in South Korea because they are the designations most commonly used by Korean activists and writers on this topic. More notes on terminology will follow.

2. See Grace Cho, "Prostituted and Invisible Bodies," in *Gendered Bodies: Feminist Perspectives*, ed. Judith Lorber and Lisa Jean Moore (Los Angeles: Roxbury Publishing Company, 2007), 210–14.

3. See in particular Cynthia Enloe, *Does Khaki Become You? The Militarisation of Women's Lives* (London: Pluto Press, 1983); Cynthia Enloe, "Bananas, Bases, and Patriarchy" in *Women, Militarism, and War: Essays in History, Politics, and Social Theory*, ed. Jean Bethke Elshtain and Sheila Tobias (Savage, Md.: Rowman & Littlefield, 1990), 189–206; Saundra Pollack Sturdevant and Brenda Stoltzfus, *Let the Good Times Roll: Prostitution and the U.S. Military in Asia* (New York: The New York Press, 1992); Katharine H. S. Moon, *Sex among Allies: Military Prostitution in U.S.-Korea Relations* (New York: Columbia University Press, 1997); and H. Patricia Hynes, "On the Battlefield of Women's Bodies: An Overview of the Harm of War to Women," *Women's Studies International Forum* 27 (2004): 431–45.

4. For more on women's varied experiences of war, see Cynthia Enloe, *Maneuvers: The International Politics of Militarizing Women's Lives* (Berkeley: University of California Press, 2000); and Lois Ann Lorentzen and Jennifer Turpin, ed., *The Women and War Reader* (New York: New York University Press, 1998).

5. Transnational adoption, also called international or intercountry adoption (and usually implying transracial adoption), refers to "the movement of mainly nonwhite children from the postcolonial so-called Third World to predominantly white adopters in North America, Northern and Western Europe, Australia, and New Zealand" (139). See Tobias Hubinette, "From Orphan Trains to Babylifts: Colonial Trafficking, Empire Building, and Social Engineering," in *Outsiders Within: Writing on Transracial Adoption*, ed. Jane Jeong Trenka, Julia Chinyere Oparah, and Sun Yung Shin (Cambridge, U.K.: South End Press, 2006), 139–49. The term "Amerasian" was coined by Pearl S. Buck in the 1950s to denote the mixed-race offspring of American servicemen (of various racial-ethnic backgrounds) and Asian women. Originally applied to Korean children, the term also gained currency during the U.S. war in Vietnam for children of U.S. servicemen and Vietnamese women. Today it officially applies to individuals born in Korea, Vietnam, Okinawa, Laos, Cambodia, the Philippines, and Thailand, among other locations. The specific social and political meanings of the term may vary from context to context. While I recognize the problems and limits of the term "Amerasian," I employ it here to signify both its social historical meanings, and its political and cultural usages by self-described Amerasians. Likewise, "adoptee" is a term that comes with a complex set of inscriptions. As Julia Chinyere Oparah, Sun Yung

Shin, and Jane Jeong Trenka suggest, because "adoptee" is a derivative from the verb "to adopt," it denotes a lack of agency on the part of those who are adopted. However, in their writing, these authors "seek to reclaim the term and boldly to declare [their] agency and self-determination." See their introduction to *Outsiders Within: Writings on Transracial Adoption*, ed. Trenka, Oparah, and Shin (Cambridge, U.K.: South End Press, 2006), 15.

6. Hynes, "On the Battlefield of Women's Bodies," 431.

7. Jean Bethke Elshtain and Sheila Tobias, ed., *Women, Militarism, and War: Essays in History, Politics, and Social Theory* (Savage, Md.: Rowman & Littlefield, 1990), x.

8. Enloe, *Does Khaki Become You?*

9. Ibid., 9.

10. Yoko Fukumura and Martha Matsuoka, "Redefining Security: Okinawa Women's Resistance to U.S. Militarism" in *Women's Activism and Globalization: Linking Local Struggles and Transnational Politics*, ed. Nancy A. Naples and Manisha Desai (New York: Routledge, 2002), 262, footnote 2.

11. Gwyn Kirk and Margo Okazawa-Rey, "Women Opposing U.S. Militarism in East Asia," *Peace Review* 16, no. 1 (2004): 59–64.

12. Fiona I. B. Ngo, "A Chameleon's Fate: Transnational Mixed-Race Vietnamese Identities," *Amerasia Journal* 31, no. 2 (2005): 54.

13. See, for example, Barbara Crosset, "When Peacekeepers Turn into Troublemakers," *The New York Times*, January 7, 1996, 6; and Gayle Kirshenbaum, "Who's Watching the Peacekeepers? Charges of Abuse and Exploitation Tarnish the Image of U.N. Troops," *Ms. Magazine* (May/June, 1994), 10–15. See also Anna M. Agathangelou and L. H. M. Ling, "Desire Industries: Sex Trafficking, UN Peacekeeping, and the Neo-Liberal World Order," *Brown Journal of World Affairs* 10, no. 1 (2003): 133–48; and Hynes, "On the Battlefield of Women's Bodies."

14. Kamala Kempadoo, "Women of Color and the Global Sex Trade: Transnational Feminist Perspectives," *Meridians: Feminism, Race, Transnationalism* 1, no. 2 (2001): 28–51; Moon, *Sex among Allies*, 1997; Enloe, *Maneuvers*, 2000; Hynes, "On the Battlefield of Women's Bodies"; Agathangelou and Ling, "Desire Industries."

15. For example, Aurora Camacho de Schmidt, Sturdevant and Stoltzfus, and Moon all refer to the popular t-shirts worn by U.S. soldiers in Okinawa and the Philippines with images of Asian women alongside the phrase "little brown sex machine" or "little brown fucking machine." "Prostitution," de Schmidt writes, "has long been associated with the life of soldiers. But military prostitution in a subjugated country has other dimensions. Race is often a central, not accidental, element of militarized sexual exploitation" (109–10). See de Schmidt, "Voices of Hope and Anger: Women Resisting Militarization," in *The Sun Never Sets: Confronting the Network of Foreign U.S. Military Bases*, ed. Joseph Gerson and Bruce Birchard (Boston: South End Press, 1991), 107–22.

16. Cho, "Prostituted and Invisible Bodies."

17. According to the U.S. Department of State (http://www.state.gov), the United States and South Korea reached an agreement in 2004 to remove 12,500 of the 37,500 U.S. troops previously stationed in South Korea by 2008. It is estimated that the relocation of U.S. troops will continue. Of ninety-six U.S. military bases, at least twenty-three have been transferred to South Korean control. See also Lolita Baldor, "Gates: Troops in South Korea Deserve Longer Family Tours," Associated Press, June 2, 2008, available at International Institute for Strategic Studies, http://www.iiss.org (accessed July 11, 2008).

18. Ms. Pak is a subject in Sturdevant and Stoltzfus's *Let the Good Times Roll*, 209.

19. Moon, *Sex among Allies*. See also Bruce Cumings, "Silent But Deadly: Sexual Subordination in the U.S.-Korean Relationship" in *Let the Good Times Roll: Prostitution and the U.S. Military in Asia*, ed., Saundra Pollock Sturdevant and Brenda Stoltzfus (New York: The New York Press, 1992), 169–75.

20. Moon, *Sex among Allies*.

21. Chunghee Sarah Soh, "Women's Sexual Labor and State in Korean History," *Journal of Women's History* 15, no. 4 (2004): 174.

22. Agathangelou and Ling, "Desire Industries," 138.

23. Ji-Yeon Yuh, *Beyond the Shadow of Camptown: Korean Military Brides in America* (New York: New York University Press, 2002); Margo Okazawa-Rey, "Amerasian Children of GI Town: A Legacy of U.S. Militarism in South Korea," *Asian Journal of Women's Studies* 3, no. 1 (1997): 71–102.

24. While this chapter focuses primarily on the experiences of Korean women, it is important to note that since the mid-1990s, Filipina and Russian women have reportedly migrated to South Korea to provide sexual services to U.S. soldiers in military camptown bars. See Cheng Sea-ling, "Assuming Manhood: Prostitution and Patriotic Passions in Korea," *East Asia: An International Quarterly* 18, no. 4 (2000): 40–78; Mary Jacoby, "Does U.S. Abet Korean Sex Trade?" *St. Petersburg Times*, December 9, 2002; and Donald MacIntyre, "Base Instincts: Filipina and Russian Women Are Being Sold into Sexual Slavery in the Seedy Bars and Nightclubs that Serve U.S. Military Bases in South Korea," *Time Asia Magazine*, August 5, 2002).

25. Cumings, "Silent But Deadly," 170.

26. Lee and Lee, *Camp Arirang*.

27. Katharine Moon, in an interview in *Camp Arirang*. Of course, not all U.S. soldiers purchase sexual services from Korean women. Many U.S. military installations offer cultural programs, tourist attractions, and opportunities to volunteer. And women and gay male U.S. military personnel may experience Korea quite differently from those heterosexual U.S. male soldiers who interact primarily with *kijich'on* women.

28. While "comfort women" were drafted from a number of Japanese-occupied territories and prewar colonies, including China, Taiwan, the Philippines,

Malaysia, Indonesia, and Thailand, the majority (80 to 90 percent) came from Korea. For more discussion of the history of "comfort women," see Hyunah Yang, "Re-membering the Korean Military Comfort Women: Nationalism, Sexuality, and Silencing," in *Dangerous Women: Gender and Korean Nationalism*, ed. Elaine H. Kim and Chungmoo Choi (New York: Routledge, 1998), 123–39; George Hicks, *The Comfort Women: Japan's Brutal Regime of Enforced Prostitution in the Second World War* (New York: W. W. Norton, 1994); Dai Sil Kim-Gibson, "They Defiled My Body, Not My Spirit: The Story of a Korean Comfort Woman, Chung Seo Woon" in *Making More Waves: New Writing by Asian American Women*, ed. Elaine H. Kim, Lilia V. Villanueva, and Asian Women United of California (Boston: Beacon Press, 1997), 177–83; and Chunghee Sarah Soh, "The Korean 'Comfort Women': Movement for Redress," *Asian Survey* 36, no. 12 (1996): 1226–40.

29. Although the *chŏngsindae* (comfort women or, literally, "military sex slave") movement has had relative success gaining visibility and the sympathy of the public, activists working on behalf of *kijich'on* women have had less success. The leaders of the *chŏngsindae* movement refuse to acknowledge similarities between the experiences of comfort women and *kijich'on* women, arguing that *kijich'on* women's militarized sexual labor has been voluntary, while comfort women had no choice. Katharine Moon, however, highlights several commonalities between the two groups, both of which have experienced intense poverty, violence, and discrimination. See Moon, *Sex among Allies*; and Yuh, *Beyond the Shadow of Camptown*.

30. Cho, "Prostituted and Invisible Bodies," 211.

31. "Jin Soo" is a pseudonym.

32. The National Campaign for the Eradication of Crimes Against Civilians by U.S. Troops in Korea was formed from the Joint Commission for Counter-Measures Regarding Miss Kum-E Yoon Case [*sic*], a coalition of twenty-three organizations, including women's groups, workers organizations, student groups, religious groups, and human rights organizations, which originated after the brutal rape and murder of a *kijich'on* women, Yan Kumi, by U.S. soldiers in 1992. See "Introduction: The National Campaign for Eradication of Crimes by U.S. Troops in Korea," http://www.usacrime.or.kr (accessed July 11, 2008). See also Katharine H. S. Moon, "Resurrecting Prostitutes and Overturning Treatises: Gender Politics in the 'Anti-American' Movement in South Korea," *The Journal of Asian Studies* 66, no. 1 (2007): 129–57.

33. Okazawa-Rey, "Amerasian Children of GI Town"; Moon, *Sex among Allies*.

34. Moon, *Sex among Allies*.

35. Susanne Thorbeck, "Introduction—Prostitution in a Global Context: Changing Patterns," in *Transnational Prostitution: Changing Global Patterns*, ed. Susanne Thorbeck and Bandana Pattanaik (London: Zed Books, 2002), 2. Of

course, not all U.S. military personnel are heterosexual. Military camptowns may also represent sites of access to the bodies of male sex workers. While cases have not been widely documented, numerous local activists suggested to me that male Korean sex workers also face exploitation and threats of violence.

36. *Sun Gu Ja: A Century of Korean Pioneers*, a documentary film by Ian McCluskey, NW Documentary Arts & Media, Portland, Ore., 2004.

37. Moon, *Sex among Allies*; Okazawa-Rey, "Amerasian Children of GI Town"; Yuh, *Beyond the Shadow of Camptown*.

38. It is estimated that as many as three thousand marriages between Korean women and U.S. military personnel take place each year (in Okazawa-Rey, "Amerasian Children of GI Town: A Legacy of U.S. Militarism in South Korea," citing B. N. Yu, "Voices of Hope and Anger: Women Speak Out for Sovereignty and Self-Determination," in *Listen Real Loud*, vol. 1–2 [Philadelphia: American Friends Service Committee, 1990], 20).

39. For more discussion of the term "military brides," see Yuh, *Beyond the Shadow of Camptown*, who employs the term instead of "war brides," to denote the fact that the majority of such marriages between U.S. servicemen and Korean women occurred postwar and during a period of intense militarism. As Enloe points out, eighty percent of such marriages end in divorce (Enloe, "Bananas, Bases, and Patriarchy").

40. Moon, *Sex among Allies*, 3.

41. Furthermore, according to *The Women Outside*, a documentary film produced by J. T. Orinne Takagi and Hye Jung Park in 2002, 80 percent of these marriages end in divorce. Third World Newsreel, New York, 1995.

42. Moon, *Sex among Allies*, 8.

43. Cynthia Enloe, "A Feminist Perspective on Foreign Military Bases" in *The Sun Never Sets: Confronting the Network of Foreign U.S. Military Bases*, ed. Joseph Gerson and Bruce Birchard (Boston: South End Press, 1991), 102.

44. In *Camp Arirang*, for example, Yon Ja Kim, a former military prostitute, discusses the governmental framing of *kijich'on* women as patriots and nationalists, working to rebuild the economy and the republic of Korea.

45. Sturdevant and Stoltzfus, *Let the Good Times Roll*; Moon, *Sex among Allies*; Okazawa-Rey, "Amerasian Children of GI Town."

46. Sturdevant and Stoltzfus, *Let the Good Times Roll*; Okazawa-Rey, "Amerasian Children of GI Town."

47. Okazawa-Rey, "Amerasian Children of GI Town"; Yuh, *Beyond the Shadow of Camptown*; Moon, *Sex among Allies*.

48. Choe Sang-Hun, "From an Ostracized Class, a Hero for Koreans," *The International Herald Tribune*, February 22, 2006, http://www.iht.com/articles/2006/02/22/news/mixed.php?page=2 (accessed July 11, 2008); Pearl S. Buck International, http://pearlsbuck.or.kr (accessed August 11, 2006).

49. Amerasians with black fathers experience greater stigma than those with white fathers, according to Okazawa-Rey, "Amerasian Children of GI Town"; Moon, *Sex among Allies*; and Sturdevant and Stoltzfus, *Let the Good Times Roll*. Similarly, women who provide sexual services for African American and Latino soldiers are deemed less desirable by white soldiers, and therefore lose a substantial base of potential customers. Also, they are more severely stigmatized within Korean society. For a detailed discussion of these themes, see Moon, *Sex among Allies*. Finally, de Schmidt also discusses the specific forms of racism experienced by black U.S. military personnel, including their placement at more dangerous positions near the demilitarized zone in South Korea.

50. Choe Sang-Hun, "From an Ostracized Class."

51. Linda Trinh Vo, "Managing Survival: Economic Realities for Vietnamese American Women" in *Asian/Pacific Islander American Women: A Historical Anthology*, ed. Shirley Hune and Gail M. Nomura (New York: New York University Press, 2003), 237–52.

52. Fukumura and Matsuoka, "Redefining Security," 255.

53. Aida F. Santos and Cecilia T. Hofmann, with assistance by Alma Bulawan, "Prostitution and the Bases: A Continuing Saga of Exploitation" (paper presented at the International Planning Meeting on Women and Children, Militarism and Human Rights, Naha, Okinawa, May 1–4, 1997); and Kirk and Okazawa-Rey, "Amerasian Children of GI Town."

54. Okazawa-Rey, "Amerasian Children of GI Town," 72.

55. Ibid., 85.

56. "Young Ja" is a pseudonym. She is interviewed for the film wearing dark glasses and in silhouette.

57. From an interview documented in *Sun Gu Ja: A Century of Korean Pioneers*.

58. Ibid.

59. Ngo, "A Chameleon's Fate," 57.

60. Okazawa-Rey, "Amerasian Children of GI Town."

61. Ibid., 99.

62. Ibid., 99.

63. Indigo Williams, "Downloading Heritage: Vietnamese Diaspora Online" (paper presented at Media in Transition: Globalization and Convergence conference, Massachusetts Institute of Technology, Cambridge, Mass., May 10–12, 2002). For a filmic representation of the effects of Operation Babylift and the U.S. war in Vietnam, see the documentary film, *Daughter from Danang*, directed by Gail Dolgin and Vicente Franco, PBS American Experience Series, Boston, 2003.

64. de Schmidt, "Voices of Hope and Anger," 112.

65. Sturdevant and Stoltzfus, *Let the Good Times Roll*, 317.

66. Toby Alice Volkman, "Introduction: New Geographies of Kinship," in *Cultures of Transnational Adoption*, ed. Volkman (Durham, N.C.: Duke University Press, 2005), 2.

67. Eleana Kim, "Wedding Citizenship and Culture: Korean Adoptees and the Global Family of Korea" in *Cultures of Transnational Adoption*, ed. Toby Alice Volkman (Durham, N.C.: Duke University Press, 2005), 56.

68. Ibid., 56. See also Barbara Yngvesson, "Placing the 'Gift Child' in Transnational Adoption," *Law and Society Review* 36, no. 2 (2002): 227–56, in which she discusses South Korea's protection of patriarchal bloodlines as part of the state reproductive policies that produce "adoptable" children, 236.

69. In fact, Kim suggests that social welfare spending and the North Korean threat may be more saliently related to militarism and transnational adoption than the actual U.S. military occupation, in that the military government diverted money to national security while installing programs designed to facilitate emigration but not to help families stay intact. In her words, "Transnational adoption became the surrogate welfare system that eased the state's population problems and placed the burden of social welfare onto agencies whose main source of revenue was from overseas placement." Personal correspondence with the author, May 2007.

70. Matthew Rothschild, "Babies for Sale: 'South Koreans Make Them, Americans Buy Them,'" *The Progressive*, January 1988, 18–23.

71. Tobias Hubinette, "Nationalism, Subalternity, and the Adopted Koreans," *Journal of Women's History* 19, no. 1 (2007): 117–22. In this discussion, Hubinette cites Youn-Taek Tahk, "Intercountry Adoption Program in Korea: Policy, Law and Service," in *Adoption in Worldwide Perspective: A Review of Programs, Policies and Legislation in Fourteen Countries*, ed. Rene A. C. Hoksbergen (Lisse, Netherlands: Svets & Zeitlinger, 1986), 79–91.

72. Hubinette, "Nationalism," 117.

73. Kim, "Wedding Citizenship and Culture," 57.

74. Yngvesson, "Placing the 'Gift Child,'" 2002. Here she also discusses the apology issued by South Korean President Kim Dae Jung to Korean adoptees in 1998, in which he described South Korea as "filled with shame," but also stated that "globalization is the trend of the times," 247–48.

75. Rosemary C. Sarri, Yeonoak Baik, and Marti Bombyk, "Goal Displacement and Dependency in South Korean-United States Intercountry Adoption," *Children and Youth Services Review* 20, no. 1–2 (1998): 87–114.

76. Saralee Kane, "The Movement of Children for International Adoption: An Epidemiologic Perspective," *Social Science Journal* 30, no. 4 (1993): 323–39; and Kim Park Nelson, "Shopping for Children in the International Marketplace," in *Outsiders Within: Writing on Transracial Adoption*, 89–104.

77. Eleana Kim, "Our Adoptee, Our Alien: Transnational Adoptees as Specters of Foreignness and Family in South Korea," in *Anthropological Quarterly* 80, no. 2 (2007): 497–531; David Eng, "Transnational Adoption and Queer Diasporas," *Social Text* 21, no. 3 (2003): 1–37. See also the Web sites for National Association of Korean Americans, http://www.naka.org, and Holt International, http://www.holtintl.org/insstats.shtml (accessed July 11, 2008).

78. Kane, "The Movement of Children for International Adoption."

79. Hubinette, "Nationalism"; Kim, "Our Adoptee, Our Alien."

80. Karen Dubinsky, "Babies Without Borders: Rescue, Kidnap, and the Symbolic Child," *Journal of Women's History* 19, no. 1 (2007): 142–50.

81. See Kim, "Our Adoptee, Our Alien," 500.

82. Dubinsky, "Babies Without Borders," 147.

83. Eng, "Transnational Adoption," 9.

84. Laura Briggs, "Making 'American' Families: Transnational Adoption and U.S. Latin American Policy" in *Haunted by Empire: Geographies of Intimacy in North American History*, ed. Ann Laura Stoler (Durham, N.C.: Duke University Press, 2006), 348.

85. Dubinsky, "Babies Without Borders," 147.

86. Briggs, "Making 'American' Families," 361.

87. *Sun Gu Ja: A Century of Korean Pioneers*.

88. Hubinette, "From Orphan Trains to Babylifts," 143.

89. Tobias Hubinette, "Comforting an Orphaned Nation: Representations of International Adoption and Adopted Koreans in Korean Popular Culture" (Ph.D. dissertation, Stockholm University, Department of Oriental Languages, 2005), 193.

90. Hubinette, "From Orphan Trains to Babylifts."

91. See, for example, Nam Soon Huh and William J. Reid's "Intercountry, Transracial Adoption and Ethnic Identity," in *International Social Work* 43, no. 1 (2000): 75–87; and Kathleen Galvin, "International and Transracial Adoption: A Communication Research Agenda," *The Journal of Family Communication* 3, no. 4 (2003): 237–53.

92. Yngvesson, "Placing the 'Gift Child,'" 249.

93. Kim, "Our Adoptee, Our Alien," 499–501.

94. Eng, "Transnational Adoption," 10.

95. Hubinette also addresses the ways in which transnational adoption is a gendered process. He suggests that the female adopted Korean today embodies a "strong nationalist concern" linked to a history of colonialism (Hubinette, "Nationalism," 118–19).

96. Eng, "Transnational Adoption," 11.

97. Moon, *Sex among Allies*; Agathangelou and Ling, "Desire Industries"; Sturdevant and Stoltzfus, *Let the Good Times Roll*.

98. Hubinette, "From Orphan Trains to Babylifts," 140.

99. While I have focused mostly on Amerasian experience within Korea, I want to note here that there are significant distinctions between the forms of discrimination experienced by Korean Amerasians in Korea and in the United States, distinctions that require further study and analysis.

100. Yngvesson, "Placing the 'Gift Child,'" 243.

101. I credit Setsu Shigematsu for raising this question in relation to my argument.

102. Fukumura and Matsuoka, "Redefining Security," 248.

103. de Schmidt, "Voices of Hope and Anger," 109.

104. Enloe, "Bananas, Bases, and Patriarchy," 190.

Conclusion

From American Lake to a People's Pacific in the Twenty-First Century

Walden Bello

Within hours after a massive tsunami hit eleven countries bordering the Indian Ocean on December 26, 2004, U.S. Navy Orion reconnaissance aircraft began flying over the affected areas to deliver emergency relief and to assess the damage. This was the prelude to a massive expedition that eventually came to encompass over twenty-four U.S. warships, over one hundred aircraft, and some sixteen thousand military personnel—the largest U.S. military concentration in Asia since the end of the Vietnam War.[1]

The grand armada was put together by the Pacific Command, the largest and oldest of the U.S. military's unified commands. Overshadowed for a number of years by the Central Command's operations in Afghanistan and Iraq, the Pacific Command's key role in the project of U.S. power and influence reemerged in the aftermath of the tsunami.

The Tsunami as Opportunity

The relief operations were not a disinterested, peacetime military mission. One immediate sign was the deliberate U.S. effort to marginalize the United Nations (UN), which was expected by many to coordinate, at least at the formal level, the relief effort. Instead, Washington sought to bypass the UN by setting up a separate assistance "consortium" with India, Australia, Japan, Canada, and several other governments, with the U.S. military task force's Combined Coordination Center at University of Tapao, Thailand, effectively serving as the axis of the entire relief operation.[2]

Displaying the flag was seen by the Bush administration as an important objective to counteract the negative relations between the United

States and many communities in the Southeast Asian region due to the war on terror, which Muslims, who were in the majority in the most devastated country, Indonesia, had seen as being directed against them. The war on Iraq was also universally unpopular throughout the area, and here was an opportunity to show a different face of the U.S. military than that of a force imposing a harsh military occupation on that Middle Eastern country.

But there were more immediate military objectives as well. The Indonesian military had been subject to a ban on arms sales from the United States and restrictions on training conducted by the United States for close to a decade because of the successful campaigns of human rights groups during the 1990s to paint the Tentara Nasional Indonesia (TNI, the Indonesian Army) as engaging in systematic human rights violations. The tsunami relief effort became an opportunity for the Pentagon to push for dropping those restrictions. As then Deputy Secretary of Defense Paul Wolfowitz put it during a visit to Jakarta a few days after the disaster, "The more we can cooperate on a peaceful basis with militaries in this region in normal times increases our capacity to respond to disasters." He then went on to say, "Everybody loses a great deal when a long period of time goes by with severe limitations on the ability of our military [to communicate] . . . when you cut off their contact with a military, whether it be in Pakistan as did for much too long a time, or here, as we've done to a lesser extent but continue. I think it is not supportive of the very goals that these restrictions are meant to achieve."[3]

The military-to-military cooperation during the tsunami relief effort became an important step in a process of the Pacific Command–led effort to restore military aid to Indonesia. In January, Washington, citing the tsunami, allowed commercial sales of "nonlethal" defense items, including spare parts for military transport planes. In February, the ban on military training was lifted, followed in May by the lifting of the ban on the government sale of nonlethal defense equipment. Finally, in November 2005, despite Congress's vote to maintain the ban two weeks earlier, the State Department, exploiting a national security waiver provision, resumed unrestricted military and training aid in order to strengthen the Indonesian military's capability for "disaster relief."[4]

Dealing with two active insurgencies, in Aceh and West Papua, the TNI will find U.S. military aid very useful, especially if the tenuous post-tsunami cease-fire that it has entered into with Gerakan Aceh Merdeka (GAM, or the Free Aceh Movement), the Acehnese independent movement, gives way again to open hostilities.

A Transnational Garrison State

The politicized and militarized posttsunami relief activities brought to global attention what people in the Asia-Pacific region have lived with for over sixty years: the massive military presence of the United States. Perhaps the best way to comprehend the U.S. presence in the Pacific is to describe it as a transnational garrison state that spans seven sovereign states and the vast expanse of Micronesia. The U.S. Pacific Command is an integrated and extremely secretive complex composed of mobile forces and fixed bases over which the host states in the western, central, and south Pacific exercise nominal sovereignty.

This complex is massive: 330,000 servicemen and women, half of them deployed in the western Pacific; about 300 bases and facilities; the world's largest naval command, with 190 ships and 35 shore installations; nearly one half of the active duty personnel of the U.S. Marine Corps; a number of Army units, including the Eighth Army, which is forward-deployed in South Korea; and several fighter wings and bomber units of the U.S. Air Force.[5]

The northern anchor of this complex is Japan and Korea; the southern anchor is the heavily fortified atoll of Diego Garcia in the middle of the Indian Ocean; and Micronesia is the great rear area. Traditionally, this Pacific garrison state has been used for power projection into Northeast Asia, the Chinese heartland, and Southeast Asia. More recently, it has also served to support the projection of U.S. power to West Asia and the Middle East.

Japan is, to use Joseph Gerson's description, the "keystone" of the U.S. military structure, its contributions consisting not only of numerous bases and facilities but also of its military, which is supported by the seventh largest military budget in the world.[6]

The U.S. military contingent in South Korea is the only U.S. military presence on the Asian mainland. The country hosts forty thousand troops, some of whom are now being transferred to Guam. While Washington justifies its military presence as necessary to contain North Korean strongman Kim Jong Il's nuclear ambitions, its deployments are actually intended to maintain the fifty-four-year-old division of the Korean nation and to make it difficult to achieve reunification except under terms favorable to the United States.

Lying about one thousand miles south of the southern tip of India, Diego Garcia's strategic location and full range of facilities make the island the last link in a long logistics chain that supports the U.S. naval presence in the Indian Ocean, the North Arabian Sea, and the Persian Gulf. A key function of Diego Garcia has been to provide long-range firepower and logistics for the U.S. military expeditions in Afghanistan and the Persian Gulf. B-52, B-1, and B-2 bombers deployed to the atoll carried out aerial bombardment of Baghdad during the U.S. invasion in March 2003.[7]

Micronesia in the central Pacific serves as a rear zone supporting the forward U.S. military presence in the western Pacific, a fallback area in the event of a withdrawal of U.S. forces in the Philippines, and an experimental site for the development of missile systems. At least sixty-six nuclear devices were exploded on the Marshall Islands from the late 1940s to the early 1960s, making nomads out of islanders who had to be relocated and subjecting many others to radioactive fallout.[8]

Aside from being employed for power projection to the Asian mainland and Indian Ocean, these bases have served as springboards for U.S. intervention in the internal affairs of their host countries. For instance, although the United States no longer maintains military bases in the Philippines, it negotiated a Visiting Forces Agreement that went into effect in 1998 that allows it to send troops to the country, ostensibly for training exercises with Philippine troops. However, training is a guise for U.S. Special Forces to work closely with Philippine troops to hunt down Islamic guerrillas as part of winning the war against terror that Pacific Command identifies as its key objective.[9]

The transnational garrison state has spawned a subeconomy and subculture that have had distorting effects on the larger economy and culture of the host societies. Wherever the United States established bases in the western Pacific, the degradation of women forced into sexual labor was institutionalized in a multimillion-dollar entertainment industry that enjoyed the tolerance of the U.S. military hierarchy, which considers sexual recreation vital for the "morale" of troops. As the Patpong area in Bangkok and the thriving red-light district in Angeles City in the Philippines illustrate, the legacy of this subculture is evident long after bases have been shut down. Also, the sexual impact of the bases cannot be contained in such enclaves: in Okinawa, rapes of women and children by U.S. servicemen have occurred outside the zones of sexual labor. These events have angered the Okinawan people, one fourth of whose territory is occupied by U.S. bases.

The conversion of Micronesia into a closed "strategic colony" of the United States destroyed the once-thriving economy of the islands and converted them into welfare states that thrive almost entirely on government appropriations from Washington. Washington's subsidies spawned a massive colonial bureaucracy that, on some islands, includes half of the adult population. It is not surprising that, because of their extreme economic dependence on the United States, the central Pacific territories opted in the early 1980s for a continuing colonial link with the United States in the form of a "Compact of Free Association." The compacts with the Federated States of Micronesia and the Republic of the Marshall Islands were renewed in 2004 and that with Palau in 2009.

It is also not surprising that, cut off from their traditions and bereft of a productive relationship to their lands and waters, teenagers throughout Micronesia have turned to suicide in alarming numbers, or that people have fled the islands in great numbers to settle in Hawai'i and the West Coast.

Meanwhile, the United States uses these so-called independent states for political cover in international affairs, for example, when it paraded the three dependencies as being part of the Coalition of the Willing standing behind Washington's decision to invade Iraq in 2003.

The Strategic Imperative

The Pacific Command traces its beginnings to the burst of U.S. empire building at the end of the nineteenth century. In 1898, when the United States erupted into Asia, grabbing Guam and the Philippines from Spain, it was clear that this was not an old-style imperial power. The United States had itself emerged from an anticolonial struggle against Great Britain slightly over a century earlier, and this mark of its birth would greatly condition and nuance its imperial engagement with empire. Though continental expansion at the expense of the Native Americans and Mexicans was popular with white Americans and accorded with their deep-seated beliefs of racial destiny, the leap to the other side of the Pacific, which was seen as empire building in the European mold, was contentious. Imperialism had to be legitimized by Washington to the American people. The emergence of the Anti-Imperialist League as a response to the U.S. annexation of the Philippines, the significant congressional opposition to the annexation, the hearings on atrocities committed by U.S. personnel like General Jacob Smith, who told his troops to convert the island of Samar into a "howling wilderness"—all this served as a warning that neither the rationale of "christianizing" the Catholic heathens of the Philippines articulated by President William McKinley nor that of Manifest Destiny promoted by the social Darwinist Senator Albert Beveridge would do. Indeed, U.S. imperialism developed into a complex phenomenon wherein the cultural–ideological dimension coexisted and interacted with two other relatively autonomous drives: the extension of the strategic reach of the U.S. state and the expansionist dynamic of U.S. economic interests.

Imperialism is often explained as being primarily an outcome of economic expansionism. However, in Asia, U.S. *strategic interests* were paramount. In contrast to Latin America, commercial rationales were formulated to support the strategic reach of the U.S. state. This was true as far back as 1853, when Commodore Matthew Perry brought his ships to Tokyo Bay, invoking commerce as his reason for his ultimatum to the Shogunate to end Japan's self-imposed isolation.

It was not unusual that a naval officer, rather than a merchant, forced Japan to open up. In the United States' century-long drive to the western Pacific, trade followed the flag more frequently than the flag followed trade. In 1898, when the United States made its eight thousand–mile leap to the Philippines, less than 10 percent of U.S. trade crossed the Pacific, whereas 60 percent crossed the Atlantic. China, Korea, and Japan were the sources of exotic imports and did not figure as significant markets except in the minds of dreamers thinking about selling a shirt to each of China's millions. Investments in the region were negligible. As Whitney Griswold noted, "American capital for the exploitation of China [was] being raised with difficulty."[10]

What lay behind the great leap westward was not a business cabal but a strategic lobby of naval and political expansionists mainly interested in expanding the reach of the U.S. state. True, entrepreneurs operating in Hawai'i, the Philippines, China, and the interstices of the dominant European empires vociferously supported the expansion, but they did not constitute the nerve center of U.S. business. That was located in New York, and New York was oriented far more toward Europe than Asia.

The U.S. Navy became particularly adept at invoking commercial rationale to promote U.S. strategic extension and its own role as the cutting edge of that mission. Acquiring bases in the far reaches of the Pacific would provide a powerful impetus to the creation of the "two-ocean navy." The two-ocean navy was necessary to achieve the goal of maritime supremacy envisioned by the fleet's leading strategic thinker, Captain Alfred Mahan.

Led by the influential Mahan and Assistant Secretary of the Navy Theodore Roosevelt, the U.S. Navy was the main force behind the acquisition of Hawai'i, Guam, and the Philippines on the heels of Admiral George Dewey's victory over the Spanish squadron in Manila Bay in May 1898. The small island of Guam in the Marianas and the Philippine archipelago were depicted as stepping stones to the riches of China, but this depiction functioned only to justify their annexation in the face of significant domestic opposition. Washington's main desire was the projection of U.S. power onto the Asian mainland, and Guam and the Philippines' geographic location was ideal for this purpose. Hawai'i had been in the control of American planters for over a decade, but it was not until the Spanish–American War of 1898 that its strategic importance was fully appreciated. During the war, the naval presence at Pearl Harbor was instrumental in projecting U.S. power to the western Pacific; following the war, moves were made to annex Hawai'i and build a massive permanent base there.

Ironically, the navy's thinking was most succinctly captured by an army man, General Arthur MacArthur, father of the more famous Douglas. Chief of the colonizing army that subjugated the country, MacArthur described the Philippines as,

> the finest group of islands in the world. Its strategic location is unexcelled by any other position in the globe. The China Sea, which separates it by something like 750 miles from the continent, is nothing more nor less than a safety moat. It lies on the flank of what might be called several thousand miles of coastline; it is the center of that position. It is therefore relatively better placed than Japan, which is on a flank, and therefore remote from the other extremity; likewise India, on another flank. It affords a means of protecting American interests which with a very least output of physical power has the effect of a commanding position in itself to retard hostile action.[11]

So important was a western Pacific presence for the institutional expansion of the navy that when army officials favored withdrawal from the region in the 1930s, arguing that the Philippines and Guam had become strategic liabilities in the face of Japan's growing might, the navy blocked any consideration of leaving.[12] This conflict set the stage for U.S. defeats in the early days of World War II.

Projection of strategic power continued to be the central impetus behind U.S. policy in the Asia-Pacific after World War II. "Forward Defense" and "Containment of Communism" were the articulated rationales, but the imperative was the strategic extension of the power of the U.S. state. Just as his father had most succinctly expressed the navy's rationale for acquiring the Philippines, it fell to Army General Douglas MacArthur to express most cogently and candidly the U.S. military's strategic imperative in postwar Asia: "The strategic boundaries of the US were no longer along the western shore of North and South America; they lay along the eastern coast of the Asiatic continent."[13]

Projecting U.S. strategic power necessitated that, as in Europe, there would be no demobilization of U.S. forces in Asia after World War II. It also necessitated the creation of a network of more than three hundred bases on the sovereign territory of seven Asia-Pacific countries. Power projection to prevent the reemergence of another power on the Asian landmass that could threaten the United States became the principal determinant of U.S. interventions in Taiwan, Korea, and Vietnam. Power projection also became the centerpiece of the U.S. grand strategy of "Containment" of the Soviet Union and its Asian allies.

In Search of Enemies

For almost half of the twentieth century, containment gave the U.S. military and its alliance strategy coherence and legitimacy that withstood both the Sino–Soviet split as well as the U.S. defeat in Vietnam. With the demise of the Soviet Union, however, a new rationale was drawn up to justify the forward posture in the Pacific. Under President Bill Clinton, the justification for the U.S. military presence in the region became that of supporting the creation of free markets and economic globalization. Despite its image of supporting multilateral—as opposed to unilateral—efforts to assure global or regional stability, the Clinton administration actively undermined efforts by the governments of Southeast Asia to make the Association of Southeast Asian Nations Regional Forum (ARF) the key mechanism to settle transnational conflicts; instead, the administration argued that unhampered U.S. military presence was the best guarantee of regional peace. Moreover, it did not hesitate to show the flag to assert Washington's solutions to conflicts in the region. In March 1996, for instance, in response to China's military exercises during the presidential campaign and elections in Taiwan, Clinton sent two aircraft battle groups to the South China Sea.

Under George W. Bush, the U.S. forward presence in the Pacific and globally was aggressively reasserted for the so-called unipolar era. The neoconservative vision that Bush endorsed when he came to power in 2001 was that which was laid out almost a decade earlier in the notorious *Defense Planning Guidance*, drawn up in 1992 under the supervision of Paul Wolfowitz, who would later serve as his undersecretary of defense: "Our first objective is to prevent the re-emergence of a new rival. This is the dominant consideration underlying the new regional defense strategy and requires that we endeavor to prevent any hostile power from dominating a region whose resources would, under consolidated control, be sufficient to generate global power."[14] There are three additional aspects to this objective. First, the United States must show the leadership necessary to establish and protect a new order to convince potential competitors that they need not aspire to a greater role or pursue an aggressive posture to protect their legitimate interests. Second, in the nondefense areas, the United States must account sufficiently for the interests of the advanced industrial nations to discourage them from challenging its leadership or seeking to overturn the established political and economic order. Finally, the United States must maintain the mechanisms for deterring competitors from even aspiring to a larger regional or global role.[15]

Sidestepped as formal policy by the administrations of George H. W. Bush and Bill Clinton, this supremacist view became official U.S. policy under George W. Bush. Institutionalized in the National Security Strategy Paper issued in September 2002, the Bush approach committed the United States to "anticipatory action to defend ourselves, even if uncertainty remains as to the time and place of the enemy's attack."[16] It put the emphasis on destroying terrorist networks and preventing what it considered rogue states from developing weapons of mass destruction. In East Asia, the Bush strategy classified China as a "strategic competitor," branded North Korea as part of the "axis of evil," and committed Pacific Command to "prosecuting and winning the War on Terror."[17]

Unilateralism, preemption, and an extraordinary sense of omnipotence created an agenda that was less conservative than radical. It destabilized long-standing arrangements with allies and neutral parties and threatened both old and new foes of the United States. But, as events in West

Asia and the Middle East would show in the succeeding years, the Bush supremacist posture also created the conditions for imperial overstretch.

An Alternative Security System

With its pursuit of a losing war in Iraq and a war on terror that has alienated so many people in the region, particularly the Muslim peoples of Southeast Asia, the U.S. strategy in the Bush era has created problems of legitimacy for the U.S. military presence in the Asia-Pacific region. Though the Asia-Pacific region is not as severely destabilized as the Middle East nor on the course of rebellion against U.S. influence as Latin America—where antineoliberal and anti-U.S. movements have come to power in countries such as Venezuela, Argentina, Ecuador, and Bolivia—people throughout the region are seeking alternatives to U.S. military and economic domination.

China has, of course, emerged as a strong counterweight to U.S. military and economic power, though Beijing is careful not to explicitly challenge the United States except on the issue of Taiwan. The governments of the Association of Southeast Asian Nations (ASEAN) are increasingly moving on an independent path from the United States. These trends pose both a challenge and an opportunity for civil society in the region.

From the early to mid-1980s, the Reagan administration's military buildup provided the impetus for the emergence of antinuclear and antimilitary movements throughout the Asia-Pacific region. The movement, called the Nuclear Free and Independent Pacific Movement (NFIP), registered significant victories, including New Zealand's banning of visits by nuclear-armed and nuclear-powered warships; the virtual disintegration of the ANZUS (Australia–New Zealand–United States) alliance; the creation of the South Pacific Free Zone by eleven South Pacific States; the upholding of their nuclear-free constitution by the people of Palau, despite strong U.S. pressure on them to scrap it; and the emergence of a strong movement that kicked out the U.S. bases in the Philippines, which also has a nuclear-free constitution.

Three features of the Pacific antinuclear movement stood out: first, the solid intertwining of principles of demilitarization, denuclearization, and nonintervention; second, vigorous transborder alliances among Third World peace movements, and between First World movements (Japan, United States, Australia, and New Zealand) and Third World movements

(Philippines, South Korea, Micronesia, and the South Pacific); and third, successful tactical alliances being forged between popular movements and governments (the NFIP movement and the governments of Vanuatu and New Zealand, for instance). Indeed, so legitimate and popular is the concept of a demilitarized region that ASEAN has declared itself as a nuclear-free zone.

Partly because of the end of the cold war, these movements lost momentum in the 1990s or were even reversed, as was the case in the Philippines, where a Visiting Forces Agreement with the United States reintroduced U.S. troops to the country. However, with the rise of U.S. unilateralism in the Bush period, a peace that is not built on military domination has again become an urgent concern of peoples and governments throughout the region.

The time may be ripe to again stoke regional energies to create a regional denuclearized and demilitarized zone. The principal mechanism to achieve this end would be a multilateral treaty for demilitarization and denuclearization that would involve, as signatories, the United States, Japan, member states of the former Soviet Union, China, India, Pakistan, and all other Asia-Pacific and Indian Ocean countries. This treaty would institute a ban on nuclear testing in the Pacific and Indian Oceans; a prohibition of the storage and movement of nuclear arms in the region; a ban on chemical and biological weapons; withdrawal of foreign bases from the western Pacific and Indian Oceans; the pullout of U.S. troops from the Korean peninsula; significant cuts in standing armies, air forces, and navies; deep reductions in naval deployments; a ban on the research and development of high-tech weaponry; and tight limits on the transfer of conventional arms via sales or aid.

The fundamental aim of an alternative security framework would be to move regional conflicts from resolution by force and intervention to resolution by diplomacy. Thus, accompanying the sanctions must be diplomatic mechanisms for the resolution not only of superpower disputes but also of regional conflicts, such as the dangerous dispute over the Spratly Islands in the South China Sea between China and the ASEAN countries and the subcontinental nuclear rivalry between India and Pakistan.

Drawing on their earlier experiences of forging tactical alliances with selected governments at the subregional level, nongovernmental and people's organizations and movements would need to craft a successful strategy for winning over Asia-Pacific governments and isolating the United States, which, being the only true transregional military power at this point, would be the state most negatively affected by a denuclearization agreement.

The twenty-first century may see either a new era of balance-of-power politics characterized by increasing tension among the United States, China, India, Pakistan, Japan, and Russia or a qualitatively new Asia-Pacific region that is denuclearized and significantly demilitarized, as well as more independent. The outcome will depend greatly on the courage and willingness of progressive forces in the region to use that rare window of opportunity for change offered by the crisis of U.S. unilateralism.

Notes

1. R. Hariharan, "Tsunami: Security Implications," Report: South Asia Analysis Group, 2005, http://www.southasiaanalysis.org/%5Cpapers13%5Cpaper1213.html (accessed December 4, 2009); Ralph A. Cossa, "South Asian Tsunami: U.S. Military Provides 'Logistical Backbone' for Relief Operation" in U.S. Department of State, Bureau of International Information Programs, *eJOURNAL USA* (November 2004), http://www.america.gov/st/washfile-english/2005/March/20050304111 202dmslahrellek0.5149347.html (accessed December 4, 2009).

2. Harirahan, "Tsunami"; and Cossa, "South Asian Tsunami."

3. Paul Wolfowitz, Press Conference, U.S. Pacific Command, Indonesia, January 16, 2005, http://www.defenselink.mil/transcripts/transcript.aspx?transcriptid =1662 (accessed December 2, 2009).

4. "US to Resume Military Aid for Indonesia," *AFX News Limited*, November 22, 2005, http://www.forbes.com/feeds/afx/2005/11/22/afx2351085.html (accessed December 4, 2009).

5. U.S. Pacific Command, "About U.S. Pacific Command," U.S. Pacific Command, Honolulu, February 4, 2007, http://www.pacom.mil/about/pacom.shtml (accessed December 4, 2009).

6. At the time this article was originally written in 2007, Japan was ranked the fourth largest. In 2009, Japan ranks as the seventh largest in terms of military expenditures according to the Stockholm Institute for Peace Research. *SIPRI Yearbook 2009: Armaments, Disarmament and International Security* (Oxford: Oxford University Press, 2009).

7. Chalmers Johnson, *The Sorrows of Empire: Militarism, Secrecy and the End of the Republic* (London: Verso, 2004), 221–22; "Diego Garcia, 'Camp Justice'" http://www.globalsecurity.org/military/facility/diego-garcia.htm (accessed December 4, 2009); Leo Shane III, *Stars and Stripes*, European edition, December 28, 2004, http://www.stripes.com/article.asp?section=104&article=26265 (accessed December 4, 2009).

8. See Glenn Alcalay, "Pax Atomica: U.S. Nuclear Imperialism in Micronesia," in *On the Brink: Nuclear Proliferation and the Third World*, ed. Peter Worsley and Kofi Buenor Jadjor (London: Third World Communications, 1987), 107–21.

9. U.S. Pacific Command, "About U.S. Pacific Command"; see also Herbert Docena, *Unconventional Warfare* (Manila, the Philippines: Focus on the Global South, 2007).

10. A. Whitney Griswold, *The Far Eastern Policy of the United States* (New Haven, Conn.: Yale University Press, 1962), 34.

11. Quoted in William Manchester, *American Caesar: Douglas MacArthur* (New York: Dell, 1978), 48–49.

12. Roy K. Flint, "The United States on the Pacific Frontier, 1899–1939," in *The American Military in the Far East: Proceedings of the Ninth Military History Symposium*, ed. Joe Dickson (Colorado Springs, Colo.: U.S. Air Force Academy, 1980), 155–56, http://permanent.access.gpo.gov/airforcehistory/www.airforcehistory.hq.af.mil/Publications/fulltext/american_military_&_the_far_east.pdf (accessed December 4, 2009).

13. As summed up in "Conversation between General of the Army MacArthur and George Kennan, 5 March 1948—Top Secret," in *Containment: Documents on American Policy and Strategy, 1945–1950*, ed. Thomas Etzold and John Lewis Gaddis (New York: Columbia University Press, 1978), 229.

14. Paul Wolfowitz and Lewis Libby, "Defense Planning Guide." 1992 draft key excerpts. Available at http://www.pbs.org/wgbh/pages/frontline/shows/iraq/etc/wolf.html (accessed December 18, 2009).

15. Quoted in Alex Callinicos, *The New Mandarins of American Power* (Cambridge, U.K.: Polity Press, 2003), 45–46.

16. The full text of President Bush's National Security Strategy is available at http://www.nytimes.com/2002/09/20/politics/20STEXT_FULL.html?pagewanted=3 (accessed on December 17, 2009).

17. Ibid.

Contributors

Walden Bello is a senior analyst at Focus on the Global South, a program of Chulalongkorn University's Social Research Institute, as well as president of the Freedom from Debt Coalition and a fellow of the Transnational Institute. He is author of numerous books on globalization and militarization, including *Dilemmas of Domination: The Unmaking of the American Empire*, *The Anti-Development State: The Political Economy of Permanent Crisis in the Philippines*, and *Deglobalization: Ideas for a New World Economy*. In 2003, he received the Right Livelihood Award, also known as the "Alternative Nobel Prize." An academic and an activist, he has been professor at the University of the Philippines at Diliman since 1997 and was recently named Outstanding Public Scholar of 2008 by the International Political Economy Section of the International Studies Association.

Michael Lujan Bevacqua is a graduate student in ethnic studies at the University of California at San Diego. He is editor for the Chamorro zine *Minagahet* and a cofounder of the Chamorro activist group Famoksaiyan. In October 2007, he testified before the United Nation's Fourth Committee on the question of Guam, and, in August 2008, he attended the Democratic National Convention as the official blogger from Guam. His research interests include American colonialism, Chamorro sovereignty, and theories of decolonization.

Keith L. Camacho is assistant professor of Asian American studies at the University of California at Los Angeles. His research examines issues of colonization, decolonization, and militarization in the Pacific Islands, with an emphasis on indigenous narratives of survival and sovereignty. His book *Cultures of Commemoration: The Politics of War, Memory, and History in the Mariana Islands* is forthcoming.

Patti Duncan is associate professor of women's studies at Oregon State University. Her research and teaching focus on race, gender, and nation, especially in relation to women of color and transnational feminist movements. Currently she is studying the long-term effects of militarism and war on women and gender in Asia, and gendered forms of violence in transnational contexts. She is the author of *Tell This Silence: Asian American Women Writers and the Politics of Speech*, as well as numerous articles about women of color, feminist pedagogy, and transnational feminisms.

Cynthia Enloe is research professor of international development and women's studies at Clark University. Among her books are *Bananas, Beaches, and Bases: Making Feminist Sense of International Politics*; *The Morning After: Sexual Politics at the End of the Cold War*; *Maneuvers: The International Politics of Militarizing Women's Lives*; *The Curious Feminist: Searching for Women in a New Age of Empire*; and *Globalization and Militarism: Feminists Make the Link*. She has lectured on feminism, militarization, and globalization in Japan, Korea, Turkey, Canada, Britain, and throughout the United States. She has written for *Ms. Magazine* and *The Village Voice* and has appeared on National Public Radio and the BBC. She serves on the editorial boards of several scholarly journals, including *Signs* and the *International Feminist Journal of Politics*.

Vernadette Vicuña Gonzalez is assistant professor of American studies at the University of Hawai'i at Mānoa. Her research currently explores the intersections of tourism and militarism in Hawai'i and the Philippines, and her areas of specialization include studies of tourism and militarism, transnational cultural studies, feminist theory, postcolonial studies, Asian American cultural and literary studies, and globalization studies with a focus on Asia and the Pacific.

Insook Kwon is associate professor in the Banmok College of Basic Studies at Myongji University, South Korea, where she teaches women's studies. She is the author of *South Korea Is the Military: Peace, Militarism, and Masculinity with Gender Perspective*, as well as several articles about militarism, sexual violence, and masculinities. She is now studying militarized college culture, female conscription, and conscientious objectors.

Laurel A. Monnig recently received her Ph.D. in cultural anthropology; her dissertation research focuses on how Chamorros of Guam negotiate the interconnected discourses of colonialism and race to manipulate social networks, construct identity, create decolonization processes, and define nationhood. She is interested in colonialism, decolonization, race, identity, and militarization among indigenous peoples colonized by the United States and continues to research ongoing processes of U.S. militarization on Guam.

Katharine H. S. Moon, professor of political science and Wasserman Chair in Asian Studies, is author of *Sex among Allies: Military Prostitution in U.S.–Korea Relations* and other publications on the U.S.–Korea alliance and social movements in Asia addressing democracy, local politics and U.S. bases, migrant workers, women, and human rights. She is writing a book on the rise of Korean social movements in alliance politics.

Jon Kamakawiwoʻole Osorio is full professor at the Kamakakuokalani Center for Hawaiian Studies at the University of Hawaiʻi at Mānoa, where he teaches Hawaiian Kingdom politics and identity, music, and indigenous research methods. He is author of *Dismembering Lāhui: A History of the Hawaiian Nation to 1887.*

Naoki Sakai is professor of Asian studies and comparative literature at Cornell University. He has published in the fields of comparative literature, comparative intellectual history, translation studies, and studies of racism and nationalism. His publications include *Translation and Subjectivity* (published in English [Minnesota, 1997], Japanese, and Korean); *Voices of the Past* (English, Japanese, and Korean editions); and *Stillbirth of the Japanese* (Japanese and Korean editions). He was founding senior editor of *Traces*, a multilingual scholarly journal series in five languages (Korean, Chinese, English, Japanese, and German).

Fumika Sato is associate professor at the Graduate School of Social Sciences at Hitotsubashi University in Japan, where she teaches gender studies. With a background in sociology, her research includes militarism, feminism, and women and the Japanese Self-Defense Forces. She is author of *Gender and the Military: Women in the Japanese Self-Defense Forces.*

Setsu Shigematsu is assistant professor of media and cultural studies at the University of California at Riverside. Her intellectual and scholarly concerns include the relationship between U.S. and Japanese imperialisms, transnational liberation movements, state violence, and comparative feminism. Her book on the women's liberation movement that emerged in Japan during the early 1970s is forthcoming with the University of Minnesota Press.

Theresa Cenidoza Suarez is assistant professor in sociology and critical race studies at California State University, San Marcos. She has a Ph.D. in ethnic studies from the University of California at San Diego and an M.A. in Asian American studies from the University of California at Los Angeles.

Teresia K. Teaiwa is senior lecturer and, from 2000 to 2009, was founding program director of Pacific studies at Victoria University of Wellington in New Zealand. Her research and publications have long focused on the cultural effects and affects of militarism in Pacific Island societies. In 2007, she was awarded a Royal Society of New Zealand Marsden Fund grant to collect oral histories and undertake a comparative feminist analysis of Fijian women soldiers in the Fiji Military and British Army. In 2008, she was appointed coeditor of the *International Feminist Journal of Politics*.

Wesley Iwao Ueunten is a third-generation Okinawan born and raised on the island of Kauaʻi, Hawaiʻi. He has a Ph.D. in ethnic studies from the University of California at Berkeley and now teaches Asian American studies in the College of Ethnic Studies at San Francisco State University. He is active in the Okinawan American community in the Bay Area as an officer in the Okinawa Kenjinkai of San Francisco and as a student of traditional Okinawan music.

Index

Note: Page references in italics refer to illustrations.

Aceh, insurgencies in, 310
activism: antinuclear, 23, 24–26, 318–20; Asian American, 116–17; by black soldiers, 112, 115, 123n55; Christian, 131; concerning militarized violence, xxiii; Japanese women's, 116; Korean women's, 125–26, 131–33, 136–37, 139; Māori, 124n72; by Okinawan women, xxii, 118, 297; of Pacific Island women, 23, 24, 27, 30n42; transpacific, 124n72. *See also* anticolonialism; *chŏngsindae* movement (CM, Korea); decolonization; *kijich'on* movement (South Korea)
activism, Chamorro, 35, 52n9, 150–51; by soldiers, 147–48, 164–65, 167–68
activism, Filipino/a, 140; antibase, 83; military suppression of, 83
adoption, transnational: coercion in, 291; colonialism through, 293, 306n95; construction of subjectivity in, 296; consumer demand for, 293; control of women's bodies in, 295; diaspora in, 293; effect of militarism on, 279–80; effect of North Korean threat on, 305n69; feminist approach to, 295–97; gendered processes of, 291, 306n95; in global economy, 291, 293, 296; globalized processes of, 294; kinship and, 294, 296; in modernization process, 291; in neocolonialism, 293; numbers of, 290–91; origins of, 290; politics of, 277, 292; population control through, 292; racialized labor of, 294; rescue narratives in, 292, 296; in South Korea, 279, 287, 290–91, 291–94; from Third World, 299n5; unbelonging in, 296; unidirectional, 289–95; as welfare system, 305n69; in Western empire building, 290
Afghanistan War, viii, 309; Japanese Self-Defense Forces in, xx; role of Diego Garcia in, 312
African Americans, urban revolts by, 110–11. *See also* soldiers, African American
Agathangelou, Anna, 279
Aguon, Julian, xxiii–xxiv
Aiuchi, Mako, 273n19
Akira, Arakawa: "The Colored Race," 104–5, 111; "An Orphan's Song," 104
Alexander, George, 156
Amerasian Children's Association, 288

327

Amerasians: association with prostitution, 288; Filipino, 289; Okinawan, 109, 287; Vietnamese, 287, 289, 299n5. *See also* children, Amerasian
Amerasians, South Korean, 277–98; as cultural contaminants, 295; derogatory terms for, 286; dropout rates of, 286–87; effect of militarism on, 278; employment problems of, 286; *kijich'on* women, 283; poverty of, 287; sex work for, 280; statelessness of, 285, 288, 296; stigmatization of, 277–78, 279, 285–86, 290, 307n99; view of United States, 277, 278
Ancho, Mr. (navy steward), 189–90
Andersen Air Force Base (Guam), 158
Angeles City (Philippines), red-light district of, 312
An Ilsun, 140
Anjŏngni (Korean camptown), 128
anticolonialism: Asian, 103; of *chŏngsindae* movement, 135; moral basis of, 135; narratives of, 72–73; in Pacific, xxi. *See also* decolonization
antinuclear movements: in Asia-Pacific region, 318–20; of South Pacific, 23, 24–26
antiwar movements, in Okinawa, 115–17, *116*
ANZUS alliance, 318
ANZUS Treaty, 25
Apter, Emily, 22
area studies, "afterlife" of, xxxiii–xxxiv
armed services, 195; desire for control in, 238–39; gender diversity in, xxviii; gender ratios in, 269, *270*; gender segregation in, 256; homosexuality in, 168; indigenous peoples in, 156; institutional preservation of, xxvii; maintenance of discipline in, 239; postmodern forms of, xxvii–xxviii; racial diversity in, xxviii. *See also* Imperial Army, Japanese; Japanese Self-Defense Forces (SDF); soldiers
armed services, American: all-volunteer, 269; citizenship and, 195; civilian accidents under, 106; gendered aspects of, xxxv, 93; Hawaiians in, 6–7, 8, 13; imagery of, 38–39; masculinity in, 159–60; Pacific Islanders in, 161; in Pacific Islands, 311; racial aspects of, xxxv, 93; sexual harassment in, 227–28; structures of domination, 163; women in, xxxix, 255, 258. *See also* soldiers, African American; soldiers, American; U.S. Navy
armed services, NATO: women soldiers in, 269, *270*
armed services, South Korean, 224; hierarchical character of, 226; living quarters of, 224, 247n7; male-on-male sexual violence in, xxxix, 223–46; masculinity in, 225, 229; psychological traits of, 248n17
Artero Sablan, Antonio, 166–67
Asagumo (newspaper), 275n49
Asia: confrontations with North America, 153–54; militarization in, vii; political geographies of, xv; remilitarization of, xxiv
Asian Americans for Action (AAA), 116–17
Asia-Pacific region: alternative security system for, 318–20; antinuclear movements in, 318; Clinton administration policy on, 316–17; demilitarization for, 320; destabilization of, 318;

geographical configuration of, xxxi; George W. Bush administration policy on, 317–18; militarization of, 311. *See also* Pacific Islands
Association of Southeast Asian Nations (ASEAN), 318, 319; Regional Forum (ARF), 316
Atomic Energy Commission, 18
atrocities: under colonialism, xvii, xxxii, 101; Japanese, 217; U.S., 313
Australia, nuclear testing in, 16
Awa, Rey, 158

Bakery Auntie (*kijich'ŏn* woman), 128–29
Balibar, Étienne, 207, 219n6
Ballendorf, Dirk: *The Secret Guam*, 44
Bangkok, Patpong area of, 312
Bataan: consumption of, 79; *Dambana ng Kagitingan* memorial, 81; Death March, 72, 75, 81; liberation narratives of, 64, 65, 66, 68, 82, 83, 85; nostalgic discourses of, 71, 72; racialized masculinities in, 69; tourism on, 63, 66, 72–73, 79, 81–82
Battle of Guadalcanal, veterans' visits to, 69
Battle of Okinawa, 98, 100–101, 121n28; displaced persons from, 108; noncombatant casualties during, 101
Beau Geste (film), 60n74
Belau, antinuclear constitution of, 23, 25
Bello, Walden, xl
Benavente, Ed L. G., 164–65
Benavente, John, 147–48
Benjamin, Walter, xxxiii, 53n24
Berger, John, 29n25
Bertram, Geoff, 149, 152
Bevacqua, Michael Lujan, xxxv

Beveridge, Albert, 314
Bhabha, Homi, 165
bikini, etymology of, 24
Bikini Atoll: erasure of history, 27; geography of, 16; marine park proposal for, 31n48; nuclear colonialism in, xxxv; nuclear testing in, xxix, 17, 28n10; population of, 17, 25; U.S. servicemen at, 188
bikini bathing suits, xxix, 15, 18–22; colonized referents of, 22; erasure of Bikini Atoll history, 27; fetishism concerning, 21–22, 26; ideological implications of, 26; introduction to United States, 29n21; Marxist analysis of, 22; mediation of social relationships, 22; negation of female body, 20; and neocolonial discourse, 20; nuclear power and, xxxv; power relations and, 19; "Swedish," 29n29
Bikini Day, 26
Bikini Islanders: dislocation of, 17–18, 22, 27, 28n13; radiation sickness of, 15; reparations for, 26; resistance by, 27; right of return, 18
biopolitics: of colonialism, 205; liberalism in, 218n4
biopower, regimes of, 218n4
Black Panther (periodical), on Okinawan antiwar protests, 115–16
Blauner, Robert, 110–11, 113
bodies: generation of knowledge, 23; militarization of, xl, 279
bodies, female: control through transnational adoption, 295; effect of militarism on, 278; exoticized, 20; fetishization of, 22; ideal, 29n28; under militarization, 280; political negation of, 20;

bodies, female (*continued*): reification of, 19; sexualized, 15; surveillance of, 295; Third World, 294
bodies, s/pacific, 22–26; decolonization of, 23
Bougainville, Louis Antoine de, 20
Briggs, Laura, 293
Broussard, Sylvia D., 233
Buck, Pearl S., 299n5
Bunch, Charlotte, 140
Burakumin, Japanese conscription of, 175n65
Burnett, Christina Duffy, 170n2
Bush, George W., 9, 33, 196; Asia-Pacific policy of, 317–18; neoconservatism of, 317; Philippines visit of, 68
Bush Masters (African American soldiers), 112
Butler, Judith, 56n42

California, bachelor societies of, 193
Camacho, Keith L., xxxvii–xxxviii, 171n7
Camatcho, Mr. (navy steward), 186–87
Camp Arirang (documentary film), 287, 303n44
Camp John Hayes (Philippines), 185
Campomanes, Oscar V., 78
camptowns, South Korean, 128; Amerasians born in, 280; social interactions within, 282. *See also kijich'ŏn* women (South Korea)
Carolinians, of Mariana Islands, 172n16
Carreiras, Helena, 276n56
Castillo, Mr. (navy man), 187
Center for Women's Global Leadership (Rutgers University), 140
Certeau, Michel De, 119n5
Chamorro Land Trust Act, 52n9

Chamorro language, U.S. suppression of, 167
Chamorros, 51n4; absences imposed upon, 43; agency of, 43–46, 46, 151; American-ness of, 37; *chenchule'* (reciprocity) among, 157, 166; civic rights of, 34, 42, 45, 51n4, 52n10, 57nn52–53, 157; collective beliefs of, 53n15; decolonized subjectivities of, 170; delegation to United Nations, 34–35; education of, 41–42, 56n46, 57n49; feminized view of, 156; gendered roles of, 149; government control over, 41; incompleteness of, 42, 43, 44, 57n50; infantilization of, 39–40, 44; intergenerational trauma of, 44; invisibility of, 44, 45; landless, 60n70, 158; liminality among, 47–48; of Mariana Islands, 172n16; militarization of, xxii–xxiii, 34; nationalism of, 178n98; number system of, 50; as other, 42; patriotism of, 35–36, 38, 45, 48, 54n29, 55n36; relocation to Guam, 175n55; resistance by, 43, 49, 148; Spanish accounts of, 160, 161; voice of, 45–46; voting rights for, 45, 58n61; warrior ethos of, 39, 148, 160, 161, 162, 163. *See also* navy men, Chamorro; soldiers, Chamorro
chattaotao (incompleteness), 43
Chen, Kuan-Hsing, xlvi in85
children, Amerasian, xl, 109, 277–78; abandonment of, 290; black fathers of, 286, 287, 304n49; of *kijich'ŏn* women, xl, 128, 139, 285, 288, 295–96; Okinawan, 109; return to Korea, 294; self-determination of, 299n5; stigmatization of, 284; transnational adoption of, 279, 288, 289–95; Vietnamese, 289, 304n63

China: Communist takeover of, 102; competition with United States, 317, 318; defense spending in, xliii n27, 273n13; Rape of Nanjing in, 211–12; relations with Okinawa, 98–99; U.S. trade with, 314, 315

China Night (film), 212

Cho, Grace, 282

Choi, Chungmoo, xxi

Chong Chin Song, 127–28

chŏngsindae movement (CM, Korea), xxxvii, 125–26; academic aspect of, 137–38; anticolonialism of, 135; anti-Japanese sentiment in, 132–33; Christian activists in, 131, 137; effect on *kijich'on* problem, 140; Ewha graduates among, 136, 137; historical studies of, 218n1; and human rights movement, 141; and *kijich'on* movement, 126–38, 140–42, 302n29; on *kijich'on* women, 127; on Korean government, 136; leadership of, 131, 132, 136, 137; lobbying of UN, 139–40; nationalism of, 127, 135, 136; organizational purpose of, 137–38; successes of, 127, 302n29; view of female sexual behavior, 134

chŏngsindae system (Korea), 125; beaurocracy in, 130; as genocide, 132; public discourse on, 134, 144n34; research on, 137–38; United Nations on, 142n3

chŏngsindae women (Korea), 125, 283; enslaved status of, 134; kidnapping of, 129; *kijich'on* experience of, 134; and *kijich'on* women, 129, 134; non-Korean, 302n28; psychological aftermath for, 127–28; reparations for, 141; Research Committee on, 137; testimony of, 142n2

Christian, Barbara, 23

Christianity, in Pacific Islands, 23–24, 30n43, 31nn44–46

cinema: American imperialism in, 206, 215; colonizer-colonized relations in, 209–10; depiction of romantic love, 209, 211, 213

citizenship: exclusionary, 182; gender and, 255; in Guam, 150; meaning among Filipino veterans, 200n65; military service and, 269–70, 276n53; role of marriage in, 182; and U.S. Armed Forces, 195

Clark Air Field (Philippines), 63, 185; entertainment economy of, 65; neoliberalism and, 64; prostitution at, 86n9; reunions at, 67; as special economic zone, 65, 67; tourism to, 68, 82–83

Clinton, Bill, 79, 196; Asia-Pacific policy of, 316–17

clothing, social control through, 24

coalitions, indigenous, xvi, 124n72

Cohen, Robin, 293

cold war: geopolitical context of, 189; nuclear testing during, 17

colonialism: atrocities under, xvii, xxxii, 101; banal, xxxv, 33–34; biopolitics of, 205; commodities in, 22; countries benefiting from, 217; demasculinization under, 182; difference in, 215; economic, xxviii, 70; effect on Chamorro males, 160–61; European, 111; fantasized situations of, 212–13, 217; gender in, xxviii, xxix, 71; homogenizing forces in, xviii; ideologies of travel in, 67; indigenous peoples' contribution to, 157; indigenous soldiers under, 165; intellectual, 100; internal, 111;

colonialism (*continued*): international encounters in, 205, 206; intrasettler, xxiv; late nineteenth-century, 217; liminality in, 47–48; local configurations of, xviii; marginalization under, 23; masculinization and, 159, 191, 228; and militarization, xv, xxvi–xxx; narcissistic fantasies of, 217; and nationalism, 207; nuclear, xxix, xxxv, 15–16, 19; obscene desires under, 41–42; in Okinawa, xxxvi–xxxvii, 97–98; power relations in, 207–9, 217; race in, xxix, 40, 71, 105, 111; in romantic films, 209–10, 212, 215; Spanish, 160, 175n55; systems of administration in, 205; trope of romantic love in, 206–10, 212; twentieth-century, 205
colonialism, American: in Guam, vii, 39–44, 48, 147–48, 167; and Japanese colonialism, xxi; justification for, xx; nineteenth-century, 151; in Okinawa, 91–92, 102–8; in Philippines, 182, 185; sexualized, 109, 110; in South Korea, vii, 289; through transnational adoption, 293, 306n95; tourism and, 75
colonialism, Japanese, xxix; and American colonialism, xxi; in Korea, xxxix, 125, 133, 135, 144n35, 282, 283; Korean resistance to, 125; liberation from, xxi; militarism in, xviii–xix; in Okinawa, xxxvii, 99–101, 111
colonizers: collaboration among, xviii, xlii n11; discourse of, 105; insecurity of, 209, 213; justification by, 212; pilfering from colonized, 211; relationship with colonized, xxxviii, 100, 208–9, 214
comfort stations, Japanese, xvii, xxxvii, 92, 205–6. *See also chŏngsindae* system (Korea)
Committee Against Tests on Moruroa (ATOM), 24
Commonwealth of the Northern Mariana Islands (CNMI), 49, 172n16. *See also* Mariana Islands
conscription: abandonment of, 269, 276n51; by Japanese Imperial Army, xix, 175n65, 229, 248n15, 251; of minorities, 156; in South Korea, 227
constitution, Japanese: Article Nine of, 252, 254, 268; feminists and, 253, 272–73n12
Convention on the Elimination of All Forms of Discrimination against Women (CEDAW), 260–61; Japanese ratification of, 266
Cordivin, Mr. (navy steward), 194
Corregidor: fall of, 64; Friendship Park, 76–77, 77, 88n28; liberation narratives of, 64, 65, 66, 68, 78–79, 82, 83, 85; Malinta Tunnel, 80; memorialization of, 74–81; monument parks of, 73; nostalgic discourses of, 71, 72; Pacific War Memorial, 78–79; racialized masculinities in, 69; sacrifice narrative of, 80; Spanish at, 64; tourism on, 63, 66, 72–73, 74–78, 88n28; tourist consumption of, 79, 80; World War II museum of, 79, 80
Cox, Susan Soon-Keum, 287, 293
Crist, William, 102
Critical Filipina and Filipino Studies Collective (CFFSC), 83
Cumings, Bruce, 282

Dae-chul Chung, 247n8
Dangerous Liaisons (film), 60n74
Davis, Mike: *Under the Perfect Sun*, 183–84
death, ethics of, 54n28, 54n30, 54n32
decolonization, xxxviii; cross-regional dialogues in, xxx–xli; demilitarization and, xvi, xxxvi; dual, xxi–xxii; for Guam, 34–35, 45, 51n2, 52n9, 148–53, 163–68; indigenous views of, 152–53; knowledge production in, xxx–xli; of Marianas, 172n16; of Pacific Islands, 152; political language of, 151, 152; Roosevelt on, 169; strategies of, 217; United Nations on, 169; U.S. position on, 151–52, 170. *See also* anticolonialism
decolonization movements: differences among, 149–50; in Guam, xxxviii, 148, 150–51, 164–65, 168–70; in Pacific Islands, 150
defense, semantics of, xix
Defense Authorization Act (U.S., 2009), xxii
Defense Planning Guidance (George W. Bush administration), 317
de la Rosa, Mr. (navy steward), 187; family responsibilities of, 192
demilitarization: for Asia-Pacific region, 320; competing interests in, xxiv; and decolonization, xvi, xxxvi; effective means of, xxviii; feminist-oriented, xvi; indigenous coalitions for, xvi; local efforts in, xxii; multilateral treaties for, 319; for South Korea, 138; transregional movements, xxv, xxxiv, xlvii n85
Derrida, Jacques: on ethics of death, 54n30
de Schmidt, Aurora Camacho, 300n15

Dewey, Admiral George, 315
diasporas: militarized, xxxviii; in transnational adoption, 294
Diaz, Vicente M., xxxiii, 153; on Japanese occupation of Guam, 188–89
Diego Garcia atoll, strategic location of, 311–12
Diokno, Maria Socorro, 290
Dirlik, Arif, xxxi
domination: colonial modes of, 70; Foucault on, 211; gendered, 64; male, 206; militarism as, 71
Donga ilbo (newspaper), 246n3
Dorn, Governor (of Guam), 57n53
Dueñas, Eddie, 162
Duncan, Patti, xl
Dvorak, Greg, xxx

East Asia, postwar hegemonies of, 216
East Asia–U.S.–Puerto Rico Women's Network Against Militarism, xlvii n85
economies, colonial: gendered, xxviii; racialized, xxviii. *See also* global economy
education, colonial: institutional absence in, 41–42, 57n49
Eknilang, Lijon, xvii
Elshtain, Jean Bethke, 265, 279
Enewetak Atoll, nuclear testing on, 17
Eng, David, 293, 294; *Q & A*, 183; *Racial Castration*, 182
Enloe, Cynthia, xlv n64, 71, 279; on gays in military, 168; on masculinization, 149; on women in military, 254, 273n15, 276n53; on women's alliances, 270
Entertainment Tonight (CBS), on bikinis, 29n28
Espiritu, Yen Lê, 164, 185

ethnicity: fictive, 207, 219n6;
in prewar Japan, 220n18
Evans, Jeff, 53n15
Eye of the Dawn (television series), 125
Eyerman, Ron, 141–42

Fallon, William J., xxv
Famalao'an, Fuetsan, xxiii
families, Chamorro: male
providers for, 161
families, extra-American, 296
families, Filipino naval, 182,
197n1; Americanization of, 196;
coconstruction of masculinity,
197; consumption of American
goods, 193; financial conflicts in,
194; gendered expectations of,
183; hardships of, 192; separations
in, 194, 195; transgressions
of the normal in, 183;
transnational networks of, 181
Famoksaiyan (indigenous rights
organization), 35, 52n9
Fangataufa, nuclear testing on, 16
fashion: effect of war on, 18–19;
relation to church and state, 28n19
fatherhood, militarized, 190–95, 197
Fedalizo, Mr. (navy steward), 187–88,
189; experience of fatherhood,
191; family responsibilities of,
191–92; on uniforms, 195
Feifer, George: *The Battle
of Okinawa*, 101
femininity: alternative constructions
for, 289; international relations
of, 181; Korean perception
of, 246; militarized, xxviii
feminism, transnational, 293–94, 296
feminists, Japanese, ix, 275n39;
on Japanese Empire, 251; and
"Peace Constitution," 253, 273n12;

resistance to militarization, 252;
and war, 267, 271n3; and Western
feminists, 268–69; on women in
military, 255–56, 260–61, 270
feminists, Korean, 285. *See also*
activism: Korean women's; *kijich'on*
movement (South Korea)
feminists, Western: and Japanese
feminists, 268–69; on
women in military, 255
Ferguson, Roderick: "The Nightmares
of the Heteronormative," 182
fetishes: concerning bikini
bathing suits, 21–22, 26;
concerning female genitals, 21;
indigenous practices as, 21
Fichte, Johann Gottlieb: *Addresses
to the German Nation*, 219n6
Fijians, in World War I, 156
Fiji Young Women's Christian
Association, 24
Filipinas: activism of, 140; immigration
to South Korea, 301n24;
racialized violence against, 84
Filipinos: citizenship for, 195;
feminized spaces of, 182; fraternity
with Americans, 76–81; legal status
of, 185; migrants to United States,
192–93; militarized fatherhood
of, 190–95, 197; Orientalist
presumptions concerning, 185.
See also navy men, Filipino
Fina'tinas Chamorro (Chamorro
cooking), 39, 55n36
Firth, Stewart: *Nuclear Playground*, 25
Fleischer, Ari, 40
Fonda, Jane, 115
Ford, Gerald, 290
Foucault, Michel: *Society
Must Be Defended*, 211
France, nuclear testing by, 16, 153–54

Franco, Mr. (navy steward), 192
Freud, Sigmund: *Civilization and Its Discontents*, 21; *The Interpretation of Dreams*, 37
Friedman, Elisabeth, 140
Frühstück, Sabine, xli n2
Fuchs, Lawrence: *Hawai'i Pono*, 6
Fujitani, Takashi, xix
Fukumura, Yoko, 297
Fune, Mr. (navy man), 193, 194; on Americanization, 195–96; experience of fatherhood, 196

Gadao of Guam, 160
Gans, Herbert, 110, 113
gaze: colonial, 20; male, 19, 29n28; tourist, 82
GEM (women's equality index), 269, 276nn55–56
gender: and citizenship, 255; in colonialism, xxviii, xxix, 71; in division of labor, 294; in global economy, 64; in Japanese recruitment posters, 261–63; Japanese stereotypes of, 217; in marginalized masculinities, 149; in militarism, viii, 79; in militarization, xv, xxvii, 148, 280; in military tourism, 74, 79, 84; in nationalism, 85; in neocolonialism, xxvii; in postmodernity, xxviii; in power relations, 226; racialization of, xl, xlvi n65, 298; in structuring of military, xlvi n65; in transnational adoption, 291, 306n95; in U.S. military culture, 183
gender norms: Japanese, 251, 252; in transnational adoption, 291, 306n95
genitals, female: fetishization of, 21
Gerakan Aceh Merdeka (GAM, Free Aceh Movement), 310

Gerson, Joseph, 311
Ghost in the Shell 2 (film), 53n25
ghosts, of wartime casualties, 35–36, 53n25
Gidra (Asian American publication), 117
"Gilda" (bomb), 19
Gillis, John, 173n35
global divisions, natural, xxxiii
global economy: gender in, 64; militarization of, 280, 297; sex work in, 279; transnational adoption in, 290, 293, 295–96
globalization, xxviii; tourism and, 70; in transnational adoption, 293–94
Glynn, Prudence, 28n19
Goldstone, Patricia, 67
Gordon, Richard, 67–69; sponsoring of soldier tourists, 84
La Goutte d'or (novel), 22
government, self-limiting, 218n4
Government of the Ryûkyû Islands (GRI), 102, 104
Grewal, Inderpal, 64, 79, 196
Griswold, Whitney, 314
Groth, Nicolas, 232, 243
Growing Pains (television series), 29n30
Guam: abortion debate in, 30n43; alliances of, xxiii, xxiv; American colonialism in, vii, 39–44, 48, 147–48, 167; American slogans concerning, 47, 60n73; antibase sentiment in, 159; "benevolent assimilation" of, 42; Chamorro relocation to, 175n55; colonial-liberal deadlock in, 46, 59n68; decolonization for, 34–35, 45, 51n2, 52n9, 148–53, 163–68; decolonization movements in, xxxviii, 148, 150–51, 164–65, 168–70;

Guam (*continued*): demographics of, 158, 176n70; discontinuities in, 52n10; economic independence for, 156; education in, 41–42, 56n44, 57n49; elections in, 151; foreign contract labor in, 158; immigration into, 157–58; independence for, xxii, 151; indigenous citizenship in, 150; institutional absence in, 41–42, 45, 57n49; Insular Guard, 49, 61n81; invisibility of, xxxv; Japanese occupation of, 35, 48, 49, 53n16, 157, 188–89; land alienation in, 60n70, 158; Leper colony in, 58n54; Liberation Day, 36, 53n15; masculinization in, 169; media in, 45, 58nn62–63; militarism in, 158, 168; militarization of, xxii–xxiv, 33–34, 59n63, 148, 155–59, 313; military fences of, 158–59; navy stewards in, 199n28; Organic Act for, 51n4, 157, 168–69; political-status options for, 151, 172n17; reparations for, xxiii; resistance in, 35, 43, 46–47, 49, 52n9, 59n68, 148; self-determination for, 148, 168, 169; in Spanish-American War, 51n4, 155; Spanish colonization of, 51n4; statehood for, 56n43, 151; strategic importance of, xxiii–xxiv, 33, 43–44, 50, 315; as strategic liability, 315; tourism in, 60n73; U.S. civil government of, 157, 168–69; U.S. naval government of, 41, 42, 148, 150, 155–56, 168–69; in war on terror, xxii. *See also* Chamorros; soldiers, Chamorro
Guantánamo Bay: closure of, 50n2; reterritoralization of empire, 33
Gutmann, Stephanie, 275n48

Hall, Gwendolyn, xlvi n65
Hall, Stuart, 154
Hanlon, David, xxi
Hara, Eloy, 165
Harootunian, H. D., xxxiii
Hattori, Anne Perez, 156; *Colonial Dis-Ease*, 40
Hauʻofa, Epeli, xxxii–xxxiii
Hawaiʻi: American presence in, 5, 6, 11; anticolonial movements in, xxxiv; Asian hegemony in, xxiv–xxv; cross-regional alliances in, xxv; gendered view of, 155; intrasettler competition in, xxiv; Japanese Americans of, 6; Micronesian immigration to, 313; militarization of, 9–14; poetry of, xxv, xxxiv; sovereignty movement, xxiv; strategic importance of, 315; during World War II, 6–8. *See also* Pearl Harbor
"Hawaiian Soul" (song, Osorio and Borden), 11–12, 14n10
Hegel, Georg Wilhelm Friedrich: on master and slave, 56n42
Hein, Laura, 171n3
Helm, George, 11
heroism: masculinized, xxxvi; in military tourism, 72–74; narratives of, 75; racialized, xxxv
Hilsdon, Anne-Marie, 84–85
Hochstein, M., 16
Hokkaido, Japanese annexation of, xviii, 99
Hokowhitu, Brendan, 155
Holt International Children's Services, 291, 293
Hom, Alice: *Q & A*, 183
homosexuality: male-on-male sexual violence and, 224, 225, 226, 243, 245, 247n11; in military, 168;

punishment of, 246n3; stigmatization of, 243, 245
homosociality: among soldiers, xxxvi, 71; in ideology of nationalism, 206; in romantic cinema, 210
Hook, Glen, xlv n64
Hopton, John, 159
Horne, Gerald, xviii
Hubinette, Tobias, 291–92, 293, 306n95
"Hui" (Hawaiian song), 3
human rights, women's, 141–42
Hye Jung Park: *The Women Outside*, 220n13
Hynes, H. Patricia, 280

identities: Chamorro, 45; gendered, xl; Okinawan, 100; Pacific Islander, 124n72; racialized, xl
Iijima, Kazu, 116
Imperial Army, Japanese: conscription by, xix, 175n65, 229, 248n15, 251; Japanese Self-Defense Forces and, xli n2; massacre of Chinese, 211–12; negative legacy of, 267
imperialism: competition in, xxvi; male domination in, 206; nostalgia for, 68, 71; objectives of, 219n4; tourism and, 70
imperialism, American: of Bush administration, 318; in cinema, 206, 215; commercial rationales for, 314, 315; cultural-ideological dimension of, 314; cultural violence of, 188; Japanese complicity in, xvi–xxii, xxxix, 216–18, 311; logic of desire in, 215; in Pacific Islands, xxxiii; in Philippines, 76–78, 196–97; Third World consciousness of, xxxvii
imperialism, Japanese: among intellectuals, 216; in Korea, 133; nationalism in, 216, 221n18;

postwar disavowal of, xx; U.S. complicity in, xvi–xxii, xxxix, 216–18, 311; Western contributions to, xviii; women's role in, ix
indigenous peoples: in armed services, 156, 165; coalitions of, xvi, 124n72; contribution to colonialism, 157; fetishization of, 21; resistance by, xxx; sacrifices by, 48, 60n74, 61n80; service in U.S. empire, 156–57; Spanish use of, 156; views of decolonization, 152–53. *See also* decolonization movements; Chamorros; Filipinas; Filipinos
individualism, universalistic, 220n18
Indonesia, military aid to, 310
Insular Cases (legal decisions), 42, 170n2
International Conference on Violence against Women in War and Armed Conflict Situations, 297
International Seminar on Women and Tourism (1988), 126, 131
intimacy: as allegory of international politics, 213–14; Foucauldian terminology of, 218n4; international politics of, 207; in male-on-male sexual violence, 234–36, 237, 245; in sexual harassment, 244–45
Iraq War: Chamorros in, 36–40, 48, 55n36, 60n75, 163; Japanese Self-Defense Forces in, 254, 255, 268; recruitment following, 161; Southeast Asian view of, 310

Jamison, Andrew, 141–42
Japan: annexation of Okinawa, xviii, 99–100; annexation of Ryûkyûan Kingdom, 91, 98, 100; anti–North Korean sentiment in, 218;

Japan (*contined*): Army Nursing Corps, 256–57; civilian job market, 258, 260; Defense Agency, 260, 266, 267; defense spending in, xliii n27, 253, 273n13, 311, 320n6; democratization in, 252; Diet, 259, 266, 274n34; disavowal of past, 217; gender norms of, 217, 251, 252; invasion of Philippines, 76; Koreans in, 251–52, 269, 272n5; in Korean War, 252; Law on Securing, etc., of Equal Opportunity and Treatment between Men and Women in Employment, 260; Liberal Democratic Party, 259; Meiji Restoration, 98; militarism in, 269; Ministry of Education, 121n28; Mutual Security Act (with United States), 253; National Defense Academy (NDA), 266; National Police Reserve, 252, 256; National Security Board, 257; nuclear bombing of, 17, 188; nuclear waste of, xxx, 25; occupation of Guam, 35, 48, 49, 53n16, 157, 188–89; Perry in, 98, 314; postwar economy of, xix–xx, 258, 260; postwar image of, 267; racial purity theorists of, 220n18; ratification of CEDAW, 266; remilitarization of, xvi, xxix, 252, 254, 270, 272n7; reparations from, xvii, 139–40, 141; reversion of Okinawa to, 117; Security Corps, 253; Security Treaty with United States, 272n9; Taiwanese in, 251–52, 272n5; U.S. occupation of, 253; wartime self-justification of, 216; Women's Army Corps (WAC), 257. *See also* colonialism, Japanese; constitution, Japanese; imperialism, Japanese; Japanese Self-Defense Forces (SDF)

Japanese, as white Asians, 216, 218. *See also* soldiers, Japanese women; women, Japanese

Japanese American Citizens League, 117

Japanese Americans: activism of, 116–17; of Hawai'i, 6; in U.S. military, 6; during World War II, xix, 7

Japanese Empire, viii–ix, xv, xvi; building of, xviii; demise of, 217; energy issues in, 13; Japanese feminists on, 251; legacy of, 267; particularism of, 216; relationship to American empire, xxiv, xxxiii, 216–18; sexualized projects of, 93; suffrage in, 251, 252; universalism of, 216, 220n18; women's role in, 271sn4. *See also* imperialism, Japanese

Japanese Self-Defense Forces (SDF), xxxix, 251–70; in Afghanistan, xx; Air Self-Defense Force (ASDF), 262; background of, 252–54; budget of, 253; constitutional problems concerning, 253, 272n12; disciplinary problems of, 258, 274n32; equipment of, 254; expansion of women's roles in, 259–65, 274n38; feminist questions concerning, 254–56; feminization of, 252, 267; gender equality in, 267, 268, 270; gender formations in, 251; Ground Self-Defense Force (GSDF), 254, 256, 257, 258, 268; heterosexist logic in, 263; image making by, 261; Imperial Army and, xli n2; in Iraq War, 254, 255, 268; Korean exclusion from, 269; legitimacy of, 253, 259, 267; male policy makers of, 258; Maritime Self-Defense Force (MSDF), 262;

masculinity of, 257; nonmilitaristic image of, 267; normalization of, 254; number of women in, 273n16; nurses in, 256–57, 273n22; opposition to women in, 258; origin of, 253; overseas missions of, 254; personnel policies of, 268; recruitment of women, 258–59, 274n33; recruitment posters of, 261–65, *262*, *263*, *264*, *265*; recruitment problems of, 258–59; sexual harassment cases in, 276n58; size of, 253; socioeconomic backgrounds in, 276n52; Taiwanese exclusion from, 269; women cadets in, 266–68; women's support jobs in, 257–59
Johnson, Chalmers, 206; *The Sorrows of Empire*, xxvii
Johnson, Donald D., 152, 170
Johnston, Agueda, 48, 61n79
Johnston Atoll, nuclear testing on, 16
Joint Commission for Counter-Measures Regarding Miss Kum-E Yoon Case, 302n32
Jones, Jennifer, 215

Ka`ahupahau (female deity), 4
Kabua, Jibā, xxix
Kadekaru Rinsho: "Jidai no nagare," 120n16
Kadena Air Force Base (Okinawa): civilian casualties at, 106; strikes at, 114; violence at, 91, 96
Kaho`olawe (Hawai`i): bombing exercises at, 25; resistance movement concerning, 9–12; U.S. Navy occupation of, 9, 11
"Kaho`olawe" (song, Bishop), 10, 14n9
Kaho`olawe `Ohana (PKO), 9, 11
Kaibara, Osamu, 257–58

Kamehameha, 11, 12
Kanaka Maoli (Hawaiian people), 4; losses of, 5; military service of, 6–7, 8, 13; view of warfare, 12; during World War II, 8, 13
Kang, Laura Hyun-Yi, 28n13
Kaplan, Amy, 51n2
Kaplan, Caren, 64, 79
The Karate Kid, Part II (film), 124n71
Kay, Leroy, Jr., 6
Kelly, Thomas, 282
kijich'on movement (South Korea), xxxvii, 125, 126, 280; access to documentation, 138; and *chŏngsindae* movement, 126–38, 140–42, 302n29; counseling centers of, 126, 129, 137, 139; cultural festival (1996), 139; human rights in, 141; on Korean government, 136; leadership of, 136–37; localized status of, 127; nationalism of, 136; NGO support for, 138, 140; organizational purpose of, 137–38; splinter groups of, 138; transitional state of, 139
kijich'on system (South Korea): economic importance of, 289; racialized-sexualized subjects of, 296; state responsibility for, 130–31, 135–36, 281–82
kijich'on women (South Korea), 126, 282–86; abandonment of, 285; Amerasian, 284; *chŏngsindae* women and, 129, 134; children of, xl, 128, 139, 285, 288–89, 295; church support for, 138; coercion of, 129–30, 134, 135; debt bondage of, 130, 135, 283; derogatory terms for, 283; diplomatic function of, 214, 220n12, 288, 303n44; invisibility of, 285; kidnapping of, 129;

kijich'on women (South Korea) (*continued*): marriage to soldiers, 284–85; motives of, 283; physical abuse of, 129, 130, 135, 137, 284; poverty among, 284; pregnancies of, 128, 285; psychological aftermath for, 128–29; racial discrimination among, 219n12; racialization of, 297; STDs of, 128, 131, 219n12; stigmatization of, 283, 294, 295–96; surveillance of, 130; video installations about, 220n13
Kili Island, Bikini Islanders at, 17
Kim, Elaine H., xxi
Kim, Eleana, 291, 294, 305n69
Kim, Jean J., xxvii, xlv n63
Kim, Jodi: *Ends of Empire*, xxxii
Kim, Private: suicide of, 223, 246n2, 246n4
Kim, Yon Ja, 303n44
Kim Dae Jung, 305n74
Kim Hyun-yong, 229, 247n8, 247n11
Kim Jong Il, 311
Kim Yang Hyang, 128
King, Martin Luther, Jr.: Okinawans' honoring of, 114
Kinjo Toyo, 95
kinship: and American militarism, 277; South Korean, 290–91; and transnational adoption, 294, 295
Kirk, Gwyn, 280
Kirshenblatt-Gimblett, Barbara, 71–72, 77
Kissinger, Henry, 25
knowledge production: alternative modes of, xxxiv; decolonized, xxx–xli; neocolonial, xxxii; transregional collaboration in, xxvi
Koehn, Tony, 287
Koji Taira, 102
Kondo, Keiko, 273n19

Kookmin ilbo (newspaper), 246n6
Korea: Japan colonialism in, xxxix, 125, 133, 135, 144n34, 281, 283; partition of, 281, 285. *See also* South Korea
Korea Church Women United, 131; Church and Society Committee of, 137
Korean Amerasian Association, 288
Korean Association of Pacific War Victims and Bereaved Families, 132
Korean Council for the Women Drafted for Military Sexual Slavery, 127, 132, 139, 141, 142n3
Korean Institute of Criminology, 242
Koreans: discrimination against Amerasians, 285; Japanese conscription of, xix, 175n65, 229, 248n15; Japanese racism toward, xix; residing in Japan, 251–52, 269, 272n5; resistance to Japanese colonialism, 125. *See also* Amerasians, South Korean; *chŏngsindae* women (Korea); *kijich'on* women (South Korea); women, Korean
Korean Sexual Violence Consultation Clinic, 226
Korean War, 282; Japan in, 252; transnational adoption following, 290
Koza (Okinawa): black soldiers at, 112–13, 114; colonialism at, 108; drug traffic in, 93; Okinawan-American contact in, 111–13; rock bands of, 108–9; segregation in, 111–12, 114; sex industry in, 93; Teruya district, 111–12
Koza Uprising (1970), xxxvi, 91, *94*, 94–98, 123n47; African American soldiers and, 108, 115; in American media, 96–97, 118; arrests in, 96;

causes of, 108–15; effect on Asian American activism, 117; historical/social context of, 91, 97–98; MPs in, 95, 96, 120n15; Okinawan image and, 117; origin of, 94–95; targets of, 95–96, 108

Kristeva, Julia, 21

Kuroyanagi, Akira, 275n44

Kwajalein Islands: Bikini Islanders at, 17; nuclear testing at, 174n40

Kwangju Massacre (1980), 136

Kwon, Insook, xxxix

Lacan, Jacques: on the dead, 54n28

LaFeber, Walter, 151–52

language, originary, 219n6

Latin America, U.S. influence in, 318

Lay, Kenneth, 40

Lee Hyo Chae, 136

Leon Guerrero, Lou, 155–56

Leon Guerrero, Victoria, 34

liberation: discourses of, 72; gendered fantasies of, 64; imperial myths of, xxi

Lili'uokalani, 11

Ling, L. H. M., 279

"Little Boy" (bomb), 19

Love Is a Many-Splendored Thing (film), 215

Lowe, Lisa, 197

Lutz, Catherine, 153

Macapagal-Arroyo, Gloria, 66

MacArthur, Arthur, 315

MacArthur, Douglas, 64, 75; on postwar Asia, 316; and remilitarization of Japan, 252; return to Corregidor, 76, 81

Magbuhat, Mr. (navy man), 187, 194

Magofña, Olympio, 147

Mahan, Alfred, 314

Malo, Juan (Chamorro character), 160–61

Manifest Destiny, doctrine of, 314

Manuelito, Kathryn, 152

Māori: commodification of, 154; liberation movements, 124n72; in World War I, 156

Marcos, Ferdinand, 78, 81

Mariana Islands: decolonization of, 172n16; Spanish colonization in, 175n55

Mariana Trench, Japanese banning from, xxx, 25

Marine Corps Air Station Miramar military base (San Diego), 198n15

marriage: arranged, 194; gendered expectations of, 200n54; during militarism, 303n39; military brides, 121n28, 284–85, 303nn38–39; role in citizenship, 182

Marshall Islanders: radiation sickness of, 174n40; remembrance by, xxx; reparation for, xvii, 18; resistance by, xxx

Marshall Islands: Compact of Free Association (with United States), 18, 313; militarization of, xxix–xxx; nuclear colonialism in, xxxv; nuclear testing in, xvii, xxix, 15, 174n50, 312; as U.S. Trust Territory, 16

Marx, Karl: on alienation, 30n36

Masaaki Aniya, 110

masculinities: of Chamorro soldiers, 148–49, 159–63, 167–68, 169; in colonialism, 159, 191, 228; competing, 229, 231, 245; cultural construction of, 149; establishment of hierarchies in, 229, 230–32; female, xxviii, xlvi n68; in Guam, 169; international relations of, 181;

masculinities (*continued*): Japanese, 218; of Japanese Self-Defense Forces, 257; in Korean armed services, 225; in male-on-male sexual violence, 228, 230–34, 245; marginalized, 149; militarized, xxviii, xxxviii, 148, 149, 159, 196, 228, 281, 288; military rank and, 228–29; racialized, xxxv, xxxviii, 69; white-based, 164, 181, 185–86
masculinity, Filipino, xxxviii; and American manhood, 196; among navy men, 181–97; coconstruction by families, 197; family responsibilities in, 190–95; heteronormative, xxxviii, 182–83, 193; militarized authorization of, 196; reauthorization of, 189–90, 192, 195
Masuda, Hiroshi, 272n7
Matayoshi, James, xvii
Matsuda, Minn, 116
Matsuoka, Martha, 297
McKinley, William, 314
memory: construction of, 71; in military tourism, 72–73; Okinawan, 97; transnational processes of, xxx, 69, 85
Men, Women, and War (conference, 1997), 141
Micronesia: American "liberation" of, xxi; Compact of Free Association (with United States), 313; Japanese imperialism in, xviii; militarization of, 311, 312–13; soldiers from, 49; suicide rate in, 313; in war on terror, 50
Middle East, Japanese forces in, xx
migration: gendered, 294, 297; to Guam, 157–58; from Micronesia, 313; militarization and, xxvi; to South Korea, 301n24; to United States, 192, 195
Miki Kiyoshi, 217, 220n18
militarism: capitalism and, 83; Chamorro soldiers on, 170; civilian elements of, xxvi, xxviii, xlv n63; effect on female bodies, 278; effect on local communities, 278; effect on women, 277, 278; in empire building, xxvii; feminist critique of, 30n33; as form of domination, 71; functions of, viii; gendered aspects of, viii, 79; and humanitarianism, xxvi; Japanese, xviii–xix, 269; long-term consequences of, 280; marriage during, 303n39; versus militarization, 173n35; self-perpetuating, xxvi–xxviii; strategic deterrence in, xix; and tourism, xxvi, 26, 63–64; transnational feminist response to, 297; women's responses to, 296–98
militarism, American: alternatives to, xl; consequences of, 279; effect on Amerasians, 279; in everyday life, 187; in Guam, 158, 168; kinship and, 277; masculinity narratives of, 66; in South Korea, 278, 296, 298
militarization: in Asia, vii; and colonialism, xv, xxvi–xxx; cross-boundary operations of, xv; cross-disciplinary dialogues on, xlviii n94; cultural transformations in, xlv n64; dehumanization through, 281; discursive constructions of, 153, 279–81; effect on Asia-Pacific migration, xxvi; effect on desiring subjects, xxviii; and femininity, 149; following September 11, 85, 161, 171n3; following tsunami of 2004, 309–10; following United Nations

missions, 280; forms of control in, 71; gendered aspects of, xv, xxvii, 148, 280; of global economy, 280, 297; of Guam, xxii–xxiv, 33–34, 59n63, 148, 155–59, 313; Japanese, xxx; Japanese feminists on, 252; and masculinization, xxviii, xxxviii, 148, 149, 159, 196, 228, 280, 288; of Micronesia, 311, 312–13; multilateral, 205; normalization of, xxix; of nurses, 256; organizing logic of, xvii; in Pacific Islands, vii, 153–55, 189; in Philippines, 64, 66, 71, 185, 313; postmodern, xxviii; pre–September 11, vii–viii; racialized, 279, 300n15; resistance to, 252, 297; role of neoliberalism in, 292; of sexuality, xvii, xl; of sexual relations, xxxvii, 110; spatial-temporal aspects of, xvi; as structuring force, xv; technologies of, xxvii; transnational, xxxvi, xlvi n64; travel and, 70; women's bodies under, 281; women's role in, xxvii, 141, 255
military brides: Korean, 284–85, 303nn38–39; Okinawan, 121n28
military technology, xxvii; feminization of, 26
Miramar Air Show (San Diego), 198n15
missionaries, 31nn44–45; clothing of Pacific Islanders, 24, 31n46
Mitchell, Kimo, 11
Miyoshi, Masao, xxxiii
modernity: colonial, 212; hegemonies of, 79; sexual violence in, 248n16
Modernization Theory, 220n16
Molasky, Michael, 105; *The American Occupation of Japan and Okinawa*, 104

Monnig, Laurel A., xxxvii–xxxviii, 171n7
Monty Python's Life of Brian (film), 43
Moon, Faye, 126; outreach by, 131, 138; separation from *chŏngsindae* movement, 133
Moon, Katharine H. S., xxxvii; on *kijich'on* women, 214, 282, 285
Moon Dong Hwan, 131
"More Like His Father Everyday" (cartoon), 40, *41*
Morning Musume (Japanese idol group), 262, *263*
Moruroa, nuclear testing on, 16, 24
motherhood, Japanese: protection of, 267
Mowforth, Martin, 70
Munhwa ilbo (newspaper), 246n5
Munt, Ian, 70
Murphy, Joe, 54n29, 59n63
My Sister's Place (counseling center, Korea), 126, 129, 137, 139

Nagasaki City, nuclear bombing of, 188
Nago (Okinawa): G-7 summit at, 118; heliport for, 118, 119
Nākoa, Sarah Keliʻilolena: *Lei Momi o Ewa*, 4
nan'yō, Japanese, xix, xxiii
Nash, Dennison, 70
I Nasion Chamoru (indigenous rights organization), 35, 46, 52n9, 59n70
National Campaign for the Eradication of Crimes by U.S. Troops in Korea, 133, 302n32
National Human Rights Commission of Korea (NHRCK), 223, 234, 239, 240, 244, 247n8, 248n13; on physical violence, 241–42; on public military violence, 225; on rate of sexual harassment, 228, on victim experience, 244

nationalism: Chamorro, 178n98; collective enjoyment in, 61n79; colonialism and, 207; ethnic, 220n18; gendered, 85; homosocial ideology of, 206; in Japanese imperialism, 216, 221n18; Korean, 127, 135, 136; patriarchal, 64; racial strategies of, 207; and romantic love, 207–8; as universalism, 220n17
National Organization for Women, Resolution on Women in Combat, 273n19
National Security Strategy Paper (George W. Bush administration, 2002), 317
nations, internality of, 219n6
Native Americans: U.S. treatment of, 172n21, 313; in World War II, 157
navy men, African American, 184–85
navy men, Chamorro, 155–59; gendered service of, 156; prior to World War II, 157; racism concerning, 165; reasons for service, 165–66; recruitment of, 186; stewards, 157, 186
navy men, Filipino: Americanization of, 195–96; arranged marriages of, 194; bachelorhood requirement for, 191; construction of masculinity among, 181–97; domesticated role of, 184–86; feminized labor of, 185, 186–87, 190, 192, 195; heteronormative manhood among, xxxviii, 182–83, 193; labor conditions for, 181; maintenance of dignity, 186–87; management of system, 186–87; patriotism of, 181, 195–97; ratings of, 184, 186–87; recruitment of, 185, 188, 189; stewards, 182, 184, 186, 189, 195; training of, 187; uniforms of, 195
neocolonialism: class in, 281; dual systems of, xxxvi; effect on Pacific Islanders, 27; gendered aspects of, xxvii, 281; in international relations, 206; militarized ideologies of, 298; race in, 280; racial aspects of, xxvii; in South Korea, 278, 284–85; transnational adoption in, 293
neoliberalism, xxviii; postcolonial fantasies of, 64; role in militarization, 292; in Third World tourism, 73
neoracism, Western European, 218
Newton, Huey, 115
New Zealand, Pacific Islanders in, 124n72
Ngo, Fiona, 280, 287
Nikkei shimbun (newspaper), on women military cadets, 266
Nixon, Richard, 196
noble savages, of South Seas, 20, 22, 163
North Korea: Japanese sentiment against, 218; troop buildup in, 311
nostalgia: concerning World War II, 69, 71, 72, 85; imperialist, 68, 71
Nuclear Free and Independent Pacific movement (NFIP), 23, 24–26, 318, 319; alliances of, 31n53; support of women's organizing, 30n42
nuclearism, violence of, xxx
nuclear technology: domestication of, 26; in Pacific Islands, 16, 187; phallic aspects of, 21; psychoanalytic discussion of, 30n33
nuclear testing: during cold war, 17; colonialism in, xxix, xxxv, 15–16, 19; decontamination from, 187–88; French, 16, 153–54;

gendered terminology in, 19; at Kwajalein Atoll, 174n40; in Marshall Islands, xvii, xxix, xxxv, 15, 174n40, 312; moratorium on, 16; in Pacific Islands, 16, 187, 199n37
Nukiyama, Eiko, 275n44
nurses, militarization of, 256

Oʻahu, warriors of, 12
Obama, Barack, xxii
Oguma Eiichiro, 99
Okazawa-Rey, Margo, 279, 280, 284, 289, 304n49
Okihiro, Gary Y., xxxiv
Okinawa: alliances of, xxiii, xxiv, xxxvii; American colonialism in, 91–92, 102–8; American-Japanese interests in, 91–92, 97–98, 118; American military government in, 101–2; American occupation of, xix, xxxvi–xxxvii, 101–8; American troop reduction in, 120n15; antiwar protest in, 115–17, *116*; black soldiers in, 112–15; civilian police, 94, 95, 96; colonialism in, xxxvi–xxxvii, 97–98; culture of, 118–19; demilitarization of, xxii–xxiv; democracy in, 104; economic exploitation of, 99–100; food shortages in, 99; Hollywood depiction of, 124n71; Japanese colonialism in, xviii, xxxvii, 98–101, 111; Japanese prefecture of, 99–100, 102; Japanese racism in, 100, 119; land seizure on, 102–3, 122n33; militarization of, 92, 102–6, 108; militarized violence in, 98, 106–8, 117–18; as nuclear arsenal, xlii n11; postwar economy of, 91; Price Report on, 103, 104, 122n33; relations with China, 98–99; reparations for, xxiii; returnees to, 108; reversion to Japan, 117; seafaring history of, 118; size of, 92; sovereignty for, xxii; strategic importance of, 104. *See also* Battle of Okinawa; Ryûkyûan Kingdom (Okinawa)
Okinawan language, Japan suppression of, 101
Okinawans: American crimes against, 105–8; censorship of, 104–5; coerced suicides of, 101, 121n28; dissent among, 118; drum dance of, 113; effect of militarization on, xxii–xxiii; feminized positionality of, 108; forced assimilation of, 100; global networks of, 118; isolation of, 93; Japanese execution of, 101; Japanese taxation of, 98, 99–100; Kenjinkai, 121n28; relationship with black soldiers, 112–15; resistance by, 103, 113; Third World consciousness of, 92, 100; Western explorers on, 124n71; during World War II, 101–2, 121n28. *See also* women, Okinawan
Okinawa Prefectural Cultural Promotion Foundation, 102–3
Okinawa Program (self-help book), 124n71
Okinawa Women Act against Military Violence (OWAAMV; organization), xxiii, 297
Oparah, Julia Chinyere, 299n5
Operation Babylift (Vietnam), 290, 304n63
oppression, feminist theories of, 30n40
Organization of People for Indigenous Rights (OPI-R, Guam), 35, 52n9
Orient, colonial discourse of, 19–20
Osorio, Jon Kamakawiwoʻole, xxxiv, 5

other: colonizalized, 28n13; discourses of, xx; as enemy, 279–80; enjoyment of, 61n79; infantilization of, 56n43; media representations of, 55n35

Pacific Daily News, 45, 54n29, 58n63
Pacific Islanders: appropriation of Western laws, 152; bathing suits of, 24; coalitions among, 124n72; effect of neocolonialism on, 27; effect of tourism on, 15, 24; gendered images of, 154–55; invisibility of, xxxv; marginalization of, xxxi, xxxv; multichronotopic links among, xxxi; in New Zealand, 124n72; postwar societies of, 153; racialized images of, 154, 162; scholars, xxxv; in U.S. military, 161. *See also* women, Pacific Islander
Pacific Islands: American imperialism in, xxxiii; American trade in, 314; anticolonialism in, xxi; antinuclear movements in, 23, 24–26; Christianity in, 23–24, 30n43, 31nn44–46; decolonization of, 150, 152; economic perceptions of, xxxi; European culture and, 20–21; Japanese defense of, xix; militarization in, vii, 153–55, 189; nuclear testing in, 16, 187, 199n37; political geographies of, xv; population of, 25; remilitarization of, xxiv; Spanish colonialism in, 160; spatial-temporal relations in, xxxii; tourism to, xx, 24, 155; as transnational garrison state, 311–13; U.S. strategic imperative in, 313–16; U.S. Trust Territory of, 16, 25; war on terror in, 312; women's sexual labor in, 312;
World War II in, 8–9, 154, 173n31. *See also* Asia-Pacific region
Pacific Rim countries, xxxi
"Pacific Way," politicization of, 27
Pak, Ms. (*kijich'on* woman), 282, 301n18
Parreñas, Rhacel, 192
particularism: fascist, 221n18; in Modernization Theory, 220n16
particularism, Japanese: and American universalism, 206, 214, 215–18
past, consumption of, 71
Pearl Harbor, 315; impact on public policy, 5; military presence at, 4–5; pollution of, 5; renaming of, xxxiv; Roosevelt's knowledge of, 13
Pearl S. Buck Foundation, 288
Perez, C. T., 158
Perilous Memories (Fujitani, White, Yoneyama), xxi
Perry, Matthew: in Japan, 98, 314; in Okinawa, 92, 98
Persian Gulf War: career soldiers in, 276n54; role of Diego Garcia in, 312
Philippine–American War, 76–77; citizen making in, 78
Philippines: American colonialism in, 182, 185; American imperialism in, 76–78, 196–97; American influence in, vii, xxxvi, 66, 74–75, 78–80, 183, 313; antibase activism in, 83; Anti-Imperialist League of, 313; demilitarization in, 67–69, 68; Department of Tourism, 68, 74, 75; discourse of security in, 67; economic dependence of, 67; Enlistment Program, 191; independence of, 186; Japanese invasion of, 76; militarization in, 64, 66, 71, 185, 313; militarized prostitution in, 84–85, 86n9; Military Bases Agreement

(with United States), 65, 66, 67, 186;
military tourism in, xxxv–xxxvi,
63–85; neocolonialism in, 72, 83;
paramilitary forces of, 83; segregation
in, 77; sex tourism in, 68; special
relationship with United States,
74–75, 78–80; as strategic liability,
315; U.S. immigration policies for,
192; U.S. Special Forces in, 312;
U.S. withdrawal from, 312; Visiting
Forces Agreement (with United
States), 66, 67, 68, 312, 319; in war
on terror, 66, 83. *See also* Filipinas;
Filipinos; navy men, Filipino
place names: Hawaiian, 4,
5; indigenous, xxxii
poetry, Hawaiian, xxv, xxxiv
Polynesian Panther Movement
(PPM), 124n72
postcolonialism, thanksgiving
narratives of, 85
postmodernity, markers of, xxviii
power relations: in colonialism,
207–9, 217; between colonizer and
colonized, 208–9, 211, 213; Foucault
on, 211; freedom in, 211–12;
gendered, 226; of intimacy, 207;
in male-on-male sexual violence,
238–39, 241; military and civilian,
xxvi, 106; between societies, 298
Preble, John M., 232, 243
Price Report (Melvin Price), on
Okinawa, 103, 104, 122n33
prostitution, militarized, xvii, 218,
281, 288; adoption following, 290;
institutions responsible for, 131; of
Okinawan women, 93, 108, 109–10;
in Philippines, 84–85, 86n9; race
in, 300n15. *See also chŏngsindae*
women (Korea); *kijich'on* women
(South Korea); sex work

"Pūpū (a`o `Ewa)" (song), 3–4
Pu'uloa (Hawai'i), xxxiv

queer studies, xl

Rabuka, Sitiveni, 30n43
race: in colonialism, xxix, 40, 71, 105,
111; in formation of subjectivity, 182;
Japanese discourse of, xviii, 220n18;
in marginalized masculinities,
149; in militarized prostitution,
300n15; in militarized violence,
xxiii, 84; in military tourism,
79, 82, 84; naturalization of
difference, 26; in neocolonialism,
xxvii, 281; in postmodernity,
xxviii; in structuring of military,
xlvi n65; in U.S. Navy, 184–86
racism: colonial, 111; concerning
Chamorro navy men, 165;
in Guam colonialism, 40;
transnational dynamics of, 281
racism, American: in Okinawa, 104–5
racism, Japanese, xix; in Okinawa,
100, 119; toward Koreans, xix
Ramos, Fidel, 79
Rancière, Jacques, 210, 219n7
Rape of Nanjing (1937), 211
Ratuva, Sitiveni, 153
Reard, Louis, 18
reparations: for Bikini Islanders,
26; for Guam, xxiii; from
Japan, xvii, 139–40, 141
resistance, viii; by Bikini Islanders, 27;
in Guam, 35, 43, 46–47, 49, 52n9,
59n68, 148; indigenous forms of,
xxx; individual, viii; to Japanese
colonialism, 125; to male-on-male
sexual violence, 236–37, 240, 241;
to militarization, 252, 297; pure, 47
Reynaud, Emmanuel, 243

Robinson, Michael, xlvii n71
Roh Tae Woo, 133
romantic love: as allegory for diplomatic relations, 211; cinematic depiction of, 209, 211, 213; international, 207, 211; versus rape, 212; as symbolic speech, 212; as trope of colonization, 206–10, 212
Rongerik, Bikini Islanders at, 17
Roosevelt, Franklin: on decolonization, 169; and Pearl Harbor, 13
Roosevelt, Theodore, 315
Rosaldo, Renato, 68
ruling classes, mystification of history, 29n25
Russell, Scott, 160
Russia, defense spending in, 273n13
Ryûkyûan Kingdom (Okinawa): dual allegiances of, 99; Japan annexation of, 91, 98, 100; treaty with United States, 98. *See also* Okinawa
Ryûkyû Islands: etymology of, 121n19; U.S. government of, 102–8, 114

sacrifice: Christian masculine, 81; indigenous, 48, 60n74, 61n80; military narratives of, 69, 80
Saewoomtuh (counseling center, South Korea), 139, 140
Said, Edward, 19–20, 100
sailors. *See* navy men
Sakai, Naoki, xvi–xvii, xxxviii–xxxix
Sala, Aaron, 14n11
Samar (Philippines), U.S. atrocities in, 313
Samawa (Iraq), SDF at, 267
Sanchez, Adrian C., 157
San Diego: Filipino naval families of, 181; militarization of, 183–84, 198n15; Pacific Fleet base in, 184

San Francisco Peace Treaty (1951), 251, 253, 272nn10–11
Sangley Point (Philippines), 185
San Juan, E., Jr., 201n69
Santo, Akiko, 259
Santos, Angel Leon Guerrero, 46–47, 59n70, 162, 178n98
Santos, Jonathan Pangelinan, 36; images of, 55n34
Santos, Nicole, 54n33
Sato, Fumika, xxxix
Satsuma, invasion of Okinawa, 98–99
Scarce, Michael, 238; *Male on Male Rape*, 231
scientific institutions, family stories of, 119n5
Securitarian (magazine), 275n48
security, militarized, xxxii; national memory of, 78
security, post–cold war, xvii
Segal, Mady Wechsler, 256, 260
self-determination: of Amerasian children, 300n5; dominant societies' view of, 152; for Korean women, 289
self-determination movements, xxi, xxiv; ethnic, 115; for Guam, 148, 168, 169
semi-Americans, 60n74; wartime deaths of, 61n79
September 11 attacks: geopolitics following, 72; militarization following, 85, 161, 171n3; militarization prior to, vii–viii
sex slavery, xvii. See also *chŏngsindae* system (Korea); *kijichʼon* movement (South Korea)
sex tourism, 92; in Korea, 125; in the Philippines, 68
sexual harassment: in American armed services, 227–28;

INDEX · 349

control thorugh, 231; intimacy in, 244–45; in Japanese Self-Defense Forces, 276n58; in workplace, 245
sexuality: of colonial modernity, 212; in conqueror-conquered relations, 217; militarization of, xvii, xl; privatized, viii
sexual relations, militarization of, xxxvii, 110
sexual violence: accountability and, 225; by American soldiers, 98, 106–8, 117–18, 127, 128, 129, 133, 213, 284; criminality associated with, 224; against Korean women, 244, 245; as product of modernity, 248n16. *See also* violence, militarized
sexual violence, male-on-male, xxxix; aggressors in, 230–31, 234–35, 237, 240, 241, 242; causes of, 226, 245; child victims of, 225; cruelty accompanying, 241–42; "everyday," 234–36; feminization in, 230, 231–32, 243, 245; frequency of, 228, 248n14; genital touching in, 240–41; hierarchy in, 233–34, 236–41, 242, 244, 245; homosexuality and, 224, 225, 226, 243, 245, 247n6, 247n11; injury to masculinity in, 228, 232–34; internalized nature of, 238; investigative reports on, 247n8; justifications for, 234, 235; in Korean armed services, 223–46; Korean media accounts of, 246nn3–6; Koreans' knowledge of, 225, 226; learned reactions to, 235–37; military authorities on, 247n7; motives for, 230, 238, 242; during national stress, 227; within nontransparent space, 245; power in, 238–39, 241; as prank, 234, 235, 236, 237; in prison, 238;

protection of masculinity in, 230–32; research on, 224, 226–27, 247n8; resistance to, 236–37, 240, 241; revenge in, 238; role reversal in, 243–45; secrecy in, 233–34; as sign of intimacy, 234–36, 237, 245; in Soviet Union, 227; suicide following, 213, 246nn2–4; terms of belittlement in, 229, 248n24, 249n25; unpublicized, 227–28; victims of, 225, 231, 232–37, 239–41, 244; victims' rationalization of, 236, 241; victims' reporting of, 227; during wartime, 227. *See also* violence, militarized
sex work: activism concerning, 125; for Amerasians, 280; bodily damage in, 127; debt bondage in, 130, 135, 143n14, 283; in global economy, 279; as means of control, 132; militarism in, 63; military institutionalization of, 85n1; in Pacific Islands, 312; patriotism in, 214–15; state-sponsored, 126, 130–31, 132; tourism in, 63
sex workers, South Korean. *See kijich'on* women (South Korea); prostitution, militarized
Shikata, Toshiyuki, 275n48
Shim, Young-hui, 248n14, 248n16
Shin, Gi-Wook, xlvii n71
Shin, Sun Yung, 299n5
Shin Hei Soo, 132
Showa Research Association (Japan), 221n18
sinthome, 40, 56n44
slave trade, African, 111
Smith, Bernard, 29n24; *European Vision and the South Pacific*, 31n45
Smith, General Jacob: atrocities of, 313
social relations, gendered, 26

Soh, Chunghee Sarah, 127, 130, 141
soldiers: career, 276n54; as first-class citizens, 269–70; grace between, 12; homosocial bonds among, xxxvi, 71; interracial fraternity among, 76; Micronesian, 49; self-control of, 239
soldiers, African American: Amerasian children of, 286, 287, 304n49; antiwar activism by, 115; black power among, 112, 123n55; Bush Masters, 112; confrontations with MPs, 113; *kijich'on* women's discrimination against, 219n12; Koza Uprising and, 108, 115; in Okinawa, 112–15, 123n55; racism experienced by, 304n49
soldiers, American: contact with colonized individuals, 205; crimes against civilians, 94, 95, 98, 105–8, 109; cultural programs for, 301n27; Hawaiian children of, 7; homosexual, 301n27, 303n35; interaction with sex workers, 215; Korean hardship tours of, 285–86; marriage to Korean women, 284, 303n38; in Okinawa, 92; Okinawan children of, 109; power relations with women, 279; relations with women of color, 281, 281–85; role as conquerors, 214; sexual needs of, 92–93; sexual violence by, 98, 106–8, 117–18, 127, 128, 129, 133, 213, 283, 312; tourism by, 84; volunteer opportunities for, 301n27
soldiers, Chamorro, 35–36, 173n31; activism of, 147, 164–65, 167–68; benefits of service for, 158; casualties among, xxxv, 36–40, 48, 49, 54n29, 54nn32–33, 60n75, 163; critique of United States, 167–68; discriminatory treatment of, 166–67; families of, 54n33; images of, 38–40, 54n33, 55n34; in Iraq, 36–40, 48, 55n36, 60n75, 163; masculinity issues of, 148–49, 159–63, 167–68, 169; questioning of loyalty, 166–67; reasons for enlistment, 157, 161, 162–63; recruitment of, 161–62; remasculinization of, 160, 162, 163, 164; resistance narratives of, 167; sacrifice by, 48; uniforms of, 44–45; veteran, 164; in Vietnam, 35, 45, 46, 49, 162; view of decolonization, 153, 163–68; view of militarism, 170; warrior ethos of, 39, 148, 160, 161, 162, 163; women, 55n34
soldiers, Japanese women: combat exclusion for, 267; expansion of roles, 259–65, 274n38; in Iraq, 255, 268; job limitations of, 268, 275n45, 276n50; at National Defense Academy, 266–68; nonfeminist arguments for, 256, 261, 267, 268; numbers of, 255, 273n16; recruitment of, 258–59, 274n33; in recruitment posters, *264, 265*; support jobs of, 257–59; understanding of national security, 259. *See also* women, Japanese
soldiers, women, 254–56; American, 258, 273n19; Chamorro, 55n34; GEM index and, 276n56; in NATO, 269, *270*; under patriarchies, 273n15; research on, 271n1; Russian, 255
somatophobia, 23
Souder-Jaffrey, Laura, 150, 152
Southeast Asia, U.S. relations with, 309–10

INDEX · 351

South Korea: Amerasians of, 277–98; American colonialism in, vii, 289; American militarism in, 278, 295, 297; anti-Americanism in, 135, 136; Base Community Clean-Up Committee, 214; Blue House Political Secretary, 214; civil society of, 127, 138–40; conscription in, 227, 243, 246; demilitarization for, 138, 289; democratization in, 135; ethnonationalism in, 141; Family Law of, 138; human rights in, 135, 141; immigrants to, 301n24; Japanese reparations for, 139–40; kinship in, 290; militarized subjects of, 278; Ministry of Health and Social Affairs, 131; modernization in, 292; National Police, 130; neocolonialism in, 278, 285; neoimperialism in, 295; perception of femininity in, 246; psychological traits in, 248n17; rape law in, 248n14; sex tourism in, 125; sexual discrimination in, 246; social welfare spending in, 305n69; Special Tourist Association, 131; Status of Forces Agreement (with United States), 133, 283, 284; STD clean-up campaign, 295; Summer Olympics (1988), 291; transnational adoption in, 279, 287, 290, 291–94; troop reduction in, 301n17, 311. *See also* armed services, South Korean; *chŏngsindae* system (Korea); *kijich'on* system (South Korea)
South Seas: conflation with Orient, 29n24; exoticism of, 29n24; noble savages of, 20, 22, 163
Soviet Union: demise of, 316; male-on-male sexual violence in, 227

Spain: Pacific colonialism of, 160, 175n55; use of indigenous peoples, 156
Spanish-American War, 315; Guam in, 51n4, 155; *Insular Cases* following, 42, 170n2
Spellman, Elizabeth, 23, 30n40
Spratly Islands (South China Sea), 319
Stoler, Ann, 207, 212
Stoltzfus, Brenda, 300n15
Stone, John: *Radio Bikini*, 28n10
Sturdevant, Saundra Pollock, 300n15
Suarez, Theresa C., xxxviii
Subic Bay Naval Base (Philippines), 63, 185; entertainment economy of, 65; military violence at, 84; neoliberalism and, 64; prostitution at, 86n9; reunions at, 67; as special economic zone, 65, 67; tourism to, 68, 82–83
subjectification, 219n7; of women, 210
subjectivities: Chamorro, xxxv; of colonized, 28n13, 170; militarized, xxv, xl; racial formation of, 182; of transnational adoption, 296
subjects, desiring: effect of militarization on, xxviii
Sun Tours (Corregidor), 75
Suruhånus, suruhånas (traditional healers), 38

Tadashi Kayama, 101
Tadiar, Neferti Xina M., 72; "Sexual Economies in the Asia-Pacific Community," 181
Taga of Tinian, 160
Tahitians, ancient Greeks and, 20
Taimanglo, Patricia, 44
Taitano, Carlos, 169
Takamine Tomokazu, 112, 114, 115
Takata Yasuma, 217, 220n18

Tanabe Hajime, 217, 220n18
Teahouse of the August Moon
  (film), 97, 124n71
Teaiwa, Teresia K., xxix,
  xxx, xxxiv–xxxv
Tengan, Ty Kāwika, 154
Tentara Nasional Indonesia (TNI), 310
Third World: consciousness of
  American imperialism, xxxvii;
  female bodies of, 294; nuclear
  testing in, 16; peace movements
  in, 318; tourism in, 70, 73;
  transnational adoption from, 299n5
time, periodizations of, xvi
Tobe, Hideaki, xxii
Tobias, Sheila, 279
Toledo, Alfonso, 115
Torres, Robert Tenorio, 160–61
tourism: effect on Pacific Islanders,
  15; as imperialism, 70; Japanese,
  xix–xx; liberalization through, 70;
  manipulation of history in, 69; to
  Pacific Islands, 24, 155; power in, 71;
  production of fantasy, 74; in Third
  World, 70, 73. See also sex tourism
tourism, military, xxvi, 26; bodily
  management in, 71; and colonial
  domination, 70–72, 75; erasure of
  violence through, 73; gender in, 74,
  79, 84; gratitude in, 83–84; heroics
  in, 72–74; memory in, 72–73; in
  Philippines, xxxv–xxxvi, 63, 67–68;
  race in, 79, 82, 84; rescue narratives
  in, 74; by soldiers, 84; violence
  in, 85; war on terror and, 72, 83
Trask, Haunani-Kay, xxiv–xxv
travel: colonial ideologies of, 67;
  freedom to, 85; gendered, 79;
  masculine modes of, 67, 69; and
  militarization, 70. See also tourism
Trenka, Jane Jeong, 300n5

True Love Mission (South
  Korea), 277–78
tsunami (Indian Ocean, 2004), 309–
  10; American influence following,
  309; as militarization opportunity,
  309–10; military cooperation
  following, 310; U.S. Combined
  Coordination Center for, 309
Tsuneo, Higashionna: Okinawa
  no shōnen, 109–10
Tydings-McDuffie Act (1934), 186

Ueunten, Wesley, xxxvi–xxxvii
Ulloa Garrido, Jose, 162, 168
Underwood, Robert, 159
unilateralism, U.S., 317
United Nations: chŏngsindae
  movement's lobbying of, 139–40;
  Convention on the Elimination of
  Discrimination against Women,
  138; on decolonization, 169;
  G-7 summit, 118; militarization
  accompanying, 281; Millennium
  Development Goals, 87n17; on
  non–self-governing territories,
  34, 51n5, 151; Special Rapporteur
  on chŏngsindae system, 142n3
United States: Amerasians' view of,
  277, 278; "civilization" projects of,
  xx; Compact of Free Association
  (with Marshall Islands), 18, 313;
  containment strategy of, 316;
  defense spending in, 273n13;
  Department of Defense, 227;
  enlightenment tradition in, 197;
  exclusionary citizenship in,
  182; government of Ryûkyûs,
  102–8, 114; hegemony in Asia,
  92; immigration to, 192, 195;
  isolation strategies for, 319–20;
  Military Bases Agreement

(with Philippines), 65, 66, 67, 186; multiculturalism of, 216; multiethnicities of, 201n69, 214; Mutual Security Act (with Japan), 253; occupation of Okinawa, xix, xxxvi–xxxvii, 101–8; position on decolonization, 151–52, 170; relations with Southeast Asia, 309–10; remilitarization of Asia-Pacific, xxiv; Security Treaty with Japan, 117, 272n9; Status of Forces Agreement (with South Korea), 133, 282, 283; territorial affairs in, 170n2; transnational adoption in, 291–93; as transnational garrison state, xl; treatment of Native Americans, 172n21; treaty with Ryûkyûan Kingdom, 98; unilateralism of, 317; urban revolts in, 110–11; Visiting Forces Agreement (with Philippines), 66, 67, 68, 312, 319. *See also* armed services, American; colonialism, American; imperialism, American
universalism: in colonial domination, 217; of Japanese Empire, 216, 220n18; in Modernization Theory, 220n16; nationalism as, 220n17
universalism, American: Japanese particularism and, 206, 214, 215–18
universals, competing, 61n80
U.S. Civil Administration of the Ryûkyûs (USCAR), 102
U.S. empire, viii–ix, xv, xvi; in everyday life, 187; indigenous peoples' service in, 156–57; insularity of, 94; relationship to Japanese Empire, xxiv, xxxiii, 216–18; sexualized projects of, 93
U.S. Navy: following tsunami of 2004, 309–10; Mess Management Specialist rating, 189; noncitizens in, 185; Pacific Command, 309; racialized domestics in, 184–86; ratings system of, 184, 186; stewards in, 157, 182, 184, 186, 189, 195, 199n28; strategic imperatives of, 314–15. *See also* navy men
USS *Midway* museum (San Diego), 198n15

Vega, Michael Aguon, 36
Vera Cruz, Philip, 192–93
Vicuña Gonzalez, Vernadette, xxxv–xxxvi
Vietnam, Amerasians of, 287–88, 289, 299n5
Vietnam War: American women in, 258; antiwar movements during, 115–17; Chamorros in, 35, 45, 46, 49, 162; Operation Babylift following, 290, 304n63; U.S. defeat in, 316
Villa, Mr. (navy man), 193
violence, militarized, xxxviii–xxxix, 280; accompanying sexual violence, 242; accountability for, 283; by American soldiers, 98, 106–8, 117–18, 127, 128, 129, 133; base-related, 84; coalitions against, 296–97; erasure through tourism, 73; frequency of, 242; against Korean women, 127, 128, 129, 284, 295; normalization of, xxv; in Philippines, 84–85; power relations in, 106; racialized, xxiii, 84; women's activism concerning, xxiii. *See also* sexual violence
Volkman, Toby Alice, 290

Wagner, William G., 233
"Waikā" (song), 12–13, 14n11

war: aestheticizing of, 78; collective memory of, 189; effect on fashion, 18–19; women's experiences of, 299n4
war crimes, Japanese: reparation for, xvii, 139–40, 141
war on terror, vii; in Asia-Pacific region, xxv; Guam in, xxii; military tourism and, 72, 83; multinational military alliances in, xxv; Pacific Island casualties in, 50; in Pacific Islands, 312; Philippines in, 66, 83; Southeast Asia and, 309–10
Watsuji Tetsurô, 220n18
Weekend at Bernie's (film), 37
Weekly Chosun (magazine), 246n4
Wesley, Christopher Rivera, 36; images of, 39, 40
West Papua: Indonesian policy in, 25, 31n52; insurgencies in, 310
"When the Lights Go on Again" (song), 8, 13
White, Geoffrey M., 69
whiteness, national fantasies of, 218
white slavery, 125
white supremacy, xviii, 201n67; military elite and, 184, 185
wianbu. See *chŏngsindae* women (Korea)
Wiegand, Karl L., 257, 261
Wilkes, Owen, 153
Wolfowitz, Paul, 310, 317
women: as absence, 19; as chaos, 21; collective self-recognition of, 265; effect of militarism on, 278, 279; experience of war, 299n4; human rights for, 141–42; as nature, 26; responses to militarism, 295–97; role in militarization, xxvii, 255; role in World War II, 257; subjectification of, 210; victim-aggressor relationships of, 244. *See also* soldiers, women
women, American: military opportunities for, xxxix, 255, 258
women, Asian: derogatory terms for, 283, 286, 300n15; sexual stereotypes of, 288
women, colonized: cinematic narrative of, 209–10
women, Japanese: in Diet, 274n34; franchise for, 251, 252; gender equality for, 275n39; role in imperialism, ix; role in Japanese Empire, 271n4; in Self-Defense Forces, xxxix, 251–70. *See also* soldiers, Japanese women
women, Japanese American: activists, 116
women, Korean: activism of, 125–26, 131–33, 136–37, 139; antimilitarism of, 132; genocide against, 132; militarized violence against, 127, 283; military brides, 284–85, 303nn38–39; relations with American soldiers, 278, 281–85; self-determination for, 289; sexual exploitation of, xxxvii, 283; sexual stereotypes of, 283; sexual violence against, 244, 245. See also *chŏngsindae* women (Korea); *kijich'on* women (South Korea)
women, Okinawan: activism of, xxii, 118, 297; black soldiers and, 113–14; crimes against, 98, 106–8, 117–18; effect of demilitarization on, xxiii; military brides, 121n28; prostitution of, 93, 108, 109–10

women, Pacific Islander: activism of, 23, 24, 27, 30n42; stereotypes of, 281; Western view of, 154–55
women, Russian: immigration to South Korea, 301n24
The Women Outside (documentary), 128
Woolford, Don, 31n46
World Tourism Organization (WTO), 70; Global Code of Ethics, 87n17
World War I: Māori in, 156; recruitment posters of, 265; women's fashion and, 19
World War II: energy issues during, 9; Hawai'i during, 6–8, 13; Japanese responsibility for, 251; liberation narratives of, 85; Native Americans in, 157; nostalgic narratives of, 69, 71, 72, 85; Okinawans during, 101–2, 121n28; Pacific Islands during, 8–9, 154, 173n31; transnational adoption following, 290–91; women's role in, 257. *See also* tourism, military

Yamashita, Motonori, 266
Yi Hyo Chae, 132
Yngvesson, Barbara, 292, 294, 296, 305n74
Yoneyama, Lisa, xvii
Young Ja (pseudonym), 287, 304n56
Youn-ok Song, 144n34
yu, Okinawan concept of, 97–98
Yuh, Ji-Yeon, 284
Yun Chong Ok, 126, 131–32, 136; separation from CM, 133
Yun Kŭmi, murder of, 129, 133, 141, 302n32
Yu Pok Nim, 126; outreach by, 131
Yu Pong Nim, 134, 138
Yuval-Davis, Nira, 255, 276n54

Žižek, Slavoj, 37, 53n24, 56n43, 58n55; on national myths, 61n79; on sinthomes, 56n44

Made in the USA
San Bernardino, CA
28 January 2020